MORAL BELIEFS AND MORAL THEORY

LIBRARY OF ETHICS AND APPLIED PHILOSOPHY

VOLUME 10

Managing Editor:

Govert A. den Hartogh, *University of Amsterdam, The Netherlands*

The titles published in this series are listed at the end of this volume.

MORAL BELIEFS AND MORAL THEORY

MARY GORE FORRESTER

Nurse Practitioner,
Albany County Family Planning,
Laramie, WY, U.S.A. and
Faculty Affiliate,
University of Wyoming, Laramie, WY, U.S.A.

KLUWER ACADEMIC PUBLISHERS
DORDRECHT / BOSTON / LONDON

A C.I.P. Catalogue record for this book is available from the Library of Congress.

ISBN 1-4020-0687-X

Published by Kluwer Academic Publishers,
P.O. Box 17, 3300 AA Dordrecht, The Netherlands.

Sold and distributed in North, Central and South America
by Kluwer Academic Publishers,
101 Philip Drive, Norwell, MA 02061, U.S.A.

In all other countries, sold and distributed
by Kluwer Academic Publishers,
P.O. Box 322, 3300 AH Dordrecht, The Netherlands.

Printed on acid-free paper

Printed in the Netherlands.

To my mother, Mary Cannaday Gore, who first taught me to care about ethics.

TABLE OF CONTENTS

ACKNOWLEDGMENTS

I would like to extend my thanks to those who have commented on drafts of this book, as well as work which preceded it — in some cases by many years — , for their interesting and useful suggestions. These include Hector Castañeda, Hardy Jones, Ron Moore, David Resnik, Bernie Rollin, and Ed Sherline, as well as the anonymous referees of not only this manuscript but of other work which contained preliminary expressions of the ideas presented here.

Above all, I am grateful to my husband, Jim Forrester, whose incisive critique of an earlier draft forced me to clarify much of the book. Without his constant support — not to mention his help with preparing the camera-ready manuscript — this book could not have been written.

I would also like to thank the University of Wyoming for being appointed a faculty affiliate, with accompanying library privileges.

INTRODUCTION

Some time ago I wrote a book (*Moral Language,* 1982) in which I argued that moral judgments are capable of being true ('truth-apt,' to use a current phrase, or descriptive and having truth-value, to use a more traditional term), that the methods of discovering moral facts are fundamentally similar to those of discovering non-moral facts, and that moral judgments may be true. What I did not do at that time was to develop a moral theory which would demonstrate how the method of discovering moral truths would work and what the criteria of truth actually are. In a later work (*Persons, Animals, and Fetuses,* 1996) I did propose a moral theory as to what the criteria for moral truth are; however, I presented it primarily as an introduction to the discussion of several practical ethical issues and did not argue fully for that theory. It is high time that I did so, because without showing that such a theory can be developed my defense of moral realism is incomplete. It is all very well to say that we can discover what moral beliefs are true, but unless we can demonstrate just which beliefs are true, the thesis that we can discover this truth cannot be fully defended.

For this reason the biggest (although not the only) challenge to showing that ethical objectivity is possible is the presence of moral disagreement — and the contention of many that such disagreement cannot be definitively resolved. The best way to handle this challenge is to develop a moral theory which represents a consensus of sound moral thinking — i.e., thinking based upon argument and defense against criticism. If it can be shown that deviations from such a theory either are only apparent, or fail to represent sound moral thinking (which I maintain is fundamentally similar to sound thinking in any discipline), then such deviations do not point to an inherent failure to resolve moral disagreement; such failure would give a death blow to the possibility of moral objectivity.

In this book I undertake the task of developing such a moral theory. It is with minor modifications the same as the theory I presented in *Persons, Animals, and Fetuses,* but includes many more attempts to answer actual and possible objections. What I shall present here is a version of naturalistic moral realism, but it is a version modified in a number of ways to take into account the important insights of relativists and other critics.

CHAPTER 1

METAETHICAL BACKGROUND

The task of justifying moral judgments consists of two parts. First, we need a method for determining which moral principles are sound, and secondly, we need to apply that method to determine what these principles are. In an earlier book, *Moral Language*, I argued that, contrary to what many philosophers and non-philosophers have maintained, it is possible to discover what moral judgments are true. I outlined a method that should enable us to find basic principles which constitute both the meaning of moral expressions and the most fundamental moral tenets. Here I will only summarize those conclusions, together with a brief discussion of some relevant arguments that have appeared in the literature since the publication of *Moral Language* in 1982.[1]

In that book I tried to show (1) that moral judgments are statements treated by speakers as having truth value, as opposed to sentences like imperatives and certain performatives which are neither true nor false, (2) that discovery of truth in moral judgments is not fundamentally different from the discovery of truth in non-moral judgments, and (3) that we have good reason to believe that there are stable truth criteria — related to human desires — for moral judgments.

I will say little about (1) in this chapter. Imperativist and emotivist theories of value judgments were originally proposed as ways of preserving the meaningfulness of moral and aesthetic sentences, given the presumption that they could not be literally true. If these theories have not been definitively laid to rest, they have most certainly taken a back seat to the much more important issue of whether any value judgments are true or known to be true. The remainder of the book will be devoted to spelling out (3). Consequently, most of the discussion in this chapter will be of (2).

To begin with I shall present some general themes in philosophy of language based on proposals of Wittgenstein, Quine, and Davidson which, if true, will support my claims. Given this overview of philosophy of language, I will briefly indicate a defense of my position that there are no differences between ethics and other types of discourse which make it impossible to define moral expressions in terms of objective properties, or to determine whether moral judgements are true.

1

1. DO MORAL JUDGMENTS STATE FACTS?

In *Moral Language* I argued that we can have moral knowledge and that moral judgments have truth value. Opposition to these positions are primarily based on the fact that people disagree widely about ethical matters. Over the course of human history, we find societies in which human sacrifice, slavery, oppression of other races, treating women and children as possessions, catering to every whim of some despot, burning unpopular people as witches or heretics, and so on, were not only tolerated, but accepted and approved of.

Yet while there can be disagreements about an enormous number of subjects, there seem on the surface at least to be problems with resolving disagreements in ethics that are not present for disputes in other areas of discourse. One apparent difference is that while we can often settle our disagreements about perceptible objects by observation, we don't seem to be able to observe moral and other value qualities directly.

This has led many to the view that there are no observable properties which would allow us to determine the answers to questions of morals, and no moral facts to discover. To some this meant that if moral judgments had meaning, their meaning is not determined by states of affairs or facts they might describe. According to this view they have no truth value; however, they certainly serve some linguistic function. Since one of the major functions that moral judgments serve is to get people to do things, several philosophers maintained that they were really a form of imperative. Another form of nondescriptivist theory held that moral judgments were expressions of approval or disapproval, for such expressions describe nothing and are neither true nor false.[2]

The most sophisticated nondescriptivist theories were much more subtle. For example, R. M. Hare maintains that moral judgments are universalizable imperatives[3] equivalent to 'Don't anybody (under the same relevant circumstances) do A!' According to Hare, actions and things have characteristics in virtue of which they are judged good or bad, but this is because we approve or disapprove of whatever has those characteristics and want everyone else to do the same. Thus even though these characteristics give some descriptive content to value terms, value judgments are fundamentally imperatives.

My case against nondescriptivism is based partly on the fact that moral judgments are far more like descriptive, fact-stating sentences than they are like imperatives and expressions of attitude, and that this resemblance presupposes that they are descriptions of states of affairs. For example, we can question or express doubt about moral judgments: for example, 'I wonder whether I did the right thing?' We don't, however, ask questions like 'I wonder whether do it.' Such questions do not even make sense, and the reason is that we only express doubt about things which might or might not be *true*. An even more important type of example, raised by Ziff, Searle, Castañeda, and Geach is the use of evaluations as the antecedents of conditionals: e.g., 'If John did wrong, he will apologize.' As such, evaluations are also used in arguments: Given the conditional stated in the last sentence, together with 'John did wrong,' it follows that John will apologize.[4] In a conditional, we state what will happen if some condition or state of affairs holds, or some other sentence is *true*. The antecedent thus describes a matter of fact. The most reasonable explanation of the appearance of evaluations as the antecedents of conditionals is that they too describe matters of fact.[5, 6]

Blackburn articulates a basic argument for the view that moral judgements cannot describe states of affairs. He maintains that naturalism (and moral realism generally) fail to account for the fact that when two different people have different moral standards, they can mean the same thing by moral expressions.[7] This is a version of the Open Question Argument, first put forth by Richard Price in the eighteenth century, later made famous by G. E. Moore, and further developed by R. M. Hare.[8] This is that if moral expressions *meant* the same as some descriptive predicates: e.g., if 'good' meant 'what promotes the greatest happiness for the greatest number,' then anyone who disagreed would not understand the meaning of 'good.' Yet a sentence like 'What's good is what promotes happiness' not only does not sound like a tautology, but it is a sentence people who are competent speakers of the language can disagree with. Blackburn maintains[9] that unless a realist can show that a moral term has a set of necessary and sufficient conditions for its application, such that whenever those conditions hold the term applies, then he would have nothing stable on which to pin moral discourse. Yet like Price, Moore, and Hare, Blackburn claims that there are no such necessary and sufficient conditions.

I believe that the Open Question Argument is fallacious, because the line between what is true and what is true by definition is not always easy to draw, and that people can understand the meanings of many words — both moral and nonmoral — about whose exact definitions they disagree.[10] All philosophers can think of many examples of debates in the literature over the definitions of such expressions as 'knowledge,' 'mind,' and 'cause.' But the main defense of moral realism against the Open Question Argument is the development of a plausible theory of what moral expressions mean — a theory that will find wide acceptance among people who have diverse political, religious, and cultural points of view. I shall present a candidate a theory which satisfies these requirements in the remaining chapters.

2. HOW IS MEANING DETERMINED?

In order to develop such a theory, it is necessary to have a method for finding out what moral views are true. I argued in *Moral Language* that this method is similar in ethics to what we do in other disciplines and in everyday life.[11] In all forms of discourse, including ethics, we find out the meaning and the truth conditions of words and expressions by paying attention to how people attempt to justify their beliefs. Thus if you and I disagree about whether Tom is a bachelor, what we will try to do (if we care enough) is find out whether or not he is married. If we do find out, this will settle our argument, for we agree that all and only unmarried men are bachelors. Not being married is a recognized *criterion*, a *truth condition*, and part of the *meaning* of the term 'bachelor.' Since it is, finding out whether or not a man is married is the way to find out if he is a bachelor. If someone learning English wanted to know what 'bachelor' meant, one way he could find out would be to observe how we settled our argument.

The sentence 'Bachelors are unmarried men' is not only true, but agreement on its truth is entrenched in the conventions of our language. To give it up — which we could if we wanted to — would require major adjustments in the meanings of other words. And if a person *denied* that bachelors were unmarried men, we would question whether he knew the meanings of at least some of the words he was using; we would find it hard, if not impossible, to understand him.

This is similar to certain views of Wittgenstein and Davidson. They maintained that in order for people to understand each other, and for their words to have meaning, they must agree on the truth of certain sentences.[12] For example, imagine discussing something like geometry when you couldn't agree with anyone on what characteristics a triangle had. You can only start getting somewhere if you and those with whom you are discussing triangles agree on the truth of some sentences such as, 'All triangles have three straight sides.' Not only must we agree on a few such sentences, but we must resist certain challenges to their truth. For example, if Greg says "I saw a triangle with five sides yesterday," you would undoubtedly say something like: "You couldn't have; either it wasn't a triangle, or it didn't have five sides." Compare this with "I saw a black tulip yesterday." Truly black tulips, I am told, do not exist (they are actually very dark purple),[13] but if you showed me a black flower shaped like a tulip, I would believe you.

But there is nothing Greg could show us that would convince us that he had seen a five-sided triangle. And the reason is that we are so much in agreement that triangles have three sides that we will not accept as a triangle anything that doesn't. Three-sidedness is part of the meaning of 'triangle,' and 'Triangles have three sides' is therefore an analytic sentence. We don't have to prove it by finding evidence for it in experience, and we won't reject it even if we seem to have evidence against it

A second premise which is important to my theory was developed by Quine: namely, that, while we must agree on the truth of some sentences if we are to talk about anything, which sentences we agree upon is not determined by the way things are, but is a matter of choice.[14] For the most part we aren't aware of making deliberate choices in what truths we are going to agree on. We normally use words the way other people in our society use them, without much thinking about their meaning, or what we would do if the facts seemed to go against what we have heretofore agreed on, or if someone challenged those beliefs. On other occasions we make conscious choices.

If, for example, we want to determine whether or not a certain animal is a mammal, we will point to characteristics of the creature which support one position or the other. I might, for example, say that the creature couldn't be a mammal because it lays eggs. You might then point out to me that it also nurses its young. We are both looking at further facts about the animal which are typically true of either mammals or non-mammals, facts which are used as *reasons* for classifying animals one way or another. If we come to agreement on which reasons are most relevant, and can agree which reasons hold in this case, then we can agree that the creature is one thing or the other. So if I insist that nothing that lays eggs is a mammal, and you agree with me, our argument will stop, and we will concur that the animal is not a mammal.

Now suppose we tell a biologist about this beast, and she tells us that it is a platypus and that it is a mammal because it nurses its young; you were right all along. Why should we accept what she says? The grounds for accepting her judgment lie in the way in which experts in her field determine criteria for classification. When biologists discovered platypuses and echidnas, they were faced with a dilemma, for these creatures did not fit into any known category. Mammals had never been known to lay eggs, but these things nursed their young, which was the criterion heretofore accepted for something's being a mammal. For the same reason what had once been thought of as great fishes, such as whales and dolphins, were now classified as mammals. To deny that the platypus was a mammal would upset this system and require a general overhaul of terminology. Biologists *might* have undertaken such an overhaul without being in any way *mistaken*. They chose not to, however; the smooth functioning of biological science was better served by keeping to the accepted criteria.

By retaining the current system, the position of nursing its young as a *criterion* of mammalhood was strengthened. As a criterion, it is a *truth condition* and a part of the meaning of the word 'mammal.' We use it to decide the truth or falsity of 'X is a mammal.' We can do so because there is general agreement among those who use this area of discourse (biology) to consider young-nursing as a criterion of mammalhood. The criterion could change, however, thereby changing the meaning of 'mammal.' Such a change would require major adjustments in biology; under some conditions, this might be warranted. It would only be warranted, however, if the progress of biology would be enhanced, if the *purposes* of that science — to advance our knowledge and understanding of the world of living things and to predict events concerning them — would be furthered.

To summarize thus far, in order to understand each other, we must agree on the truth of some sentences to the point of not being willing to accept facts as evidence against them. These sentences we may consider true by definition. Most of the time we do not concern ourselves about whether the sentences we believe true are true by definition or true because there is strong evidence for them. Only when we have a dilemma like the one faced by biologists when platypuses were discovered, do we need to analyze the status of these sentences or make decisions about what is to count as true by definition and what we will consider true only when the evidence warrants.

When we do analyze the status of the sentences we have heretofore accepted, a good way to determine what people mean by the terms in those sentences is to see how they argue for the truth of the sentences in which they appear. When we discover what people ultimately appeal to in deciding whether to apply a term, we discover the meaning, or truth conditions, of that term. If we can't make such a discovery because there *is* no consensus about criteria, we may find it useful to *legislate* a definition, as the biologists did.

Whether meanings are discovered, or whether they are legislated, there is nothing to prevent them from changing over time. Meanings change when the fundamental beliefs we have about a subject are altered. What guides meaning change is what is useful, convenient, and serves the purposes of a particular discipline in which the terms in question are employed.[15] I do not wish to maintain that this theory of meaning is the only defensible one. It is, however, highly plausible. A less conventionalistic competitor would have a heavy burden of proof, and one which is more conventionalistic would be unlikely to show that moral judgments are less objective than others, for *no* judgments would be objective. What I wish to show is that moral judgments are *no less* objective than others. I will discuss a few objections here, but a detailed discussion must wait for another volume.

3. THE MEANING OF MORAL EXPRESSIONS

This general view of meaning holds for ethical terms just as well as for others. Although there is much disagreement about ethics, there is disagreement in many fields. But in ethics, as well as in other areas, people argue. When they do, they appeal to certain features of the actions they are judging, such as kindness or cruelty, fairness or injustice, to support their beliefs that those actions are right or wrong. People may disagree about these characteristics as well: not only as to whether an action has them, but also as to which of those characteristics takes precedence in cases of conflict. Thus if you and I disagree as to whether it is better to lie to someone than to tell her a painful truth, neither of us denies that it is generally wrong to lie and generally wrong to cause pain. What we disagree on is which, in these circumstances, is worse. When we argue further, we will point to other considerations. We might argue for telling the truth by appealing to respect for her autonomy. Or we might look at the person's character and situation to determine whether she is likely to be able to deal constructively with the pain and use the truth to make the best of her bad situation: in other words, will knowing the truth be for her overall good? We must also consider the effect of lying in any one case on the useful practice of truth telling. Also we may consider that it is unfair to take special advantages for ourselves by lying when other people tell the truth, since we would be taking advantage of the atmosphere of trust which their having been truthful when it was to their disadvantage has created, which trust makes it possible for a lie to be believed.

In arguing we point to more general features of the respective actions: e.g., that lying is *unfair* and shows disrespect for the autonomy of a person, and that pain caused must be assessed in the light of whether it is or is not in the person's overall best interest. We find out what the truth conditions of moral judgments are by looking at these general features to which people appeal in arguments.[16] We can test whether some general feature is a moral truth condition by seeing whether it enables us to derive certain particular moral judgments which are *well-established*. A well-established moral judgment is one which has stood the test of time — has been accepted by many people in different cultures under conditions which allow the free exchange of ideas and open debate. In a closed society the powerful and influential can impose their beliefs upon others and prevent those others from being exposed to the views of outsiders.[17] Absence of debate can also result from physical isolation; indeed, until recent times relatively few people could travel to other parts of the world -- or even read and hear about them. In the modern age, however, we have wide access to information about how others live and what they believe, and we can compare their ways with each other and with our own. There is much more material for argument over what is the best way to live and treat others. Consequently, comfortable beliefs that our own codes of behavior are best are under constant challenge.[18]

Yet beliefs that survive these challenges (in the sense of being widely believed despite the challenges) survive, if I am right, because they have been more extensively justified by appeal to broader criteria that all — or virtually all — people find acceptable. According to what I have proposed, these broad principles are the fundamental criteria for application of moral terms and are, in fact, the truth conditions which determine the meaning of moral expressions. Well-established beliefs are those which are adopted in some form or another by nearly all known societies. People appeal to them to settle arguments in specific cases; also, however, there may be conflicts between such beliefs. In these situations, disputants who are looking for a rational solution (as opposed to appealing to authority, or refusing to argue) will go beyond the specific rules to looking for the point behind them. Why, for example, is honesty important? In attempts to elucidate these points still more general principles, such as the value of trust and the unfairness of making oneself an exception to a rule one expects others to follow, may be brought into the discussion. These general principles support the well-established beliefs by being their *raison d'être*.

Not everyone, of course, is interested in elucidating such reasons. Aside from philosophers, those who are interested are probably primarily concerned with solving a practical problem: e.g., What should I say to Eric right now? or Should we have a tax cut, and if so, whose taxes should be cut and by how much? To the extent that people have the time and interest to pursue the issue, they typically appeal to these general principles. It is these principles that are the fundamental criteria for the application of moral terms. When the well-established beliefs are under challenge, their rational supporters (who are free to discuss their views) look to the fundamental criteria which supply the point to those beliefs and which can, in turn, explain why they are well-established. Such criteria include fairness, helping and not harming, respecting a person's autonomy, being honorable, and supporting the community. It is among these criteria, I believe, that the truth conditions of moral judgments can be found. An adequate *moral theory* is one which codifies these fundamental criteria in such a way that they form a coherent account both of the criteria and of the more specific beliefs that have been held worldwide. It should also go some way to explain differences in the forms which these beliefs may take — how the circumstances of a society might influence what counts as dishonesty or as cruelty. Furthermore, it should flesh out the meaning of seemingly vague terms like 'harm,' 'interests,' and 'justice' in such a way as to allow solutions to particular problems.

There may be a number of distinct adequate moral theories — mutually consistent — that can do this, giving different criteria primacy over others, for example, or providing differing definitions for such terms as 'fairness.' Two different scientific theories might explain the phenomena equally well, but differ in what models, laws, and hypotheses are taken as basic and defining; the same will undoubtedly be found to be true of moral theories. A moral theory or basic set of principles can be indirectly justified by showing that well-established moral principles are part of or consequences of the theory. Conversely, a theory can be criticized on the grounds that it has consequences which go against some well-established moral beliefs. What I shall do here is to present one theory which I believe is adequate, for only if at least one can be found can a full defense of moral cognitivism be made.

If we may suppose that meaning change is primarily based on pragmatic concerns, then just as biologists classify animals based on criteria which enhance the ability to explain and understand phenomena, our choice of what moral theory to accept is also based on the purposes for which we engage in moral judgment. These purposes have to do with people's pursuit of their goals.[19] We generally want everyone to behave in ways that are at least not going to obstruct our realization of our purposes. And if our purposes conflict with those of others, we want some assurance that our interests will not be ignored. We might like to win out in every conflict, but we can hardly expect others to acquiesce in this, so we must work out some sort of reciprocal arrangements to balance the interests of one person against those of another. These requirements impose certain limits on the sorts of moral principles that can be widely accepted — accepted widely enough to be considered part of the meaning of moral expressions.

Support for the view that there is everywhere wide acceptance of the same basic moral principles is given in the work of James Q. Wilson, who maintains[20] that human *sociability* provides a motive for developing moral systems that have basic values in common. Virtually all children, in all kinds of societies, grow up with a desire to please and be accepted by others. Acceptance requires certain behavior that everyone wants from other people. Hence children have strong — although obviously not always sufficient — motives to help, or at least avoid hurting, others; not, for the most part, to take more than what is considered by the group to be their fair share; to fulfill whatever obligations are laid upon them; and to control such impulses as might cause destructive conflict with others. For example, hunter-gatherer societies in general have rules of sharing and reciprocity (at least amongst themselves, although not always applied to outsiders) that may well be evolutionarily based, in that groups which have these rules are more likely to survive and leave descendants.[21]

Obviously, to prove that all people past and present who have been able to compare their moral views with those of others and discuss them freely would affirm the basic principles set forth here would require an enormous volume of anthropological research, which research could not include those innumerable societies about which we know nothing. What I am proposing here is a hypothesis based on information about the fundamental principles accepted by a wide variety of societies. Not only do I discuss some of this information, but the principles also seem to reflect basic truths about human nature: namely, that people are goal-oriented, having a stake in attaining their goals, and furthermore that they want from others behavior which at least does not interfere with their pursuit of these ends.

Wilson points out that while there are numerous differences among the ways human beings give expression to their moral sense, contact with other societies has lessened some of the differences, as well as broadened the moral concern people may have for those who are not a part of the community in which they grew up.[22] As the book progresses I will discuss many indications that there is indeed such agreement about moral basics.

4. SOME OBJECTIONS

Hare[23] has accused descriptivists — I. e., those who hold that value judgments can be true or false — of maintaining that meaning is identical with truth conditions. The meaning of a sentence is indeed broader than its truth conditions, and the meaning of a term broader than its necessary and sufficient conditions of application. The truth conditions specified in physics for 'X is red' are that X reflects wave lengths of light having a specific range of frequencies, yet most people don't think of 'red' in terms of electromagnetic radiation, but rather the visual sensation that red objects produce in them, and this sensation is what they mean by 'red,' even though what makes that sentence true is the car's reflecting those particular wavelengths. A person may be using 'red' correctly — i.e., the cars one calls red actually do reflect the appropriate wavelengths — , but never have heard of electromagnetic radiation. In such a case, the speaker might be said to have a lesser grasp of the meaning of 'red,' than does someone else who knows the wavelengths of red light, but just isn't thinking about them when speaking. Both, however, know at least in a rough sense what 'red' means. Furthermore, if many things that reflected the proper wavelengths didn't look red to people, or if things that looked red reflected different wavelengths of light, speakers might abandon the scientific characterization of redness. Whether they would keep the common meaning, the scientific meaning, or retain both for different purposes would, on my view, depend upon pragmatic concerns.

The broader meaning of a term is akin to what Putnam[24] has called a *stereotype*. For example, we think of tigers as large orange cats with black stripes, that are fierce and dangerous. Yet some tigers are white, so being orange is not a necessary condition of tigerness, and the sentence 'That tiger is white' is not a contradiction. Alternatively, if there were many white tigers, the stereotype might change.

Implicatures given by choice of words may also be part of meaning, as Grice pointed out.[25] Thus "She was poor but she was honest" differs from "She was poor and she was honest," not in truth conditions, which are the same for both, but in the suggestion found in the first — but not the second — sentence that there is some contrast between poverty and honesty.

The core meaning of a sentence includes (1) its propositional content and (2) what I have called "mood"[26] and which is similar to but not identical with what Hare[27] called the "trophic." The mood, which is indicated by such grammatical features as the mood of the verb (e.g., declarative or imperative) and word order (e.g., forming a question by inverting subject and predicate), or by specific added phrases such as 'I promise,' 'I hereby pronounce,' or 'I bet,' indicates something about the relationship of those persons who might speak or hear the sentence to the type of state of affairs indicated by its propositional content.[28] Another way of putting it is that the mood indicates what type of illocutionary act is most typically performed with the sentence. Thus 'John will close the door,' 'Please, John, close the door,' and 'I (John) promise to close the door' all express a different relationship of speakers and hearers to the state of affairs which is John's closing the door at some time in the future. While 'John will close the door' would normally be used to claim that the state of affairs of John's closing the door will hold, the second sentence is normally used to instruct John to make that state of affairs hold, and the third would typically be used by John to make a commitment to bringing about a state of affairs of that type.[29] As noted above, sentences may be used to perform illocutionary acts different from those for which they are usually employed. While under certain circumstances someone's saying "I will pay her tomorrow" — normally a simple assertion — might constitute a promise as well, its being a promise is not part of its meaning. On the other hand, 'I promise to pay her tomorrow,' has the mood of a promise *and* being a promise is part of its meaning.[30]

The core of propositional content is the truth conditions of the sentence. Truth conditions apply only to the propositional content of a sentence, and not the mood. We use them to see if an assertion is true, a command has been obeyed, or a promise kept in order to determine whether the type of state of affairs described by the propositional content is realized. Thus truth conditions are important for all sentences. They hold, however, a more central place with assertions than with sentences having other moods. This is that they determine the *truth value* of assertions. 'John will close the door' is either true or false, but 'John, please close the door' is neither. The imperative may be fulfilled or not, depending upon whether John in fact closes the door. Non-assertoric sentences may have some other value like 'satisfaction' or 'termination' which replaces truth value,[31] but truth and falsity do not apply to them. Another way of putting this is that the truth conditions/conditions of application are what enable one to pick out a state of affairs, individual, or property from others. In short, meaning and truth conditions are not identical, but truth conditions are a central component of meaning.

Some question whether truth conditions play any significant role in meaning at all. Wright, for example, holds that meaning consists primarily of assertibility conditions, of which truth conditions are a subclass only where the object is directly present to the observer. He asks what is it that a person knows when he knows the meaning of a term, and concludes that we cannot know what we cannot perceive.[32] Knowing the meaning of a sentence is being able to use it correctly in response to our experience; if we cannot experience its truth, we cannot understand it.[33] Therefore, Wright argues, we cannot understand what it is, for example, for an event to have occurred in the past or what it is like for another person to have a sensory experience.

All that we can observe and understand are certain effects we attribute to past events or others' mental states, such as a large crater in the earth or someone's crying. These are at best *criteria* for there having been a collision of a giant meteor with the earth or for a person's being sad. Not only do we have no epistemic justification for supposing that there was a meteor collision fifty million years ago or that Samantha is sad — neither of which we can observe — , we don't even know what these sentences could mean apart from such criteria as suggested above.

Like many before him, Wright collapses the distinction between meaning and verification, on the grounds that if we cannot verify a statement in principle, we wouldn't know what we had found if we did verify it. But there are many degrees and kinds of ability to verify a sentence. Probably the only sentences — if any — we could verify totally and completely without possibility of error are sense datum statements, as Wright briefly acknowledges[34]

To go beyond the solipsism that would be imposed by allowing oneself to believe only what could be conclusively verified, one must make a few assumptions. The most crucial is the realist assumption that everything doesn't go out of existence the moment it leaves one's own perceptual field. This is an assumption that can, of course, never be conclusively verified — or falsified either, as Wright admits.[35] Part of the realist assumption is that not only are there things and events which exist when we don't actually perceive them, but that they can and do exist even when we will never be in a position to observe them.

Moreover, realists — as well as all people in ordinary circumstances — assume that at least a significant proportion of such events and objects bear some resemblances to those of which we are aware in the present. If so, then we can understand what it would be like for those events to occur and objects to exist, even when we cannot verify conclusively that they are (or were or will be) as we suppose. Thus we know what it means to say that a meteor collided with the earth fifty million years ago because some have observed similar events, and a major way that we can know what it is for Samantha to be sad is our having been sad ourselves. Our evidence is only indirect, of course, and we know that there may be other explanations of what we take as evidence. The crater we think was left by a meteor might have been a great excavation made by aliens. Samantha's tears might be tears of joy or mere crocodile tears.

The statements that a meteor fell in Siberia fifty million years ago and that Samantha is sad are defeasible, *just because* they aren't identical with the statements of the evidence for their truth. New evidence might disconfirm them, or it might tend to confirm them by disconfirming competing hypotheses. Hence these statements mean something different from their assertibility conditions even if we take assertibility conditions to be the best evidence we have, or even the best evidence we could get, as Putnam[36] suggests, and even if we have what Wright calls 'superassertibility' where the statement is not only warranted, but no further evidence would impugn its warranted status.[37]

Indeed, what makes a particular fact evidence for or against a particular statement is based upon what that statement *means*. If it were the case that a meteor landed in Siberia fifty million years ago, what might we expect to find? If Samantha is sad, how would we expect her to behave? These expectations result not only from what the statements in question mean, but also from our beliefs about how the world works. If all goes as we expect it to, we take this as confirmation of our beliefs and hypotheses; otherwise we need to revise them. Having an idea of what effects would result from the statement in question's being true is what allows us to know what evidence would confirm or disconfirm it. We must know, in other words, what it would be like for that statement to be true — in short, what it means.

At times the best that anyone can do in specifying the meaning of an expression is to say that it is whatever-it-is that produces certain observations. Subatomic particles, for example, which can never be perceived directly can be distinguished only by effects physicists perceive. In other cases — e.g., the notion of infinity, or the universal quantifier — , we can only grasp what something means by projecting from what we already grasp directly. Wright argues that such extensions are illegitimate.[38] We can't really grasp these unobservables, but only imagine that we do. On the contrary, imagining is precisely what we *cannot* do here. Even to describe what one is directly aware of and to suppose that the referents of the terms do not alter from one moment to the next is to presuppose a language — which language can only be acquired in a context of communication between individuals, and where there is at least a supposition that there are stable, recognizable objects to which terms refer — including the individuals who speak the language.

In short, if there is no reality beyond what is directly evident to our senses, we cannot have language, much less knowledge. Granted this knowledge never amounts to certainty — except insofar as we stipulate conventions (see below), but we must for practical purposes rely on what is coherent with our observations and beliefs. As McDowell points out,[39] while experience is necessary for meaning, this implies neither that any particular experiences are required for a specific term to have meaning[40] nor that what we cannot perceive has no meaning.

Richard Miller has presented an important challenge to my project.[41] He proposes a theory of how meaning is determined which closely resembles my own in the following respects. What determines the beliefs which are most central and which constitute meaning are the projects people have which are related to the area of discourse. Thus what scientific statements are taken as comprising meaning depend upon what best promotes the goals of the science: to explain and predict, or to create useful objects and procedures. Likewise in ethics we want to promote our ends and resolve conflict.

In scientific discourse common words which most people understand like 'water' and 'energy,' have more technical definitions such as 'water = H$_2$O' and 'E = mc^2' whose correct application is dependent on certain theories like the atomic theory of matter and relativity theory. A person can know what 'water' and 'energy' mean without knowing the scientific definitions. Miller argues that we can also have a difference in the meanings of moral terms as well. The term 'just' can mean loosely what is the right way of distributing goods, etc., or it can also have a theory-laden meaning like 'what creates the greatest happiness for the greatest number,' or 'what gives equal goods to everyone.' Two people might very well accept the common meaning — probably anyone would — yet not agree on the theoretical meaning. Likewise, people from very different backgrounds, having different social goals, might give different specific meanings to a term like 'just.' Rather than bringing about equality, what is just might be taken to be what best holds the clan together or what enables the society to produce the highest intellectual achievements. Between two people who have such different frameworks, Miller maintains, there can be disagreement which no amount of new information or rational argument can resolve.[42]

On the contrary, there *are* ways of resolving disagreements among people as different from us as, to use Miller's examples, the Tiv people of Nigeria and Aristotle. The Tiv believe that resolution of disputes ought to be carried out so as to preserve the ties of the extended family, regardless of the wishes of individuals. Often a man's wife or child who vigorously objects to living with him is forced to do so. Miller is right in supposing that we regard the interests of the individual person as having greater weight than the Tiv seem to do. And Aristotle believed that it was better to have a society in which a small number of individuals had the wealth and leisure to spend the better part of their time in rational activity in accordance with virtue — and thus be happy. He thought this best even though the elite required numerous people to serve their needs through menial activities which not only left them no time for much rational activity, but were actually degrading and contrary to virtue and happiness.

Both the Tiv and Aristotle would seem to most contemporary Westerners to have very skewed systems of what is right and wrong. Unlike Miller, however, I think we can say that there is something *objectively* wrong with both systems. They are defective because a great many people in both systems are excluded in the sense that their interests and purposes are given virtually no consideration at all for reasons having nothing to do with their deserts or contributions to the society. A moral system in which many people have no say in their fate and whose interests are ignored will not be widely accepted, even in a society which follows that system. The system may be stable because those whose interests *are* considered are powerful enough to enforce compliance, but it will not be acceptable to those who are kept down. It will certainly not be accepted broadly enough to be considered, even within the society itself, constitutive of the *meaning* of 'right,' 'just,' or 'ought.'

Another objection which can be made to the view I have proposed is that if basic moral principles are considered true by virtue of being part of the meaning of what is right, and if meanings can change, then what is to stop these basic principles from changing? Indeed, G. J. Warnock, whose view of ethics is similar in many respects to my own, holds that there is no good reason why morality as defined in any particular way might not be rejected entirely.[43] I agree that one could, without necessarily being irrational, adopt a very different concept of morality with basic principles much at variance with those of beneficence and fairness. But several factors set definite limits on the extent to which this is likely. First of all, if only one or a few individuals did this they would run the risk of not being understood by other people when they talked about moral issues. They would not share enough beliefs with the rest of us to make communication possible. Suppose there were individuals who claimed that everyone ought to cause as much pain as possible — not because pain leads to anything desirable, but because it is good in itself.[44] How would you talk with such a person about a moral question? You would first need to know what he meant by not only 'good' and 'ought,' but also by 'pain' and 'much.' You might, for example, wonder if he meant the same thing others do by 'pain.' It would be as easy to suppose that he used 'pain' to signify what other people call 'pleasure,' or 'much' as the rest of us use 'little' as to suppose that he is using 'good' or 'ought' differently from the way we do. We could only find out by trying to find a few points of agreement. And this would be very difficult.

Furthermore, it is very unlikely that any wildly different moral concepts from those encompassed by beneficence and fairness would ever become well-established, for most of us have a large stake in seeing that other people behave in accordance with these principles. We may not always want to follow them ourselves, and many people ignore them whenever they think they can get away with doing so. But everyone has goals — things she wishes to achieve or obtain — and does not want others interfering with her pursuit of them. Many of our goals would be hindered by our letting it be known that we have no regard for the goals of others. So we not only have a strong motive to make other people follow rules which promote our interests, but also at least to pretend to follow them ourselves. This requires us to use moral words the way other people do. Thus even if there are moral nihilists[45] or others whose moral concepts and beliefs are markedly different from those of the vast majority, they are likely to keep them to themselves and therefore not contribute much to discourse and the evolution of moral language.

If the meaning of moral terms is as I have claimed, then morality may seem not to be objective. If it were objective, it would be possible for everyone to be wrong about what is morally right, and, of course, my view precludes this.[46] In the same way, though, it would not be possible for everyone to be wrong about what is red or what mammals are, for there must be agreement on meaning criteria for there to be any mutual understanding in discourse. Given a certain definition of 'mammal,' however, everyone could be wrong about whether a particular creature is a mammal. And given that certain characteristics of actions define them as right (because of near-universal belief that these characteristics confer rightness), it would be possible for everyone to be wrong about whether some specific action or class of actions is right. Particular, synthetic statements — both moral and non-moral — can in this sense be objective. On the other hand, analytic statements which determine the meanings of terms are determined by mutual agreement and in that sense are not objective; this applies to both moral and non-moral judgments.

Harman[47] maintains that so-called moral argument is not really argument in the sense of looking for a correct answer to a question, but rather a process of bargaining. If so, then it would seem that moral disputes are not conducted by appeal to principles which all the disputants hold true and which are thus well-established. There is, however, a major difference between bargaining and looking for a right answer. When two parties bargain, they try to negotiate a settlement that they can both live with. Part of the process involves each party's giving up some of what it wants in order to get concessions from the other. Bargaining does *not* require a change in the values of the respective parties. Union members, for example, still want and think they *ought* to get a $2.00/hour raise, but they are willing to accept a one-dollar raise because they know management won't give more. Management, in turn, thinks the employees are paid as much as they ought to get already and does not want to give any raise at all, but they are willing to give the one-dollar raise to prevent a strike. Neither the interests nor the values of labor or management change in this process; bargaining is a practical solution for people whose interests are opposed and who may (or may not) think they are morally — as well as prudentially — justified in their demands.

There are, moreover, some shared values which make bargaining possible in the first place. One is that negotiated settlements are better (more in the interests of each party) than continued conflict or resolution by force. Another is an acknowledgment that all parties to the dispute have interests that deserve consideration — or at least that no one will benefit by ignoring the interests of the other party. In short, bargaining presupposes the recognition that people's wants and interests are important and that all people's interests should receive consideration — i.e., two fundamental, well-established moral principles, to which people constantly appeal in argument.[48]

Crispin Wright[49] has argued that moral judgments are not objective in that they lack *cognitive command*. A discourse has cognitive command when it is *a priori* that any difference in opinion between two individuals is entirely accounted for by divergent input, which is usually some cognitive shortcoming by one party or the other.

It seems unlikely, however, that it is *ever* an *a priori* truth that disagreements between two persons are due to cognitive shortcomings (except perhaps in the simplest observation statements). Nor is it likely that it can be shown that any moral disagreements are *not* a result of some such shortcoming. For Wright 'cognitive shortcomings' covers a lot of territory -- not necessarily things the person is to be blamed for. Cognitive shortcomings include ignorance of fact, as well as prejudice, or working under "unsuitable conditions" (such as inattention and distraction). Disagreements in judgments within a discourse that has cognitive command may also be due to vagueness (144) — in meaning, or in the criteria, standards, or boundaries of application of some of its terms.

How can it be *a priori* that a disagreement on any matter be attributable to differences in input? Given the wide variety of instances which Wright considers input differences, it seems highly unlikely that we be sure that other sources of disagreement are not also so classifiable. After all, if two people disagree upon whether a certain body of evidence is sufficient to confirm a hypothesis (as in one of his examples, in *Truth and Objectivity*, 144), this seems much more likely to be a result of their different temperaments or training than of any input or to vagueness of the criteria for what is acceptable (e.g., Jones is a scientist of skeptical bent, whereas Smith tends to be slightly more accepting of what he reads, but both judge within the limits of what is considered a reasonable conclusion). Certainly, the differences in what they conclude are quite independent of the data available to them.[50]

A clue as to what Wright really means by cognitive command is his statement[51] that we think *intuitively* that judgments having cognitive command have only cognitive content. In short, we *suppose* that they are statements of fact and are representative of what is the case. Such a supposition is *a priori* in that we don't allow any evidence to refute the factuality of the statements we believe to state facts. If there is a disagreement that we can't account for by something obvious, such as one party's ignorance of a body of relevant observational data, we look for another explanation, such as the person's insensitivity or lack of attention or the vagueness of the terms. I don't deny that such explanations are perfectly just; what I do claim is that it is not a matter of *fact* that such explanations of disagreement will always be forthcoming, but rather a determination on our part to keep looking for them.

Wright claims that there are some bodies of discourse for which there is no such intuition that their statements represent the way things are, and that such discourses include morals and comedy. Certainly it is true that what we find funny varies greatly with individual temperaments, beliefs about the world, and values. There is, however, an important difference between comedy and morals. What is funny — like what is pleasant, delicious, or soothing — for individuals varies enormously. There are certain things that are widely — although by no means universally — considered funny. Jokes and comedies tend to have certain characteristics which make them funny to most people: e.g., citing shared stereotypical beliefs about some group, an element of surprise, or poking fun at common foibles and unpleasant situations. Yet whether a particular person would find a particular joke funny depends upon his own beliefs, personality, and situation.

Similar remarks may be made about what is pleasant, delicious, or soothing. How people attribute such characteristics varies widely with the individual's temperament and past experience, but each adjective tends to mark some general features that tend to bring forth such assessments. But for each, there are also many people who do not consider those items pleasant, delicious, or soothing. So while there are some objective features of items described by these adjectives, those features do not elicit uniform reactions in all. We may scorn the tastes of those who react differently or think that more experience would change those tastes, but we do not consider people with different tastes cognitively at fault. The adjectives 'funny,' 'pleasant,' 'delicious,' and 'soothing' connote primarily subjective responses to things and events rather than objective characteristics.

Our moral judgments, however, are different in that we do not tolerate differences in judgments in the same way. A person who thinks it all right to set a living creature on fire or to cheat on exams is *not* thought just to have different tastes, but to be *wrong*. An individual who does not see this can be brought to realize it by having certain facts pointed out. Thus we can teach a child that cheating is wrong by pointing out that doing so gives one an advantage at the expense of others, and that doing damaging things to sentient beings causes them pain. Pointing out such matters need not lead a person to *care* about the feelings or interests of others or to change his behavior, and those who don't care may attempt to justify their actions by, for example, claiming that others deserve punishment or that they themselves deserve special treatment. What they cannot do is credibly claim that it is morally all right to cause needless pain or to attain advantages by denying similar advantages to others.

In short, common usage suggests that we *do* think of moral judgments as having cognitive command in Wright's sense. We argue about whether an action is morally acceptable or not, whereas we don't argue about whether a joke is funny or a dish is delicious. We are content to allow that individual tastes determine what strikes one as funny, pleasant, delicious, or soothing, at least as much as this is determined by objective characteristics of the things to which those adjectives are applied. We don't have this same contentment about moral issues, because we so frequently attempt to change others' minds by pointing out reasons why an act is right or wrong. True, we often stop debating before agreement is reached, but that is because the complexity of the issues exceeds our time for, interest in, and capacity for argument. But we don't conclude that both parties are equally correct or that agreement cannot eventually be reached, any more than we do for complex non-moral issues that we give up on debating.

David Wong[52] has maintained that certain fundamental differences between ethical beliefs of societies are irreconcilable. As an example, he points to the difference between contemporary Western societies' emphasis on individual rights and the centrality of the good of the community in the moral codes of traditional Eastern cultures. I do not see, however, that these differing values are at all irreconcilable. Many thoughtful Westerners have come to deplore the loss of a sense of community in contemporary life. Human beings have as one of their greatest needs a connectedness with others, which requires reciprocity and concern for those around us. Those who neglect their relationships with other people find their lives impoverished, and people living in societies where traditional roles have broken down and nothing comparable has replaced them often suffer greatly.

On the other hand, while we need close and healthy relationships with others, some traditional arrangements are better than others for fostering the well-being of the group and the individuals within it. In countless societies a part of the population has endured actual or virtual slavery. When the voices of these oppressed people have been heard, they have *not* praised their traditional roles in which their interests were subordinated to those of the group.[53] People need and want both individual freedom and close relationships, even though finding the proper balance between them may be extremely difficult. Reflective individuals from both East and West may come to recognize these dual needs and try to find a moral path that provides for both, thereby combining the best of both worlds. This would be indicative not of relativism, but of people's having a vision of what constitutes a good life and right action that may transcend limited local traditions.

Nondescriptivist philosophers have revived the Open Question argument by claiming that it is not possible for evaluations to have the status of definitions.[54] If so, they argue, evaluations could not guide action; moreover, they would sound trivial if stated and their denial would be clearly absurd.

A major difficulty with the Open Question argument is that it is *not* always peculiar to ask questions of the form 'Is F G?' when 'All F's are G' is analytic; doing so does not show that the questioner is not a competent speaker of the language. Analytic statements may be very complex. An intelligent and skilled speaker of the language might well ask whether some proof in logic or mathematics is valid, or, as in earlier examples, whether an analysis of some philosophical term is adequate. If the proof is in fact valid or the analysis adequate, we would still find nothing peculiar about the question. The Open Question argument is persuasive primarily because what is offered as examples of definitions of value expressions are so clearly inadequate — e.g., "Good is what is conducive to pleasure."[55]

The primary support for the open question argument is the view that evaluations have an essential nondescriptive component — in particular, that their action-guidingness is part of their meaning. The descriptive content of value terms does not exhaust their meaning, so no definition couched in descriptive predicates is adequate.[56] As some others have put it, moral definitions are essentially contestable. J. L. Mackie maintained this,[57] and more recently Stephen Darwall, Allan Gibbard, and Peter Railton[58] developed the thesis further.[59] They claim that for any proposed definition of 'good,' 'bad,' 'right,' or 'wrong,' we can suppose that some perfectly rational, well-intentioned persons might not have a reason to acquire or avoid something, act or refrain from acting, just because a thing or action fits that definition. People are not willing to have boundaries set by definition because they can suppose that the definition may apply to a thing or an act without giving them a reason for action. This, they say, explains why no proposed definition of moral terms has found general acceptance, and all efforts to do so have been such spectacular failures. They contrast this with science, where people are content to settle meaning indeterminacies by fiat.

Certainly no proposed definition for 'good,' 'ought,' or 'right' has received universal acceptance. But neither have definitions of many other important philosophical terms. Furthermore, there are good reasons why it is difficult to arrive at definitions of moral terms. Most moral discussions involve settling conflicts of interests and desires. Because of the scarcity of goods, any effort we make to promote the welfare of any individual runs the risk of harming the interests of another. Any effort to share and balance benefits and burdens will require sacrifices on the part of some. Those who are concerned with morality find it difficult to accept a moral system which permits damage to the interests of anyone. Yet almost any proposed solution to a really difficult moral problem will result in harm being done or good foregone to individuals or the violation of valuable practices or principles.

Proponents of the Open Question Argument say that moral definitions are contestable in that a person might not have a reason to act just because that act fits a particular definition. Given any definition, we may still ask why we ought to act in accordance with that definition.[60] A person's having a reason to act can, however, be one of two things: (1) the person is actually motivated to act, or (2) the person considers himself justified in acting. If we take sense (1), X's being motivated to do A is neither necessary nor sufficient for its being the case that X ought to do A. There is, for example, no logical contradiction in a woman's saying to her son, "I know you ought to enlist, but please don't!" As Darwall, *et. al.* point out, the mother — by using 'ought' — implies that — despite her own preferences — there are conclusive moral reasons for her son to join the army.

As for (2), justification for action can be either moral or non-moral. If 'X ought to do A' means that there is non-moral justification for X's doing A, it is incumbent on anyone making that claim to state what sort of non-moral justification he means (e.g., prudential, ought-everything-considered, etc.) I will discuss these issues in Chapter 2.

If 'X ought to do A' means that there is moral justification for X's doing A, then whether X actually ought to do A depends upon whether there are conclusive moral reasons for doing A. Whether 'ought' defined in a specific way entails such reasons depends upon what that specific definition is. To reject *a priori* the possibility that *any* definition can supply such reasons is premature. The full response to an objection that a person might not consider himself morally justified in acting as he ought-under-definition D requires a full exposition of D. The remainder of this book is an attempt to provide one. What is necessary to condemn a definition of a moral expression is an objector's being able to show that acts required according to the definition are not morally required — or even wrong — or, alternatively, that acts wrong by the definition are either acceptable or required. If noncognitivism is true, then — for any definition — not acting in accordance with that definition could be rationally justifiable. But what sense of 'rationally justifiable' is consistent with noncognitivism? Presumably this sense would be that a person can be morally justified in not acting in accordance with the definition. For example, one could say with Hare that someone might intend that everyone in the situation in question not act in that way. But just that someone *might* intend this, does not make it rationally justifiable to fail to act. Unless we already presuppose that there are no objective standards of right action which can dictate that failure to act is not justifiable, we cannot assume that for every possible definition a failure to act as it requires would be justifiable.[61]

In earlier work, Darwall[62] defends the view that what we ought to do is what is rational, and that this in turn is what one would want to do if one were totally impartial and considered all the relevant facts. This would explain, he maintains, how value judgments are essentially action-guiding without requiring that people always be motivated to do as they ought. Since, however, no one ever attains such a state of impartiality and knowledge, we do not know how we would choose if we did. The best we can do is try to remedy specific instances of ignorance and prejudice, and we do this when trying to decide the right course of action, not because we value impartiality for itself, but rather because we believe it unfair and hence wrong to put our own wants and interests (or those of persons we favor) ahead of the wants and interests of others. And the justification for maintaining that what is right is what we would *want* under the conditions of total objectivity is based on the moral value we ascribe to human purposes. In other words, the conditions under which Darwall (as well as Rawls and other contract theorists) maintain determine the right choice presuppose certain moral principles, specifically the rightness of promoting interests and of doing so without allowing one person to benefit at another's expense. Hence Darwall's characterization of right action does not help us determine the basis of those principles.

Michael Smith[63] proposes a similar view, according to which what we ought to do and value is what we would all come to have pro-attitudes toward if we all had a maximally coherent and rational set of attitudes. But if to be coherent one's attitudes must simply be mutually consistent, this is hardly sufficient to determine moral rightness, for a person could have perfectly consistent, but selfish or malicious. If coherence of attitudes entails their coming together to support a specific purpose, then whether coherence confers moral rightness depends upon whether that purpose is morally good or acceptable. If it is, then coherence is trivially what we ought to pursue; if not, then we must have a further justification for supposing coherence to confer moral value. We must also ask what makes an attitude rational? If to be rational an attitude must be impartial or suited to some human purpose, Smith's criterion runs into the same difficulties faced by Darwall's; it already has already has moral content built into it, making it circular.[64]

My own procedure may appear to do precisely what Darwall, Smith, Rawls, and other contract theorists do: namely, set forth conditions under which people decide on the moral principles they will accept — in which case, it would still be necessary to say why these conditions and not others should be the right ones under which principles are chosen.[65] The difference is that on my view the conditions under which the most fundamental moral principles are discovered are those under which the truth conditions of any judgment — moral or otherwise — are determined. The fact that it is necessary to have free and open discussion to find out what these are, and not to exclude anyone from participating, is an important condition for finding any type of truth. This condition needs to be explicitly stated in discussing the conditions for seeking fundamental moral criteria because it is so frequently in the interests of dominant groups to suppress the opinions of subservient classes. No one particularly cares what the truth conditions would be for 'This figure is a triangle,' whereas a great many people would have a stake in what the truth conditions are for, say, 'It is wrong to deny women the vote.' Nevertheless, if there were a large number of individuals who maintained that triangles had seven sides, it would be important to removing misunderstanding and the advancement of geometry to bring this group into the discussion of what was meant by 'triangle.' Thus the basis for requiring open discussion as a means of discovering basic moral principles (i.e., the truth conditions of moral judgments) is — on my view — a matter of linguistics. Open discussion happens also to support principles of equality and promoting human aims and goals, because people want others at least not to interfere with their aims and to give them equal footing with others. It is not always clear, however, why contract theorists set the conditions that they do; if, however, as seems likely, they select the specific conditions because these conditions result in the principles they want to generate, there is definitely the appearance of presupposing what they try to prove. My view has the advantage that the primary justification for accepting what moral criteria come out of open discussion has a basis other than its generating desired principles — namely, that it is a requirement for discovering any meaning criteria.

There is, however, another intuition to which the Open Question Argument appeals, even to some moral realists. David Copp, for example, argues that moral judgments are propositions asserting that an action is in accordance with a justified moral standard.[66] Moral standards in turn are, however, prescriptions, and what justifies them is that they meet the needs and support the values of the society which holds them. Thus sentences which assert that an act ought to be done, as well as sentences asserting that a given standard promotes the needs and values of the society in question, are propositions. On the other hand, standards themselves are not; rather, they ascribe "to-be-doneness" to certain types of behavior. They are like rules, which are always expressible as imperatives; although they may sometimes be stated as propositions, they are essentially imperatives.

There is, however, an important difference between 'You ought not to kill' and 'Thou shalt not kill.' An imperative does not necessarily apply beyond the immediate situation or the person(s) to whom the command is addressed, nor does it imply that there is any reason or justification for the command. It is always open to someone to ask, "Why should I do that?" To say, on the other hand, that one ought not to kill, implies that it is immoral for anyone to do so (at least *prima facie*), and that there are reasons (applicable to all in like circumstances) why killing should not be done. This may seem to support Copp's view: 'You ought not to kill' states that there is a standard, 'Thou shalt not kill,' which is justified because killing people interferes with their satisfying their needs. The question, however, arises as to how we distinguish between specific moral judgments and standards. Would Copp say that 'It is wrong to kill Jones' is a specific moral judgment with a truth value, while 'It is wrong to kill anyone,' is the propositional form of a standard which is essentially 'Don't (or thou shalt not) kill?' But then could we not equally well say that 'It is wrong to kill anyone' is a specific moral judgment asserting that not killing conforms to the standard, 'Don't prevent people from attaining their goals?' In short, it seems that both moral judgments and standards have varying degrees of specificity, and either may be considered an application of one which is more general; there seems to be no grammatical difference between them. True, we can order people to do whatever we consider to be the right thing to do — e.g., 'You ought not to be so rude to her' vs. 'Don't be so rude to her.' And we can justify our commands by pointing out that it would be wrong to disobey them, and we justify them further by showing what it is about disobedience that makes it wrong. The commands connected with moral judgments are not necessary to the status of those judgments, and moral discussions can proceed without ever using them.

On the other hand, Copp claims that a standard's prescriptive nature does not lie simply in its grammar, but rather than in the fact that they are *subscribed to*. That is, people want (in general) to live by them and want others to live by them as well; furthermore, they think that anyone who violates them is deserving of some sort of blame. We do not, however, have to suppose that standards are *prescriptions* in order to accept that people subscribe to them in this way. People generally do not want to harm others (unless, as in all too many cases, they have something to gain by it), and they certainly don't want others to harm them. They also consider blame appropriate in that they are so concerned not to be harmed that they think people should be pressured in some way not to harm. We want not harming to be a guide to life, and thus we subscribe to it. But as Copp himself admits, people frequently do not want to conform to certain specific moral standards in specific situations, so that subscribing does not entail sufficient motivation. Copp also recognizes that believing that a particular moral rule is justified does not entail subscribing to it, so that we can believe in the truth of a moral judgment without subscribing to the standard on which it is based, and vice versa. Ed might believe that a rule against driving over a certain speed limit is justified (on the grounds of promoting highway safety) without wanting anyone, himself included, to stay within those limits, or be fined for any but the most flagrant disobedience. It would, of course, be very odd to suppose that one could have such a fractured attitude to a great many rules, but why this is so must be seen by appealing to what it is about a rule that makes it justified. Copp maintains that a rule is justified through satisfying the needs and values of the society which has that rule, and this has much to be said for it; if I am a member of a society whose needs I care about and whose values I share, I will certainly subscribe to the majority of its rules. This criterion of justification, however, itself stands in need of justification — or at least an explanation of its unique status — , and on this Copp's explanation does not appear satisfactory. He says that the criterion is indeed a meta-standard, but that he can avoid the need for an infinite regress of standards to justify further standards by using not moral standards but general standards of philosophical reasoning (p. 45). A society would be *rational* to choose standards which promote its needs and values, because these are *self-grounded*, in that "in order to cope with things we need to think that some choices are better than others and that some choices are rationally defensible" (p. 168). Thus we must act on the assumption that some self-grounded reasons are rationally justifiable. But there is a large jump from supposing that we must assume that some choices are better than others to supposing that it is better to choose on the basis of our needs and values. Of course, most of us most of the time (when not suffering from akrasia) *do in fact* choose on the basis of what we need and value, and, in the case of what we value at least, we usually believe that it is better to choose so. If Copp *means* by this that such choices (by individuals and societies) are rationally justifiable, then acting on self-grounded reasons *is* rationally justifiable in his sense. But if we use the term in just this way, we cannot then jump directly to the conclusion that what is rationally justifiable is also *morally* justifiable.

Mackie argues[67] that even though saying that something is good is connecting it with the realization of human purposes, and that this does place limits upon what can count as good, this is perfectly consistent with subjectivism, for it does not rule out the existence of a commending (or emotive, imperative, approving, or endorsing) component to the meaning. Words like 'brave,' for example, have descriptive content, but also, when used, include a commendation of the individual described as brave. Williams[68] gives an argument similar to Mackie's. He remarks that we cannot understand what an evaluative term means unless we see it as action-guiding. Thus to call someone a coward is to condemn him and attempt to keep others from being like him.

No doubt this is frequently what we do by ascriptions of cowardice. Yet while we don't as a rule want people to be cowards because this tends to limit our ability to protect and advance our goals, it does not follow that the term 'coward' has action-guidingness as an essential feature. If a historian describes some king or general who lived many centuries ago as cowardly, she not only has no opportunity to affect the behavior of the personage in question, but she is probably not providing moral lessons for her readers so as to make them more courageous. Readers may draw conclusions about what to do in their own lives, but they are not being *told* to do so. Note that I am not denying that 'coward' is an evaluative word entailing beliefs about good and bad, but only denying that such terms are essentially action-guiding.

It might appear that if we restate conditional sentences which have evaluations as the conditioning clause as alternations or conjunction, the grammatical and logical problems with supposing evaluations to be imperatives or performatives can be eliminated. 'If that movie is good, I will go see it' could be read as 'Either [not (that movie is good) or I will go see it]' or as 'Not [that movie is good and not (I will go see it)].' This seems to avoid interpreting 'That movie is good' as a description of a state of affairs. But the problem reappears when we consider how to interpret 'Not (that movie is good).' The natural way is 'It is not the case that that movie is good,' but what imperative or expression of attitude or feeling might this be? It is clearly an evaluation, covering the possibilities that the movie is anything from mediocre to awful. Yet there seem no imperatives or expressions of attitude that might correspond to this. 'Don't see that movie' or 'Boo to that movie' fail because denial that the movie is good isn't equivalent to declaring it bad.

Blackburn[69] suggests that the negation of 'Hooray p!' is 'Tolerate not-p!' (And the negation of 'Boo p!' can be interpreted as 'Tolerate p!') One can then translate an argument like 'If it is wrong to lie, it is wrong to get your little brother to lie. It is wrong to lie. Therefore, it is wrong to get your little brother to lie.' into non-assertoric terms. The above argument would become 'If B! Someone tells a lie, then B! You get your little brother to lie! B! Someone tells a lie. Therefore B! You get your little brother to lie.' The second premise denies the first horn of the alternation of the first premise, so a person cannot have consistent attitudes by assenting to the premises, but not the conclusion.

The problem with this move is that 'Tolerate p!' is not an adequate negation of either 'Hooray not-p!' or 'Boo p!,' nor is 'Not-Tolerate p!' a negation of 'Hooray p!' 'Hooray' and 'Boo' may be interpreted as expressions of feeling or as expressions of an attitude. These, however, are not the same thing. A feeling is a momentary reaction to a situation, which is subject to change; while it may be and frequently is influenced by our values, it need not be. An attitude, on the other hand, is a complex entity, consisting of various beliefs and dispositions to feel in certain ways. Let us consider the case where Blackburn's operators are interpreted as expressions of feeling. If I am angry with someone it may or may not be because I believe he has wronged me or behaved badly, and the feeling is apt to pass, even though whatever evaluations I have made remain the same. If 'Boo! John said he didn't care for the paté (which, unbeknownst to him, I spent all day preparing)!' is simply an expression of my negative feeling, it is not necessarily an evaluation of what John said.

Toleration, however, is not just a feeling. It can go with feelings, of course. Tolerating p is consistent with liking p, but does not always involve a positive feeling (e.g., 'I can tolerate the pain' certainly doesn't mean you like having it!). In other words, tolerating something is not a feeling, but rather involves the absence of a strongly negative feeling. It is primarily an attitude which includes a variety of beliefs and dispositions to act or feel. If evaluations are expressions of feelings, we need a feeling-expression which indicates the negation of those expressed by 'Hooray' and 'Boo' to represent 'It is not the case that X is good' or 'It isn't wrong to A,' which *are* evaluations. One might try 'Ho hum' — but that only covers indifference, not feelings opposite to either 'Hooray' or 'Boo.' 'It is not the case that X is good,' however, includes *both* indifference and negative assessments of X.

Let us now suppose that 'Hooray,' 'Boo,' and 'Tolerate' are not merely expressions of feelings, but expressions of attitudes, such as approval, condemnation, and toleration; this is how I think Blackburn really wants them understood. As I have argued elsewhere,[70] however, approval of some thing, act, or person in virtue of its possessing a certain characteristic has only one *essential* feature. This is a *belief* in the goodness of that characteristic, or of items to the extent that they possess it. Attitudes such as approval may be expressed in many different ways, always including overtones of feeling, but none of these are *required* for approval apart from that belief in the goodness of the item approved.[71]

Thus if I approve of John's work as a philosopher, I might recommend him for a job, or buy his books, or feel excitement on learning that he is coming here to speak. But no one of these actions or feelings is required. And under peculiar circumstances, I might do any of these things *without* approving of his work — e.g., I might buy his books and look forward to his speaking because I have plans to write a paper tearing his work apart. On the other hand, if I don't believe his work is good, I don't approve of it; and if I do believe his work is good, then I approve of it, regardless of what actions or feelings *express* that attitude.[72]

In short, such attitudes as commendation, approval, endorsement, etc. may be expressed by a variety of actions and feelings; none of these, however, are essential. What is essential to the attitude is a belief in the goodness of the item toward which one has the attitude. And condemnation, disapproval, etc. essentially involve a belief in the badness of the thing toward which one has that attitude. Toleration, on the other hand, does not essentially include an evaluative belief, but rather a belief that whatever one thinks of the item tolerated, one is able to accept it. This does not, of course, preclude valuing it highly.

In short, claiming that an evaluation of something as good or right entails a pro attitude of some kind does nothing to support subjectivism. If as Blackburn clearly seems to want, we interpret H! and T! as analogous to the Obligation and Permission operators in deontic logic, it is even more obvious that they include a belief in the requirement (or non-requirement) of certain actions or states of affairs. Because I hold that it is impermissible to lie, a liar may make me angry or distrustful, and I may recoil from lying myself; however, I could have these same feelings and reactions without believing that lying is wrong, and I could hold lying to be impermissible without having any of these specific reactions. What that attitude has essentially is a *belief* that lying is wrong.[73]

Even if we have a proper negation for imperatives or expressions of attitude that can be used in arguments involving nonassertoric sentences, we still have no interpretation for complexes that correspond to truth-functional compounds of assertions or an account of our ability to make inferences. What, for example, is the non-truth-functional value to be ascribed to 'If Lizzie murdered her parents, then she ought to be executed?' We could read it as an imperative or commitment and say that it is satisfied or not satisfied, depending upon whether Lizzie is executed or not, given that she murdered her parents. But if we read it as 'Either it is not the case that Lizzie murdered her parents or execute her,' it is not clear whether the natural reading of the whole conditional as a commitment, as Blackburn suggests,[74] is appropriate. As Hale[75] points out, if we interpret it as a commitment (or imperative, or expression of attitude), then either the commitment applies to each disjunct

separately or to the disjunction as a whole. If it applies to each separately, then either
the speaker is committed to the falsity of 'Lizzie murdered her parents' or she is
committed to 'Execute her!' Carrying out an inference in this situation (e.g., 'If
Lizzie murdered her parents, she ought to be executed; Lizzie murdered her parents;
therefore, she ought to be executed'), however, demands a truth-functional
interpretation. The speaker must either be committed to the falsity (in believing it
false) of 'Lizzie murdered her parents' or be committed to (in having a pro attitude
toward) Lizzie's being executed. But it is not the speaker's *believing* the truth of the
antecedent that allows the inference. Rather it is the actual truth of the antecedent.
Considering the commitment to apply to each disjunct separately, therefore, admits
the fundamental truth-functional nature of such judgments, even where the
consequent — and the conclusion — is nonassertoric. Similarly 'If it's nine o'clock,
go home. It's nine o'clock. Go home' allows the conclusion because the antecedent
is true, not because the speaker (or hearer) believes that it is nine o'clock.

If, however, as Hale believes Blackburn desires, the commitment applies to the
disjunct as a whole, then there is no way to carry through an inference. The first
premise is a commitment to the alternation, while the second premise 'Lizzie
murdered her parents' is an assertion. It cannot, therefore, negate the first horn of the
alternation, since the first horn is not the negation of 'Lizzie murdered her parents,'
but a sentence imbedded in a nonassertoric compound. As more than one of
Blackburn's critics has suggested,[76] if he makes evaluations enough like assertions to
carry through inferences, then there is little to distinguish between them and
assertions. If he tries to maintain the nonassertoric quality of evaluations, he is
unable to use them in the sorts of inferences people ordinarily make with them.
Blackburn attempts[77] to develop a complex inference system using closer
approximations to evaluative perfection (where all positively evaluated states of affairs
hold). I will not try here to determine whether this is successful, but it is abundantly
clear that no one actually makes inferences in this way with evaluations. In normal
linguistic usage, evaluations are treated as assertions.

`   In more recent work,[78] Blackburn seems to abandon his efforts to give a non-
descriptive interpretation to arguments involving evaluations. They can be treated as
descriptions for the purposes of logic and grammar, but this does not mean that they
are descriptions. When we use evaluations in conditionals or in arguments, we are
making connections between attitudes, or between attitudes and beliefs. Conditionals
express "the endorsement of a movement of thought;" a person who states or believes
'If p, then q' is 'tied to' the alternation 'Not-p or q,' regardless of whether the
sentential variables are descriptions or expressions of attitudes. What Blackburn
appears to be saying is that certain combinations of beliefs and attitudes are consistent
or rational. It is just as irrational to approve of, say, p.q but not approve of p as it
would be to believe p.q, but not believe that p.

What is irrational about such a combination of attitudes — or beliefs? Of course, it is reasonable to hold compatible beliefs and attitudes since this usually serves our practical purposes well, but there might be occasions when it would not be — e. g., one might achieve more of what he wants by holding some incompatible set of beliefs and/or attitudes. A white southerner might have black friends whom he respects more than many whites, while holding that blacks are inferior; by having these incompatible stances he can keep his friends, but at the same time feel comfortable with his reactionary political views. If he suspects anything inconsistent in his beliefs, he avoids thinking about this sufficiently to recognize this inconsistency. What is consistently irrational, however, about holding incompatible beliefs is that they can't all be true. Likewise, the states of affairs toward which one has the incompatible pro-attitudes (i.e., p and not-p) are inconsistent because they cannot both be realized. And the incompatible attitudes are derivatively incompatible because statements describing these states of affairs cannot both be true. Our southerner's attitudes toward blacks are incongruent because 'All blacks are inferior to all whites' and 'Some blacks are superior to some whites' cannot both be true. In short, we can certainly have a logic of attitudes or of nonassertoric sentences generally, but it would need to be based upon assertoric logic. To draw inferences we need to recast non-assertoric premises into assertoric terms as the states of affairs which would be realized if what one approved of (or commanded) was to happen.

A further argument that moral judgments are essentially action-guiding is that, if they are not, we cannot explain why people are motivated to act morally.[79] There are, however, many motivating reasons, but none of them entail that being motivating is part of the meaning of moral judgments. Clearly the reasons people have for doing what they ought are not sufficient to compel them to act morally. Otherwise, how could anyone knowingly do wrong? Our reasons to do as we ought include primarily our desires to avoid conflict with others (including others' desires to retaliate for such harm as we do) and to establish warm relationships with a sizeable number of persons[80] These desires usually keep people well motivated to act in accordance with what they hold to be right most of the time. On the other hand, all of us are occasionally tempted to do what isn't right in order to pursue some personal end, and we sometimes give in to these temptations. An anti-realist could argue that moral judgments don't entail that the person who accepts them will be fully motivated to perform the required act (or demand it from others) — an entailment which would be fatal — , but that there must be *some* motivation. The burden is then upon him to say what sort of motivation and how much. Certainly the degree of motivation connected with a particular moral judgment is dependent upon many factors. For example, it is difficult to see what kind of motivation is attached to a judgment that Henry VIII ought not to have beheaded two of his wives. Actions so removed in time and place are unlikely to arouse much feeling in us. I will discuss this issue in more depth in the following chapter.

Several contemporary philosophers have tried to show that moral qualities are irreconcilably different from other qualities. For example, Blackburn[81] criticizes efforts[82] to assimilate moral predicates to secondary sensible qualities. He maintains that perception of secondary qualities correlates with specific brain changes, whereas there is no such correlation with moral qualities. Rather than describing the way things are, moral predicates are assigned to the way we *want* the world to be. A moment's thought, however, will make it clear that what any person or group considers right and wrong does *not* correlate exactly with what that individual or group happens to want. At the same time, as I have stressed above, what we want has a lot to do with what we think right and good. In the same way, my perceiving something as red does not necessarily correlate with its being red, but redness is closely related to what people usually do perceive as red. As children we learn the meaning of 'red' through being shown examples and through having our color ascriptions corrected by others. And 'red' can stand for the property that tends to induce certain sensations, even though people may be mistaken in thinking that particular things are red and others are unable to perceive that color at all.

Children learn moral terms similarly — good people and wrong acts are those which by and large elicit pro and con feelings, but with time they elicit not only feelings, but recognition of moral attributes of people and events that are independent of our particular feelings and desires. Over time the child who claims that anything anyone does that he doesn't like is "not fair," comes to realize that fairness does *not* always coincide with what he wants — at least most people eventually become sufficiently mature to tell the difference. Good people *generally* help others to get what they want, and wrong acts are generally those we don't want done, but as our experience of life grows we discover not only exceptions, but reasons for those exceptions. Values are not just like secondary properties,[83] but in the respect of being primarily understood through their effects on individuals, they are similar.

Properties of objects and events may be roughly classified into two types — those which are considered to be had by the object or event regardless of other events, including how they affect or are interpreted by those who perceive them, and those which are dependent upon other events, including the effects upon and interpretations of perceivers. For example, suppose that Tommy Tucker pushes Miss Muffett to the ground. His physical motions are the same regardless of how they affect Miss M., or what else is going on around them, or how these motions are interpreted. Let us suppose that a train is coming when TT pushes MM. If TT pushes MM away from the train, he has saved her life and performed a heroic deed. If he pushes her onto the track, he has caused her death and, indeed — assuming this no accident — has committed murder. 'Saving a life,' 'doing something heroic,' 'killing MM,' and 'committing murder' are all action descriptions ascribing to them properties of the second sort.

Simple properties such as primary and secondary qualities belong to the first class, as do the properties of belonging to certain natural kinds.[84] The characteristics of actions are generally of the second. Moral properties must certainly be of the second class; by and large they hold because of certain sorts of effects upon people and in virtue of human institutions, interpretations, and practices. Consequently, a person's goodness or an action's wrongness could not be perceived immediately; rather they would have to be inferred from other immediate perceptions together with information about the desires, beliefs, and practices of those who interact with the agents. Not only do we need to know something of the interests and goals of all those affected by an act, but also how its effects are distributed among those involved. This knowledge requires considerable information about non-moral factors, much of which is often unavailable, so that our apprehension of moral properties is not only indirect, but an extrapolation from what we have been able to determine. None of this entails that moral properties are subjective — only that they are complex.[85] There are a great many other properties that share such complexity. For example, that a situation is dangerous or presents opportunities for accomplishing something is often not immediately apparent; such properties of situations must be inferred from other aspects of the situation which are more directly perceived. Moreover, such properties are not always perceived by those who do not have certain kinds of knowledge or special interests. Thus it takes considerable medical knowledge to realize that certain symptoms — e.g., stiff neck in a person with fever or headache — can indicate a dangerous illness. And a person who is not particularly concerned with advancing a business may well not perceive an opportunity for making money.[86] That a moral property is dependent upon human desires and institutions does not thereby make it relativistic.[87] It would be relativistic only if given *exactly the same* circumstances, desires, beliefs, and practices, incompatible moral properties could be legitimately ascribed to the same person or act.

One objection to moral realism has been that moral properties of acts or individuals cannot serve as explanations of events.[88] We do in fact use moral judgments as explanations — e.g., that the injustice of a government caused rebellion. Critics, however, would say that it was not injustice, but people's belief that the government was unjust that caused them to revolt. In response to this criticism, one may point out that one important cause of a person's believing that p is the truth of p. Unless we have an alternative explanation which accounts for the belief and also reason to think that p is false or unknowable by the believer, that-p should be accepted as part of the explanation of the belief that p. To suppose that moral properties *cannot* be explanations of events seems to presuppose that they are unknowable.

One might also say that a rebellion is explained not so much by injustice as by such specific events as arrests and beatings. I am not sure that this is so, because arrests and punishments by authorities (even beatings in some times and places) are generally accepted by citizens if they see them as justifiable. It is when arrests are seen as arbitrary and undeserved (i.e., unjust), or punishments as cruel (i.e., unjustifiably causing pain), that people (other than those punished, at least) object. Even so, it is true that many large-scale events or situations are complexes of smaller, interacting episodes which are more directly responsible for certain effects. Either the large event or the small occurrence might be cited as the cause of a particular effect. Thus the death of a Honduran farmer might be attributed either to Hurricane Mitch or to the landslide that buried his house. The hurricane can be rightly called the cause of his death since it consisted of a violent pattern of winds and rains that caused many such landslides. Nevertheless, if we want to know more specifically what happened, the particular wind and rain patterns that caused the landslide will explain the event more precisely. Likewise we could say that a rebellion was the result of governmental injustice. We might, however, also attribute it to more specific actions of the government, such as the killing of a popular leader.

On the other hand, as Sayre-McCord points out,[89] sometimes a more general term serves better in an explanation than a more specific one. If, he suggests, we explain why a square peg goes into a square hole by describing the molecular structures of both the peg and the hole, we will not be able to generalize the explanation to include other pegs' going — or not going — into certain sorts of holes. If, however, we use the broader term 'square,' we can understand just why square pegs fit more easily than, say, round or triangular pegs, into square holes. And if we say that the farmer was killed by Hurricane Mitch we place his death in the context of a particular natural disaster. Furthermore, the injustice of a government is what was common to many of its actions which aroused the people to revolt. In short, explanations have different purposes, depending upon what sort of understanding we ask for, and wording them differently can answer to these different needs. In this way, moral properties, as well as other general and complex properties, can and do serve in explanations.

Wright maintains that — while moral judgments may sometimes be used in explanations — , they do not have what he calls a 'wide cosmological role'.[90] A type of discourse with a wide cosmological role is one in which the states of affairs its statements cite appear in explanations of events which are not simply attitudes towards those states of affairs. The explanations in which such a discourse could contribute would also include events or states like sensations felt by individuals, direct physical effects on people, and effects on inanimate objects, as well as on the beliefs and attitudes of individuals. Thus Wright says that while a state like the wetness of some rocks can figure in explanations of all these kinds, a state like the wrongness of an act cannot.

While we do not cite the goodness or wrongness as such of an action in explaining these varied types of events, we *do* cite more specific moral explanations which indicate the respect in which an act is good or wrong. Thus because of Lucinda's kindness to him a beggar was able to turn his life around (e.g., she gave him food and shelter for the night, helped him find a job, and generally restored his faith in human nature); the beggar's turning his life around included his becoming self-supporting, getting more education, and staying away from drugs. Wright might argue that we could explain these same events by citing only the descriptions of what was done to the persons concerned and not by bringing in any moral characteristics of the actions. But we could also explain the death of the farmer in Honduras without specifically mentioning Hurricane Mitch. Saying only that a hurricane occurred explains particular events less well than pointing out the particular features of the hurricane, such as the torrential rain that caused a mudslide in a particular spot. And we understand more exactly how the beggar was helped by Lucinda, when the particular actions in question are cited than we would if we were simply told that they were kind. These latter terms are much more general and cover many different sorts of actions, just as 'hurricane' applies to a variety of different storms. Wright might say that calling a particular weather pattern a hurricane is describing it, in a way that calling an act wrong is not. If he does, though, he is presupposing what he is attempting to show.

But even if it can be shown that moral discourse does not have a wide cosmological role, why is this relevant to its objectivity or lack of it? Many other terms widely considered to refer to real properties are similar. If we hear simply that a person is sick, this alone (without any details as to what sort of sickness) can do little more than arouse sympathy or worry (i.e., attitudes), and even these tend to be free-floating when we have no idea how serious the sickness might be. Without details of the nature of his sickness, we know nothing about what effects his illness might have on himself, his family, or his ability to engage in activities, or how long the effects may last. Nor can we explain any of these effects very well merely by saying that the person is sick. Likewise, the usefulness of explanations citing the moral quality of actions runs the gamut from thin concepts (like wrongness), which explain little, through thick concepts (like cruelty), which explain more, to specific descriptions (like beating a small child).[91] If anyone were to say, as some no doubt will, that the last is a description of an objective state of affairs, while the former two are not, it is worth pointing out that this begs the question at issue.

Whether or not moral predicates can figure in the explanation of events, however, their primary role is not explanatory; this, however, does not count against moral realism.[92] In the sciences there is a place for both explanation and classification. Subatomic particles, chemical elements, organic compounds, and orders and classes of plants and animals are distinguished by certain characteristics they have. Assigning them to a particular category is classification. How these things behave and interact with one another is the domain of explanation. The characteristics they have determine how they will behave and interact. Classifying them enables us to express our explanations more succinctly, but classification is not itself explanation, unless it comes with an understanding of what properties the individual has which cause it to appear or behave in a certain way. While the classifications we use are conventions, this hardly shows that the things we classify are not real, or that the classificatory terms we use do not refer. For example, having a negative charge is one of the properties of electrons; we classify electrons as particles which have a certain mass and a negative charge. That we so classify them explains nothing; however, that they have a negative charge and a certain mass explains to those familiar with physics how electrons behave in innumerable interactions.

Likewise our moral expressions are more classificatory than explanatory. We classify actions as right or wrong, and individuals and situations as good or bad because of certain properties they have and certain ways these properties affect people and things. If we say that John did wrong, we aren't saying specifically what he did or what characteristics his action had; we do, however, suppose that it fell within a certain range of actions types — e.g., that it hurt someone unnecessarily or was unfair. The characteristics of actions can enter into explanations of events. That John cheated on his wife and gave her gonorrhea explains why she is divorcing him. That his so cheating is classified as a wrong action doesn't add very much to the explanation.

In short, while classification can help with explanation, that is not its primary purpose. We classify in every area of discourse, and our classifications are conventional, in that we are perfectly free to classify things differently from the way we do. It does not follow, however, that what we classify does not exist or does not really have the properties according to which we classify it. These properties are, in fact, what explain the behavior of the entities that have them, and how these entities interact with other things. Moral terms classify individuals, things, and actions largely according to the manner in which they affect our ability to attain our goals and support social interactions. The specific effects of individuals, things, and actions upon our goals are more likely to explain particular events, however, than is the bare fact of their goodness or badness, or rightness or wrongness.

The above observations can explain a difference between moral and scientific theories which is probably behind objections like Wright's. A scientific theory can be used to predict new observations, which — if those observations are actually made — tend to confirm the theory. Moral theories aren't used in this way. Consequences of moral theories are tested not against observations, but against well-established moral beliefs. Well-established moral beliefs form the bedrock of testing, not because they are observable data, but since they have been successfully defended against challenges, there is good reason to think that they are based upon what we mean by our use of ethical terms.[93]

This, however, does not mean that moral theories cannot be objective while scientific theories are. Since stating that an action is right or wrong is primarily classifying it, it does not play the primary role in predicting events or states of affairs. What does any predicting using moral theories is not this classification alone, but the classification together with a multitude of other facts and considerations. This is true of both moral and scientific theories. We can predict, say, that ingesting the bacterium *Helicobacter pylori* is likely to cause peptic ulcers. We also know that ulcers are painful and even life-threatening, and from this we can infer that (unless there are mitigating circumstances) feeding these bacteria to a person without his consent would be wrong, just because we normally classify acts that cause pain, especially when the person who suffers does not consent, as wrong. We classify causing pain as wrong, because people generally don't want to experience pain, and we classify deception as wrong because it is unfair and shows disrespect for the person. We classify acts as right or wrong on the basis of what people want and on the basis of equal consideration of people's wants, because the point of having moral rules in the first place is to control behavior in such a way as to enable people to have what they want and to resolve conflicts between people when their wants conflict. Classifying certain kinds of organisms as bacteria doesn't explain what bacteria do, but enables us to know whether an organism is a bacterium based upon what characteristics it has; it is these characteristics that in turn enable us to predict what bacteria will do under particular circumstances. Likewise, classifying certain kinds of actions as wrong doesn't explain their effects, but enables us to know whether a particular act is wrong based upon certain observable characteristics it has; it is these characteristics which cause the predictable effects of the action. All this, of course, presupposes that we can reliably connect the moral qualities of an action with empirically observable characteristics. To show that this is so is the task of the remainder of this book.

CHAPTER 2

THE MEANING OF 'OUGHT' – A FORMAL SCHEME

The challenge before us now is to provide an account of the meaning of moral expressions which is generally acceptable. If this cannot be done, then my contention that the meaning and truth of value judgments is to be found by discovering the moral beliefs that people in general hold most deeply will fail to be substantiated. The task consists of two parts. The first and easier is to spell out a schematic account of what the term 'ought' means; this schema is, I think, applicable to most moral theories. The second task is much more difficult, for it will require fleshing out the meaning of 'ought' in ways that assert the truth of ethical principles, which — though general — have definite content capable of allowing solutions to moral questions.

I shall contend in the first component that — in general — 'oughts' refer to the meeting of some standards or other; in the second component I argue that moral oughts tell us what is necessary to attain a particular end or purpose of morality which is the greatest happiness for all consistent with a like happiness for everyone. It is not hard to see that many will accept the first who will find the second problematic.

In this chapter and throughout the remainder of the book, I will frequently appeal to those widespread moral beliefs which I called well-established, as well as to those very general principles which are typically cited as justifications for the well-established beliefs and for their application in specific circumstances. These principles, which are statements asserting that fundamental criteria apply, need not be universally held, but they are held by the vast majority of *reflective* persons — i.e., the sort of people who attempt to justify their moral beliefs to themselves and to others. They are the considerations to which people disputing ethical questions appeal and use to resolve their conflicts. In many cases where it appears that such thoughtful people hold some view contrary to those I claim are fundamental, I try to show that their views rest upon misunderstandings and that properly clarified they fit with views which I do consider well-established.   As indicated in the previous chapter, a theory of meaning (for any type of discourse) like the one I shall present need not be shown to be the only correct theory, for which truth conditions of several alternatives we accept is a pragmatic matter. On the other hand, a correct theory must be consistent with and explain, by giving a coherent account of, the discourse in question. It must be consistent with those well-established beliefs which people using the discourse hold in common to be true.

1. OUGHTS AND STANDARDS

A core feature of the meaning of oughts, which applies to all kinds of ought expressions and which is probably acceptable to all theorists about the nature of deontic language, is that the item in question (event, state of affairs, or action) meets some standard. A standard sets forth a criterion for ascribing value. If X ought to do A, then A is in accordance with a standard of behavior moral, prudential, or some other. If it ought to be that p, p's being true is appropriate to some ideal; it fits with a standard, or criterion, for goodness of the world. A third type of ought is the epistemic ought. In expressions like 'Ralph ought to be dead by now,' we are not saying that Ralph's being dead would meet a standard, but rather that — given what we know — one who concluded that Ralph would be dead by now would have used proper standards of reasoning.

Standards are sentences which set forth properties as criteria of value; they are *norms*. For the purposes of this chapter the nature of norms may be kept open, as there is considerable disagreement about their nature, but not about the role they play in evaluative discourse. What I have to say in this chapter about standards is consistent with norms' being either propositions with truth value or prescriptions grammatically different from propositions. The truth of descriptivism and moral realism are thus not implied by the view that what ought to be or what someone ought to do is first and foremost what meets standards. The remarks about standards which follow are compatible with both nondescriptivism and anti-realism. Wherever there are standards or criteria of appropriateness, these reflect value attributed. Those who ascribe to the standards believe that what meets them has some value, whether or not having value entails the truth of a statement. Where there are standards of behavior, behavior meeting those standards is more valued by those who subscribe to the standards than behavior which does not. A speaker who says that someone ought to do something or that something ought to be asserts that the something in question meets standards to which she subscribes, i.e., considers to be sound criteria of value. Furthermore, standards and criteria of appropriateness are set up in order to protect and enhance what people consider valuable. They reflect their ideas about what is and what is not of value. Thus if a person states that something ought to be or an act ought to be done, she implies that it is either valuable in its own right[1] or that it contributes to something else of value. What we value dictates what we say we ought to do or what ought to be. These statements about what people mean when they use oughts do not, however, entail that there are objective standards of value and behavior, or that — of competing standards — some are better than others. They are consistent with some forms of nondescriptivism — e.g. Hare's, according to whom an acceptable standard must meet the requirement of universalizability.

A further feature of oughts which is common to them all is that ought expressions imply that the action or state referred to is a strong requirement for meeting the standard. While other acts or states might be acceptable, or even good, according to the standard, the standard might be met without them, but if what ought to be, or to be done, is not, the standard will be met only with difficulty or not at all. For example, if you ought to drive to Chicago, then even though walking or flying might get you there, driving is the one way which will meet the relevant standards (which would no doubt include time and financial constraints). If driving and flying were equally appropriate, then neither is *the* means of travel you ought to take. Rather, you ought to either drive or fly (as opposed to walking or taking a cab). As another example, if both p and q are incompatible statements equally supported by the evidence, then 'It ought (epistemically) to be that p' is not true. Rather, it ought to be that *either* p or q, assuming that no alternative conclusion r is at least equally justifiable.

A third feature which I believe is common to all forms of ought is that, if an act ought to be performed or a state of affairs ought to be, then not only is it required for meeting *some* standard, but that standard is correct. If I were to maintain that a criminal ought to be hanged, drawn and quartered on the grounds that this meets a standard of justice held in medieval Europe, this would not suffice to justify my contention.[2] I would need to justify the standard itself. If I could not adequately defend the standard, I would not be able to defend the judgment, even though the action I said ought to be done met the standard. Such a defense could, but need not, entail showing that it is true that what meets the standard has value. If one is a nondescriptivist, one might have other criteria of correctness, such as that the speaker would prescribe the act for everyone in the given circumstances or that it was an accepted standard of behavior for the speaker's society. Obviously, what standards are considered correct depends upon one's moral theory, and whether they are actually correct depends upon whether the theory itself is correct.

Three things valued almost universally are reflected in the three major sorts of oughts mentioned here. People value what would – in their opinion – constitute an ideal, or at least a better, world. Anything which would be necessary to its realization is something which ought to be. Secondly, we value truth and knowledge, and good reasoning is necessary for attaining these. Standards of reasoning are dictated by what procedures are needed to reach knowledge and truth. This gives rise to epistemic oughts: the conclusions we ought to draw from given evidence. Finally, the objects of goals and purposes are valued, and we consequently value actions which are required for their realization. This is the source of the ought - to - do.[3] Whether these three valued things — ideals, truth, and realization of our purposes — are in fact valuable is another matter; nevertheless, a sentence of the form 'X ought to do A' or 'It ought to be that p' implies that A or p has value, be it intrinsic or instrumental.

The connection with appropriateness or meeting standards had by all forms of oughts does not entail any logical relationships between ought - to- be's and ought - to- do's. In fact, there are probably at most pragmatic relations between them.[4] If this is correct, then the fact that it ought to be that p does not imply that anyone ought to perform any action, and that X ought to do A does not imply that any state of affairs ought to be. Since this is a book about ethics, my major concern will be with ought- to-do's, although there will be occasional need to bring in ought-to-be's as well. Unless otherwise indicated, then, the remarks which follow will apply to the ought-to- do. I will not discuss epistemic oughts any further in this book.

2. OUGHTS AND GOALS

Thus far, I do not believe that anything I have said is likely to be disputed. From here on, however, the path becomes more difficult, for I must spell out the, or at least a, correct standard for ought-to-do's. Most — but not all — would agree that — with the exceptions to be discussed below — people ought to do what is needed to achieve their own goals and ought not to do what will frustrate their achieving those goals. We also suppose, however, that it is permissible to use a certain means to an end only when one's so doing does not frustrate the equally important — or more important — ends of oneself or of others. What one ought to do and what is an effective solution to one's practical problem may not be the same.

The relationship between them is, however, a close one, and in order to unravel it, we need to consider the meaning of deontic sentences in some detail. In determining what a statement like 'X ought to do A' means, we must pay careful attention to its actual use, because, as I argued in Chapter 1, what people not only agree to be true, but appeal to in order to settle disputes, is central to meaning. The analysis which follows does, I believe, represent a formalization of what people mean when they make such statements.

I shall propose below a formal scheme of analysis of the statement 'X ought to do A,' and then defend it against some actual and possible criticisms. That a person ought to do A means that doing A is either logically or causally necessary (or at least strongly required) for attaining one of a certain range of goals, in that his failing to do A will place significant obstacles in the way of achieving that goal. The standard which actions must meet if 'X ought to do A' is true is that X's doing A would attain a goal within that range. 'X ought to do A,' is sometimes used in a weak sense, to mean merely that A is not something X ought not to do. It is primarily used in a stronger way, however, to mean that A is in some sense required; I shall try to show that what it is required for is the realization of certain sorts of ends.

The statement form 'X ought to do A' is used in a variety of contexts, which may be classified into three groups. We use oughts in the *specific goal* context when we say that X ought to do A because A is necessary for X to in order to attain some goal X has. X ought to do A in the *prudential* context when doing A is required for X to in order to attain what is in his own best interest, or his own good. Finally, 'X ought to do A' is used the in the *moral* context when the speaker maintains that X's doing A is morally required.

The context in which an ought statement is being used is generally clear from the overall context, although it may not be. Alice might say to in order to Bob, "I ought to go to Charlotte's party," and Bob might reply, "Why? You didn't promise, did you?" (taking the ought to be in the moral context). Alice might then say, "No, but Dave will be there and I need to in order to talk with him about my investments." Here Alice is using the ought in a specific goal or prudential context, but even with this clarification, it is not apparent which of these two is being employed. What we do know is that Alice considers her going to the party a necessary step for attaining some purpose, which might be a specific desire on her part, or her overall best interests, or possibly even moral, if she thinks of caring for her investments as a duty which affects others besides herself. And certainly there are times when what one ought to do fits more than one context. This could be the case with Alice, if she wants her investments to in order to succeed regardless of their effects on her best interests or those of others, but also knows that their success is important to her good and that of her dependents.

Although there are often overlaps among them, and a given ought statement may be used simultaneously in more than one context, we may discuss each of these contexts for practical oughts separately. The specific goal use of ought statements is employed when we say that in order to achieve some end — either stated or not — had by X, X ought to do A. A necessary condition of the truth of "X ought to do A," used in the specific goal context is that A is needed to in order to attain X's goal. Thus if Ellen desires to lose weight, then she ought to consume fewer calories than she expends, because in no other way can this goal be achieved.

There may be more than one means of attaining a given end, and we can never show that there is *not* more than one means.[5] When there is more than one equally effective means, the agent needs to consider the effects of each of these means on his other ends. If there is no effect, none of the means is *the* one the agent ought to pursue; he ought, however, to adopt *one* of them: i.e., if the various means are A_1, A_2....A_n, then he ought to do A_1 or A_2 or...or A_n.

On the other hand, if the alternative means have differing effects on the agent's other ends, he ought (subject to in order to the restrictions which I will discuss below) to adopt the means that will enable him to realize the greatest number of his ends, or those most important to him, and avoid, if possible, those which would frustrate his other ends. People generally believe that an agent ought not to pursue one end at the cost of frustrating those he values more. Thanks to the miracles of liposuction and other forms of surgery it might not be necessary to establish a negative calorie balance in order to lose weight (although if Ellen continues to eat as she used to, she will gain it back). Even if liposuction were successful, however, she would have to consider possible adverse effects upon her health resulting from surgery, as well as the financial costs of such a procedure. What she ought to do in the specific goal context would be what she must do to maximize what is valuable to her (i.e., maximize the realization of all her specific goals).

If no action is needed on the part of the agent in order to attain something she desires, then there is nothing she ought to do with respect to that end. But if the end cannot be achieved without her doing something, then she ought to perform some one of the available means.[6] If a given action is required in order for some end to be achieved, and there is an essential step involved in it, then the agent ought to perform that step. On the other hand, if a particular step is not necessary, but other measures will do as well, it is not the case that the agent ought to perform that particular step. Nevertheless, he ought to perform some sequence of steps or other. For example, Ellen might choose a diet, an exercise program, or some combination of these. No one of these plans need be *the* one she ought to follow, but she ought to follow one of them, given that her goal is to lose weight. Because individual necessary steps are things that ought to be done, even though they alone will not result in the attainment of a given end, that X ought to do A does not entail that A is sufficient for X's attaining some end. Nonetheless, X ought, subject to the restrictions outlined below, to adopt some sufficient means or other for attaining her ends.

It is neither necessary nor sufficient for the truth of "X ought to do A" that X or anyone else believe that A is required for achieving a given end. It might be thought that what a person ought to do is not what will in fact enable her to attain her ends, but rather what has the highest probability of doing so.[7] Even if a certain course of action is the most rational, however, it does not follow that it is the one that ought to be performed. For example, suppose that, to the best of my knowledge, my driving to Denver for some errand is necessary for some end. A sudden, entirely unexpected snowstorm, however, keeps me stranded on the Interstate for two days. I might truthfully lament that I ought not to have come. That I ought not to have come, however, does not entail that I chose stupidly or irrationally — provided that I pursued the course of action that was most reasonable given the evidence available to me. Since we often use ought expressions prospectively, what we see as needed for attaining our goals is the only standard we have for judging that we ought to do something. Retrospectively, of course, what we thought we ought to do, and what was subjectively reasonable for us to do, may often turn out to have been wrong.

In other words, we distinguish between what one actually ought to do and what it seems one ought to do, given the information to which one has access. Provided an individual has made reasonable efforts to obtain relevant information, and has not made foolish inferences from it, the accusation of irrationality is not appropriate, no matter how badly her actions turn out. We still say, however, that she (actually) ought not to have done A, even though she was rational in concluding that she ought to have done A. We commonly make this distinction in such statements as "It seemed the right thing at the time, but now I know it wasn't;" "I ought never to have let her go, but I knew of no reason then to keep her at home;" "He took every precaution that anyone could reasonably expect, but still ought not to have done it." Obviously, before an action is performed and its consequences known, we reasonably conclude that the agent ought to do what has the greatest probability of success; after the fact we might alter this assessment.

That one may be tempted to suppose that a person ought to do what all the evidence available to him supports has to do with considerations of blame. Blame for a person who did what he ought not to have done is only appropriate if that person's decision was based on poor reasoning or faulty standards. As I shall argue in Chapter 8, what we ought not to do is not necessarily what we deserve blame for doing.

Occasionally the best means for achieving a goal is to perform an action which the agent desires to perform for its own sake. For example, if I want to see a film, then, unless there is some overriding reason why I should not, I ought to see it. In this case, both the goal and the action which realizes it are the same. The fact that we often say a person ought to do things that he wants to do, as well as our saying that he ought to do what will best enable him to achieve what he wants, indicates that we believe a person's wanting a thing is a reason — although not a sufficient reason — for considering it something worth his having.

3. PRUDENTIAL AND MORAL OUGHTS

The reader who has proceeded thus far will undoubtedly have misgivings about specific goal uses of 'ought.' After all, that someone wants something doesn't always imply that she ought to do what is necessary to obtain it. What if doing that thing is morally wrong or bad for her? What if she shouldn't want the object of her desire in the first place? This is where the restrictions to which I alluded above come in. I shall argue that it is not only true, but imbedded in the meaning of 'ought,' that there is a hierarchy of contexts. The specific goal context has the lowest place, the prudential context is next, and the highest is the moral context. What this amounts to is that if a specific goal conflicts with the agent's overall good or with moral demands, the agent ought to put his specific goal aside. The theory of the hierarchy of contexts also implies that prudential considerations ought to give way to moral considerations in case of conflict. While people are not always *motivated* by moral considerations before prudential considerations and their own goals, when people attempt to *justify* what they believe or do, the justification will not be considered complete by parties who disagree with particular ought judgments unless it follows this hierarchy. The hierarchy is well-established in that it is common to nearly all moral systems and fundamental in that it is appealed to in cases of disagreement about practical matters. I doubt that there are any societies in which imprudence and selfishness — however widely practiced — are condoned as such by those who look objectively at such behavior, although what one society considers imprudent or selfish may differ from the assessment of others. Thus the custom of the potlatch practiced by some Native American people on the Pacific coast strikes most Americans as highly improvident and self-centered. The competitive giving of more and more gifts could drive one into extreme poverty, and those who win at this competition gain advantages at the expense of others. Yet the people who engaged in potlatches viewed the status they obtained as worth more than the goods they sacrificed, and considered the custom as a morally acceptable furthering of their own interests.

That the hierarchy incorporates what people mean by ought expressions is suggested by the following situations. Suppose an alcoholic is extremely anxious about some problem in his life. He knows that taking a drink is the only thing that will calm him. He also knows, however, that the drink will not solve his problem, and that it will impair his ability to deal with it. He is also fully aware of the deleterious effects of his excessive drinking on his health and his relationships with others, and of the fact that once he begins drinking it is very difficult for him to stop. In short, while taking a drink might be necessary to reach his immediate goal of becoming calm, it would be bad for him overall. And given that this is so, it is false that he ought to drink, and I think it highly unlikely that anyone, knowing of his addiction, could believe that he ought.

Another example which illustrates the hierarchy is this. Suppose that Evelyn has done something wrong and is likely to be found out. If she asks Frank what she ought to do, Frank would hardly say that she ought to throw suspicion on Gina, even though that might be the only way for Evelyn to get out of the difficulty and even be in her best interest in the long run. It is possible that Frank might advise Evelyn to do this; he might simply tell her to do it, or he might say, "This is what you have to do," or "There is no way out for you but this." However, if Frank said that Ellen *ought* to throw suspicion upon Gina, this would be false. His saying so would indicate that he was impervious to the moral wrongness of what he was advising Ellen to do, or that he was being deliberately misleading. A person might, of course, say such a thing — and certainly Ellen might not be motivated by moral considerations — , but remember that the structure here is what would be used in situations where justification would be called for. Frank might say something to Ellen like "If you are going to get out of this mess, you ought to thrown the blame on Gina," relativising the ought to the specific goal (or her own interest). Perhaps the best way to put my position is to say that detached oughts, not tied to a condition, more clearly follow the hierarchy than those which are relativised to a particular purpose. In other words, Herman, on hearing Frank's advice, might justly respond, "But Ellen really ought not to do that; that throwing the blame on Gina will get her out of her present difficulty is not sufficient to justify her acting so."[8]

The second context in which oughts are used is the prudential. Used in this context, "X ought to do A" means that A is needed to promote X's interests overall, what is best for him, or what is conducive to his greatest good. One's best interest is a goal which overrides one's particular desires, in that, where an end, or a means to that end, conflicts with one's best interests, it is not true to say that one ought to pursue that end or pursue it by that means. This accords with common usage; we often say that a person ought not to do such things as smoke, drink excessively, gamble with large sums, etc., since these things — however much we enjoy them — are ultimately detrimental to our best interests. The belief that we ought not to pursue our particular ends when these, or the means to them, conflict with what is best for us is virtually universal.

There is one exception to prudential oughts. We are often required by moral demands to do what is contrary to our interests. And in general, even though an action is in one's best interest, it is not the case that it ought to be performed if its performance would be contrary to moral principles.[9] Although it might be in my interest to poison my rich uncle who has generously provided for me in his will, it is certainly not true that I ought to murder him. That moral ends thus override prudential ends, just as prudential ends override particular desires, is so pervasive a feature of the way in which ought expressions are actually used that it seems accurate to say that they are part of the meaning of such expressions. In the specific goal context, 'X ought to do A' entails that A is needed for obtaining some goal had by X and does not conflict either with moral demands or with X's overall good. In the prudential context, 'X ought to do A' entails that A is in X's best interests and is, in addition, morally acceptable.

Uninterpreted, this claim would no doubt be controversial. I think the most efficient way of discussing the possible problems and how they may be answered is to state first what 'X ought to do A' in the moral context means, and then to clarify some possible misconceptions about its use in both the prudential and moral contexts. When we say 'X ought (morally) to do A,' we mean that X's doing A is morally right. Another way in which this might be put would be that A is strongly required for X to achieve moral ends. It may be thought that this is not merely an alternative way of saying that X's doing A is morally right, but an assumption of the truth of a teleological moral theory. It is not. A moral end might, for all I have said here, be moral action itself: i.e., if moral action is something which ought to be achieved for its own sake and not for the sake of any other end, such as the greatest happiness for the greatest number. If so, then just as we ought, other things being equal, to do what we want to do, we ought, absolutely, to do what is morally right; it may be that the best way of achieving moral ends is to act morally, because acting morally is an end in itself, the most worthy end to be achieved, even if it leads to no other good beyond it.

Moral ends — whatever they are — take precedence over both the prudential and particular ends of any agent in the following sense: where moral ends conflict with either prudential or particular ends, the agent ought to serve the moral ends. This is true, regardless of whether the agent cares about doing what is morally right. I still ought not to murder my uncle, even if I happen to believe that murder for personal gain is morally justified or if I have no concern whatever with being moral.

To summarize, the position I have set out here is this:

'X ought to do A' means that either (1), (2), or (3):

(1) A is required for X to achieve some goal(s) that X has, and doing A will not frustrate other goals which are more important to X, and A is not contrary to X's best interests or morally wrong.

(2) A is required for X to achieve what is best for X overall, and A is morally permissible (i.e., not contrary to the goal of moral ends).

(3) A is required for X to achieve moral ends.

I believe that all cases in which we say that someone ought to perform an action can be fitted into one of these three contexts. If X's doing A is not needed to achieve one of these kinds of ends, A is not an action that X ought to perform. Actions which are not morally required, do not contribute to one's best interests, and do not lead to the achievement of anything we may want are not actions which we ought to do. It does not follow, of course, that we ought *not* to do them.

The analysis which I have given above is only schematic, specifying but a few aspects of the content of ought judgments. Basically, it rests on the following postulates which are consistently appealed to in arguments for and against particular ought judgments, and it is difficult to think of defensible counter examples to them. They are:

(1) That what we ought to do is what is needed to attain goals; that if a particular action could have no effect upon whether some objective could be achieved, there would be no grounds for saying that it either ought or ought not to be done.

(2) That one ought to do what is needed to realize one's greatest overall good if one's personal goals conflict, and ought to do what is morally right when the goals and interests of more than one person conflict.

I would further argue that persons using ought expressions in a manner contrary to these postulates might not be understood by others. Consider how peculiar the following sentences seem. "I know it would be bad for you on the whole, but you ought to go ahead and do it, just because you feel like it" and "Of course it is morally wrong to do that, but you ought to anyway because it is in your best interests." It is at least questionable whether anyone seriously uttering such sentences would mean the same thing by "ought" that the rest of us do.[10] A further indication that ought judgments imply moral acceptability would be that if Joe tells Karen that she ought to have an abortion and Karen is opposed to abortions, she would vigorously dispute Joe's statement. If he then said, "I just meant this would be best for you," she would be inclined to point out that there were other considerations besides her personal interests which determine the rightness or wrongness of actions. Joe could only convince her that she ought to have the abortion if he could convince her either that nothing but her own well-being need be considered or that she was mistaken in thinking abortions were morally wrong. The natural interpretation of ought judgments is that they are at least consistent with moral demands,[11] and to use them in contrary ways demands explanation.

Postulate (1) implies that it would not be possible to justify a statement of the form 'X ought to do A' if A could not be shown in some way to be conducive to an end that some person(s) either cared about or might conceivably care about. Consequently, I think that this formal scheme for the use of ought expressions is one of their truth conditions. It does not exhaust them, of course, for it does not include the full content of moral judgments, but only some constraints upon them.

On my theory, we can discover the meaning of terms (and the truth conditions of sentences containing them) by finding out what considerations are used to justify the application of those terms. It does not follow that every person who understands the term and uses it correctly has thought about such justifications or would be able to produce one on the spot. If, however, one of her judgments is questioned, one who fully understands a term should be able to argue for it by appeal to criteria which either are fundamental or could in turn be justified by fundamental criteria. The junior officer who is told by a superior that he ought to do something (as opposed to being ordered to do it) will have no trouble understanding not only what he is to do, but, because it is his captain who is speaking, he knows he had better do it. On the other hand, the captain's *ought* statement might be questioned — e.g., by her superior officer — , in which case she would need to justify it in terms of the goals of the army or the particular unit, the interests of the lieutenant, or even moral reasons. If she understands what she has said to the lieutenant, she should be prepared to offer such a justification.[12]

A major objection to (1) is that what is morally right need have nothing to do with people's goals.[13] The consequences of an action are not what determine its rightness or wrongness, and therefore what we ought to do cannot be decided by seeing whether or not the actions in question are conducive to the realization of goals. The precise relationship between what people want and what is right is a complex one, which I shall be discussing in later chapters, but the fact that it is not invariably right to act so as to get people what they want or invariably wrong to frustrate a want does not show that what we ought to do has no relationship to goals and objectives.

4. OBJECTIONS TO THE HIERARCHY

The primary objection to postulate (2) is that it is not true by definition — and may not be true at all — either that (a) moral ends ought to take precedence over the interests and specific goals of the agent, (b) the overall good of the agent should always take precedence over his particular goals, even when moral issues are not at stake, or (c) there are no other types of oughts which need to be considered. Each part of this objection deserves a detailed reply.

(a) (i) It might be thought that the fact that there are ethical egoists shows that it cannot be true by definition that moral ends should take precedence over prudential ends. What a theoretical egoist typically maintains, however, is not that a person's self-interest takes precedence over what is morally right, but that what is morally right is identical with each agent's pursuing her own interests to the greatest extent possible. Some egoists such as Nietzsche[14] maintain that certain individuals have greater worth than others and that even if their pursuing their own interests harms those others this is morally acceptable.[15]

Most egoists – Spinoza for example[16] – maintain that the interests of all are best served by everyone's pursuing what is in his own true interests. On this view the kinds of actions which result in harm to others are not truly in the interests of the agent. Thus if Spinoza is right it is not in the best interests of anyone to attain excessive wealth, power, etc., which others cannot share.

Others — no philosophers among them, to my knowledge — say that a person should look out for himself, and not bother with anyone else. Usually when someone attempts to justify this claim, he bases it on the view that if you don't look out for your own interests, no one else will. Such people seem to hold a view of the world similar to Hobbes's State of Nature, in which mutual aid and protection from harm are not available. This position might be interpreted in one of two ways. Either its proponents think that what is morally right is the same as looking out for your own interests, or they don't think so. If they think it is morally right to do so, they would probably say that in a State of Nature no one's interests would be served by his failing to take care of his own needs first of all. Such egoists would view morality as what creates good or promotes interests and deny that given the world as they see it being altruistic will do this. Consequently, it is, if they are right, wrong to do what people usually think of as moral. If they hold this, then the same remarks apply as those I applied to Spinoza.

On the other hand, if they hold that there is a difference between what is prudent and what is morally right, then they are expressing a decision (or advice) not to act morally. They oppose acting morally because they want what is in their interests more than they want to do what is morally right. Such egoists espouse a flawed position. As Brian Medlin pointed out,[17] they must either recommend that others besides themselves ought to ignore morality or not recommend this. If they do recommend it, doing so could go against their personal interests and hence their view is self-defeating. Suppose, on the other hand, some egoist (call him Egbert) maintains that he alone ought to put his interests above moral concerns. Other people, however, ought to do nothing to interfere with Egbert's interests. Egbert's position is consistent, but he can hardly expect anyone else to accept it. I do not wish to maintain here that everyone who claims to be an egoist has thought out these implications of his theory; rather, an egoist who attempted to defend his views would need to face those implications..

To summarize, in no egoistic theory even remotely worthy of belief does the proponent really hold that there are moral demands distinct from maximizing one's own good, which demands are subordinate to one's own good. Certainly, many egoists maintain that society's requirements that people sacrifice themselves for others are wrong. According to their views, these rules can be legitimately ignored and may even be immoral.[18] This claim, however, is that certain social demands are not morally required or even worthwhile — not that we should avoid doing what is morally right. Furthermore, all views about ethics that anyone happens to have had are not data worthy of supporting a moral theory, but only those which have stood up to discussion — whether by philosophers or by intelligent people generally. A great many people seem to confuse what they believe to be right with what they want — in fact, probably most of us do this on occasion, but such confusion is easily exposed when the issues in question are discussed impartially. What counts as data for a moral view — i.e., well-established beliefs and fundamental criteria used in justification — are what have survived criticism and cultural change, and not the views of just anyone who has an opinion about morals.

(ii) Another possibility which would create difficulties for my position has been raised by James Forrester.[19] It is that, while in general moral considerations take precedence over prudential ones, this is not necessarily the case. If, for example, one's important personal interests would be harmed by fulfilling a minor moral obligation, one surely ought not to fulfill the obligation. Most persons would think it wrong to risk getting the job I have always wanted in order to keep a promise to meet you for lunch or put flowers on your grave on your birthday. If so, this suggests that prudential considerations may sometimes outweigh moral considerations.

The appearance is dispelled, however, when we look at the manner in which someone might attempt to justify putting the prudential concern first. The most likely manner of arguing would be to say that the balance of *moral* good over harm would be greater if I pursued the job rather than keep the trivial promise. One feature of virtually all moral theories is that the agent's good counts equally with that of others: i.e., that it is morally, as well as prudentially, relevant. Even Kant, who would not allow anyone's placing one's own interest above fulfilling minor promises, would give overriding moral weight to the agent's interests in some cases — e.g., the perfect duty of not taking one's own life presumably outweighs the imperfect duty of helping others in need.

Other major theories clearly allow putting one's own major interests above the lesser interests of others. In utilitarianism, for example, the agent counts for one just as everyone else does, so that if more good can be done by doing something for herself than by doing something for someone else, she ought both morally and prudentially to help herself. According to ideal observer theories and social contract theories like that of Rawls, the method of choosing what actions or rules to adopt involves considering what an impartial individual would do, i.e., one who would not, or could not, make choices based upon the identity of the persons affected – including whether one of the persons affected is oneself. The right answer to a question of whether an agent ought to act in her own interest or that of another is therefore in such theories independent of the fact that the agent's interest is involved. Whether X ought to help X rather than Y is determined by the same considerations that determine whether X ought to help Z rather than Y. Jews and Christians are supposed to love their neighbors *as* themselves — not necessarily more than themselves. Thus, one's own interest can outweigh some interests of others in some circumstances in all major classes of moral theory. This, however, does not show that prudential considerations sometimes outweigh moral considerations, because it is sometimes *morally* right, as well as prudent, to put some concern of your own ahead of some concerns of others.

Perhaps, however, there are some *non*moral grounds for arguing that one ought sometimes to place one's own interest ahead of a moral obligation. Two candidates seem possible: first, prudential reasons, and, second, some other nonmoral, nonprudential ought. I shall discuss the second possibility below under (c). As for the first, if I were to try to justify on prudential grounds the contention that I ought to pursue an attractive job opportunity rather than meet you for lunch, I would say simply that it is better for *me* to pursue the job than to keep the promise. What is most striking about such a defense is that, despite the quite obvious truth of the stated premise, it *ignores* your interests. No one would be satisfied by it, whereas a defense which took your interests into account and found them less weighty than mine in these circumstances would be quite acceptable. My action would not be considered justified merely by my pointing out what was best for me, because I would have ignored the relevant moral considerations: i.e., your interests and the value of promise-keeping.[20] Not only would using such a defense show me up as a selfish, unfeeling person, but also and more importantly, justifying an action requires showing it to be morally acceptable; otherwise the justification is considered incomplete by people who engage in moral discussions. This is evidence for a shared belief in the primacy of moral oughts.

(iii) Another objection, which has been suggested by Jonathan Harrison,[21] is that there are nonmoral virtues, and, by extension, goals, which might take precedence over doing what is morally right. As examples, he cites competence at one's job, or the development of an outstanding artistic talent. Would you not prefer, he asks, to have your neurosurgeon be superlatively skilled than to be a morally good man, or to hear the works of a great composer who has a few moral failings than those of a second rater who does everything he "ought" to do?

Harrison does not claim that professional or artistic excellence is necessarily incompatible with moral goodness, but he does point out — correctly — that some of the qualities which may make a person supremely good at his work may also be qualities that can lead to moral failings. Furthermore, the time and energy expended in seeing that one does his moral duty may be taken at the expense of perfecting one's other abilities. A great neurosurgeon, for example, must have a very high degree of self-confidence, which may easily become arrogance. He cannot afford to tolerate incompetence on the part of those who work with him, and this may lead him to be unduly offensive to his underlings. A composer, if he pays his bills and provides for his children's education by working at a full time, mind-deadening job will accomplish less musically than he might if he ignored some of these responsibilities.

Answers to this objection vary depending upon one's view of what is morally right. According to utilitarianism, whether Jones and Smith are morally justified in their actions depends upon what is the greatest good for the greatest number. If Dr. Jones would be a less than excellent surgeon if he refrained from throwing instruments at the operating room staff, and if Smith would not have written his marvelous symphonies had he kept up the mortgage payments on his house, the world would lose much. It would probably lose much more than it does by the failings of the individuals concerned, and thus Jones and Smith would be morally justified in behaving as they do. Thus a utilitarian could say that it may very well be morally better, as well as better in some nonmoral sense, for Dr. Jones to concentrate more on improving his skills than on controlling his temper and for Smith to be gainfully employed only sporadically so that he can spend more time on his music.

We might look at Harrison's examples from another point of view, as well. Given a theory of morality in which subordinates creating great good to meeting certain specific sorts of obligations to others, such as being courteous or paying one's debts, what Jones and Smith morally ought to do would be quite different from what it would be in classic utilitarianism. We might, of course, *prefer* that these gifted individuals put their efforts into realizing their talents rather than meeting their moral obligations. ("We" here presumably refers to the beneficiaries of the talents, and not to nurses hit by flying scalpels or Smith's hungry children.) That most people would prefer to have the talents developed than the obligations met, however, does not imply that the surgeon and the composer *ought* to act as they do. The fact of preference would govern only a specific-goal ought, and might very well be outweighed by moral considerations, including the preferences of particular victims of ill temper and insolvency. According to a theory like Kant's, which gives much greater weight to following universalizable principles than to producing good, talented persons ought to fulfill their perfect duties rather than develop their gifts to the greatest extent, when they cannot do both. Furthermore, on practically any moral theory, if Jones and Smith actually harm others, the development of their talents is probably not a sufficient excuse for their behavior. It is hardly necessary for Jones to throw scalpels at nurses in order to be superb at his craft; he could surely criticize less violently.

And if Smith is unwilling to take on family responsibilities, he should not have children. In short, Harrison's examples do not show that people ought sometimes to do what is not morally preferable.

Harrison also brings up the case of Mark Twain's Huckleberry Finn. Huck has the opportunity to turn in his friend, the runaway slave Jim. He believes that he ought to do this; like the rest of his society he believes that slaves are property and that by helping Jim escape he is actually stealing. He cannot bring himself to betray Jim, however, and suffers pangs of remorse because he believes himself a thief. Twain clearly suggests that Huck is a far better person for his loyalty to Jim, and contemporary readers almost certainly agree. Could this be used as an argument for saying that it is not a fundamental moral belief that moral considerations trump others? Not at all. Huck clearly thinks he ought to have turned Jim over to the slave hunters; he believes that this was the morally right thing to do and that his inability to betray his friend was weak and bad. We (modern philosophers, like Huck's creator) think he did right and that his actions showed him to be a fundamentally decent person, but we believe this because we believe that slavery is morally wrong and that helping a person escape his bonds would be morally praiseworthy. Consequently, we think Huck's action was justified, even though he does not. Jonathan Harrison and Huckleberry Finn both think that Huck ought to have done what is morally right; they differ in their view of what actually *was* morally right. In short, the example of Huckleberry Finn is not a counter-example to the view that people generally believe that moral considerations trump one's personal preferences and interests.

(b) It is a fairly popular view among laymen and literary people that prudence is not a greater virtue than pursuing certain other goals which may be contrary to one's best interests. There are those who maintain that a person ought to sacrifice all for love, for art, or for any of a variety of ends, none of which have any obvious connection with prudence *or* morality.[22] The kind of life which such persons criticize does not, however, really seem to be that of seeking one's greatest good; rather it is a narrower characteristic — namely, a cautious regard for what is safe and avoids risk. One's true good, such people would maintain, requires commitment and sacrifice of certain goods, all for the sake of a higher good. The view that one has not really lived until he has been passionately in love or has done something creative suggests that the real position here is that such experiences are an essential part of a good life. They constitute part of one's good, and thus may be considered in one's best interests overall, even though attaining them may frustrate certain other goals and interests. (I will discuss these considerations more fully in the next two chapters which deal with individual good.) In other words such claims might be justified — if they can be justified at all — on prudential grounds (whether or not their proponents would agree); if they are not, it is difficult to see how they could be justified to anyone's satisfaction – with the following exception. Certainly, people who take risks and bear burdens contrary to their own interests for the benefit of others are considered not merely justified, but heroic. We may, of course, admire those who take risks like jumping the Snake River on a motorcycle. Yet we admire them because of a virtue they exhibit, such as courage. In turn, however, we admire courage because it enables people to do what is needed for the good of themselves and others. On the other hand, if we ask whether a biker *ought* to take such a leap, we would appeal to such considerations as responsibilities to others (e.g., his young children) to stay alive and whole, or what will bring him the best life overall (which might, given his personality, include doing some things that the rest of us would find utterly foolhardy). And of course, people often do the most imprudent things without thinking at all; we are considering, however, the way in which people attempt to justify what they have done – not just what anybody might actually do.

5. OTHER KINDS OF OUGHTS

(c) (i) It has been argued that there are a number of other contexts in which people ought to do things: e.g., legal, religious, in accordance with customs, or as a result of some kind of contract, and that these may have little or nothing to do with what is morally right, in the interests of the agent, or needed for the attainment of his goals.[23] Indeed, according to Kierkegaard, what one does as an act of faith in response to a command from God may override the requirements of morality. Hence Abraham was justified in being prepared to sacrifice his son, since God had ordered him to do so.[24] Kierkegaard points out that only such an act of faith justifies us in violating a moral principle, and the person who does so is and should be in a state of dread, for what he took to be a divine injunction may not in fact have been so. Nevertheless, there are occasions when moral obligations may be overridden by the demands of faith.

While legal, religious, promissory, and other obligations do not generally seem to be derived from moral obligations, and appear to have a life of their own, the reasons which are generally employed to justify (as opposed to people's motivations for following) them are, ultimately, moral, prudential, or for the attainment of some goal. So also are the reasons we could cite for choosing to fulfill one form of obligation rather than another in cases of conflict. An example is the Quaker who decides to violate his legal obligation to serve in the armed forces in order to fulfill his religious obligation not to fight. In concluding that his religious obligations ought, either in general, or in this particular case, to take precedence over his legal duties, he must, in order to justify his choices, have some means of determining which obligations are most important.

I do not deny that people could derive moral obligations from legal or religious obligations, or consider some of these alternative types of obligations as independent. Rather, I hold that when such obligations are questioned or challenged, or when conflicts between them occur, what we in fact appeal to ultimately when pushed is most likely to be moral or prudential considerations. Furthermore, the fact that we do appeal to them is good grounds for considering them more fundamental, just because it is by observing such usage that truth conditions are discovered. I will illustrate by concrete examples that we do cite moral and prudential considerations in justifying other kinds of oughts.

We can, and often do, justify a given action on the basis of its legality, its aesthetic value, or its conformity to the demands of some religion. But sometimes the legal, aesthetic, religious, or other principles conflict with one another, or they may themselves be challenged. One could in some instances defend one such principle on the basis of another, for example, by defending a social obligation by pointing out that it was required by one's religion. But then suppose that it was questioned why one ought to do what one's religion requires. A person could, of course, say "One just ought, that's all." (Not everyone is interested in justifying their beliefs and actions to those who disagree.) But other people of a different — or no — religion, would not consider that person to have justified her stand. Particular individuals of the same religious persuasion might be satisfied, but others would not be. On the other hand, if someone maintains that she ought to do something her religion demands because it is also morally right, or in her best interests, or something she wants to do, which is neither bad for her nor immoral, and if she convinces those with whom she is arguing that this is true, then she will almost certainly satisfy them.

That people do so respond is indicated by the fact that Kierkegaard's suggestion that Abraham would have been justified in sacrificing Isaac had God not taken back his order sounds shocking, and, indeed, Kierkegaard himself expected this reaction. It is less shocking if we think of why a person would hold that he should act from religious faith. There seem to be two fundamental types of religious motivation: fear and love. If one does what he supposes that deities command because of fear, his reasons are prudential — to avoid disaster in the present and damnation in the future. On the other hand, if he loves God, he loves Him for a reason — either because of a supposed personal relationship — e.g., God cares about *him* (and perhaps others of a chosen group), or because he believes that God loves all mankind and will — despite any appearances to the contrary — bring about what is ultimately best for every individual. If the former, the motivation to obey God is to attain a specific goal (to foster the special relationship); if the latter it is moral (God is the ultimate expert on what is right). Of course, there are undoubtedly people who simply believe one ought to obey God, regardless of whether God's commands have independent moral worth. You just do what (you think) God has told you to do, possibly because God's will is the criterion of what is right. In this case, we have two possible accounts. Either the person holding such views does not attempt to justify them, or — if he does — he identifies God's commands with what it is morally right to do. There are indeed people who maintain that what God wills is the standard of what ought to be done, by which all other oughts, including moral oughts, are to be judged. But given the multiple conflicts between what different groups and individuals have claimed that God has commanded, it is virtually impossible to attain wide consensus on what God wills. Some outside standard is needed to determine whose interpretation is worthy of belief, and, since there are no broadly accepted epistemic standards for evaluating religious beliefs, there seems no better standard than whether the supposed divine commands are morally worthy.

Indeed, it seems that only the complete righteousness of God (either because his commands are themselves the standard of goodness or because they invariably conform to some independent criterion of moral rightness) which would justify a person's acting against established moral principles in response to what he believed that God had commanded. If God could be evil or ignorant, and thus tell a person to do something morally wrong, then the believer's faith would be misplaced and his actions wrong. And likewise if a person were to believe falsely that God had told her to do something which harmed another or required the violation of a moral principle, she would be wrong to follow the supposed divine command. I think that all religious persons — including Kierkegaard[25] — would agree.

We consider ourselves bound to obey the law, sometimes because we are supposed to have made an implicit contract by consenting to live in the society in question, or simply because it is believed to be, in the normal case at least, in the interests of all for everyone to obey,. Violations of the law are sometimes considered morally justified when doing so will correct injustices, and individual laws are justified or criticized on the basis of whether or not they promote the common good (even though this may not be the actual motive behind their adoption or repeal). Correcting injustices and acting for the common good are moral ends, and laws which promote neither these nor any other moral end are difficult to justify.

When our children question the sometimes mystifying rules of etiquette we generally point out that following them is frequently necessary to avoid hurting the sensibilities of others — with the implicit assumption that hurting people is morally wrong. We may also point out to them that if they want the good will of others, they will be polite; thus we give them a prudential reason for following social norms. Those who reject the religious obligations they were taught in childhood may do so on the grounds that since there is no God, or since He is unlike what they were led to believe, no harm can be done by ceasing to obey these rules. They may contend that such tenets are not obligations at all, for there is no moral wrong done in ignoring them. Usually, however, such apostates do consider themselves bound by some of what was once presented to them as religious obligations — namely, those injunctions which they consider to have some moral point apart from religious doctrine. For example, "Thou shalt not bear false witness" is justifiable on any moral theory, independently of religious considerations.

In short, in attempting to justify particular types of obligation or the specific demands that they impose upon us, we generally employ moral or prudential reasons. Alternatively, we may value the institution, such as religion, the law, or good manners, for its own sake. In this last case, we have a specific goal in promoting those institutions. Such specific goal oughts may be overridden. Thus a person who breaks the law in order to save someone's life (e.g., someone who protected Jews in Nazi Germany) is normally praised. Alternatively, a person who sticks to the forms of etiquette even when doing so hurts others is considered to have acted wrongly; this shows that we consider morality to take precedence over etiquette.[26] These examples show that people share the belief that we ought to choose first and foremost in accordance with what is morally right, or, if we do not believe there is a moral basis for a supposed obligation, then in accordance with what is prudent. In deciding whether or not we ought to obey a given law most people consider both whether there is some moral point in doing so, in which case they decide we ought to obey it, and whether, if there is not any moral reason, whether prudence requires obedience. Obviously, our actual motivations may be neither moral nor prudential, but if we are pushed to defend our position, these are the considerations upon which we fall back.

If there are neither moral nor prudential reasons for obeying a given law and no personal end is served by doing so, it ceases to be a justifiable obligation. There is, of course, a fairly strong case to be made for saying that there is some *prima facie* moral reason to obey any law. And unless a particular law is a dead letter, it is also usually prudent to obey it.

(ii) Castañeda proposed[27] that there is a type of ought which overrides both moral and prudential oughts, as well as any other sort. This is what he called the 'ought-everything-considered,' or ought$_e$. What one ought$_e$ to do is what one ought, absolutely, to do. This ought is the expression of the individual's motivational structure: what he wants most, given all the considerations that matter to him. By considering what we want most, value most, or consider most important, we can resolve conflicts between different oughts.[28]

I do not think, however, that it is necessary to have an extra-moral, conflict-resolving ought$_e$. If A ought, morally, to be done, then it ought to be done, regardless of whether other considerations weigh against it. And prudential, legal, and other oughts are valid only if they are morally acceptable. Hence the moral ought can be used to resolve conflicts among lesser oughts.

The main reason why I think my analysis is preferable to Castañeda's on this point is that people generally do not think that an agent actually ought, in all cases, to do what realizes the ends he is most motivated to pursue, or even those which he considers most valuable or important. (Just ask if Hitler ought to have pursued what was most important to him!) Even in ordinary cases, no matter how many other people an individual cares about, he is hardly likely to care about the interests of every single person, and certainly does not care about everyone to the same degree. Yet people generally believe that one ought at times to consider, and even give equal weight to, the ends of persons for whom one cares nothing. Morality is concerned with the ends and interests of all persons, and our ought judgments reflect this concern.

The main problems with Castañeda's ought$_e$ come to light when we say that someone else ought to do something. Do we mean that she ought to do what her own motivational hierarchy dictates? Certainly this is not invariably true. Most of us have thought on a occasion that a person ought, all things considered, to do a thing, when the person herself thought that, all things considered, she ought not to do it. Do we then mean by 'X ought$_e$ to do A' that X's doing A is demanded by the motivational hierarchy of the speaker? This does not seem right either. I might say, for example, that John ought to move his bishop to K-5, even though I don't care in the least whether he wins his game. If I'm playing against him, I certainly don't want him to win or to make the best move. We often say what a general or athlete ought to have done, even when we favor the opposite side. I believe that Nero ought not to have murdered his mother, despite the fact that I care nothing for either of them. One might say that it is part of my most cherished ends that no one murder anyone; perhaps so, but this does not apply to the past, which nothing I, or anyone else, can do will affect. If non-murdering is one of my ends, it can only be to prevent future murders.

In short, when Y says that X ought to do A, she is appealing to a standard that goes beyond both what X wants most and what Y wants most. This moral standard is, I think, dictated by what people in general want in the way of behavior from everyone. The standard may change, and certainly has over time, with consequent minor changes in the meaning of 'ought.' Nevertheless, the degree of change is limited by the fundamental fact that human beings have ends and use ought expressions to classify actions with respect to their effects on these ends.[29]

One feature of Castañeda's ought$_e$, which many would consider an advantage, is that it can easily explain how people can be motivated to do what they ought. Such philosophers as Hare, who consider the action-guiding aspect of moral language to be central to its meaning find this a difficulty with descriptivism.[30] Assuming the ought$_e$ is what one wants most to do overall, everyone will want to do what he or she ought$_e$ to do. My own analysis does not provide such a tight connection between what we ought to do and what we are motivated to do, and this is, I think, an advantage. Virtually everyone wants what is in his or her own best interests, and is thus strongly motivated to do what is prudent, yet even so we all fail at times to do the prudent thing. There is an even looser relationship between what one morally ought to do and what one wants to do. Not only do morally weak people fail to do what they ought to do despite wanting to do the right thing, but some are perverse enough not to care about doing the right thing. The trouble with making the connection between ought and motivation too tight is that weakness of the will, moral weakness, and perversity cannot be readily explained. If, however, there is no necessary connection between X's believing that she ought to do A and her coming to intend to do A, it is nevertheless possible that an adequate characterization of the descriptive meaning of ought expressions will explain why people are usually motivated to do as they ought.[31]

Even though a moral ought, as I have analyzed it, does not provide sufficient motivation for *all* people to do as they ought, it does give most people most of the time reason for wanting people in general to act as they ought, especially when the agent is the target of the actions of others. Suppose, for example, that I believe people ought not to steal. I certainly don't want people to steal from me, or from anyone I care about. Nor do I like it when stealing is so common that no one (including me) can feel secure about her possessions. Nor do I want to steal in situations where I might be caught and punished. As a matter of fact, I and, I believe, the great majority of others, don't want to steal because we don't like the idea of hurting others or being unfair to them. For most people, then, who believe that stealing is wrong, there is ample motivation to keep them from stealing. The existence of these motives does not imply that being motivated to do what one ought is a part of the meaning of "ought." And they are easily compatible with the fact that there are people who believe that stealing is wrong, but do it anyway.

In short, I think the hierarchy of types of ends is so deeply embedded in our beliefs about what we ought to do that these supposed counterexamples can be easily answered. And because these beliefs are fundamental to moral argument, there is a presumptive reason to include them among the truth conditions of ought-to-do's. As with any other expression, these truth conditions (and meaning) may change, but this does not affect their present status.[32]

6. WHY SHOULD I BE MORAL?

This question can have any of several possible meanings. These are: (1) Why is it right for me to be moral? (2) What motivations might I have for being moral? (3) Why should I follow the moral code of (my) society?[33] (4) What would make it rational for me to be moral? (5) What justifies me in being moral? My answer to (1) is that it is trivially true, since moral oughts trump others.[34] That is, they should always be followed and inconsistency with moral demands invalidates other ought claims. (2) has already been touched upon in the previous section; a person can be motivated to act morally for both prudential and altruistic reasons. Between society's enforcing certain moral rules by rewarding compliance and punishing deviations, on the one hand, and, on the other, individuals' caring about the feelings and rights of those with whom they typically come in contact — not to mention the desire to maintain closeness with others and their good opinion — most people most of the time have ample motivation to do what they believe is morally right. Obviously these motives are not sufficient, however, to make all people moral all the time. Since people frequently act against what they acknowledge to be right, a theory which makes moral motivation part of the meaning of 'morally right' is suspect. Question (3) should be answered, "Yes, provided that what one's society's moral code requires is consistent with what is really morally right." As noted above, there are good reasons for following the rules and traditions of the society of which one is a member, but these reasons are not absolute, and there are times when following them would be contrary to the demands of morality. In the latter case, we shouldn't be moral in sense (3).

As for (4), the answer depends upon what sense of 'rational' one uses. In a Humean sense what is rational is what will enable the individual to attain his ends. In that sense, it is not the case that one should always be moral, for our goals sometimes conflict with what morality demands, although it is probably usually rational for most people to act morally. In another sense being rational is acting impartially. Being impartial does normally lead one to act morally, because doing so treats everyone equally. This is an important part — but is not the whole — of morality. One could be perfectly impartial in dealing out pain and suffering, and one could also make all people equal by destroying whatever some have that makes them better off than others.

Another sense of rationality as impartiality combines the two above and can be seen in the work of Darwall, Firth, Rawls, and any who espouse an Ideal Observer theory. In this case what one should do is what one would want if one were completely impartial. This comes much closer to what would in fact be morally right, for it takes into account both what people want and what would be fair. To the extent that Ideal Observer theories adequately determine what is morally right, then to say that a person should be moral — i.e., be rational in that sense — would be trivially true. I shall discuss the adequacy of such theories more fully in Chapter 5.

Christine Korsgaard has argued that the answer to question (5) is "yes," in that being moral is justified by the fact that human beings can make rules for and demands on themselves.[35] The act of making a choice among the alternatives with which one is presented affirms that choice as being good and gives it the force of a command, thereby obligating us. The ability to reflect, choose, and command ourselves makes us autonomous agents. Our reflections enable us to decide which of our impulses are consistent with the practical conceptions we have of our identity — i.e., the roles we have, such as parent, citizen, etc.. And our specifically human identity is what allows us to reflect upon these roles and choose which we should retain and how to resolve conflicts between them. Treating one's human identity as normative — a source of reasons and obligations — is our *moral* identity; it is valuing our humanity. If we do not treat our humanity as normative, Korsgaard says, we have no reason to act at all, because our other, subsidiary practical identities are founded upon it and derive their authority, or normativity, from it.

The fact that we are autonomous does not, of course, guarantee that we will make the choices we ought to make. Korsgaard attempts to show that the only rational choices are those consistent with respecting the humanity of all persons. She does this by maintaining that choosing is an affirmation of our own humanity, because it is the ability to reflect and choose which makes us human. It would thus be inconsistent to support this ability in ourselves but ignore its claims in others. We all think others have obligations to us in that when they hurt us they have a reason — and thus an obligation — to stop. "But if you are a law to others in so far as you are just human, just *someone*, then the humanity of others is also a law to you." (p. 143)

Interpreting decisions as the formation of intentions and a type of self-command is highly plausible and thus gives them force. Yet it is our desire for what we choose or what that choice is expected to bring that provides the force behind the intention, not merely its status as a command. We can ignore commands when we neither fear nor wish to accommodate the commander. (Just before dinner your child demands "Give me a cookie!"). And, as Cohen points out in his reply to Korsgaard,[36] we have the power to change our minds when we no longer desire to do what we have previously decided to do.

But normativity is clearly more than what provides us with motivating force; it also includes authority. Can we say that our decisions have authority, in the sense that we have a right to make them and an obligation to obey them? In other words, if our choices are normative, they are justified. When we have made a decision, we usually also think that some good will come of it which good will justify the decision. On the other hand, — as in cases of akrasia or perversity — we may be perfectly aware that whatever good may come of a particular decision, it is not justified. And even when we believe our choices justified, we can be wrong through ignorance or stupidity. Whether a decision is justified depends upon whether it meets whatever qualifications make it *right*. It may well be that, as Korsgaard says, good and justifiable choices affirm humanity in ourselves and others by being consistent with our integrity and respecting the same in others. The point is, however, that justification is on other grounds than the fact that we can command ourselves. Even granted that the ability to do so is what makes us human (Yet do we *know* that no other animals can command themselves?), what makes our humanity the ultimate source of value and rightness? A case can, no doubt, be made for saying that this autonomy is our most valuable attribute, but it needs to be argued — perhaps on the ground that we do, after sufficient reflection, value it more than any other, as it enables us to do so much and have so much control over our destiny. Moreover, the fact that I value humanity in myself does not automatically entail that I must — on pain of inconsistency — value it in others. I might, for example, make the maxims of my action conform to whatever promotes *my* own interest. Unless I *already* believe that others' interests have equal weight, there is no inconsistency in my ignoring their concerns.

Korsgaard argues[37] that to make a choice is to choose on the basis of reasons. If R is a reason for action, this entails that it is also a reason to act in the same way in the same circumstances, should these arise again. And if it is a reason for me to act, it is also a reason for others, should they be in the same circumstances. And if R is a reason for me to desire certain behavior on the part of others, it is also a reason for me to act in the same way towards them. Thus reasons have a universalizability that mere impulses do not have. Note here that a great deal of weight is given to the term 'reason;' if the argument is to work, it must imply justification. But whether a reason is in fact a justification, it must pass the tests of morality, prudence, or whatever other standards of justification there may be. And if R is a reason for others to behave in a certain way toward me, it will only be a reason for me to behave similarly to others if their interests count as well as my own. What is operative here is not a demand for consistency, but an implicit assumption that the needs of all have equal weight — a substantive moral principle. In what follows, I hope to show that a morality of the kind Korsgaard envisions, in which the humanity of all persons is given equal consideration, can indeed stand behind whatever reasons for action are justified. I do not, however, think she succeeds in showing that such a morality can be derived directly from our human capacity for deliberation and choice.

7. OUGHT AND CAN

No discussion of the general meaning of 'ought' is complete without considering whether 'ought' implies "can." One who holds that 'ought' implies 'can' would also hold that A's being necessary for X's attaining one of the three kinds of ends is not enough to make it true that X ought to do A. A must also be in some sense open to X. If a newborn baby's best interest can only be promoted by its going out and earning its own living, we would hardly insist that the infant ought to do this. Something which X could not possibly be expected to do is surely not something which he ought to do.

It is not, however, universally believed that we ought to do only what we are able to do. As James Forrester has pointed out,[38] there are ethical systems which do not accept this tenet. For example, certain forms of Christianity set up the impossible moral demand that we ought always to act as Christ, who is perfect, would act. This is not simply an ideal to strive for. Our failure to achieve this impossible perfection makes us guilty and worthy of damnation, from which only the grace of God can save us. Forrester concludes from such examples that "'Ought' implies 'can'" cannot be a part of the meaning of 'ought.' Rather it is an implicature; the most common use of deontic language is to influence action, but we can't influence people to do the impossible (although we can get them to try). Consequently, it is at best silly and at worst cruel to make impossible demands, but it is not logically contradictory to do so. This is the reason why we would never say that a newborn child ought to earn its own living, or that Sophia ought to square the circle. Such sentences are not, however, analytically false. This is an issue to which I shall return in subsequent chapters, but for the moment I shall assume that it is not part of the meaning of 'X ought to do A' that X be able to do A.

8. CONCLUSION

The scheme proposed above does not depend for its truth upon any particular moral theory or any view of what is good for people or in their interest. This analysis is not necessarily even teleological, despite its emphasis on what we ought to do as being means to ends, for it allows that when performing an action is an end in itself (and this may include acting morally for its own sake), then we ought to pursue it, other things being equal. Nor does the scheme depend upon the truth of descriptivism. Even if moral and prudential standards are entirely subjective, what we say we ought to do is what meets those subjective standards.

A major challenge to my analysis is how to answer someone who doesn't agree that moral judgments take precedence over prudential and other kinds of oughts. What right do I have to say that he or she is wrong? Even if the great majority, or even everyone, agrees that one's own best interest should take precedence over particular desires, but a back seat to moral concerns, how do we know that this is *true*?

I have claimed that this hierarchy is part of the truth conditions (and hence meaning) of 'X ought to do A' on the grounds that this hierarchy fits with widely held and extensively defended beliefs about what sorts of practical considerations take precedence over others. If the argument of Chapter 1 is correct, this criterion will let us determine what is part of the meaning of any expression, moral or otherwise.

CHAPTER 3

INDIVIDUAL GOOD AS HAPPINESS

The purpose of the next two chapters is to provide an analysis of individual good: that is, for a given person, what is good for that person. This good may differ from what the person ought morally to do or what will achieve some ideal — either one of his own or one which society commends. I will try to show that individual good is identical with happiness, appropriately defined. In subsequent chapters I will argue that there is a central purpose of morality which is (1) to bring about as much happiness for all persons as is compatible with like happiness for all other persons, and (2) to bring about as much happiness for sentient nonpersons as is compatible with (1). Further, I shall argue that an individual ought to do what is strongly required for avoiding hindrance of this purpose,[1] and that the best thing someone can do, morally speaking, is to do what is, of all that is within his power, most apt to advance that purpose. By a "strongly required" action I mean that unless that action is performed it will be difficult if not impossible for the goal in question to be attained.[2]

Such an analysis clearly puts individual good at the heart of moral theory by claiming that the best we can do is to promote the happiness of persons and sentient nonpersons. The sole restriction I propose is that we may not promote the happiness of some at the expense of keeping others from attaining a like degree of happiness. But there are those who maintain that morality is not the promotion of individual good, and that what we ought to do is not determined by how much good our actions can accomplish. Others claim that goodness is not the sort of thing that can be measured at all. Still others deny that individual good can be even roughly equated with happiness or with what we want.

There is clearly much that is controversial here. Some of the questions which I will address in this chapter and the next include 'What, precisely, is happiness?' 'What else, if anything, besides happiness — as I have defined it — is part of

61

individual good?' 'If happiness does not encompass the whole of good, then is there not some other criterion of goodness, and, if so, what is it?' 'Is there a single criterion of individual good, or are there several (the claim of pluralism)?' 'What is the relationship of individual good to desires?' and 'Can goodness be measured?' Later on I shall discuss where the concept of individual good fits into an overall moral theory, including how can we make decisions about distribution or in cases of moral conflict. If the arguments in Chapter 1 are correct, goodness is at least possibly a real property, and sentences claiming that something is good could have truth value. Showing that goodness *is* a real property, however, depends upon providing an adequate realist analysis.

The plan of this chapter is as follows. First I shall discuss the meaning of 'good' in general. Secondly, I shall outline some desiderata for an analysis of individual good — certain requirements that would make sense of what people generally believe about what is good for a person. Then I shall discuss the popular group of theories which equate individual good with what satisfies our desires, or with desires of a certain restricted sort. These theories, unfortunately, have major flaws, but I believe that they are on the right track and that their difficulties are instructive. Subsequently, I shall develop an account of individual good as happiness, which is living in a way that the individual wants to continue. This position can, I hope, combine the advantages of desire and certain non-desire accounts while avoiding their difficulties. In Chapter 4 I will discuss some actual and possible objections to this sort of analysis.

1. 'GOOD' IN GENERAL

When we call a person, thing, or event good, we are saying that it meets some kind of standard to a relatively high degree. It has a high rank on a scale which could go from very poor to excellent. This is a characterization of 'good' which cuts across numerous metaethical views. Thus the prescriptivist Hare and the realist Elizabeth Anderson[3] both use it; what distinguishes them is their views of whether the standards themselves are objective.

The overall notion of goodness as meeting standards accords with common usage. Standards for a good tool or appliance are characteristics which enable one to do effectively the jobs for which that thing was intended, so those characteristics are considered marks of goodness in tools and appliances. For example, they do not break down under normal use. The more a thing has these properties, the *better* it is. Thus the more miles you get per gallon from your car, then — other things being equal — the better your car. Animals, too, may be considered good or bad, depending upon what uses we have for them, which uses set the standards. A dog or cat is a good pet if it is gentle and affectionate. Being a good pet may or may not be compatible with meeting other standards of goodness for these animals, such as being a good watchdog or a good mouser.

People, too, are called good X's when they fulfill well certain functions people have. Thus a woman could be a good lawyer or a good mother or a good athlete, meaning that she performs well in these roles. Alternatively, we often speak of persons as good overall, and by this we usually mean that they are morally good. We wouldn't, for example, call someone a good *person* no matter how good a lawyer she was if she was ruthless in court or neglectful of her family.

Things and people are called good only when they meet standards of functioning and behavior which are themselves at least acceptable. As a rule, fulfilling roles and functions which are considered bad or useless does not entitle one to being called 'good,' no matter how completely one carries them out. Hence there is no such thing as a good murderer or rapist. We sometimes, of course, speak of good — i.e., successful — liars, perhaps because it may be acceptable and useful to lie in certain circumstances — e.g., when trying to escape from enemy territory.   Most often, however the expression 'good liar' is used in a tongue in cheek way to deny that a person is one — i.e., has no skill at deception. Thus one may say with some pride, "I'm not a good liar." Occasionally, too, we could speak of someone as good at doing something which is morally bad — but in a context in which it is clear that we mean simply that he is effective.

Events and states of affairs are also considered good when they meet certain standards. Thus a good performance of an opera is one in which the voices, acting, and orchestral accompaniment are skilled and aesthetically pleasing.   A good party is one where the guests enjoy themselves — and no one causes trouble for the hosts or neighbors. A man is in a good situation when circumstances are favorable to his advancement — professionally, personally, or economically. A house is in good condition when there are no portions broken or unpainted, the plumbing works, and its roof, windows, doors, and basement are secure against the elements. We say "Oh good!" when we hear of some event or fact that bodes well for an individual — e.g., when a biopsy shows no malignancy or a wayward child has finally graduated. In all of these cases 'good' is appropriately applied because the people, objects, and events meet standards we have for operas, parties, houses, and personal fortunes and character.

Thus the truth that lies behind the pluralists' claims[4] is that there are a lot of things that are good. Primarily because we desire and enjoy many things for many different reasons, those things and events which bring good to our lives are widely various. There are enormous differences between eating a tasty meal when hungry, listening to a fine performance of your favorite symphony, realizing that you have done an excellent piece of work, and being in love. The characteristics of each of these experiences, and the reasons why they are desirable, appear to have little in common. The first and third are more apt to bring a sense of satisfaction, while the second and fourth more excitement. The first and last are more physical, the second and third more intellectual. Yet they are all experiences that people seek and are glad to have had, as well as apt to enjoy while they are happening. We seek them or try to prolong or repeat them, however, not just because they will satisfy a desire we may have, but rather for certain specific characteristics of those experiences. I go to a concert not because I want to satisfy my desire to go to a concert, but because I want to hear beautiful music. I try to do my best work not because I want to satisfy a desire to recognize it as good or even to experience it as good, but because I want it to *be* good. Yet while the character of the goodness of one experience, and the reason why it is sought, may differ from the character of the goodness of another, both are good because they have a tendency to a certain degree to meet standards, which standards are determined by our individual or collective goals.[5]

And in general, a fact or event is good *for* someone if certain features it has contribute to the well-being of that person — or perhaps an animal or an aggregate of individuals like cities or ecosystems. In an extended sense things can be good for plants or other inanimate objects — e.g., that watering trees is good for them or that it is good for cars to get their oil changed regularly. Goods for inanimate objects keep their functioning or appearance up to our standards. The characteristics of things called good meet certain standards which are set by the speaker's standards, or those recognized in his or her society, for what is good for individuals, which enable them to fulfill their goals, and which bring them enjoyment or happiness — without accompanying pain or disadvantage. At least whatever drawbacks they may have are significantly outweighed by the advantages. Hence a thing may be good for someone overall through having a greater balance of advantageous features over disadvantageous.[6] Often we consider the good of some non-human item (usually plants or animals whose existence and well-being we value) as being not so much what is conducive to our uses, but rather what makes that thing flourish. Hence, food that is good for a horse is what makes it strong, energetic, and resistant to disease; in this we are not merely supposing that these characteristics in horses are useful to us (which they generally are), but that they are analogous to characteristics that are good for people, and – by extension – any other living thing. We may also speak rather ambiguously of something's being good for a thing we'd like to be rid of. If, for example, someone says "X is good for tumbleweed," X could refer either to something that will kill these weeds or to something that will make them grow, but it is more likely to refer to the former.

Because our standards of well-being include good health and being educated, hearing of the benign biopsy or the young person's graduation is good news. The standards for houses include those features that make it comfortable and easy to live in; houses that meet these standards are good because anyone would want to live in one. On the other hand, a party where the guests have fun but break up the hosts' furniture and keep the neighbors awake all night isn't really a good party overall, for what may have been good for the guests was not good for the hosts and neighbors.

Thus many things are good for many reasons, but there is a common thread that runs through attributions of goodness. Directly or indirectly, what is good has a tendency to promote the well-being of individuals: i.e., to be *good for* those individuals. Often the connection is tenuous. For example, a good cigar or good chocolate cake is rarely good *for* anyone. They are good in that they have certain characteristics like a rich, smooth taste that contribute to the pleasure of those who enjoy them, but they also have a tendency to undermine the health of people who indulge too frequently. Having pleasures, however, *is* good for people in that having them makes their lives happier overall. Pleasures are only bad for you if they interfere with this happiness; thus cigars and cake can be good for you when you partake of them sparingly enough to avoid ill effects. Pleasures may thus be good even if they are not good for you, so long as they are not positively bad for you. (Yet on the view I shall defend anything that gives you pleasure, and does not bring pain or preclude deeper or more extended pleasure, is good for you since it is by definition something you want to continue. Once you stop wanting it to continue it is no longer a pleasure for you, or good for you to have it – at that moment.[7])

There is a difference between what is good for an individual and what is good overall. Just as a thing is not good to the extent that it is bad for the persons affected, it is not good overall if, in spite of being in the best interests of a particular individual, it is morally bad or is contrary to the interests of others. We might say that a particular war was a good thing for General Jones because he distinguished himself in battle, was never wounded, and as a direct result of the war embarked upon a successful military career. But we qualify it by saying it was good *for him*, not good overall. Likewise, something can be good overall without being good for a particular person. For example, the state of the nation's economy may be good overall as a result of increasing technology, but Smith may be worse off by losing his low tech job – although if there is no safety net or retraining provisions, for people like Smith, we might hesitate to say that the economy is good overall.

Overall goodness appears to have a hierarchical structure similar to that of what ought to be done. That is, it meets some particular standard without being against the interests of an individual or morally bad, or it promotes interests of individuals without being morally wrong, or it furthers the realization of moral standards. What is good overall and what is good for an individual share the feature of meeting some standard — the standards being respectively, for the general good and for individual well-being.

In contrast with oughts, if X is good, it is *sufficient* for meeting standards to a certain degree, or it helps to meet a standard, while if X ought to be or to be done, it is *required* for meeting standards. What is good may go beyond minimum requirements and is looser and more varied. There may be many different ways — none of which is necessary — of obtaining what is good, but if something ought to be or be done, *it* must be or be done to satisfy the standard. Likewise, if something is good for a person it suffices or at least helps to meet a standard of well-being, but may not be necessary, for the standard might be reached to the same degree by other means. On the other hand, if one ought prudentially to do something, that action is required for one's well-being.

The above remarks provide only a schematic account of 'good,' which is consistent with many theories of what is in fact good. What we must now consider is what constitutes correct standards of well-being — the substantive, not merely the formal, content of the concept of goodness.

2. WHAT DO WE WANT FROM A THEORY OF THE GOOD?

To begin with, it will be useful to set out several desiderata for an account of goodness. These desiderata are features of what people in general appear to believe about goodness. Such beliefs may be muddled at times, but it is the job of philosophers not only to clarify these beliefs but to give reasons why those that are untenable have taken such a hold. In what follows, I shall, for the reasons discussed in Chapter 1, assume the truth of J. L. Austin's dictum that while ordinary language may not be the last word, it is always the *first* word.

(1) *Variability*. An adequate analysis of the good needs to allow for the fact that good for different individuals and good for a given person at different times can vary.

(2) *Commonality*. Despite these differences, however, there is apparently some common core. While the specific things that are good for me may differ from those which are good for you, we generally presume that there is something about those specific things which makes them good for one person but not for another. Throughout the history of philosophy, many theories have been proposed: what is good is what participates in the Form of the Good, it is rational activity in accordance with virtue, it is what is conducive to pleasure, it is a simple, unanalyzable quality, it is that which is in accordance with God's will, it is what contributes to human flourishing or what is in accord with one's *telos*, it is what satisfies our desires, or certain sorts of desires, it is that which we approve of and want others to approve of as well. Each of these views of the good for an individual has been widely criticized, but it seems reasonable to think that an adequate analysis of the concept will need to incorporate some elements of at least some of them.

(3) *Comparability*. A theory of goodness should allow for comparisons and degrees. We commonly say that one thing is better, or better for someone, than another, and even that something is better for one individual than it is for someone else. For the purposes of a moral theory, it would be difficult without this comparability to settle questions of distribution — e.g., to say of some commodity that one person rather than another should get it, or, if it could be divided, how it should be shared. While there may well be goods which are incommensurable — like, perhaps, health and being loved — and while, according to nonconsequentialists, what we ought to do is not determined by the amount of good we can bring about, we still make comparisons of good. It would be useful to know what we are talking about when we do this, and, if we have no rational basis for making these comparisons, to know why we think we do.

(4) *Comprehensiveness*. There are an enormous number of things which people have judged as being good for individuals: including, but hardly limited to, knowledge, pleasure, wealth, love and intimacy with others, freedom and autonomy, security, health, accomplishment, beauty, and oneness with God. We need a concept of goodness which allows us to say that all, or nearly all, these things are good and why, as well as how it can be that some of them are sometimes *not* good for a

particular person. The concept needs to be sufficiently broad to do this job, yet also allow us to make judgments in specific cases, given specific conditions — e.g., would it be good for John to have a glass of wine right now. In other words, we want a concept of goodness that is inclusive, but not so broad as to be useless in practical reasoning.

3. GOOD AS SATISFACTION OF DESIRE

One way of fulfilling the above desiderata appears to be identify the good for individuals with the satisfaction of their desires. And indeed, most people think that goodness for an individual does have some connection with the satisfaction of her desires. If she desires two things, but cannot have both, it is usually better for her that she have what she wants most. It is difficult to believe that anything which nobody either wants or is ever likely to want could be good for anyone.[8]   If goodness for an individual is unconnected to desire, we would need an account of why most people believe otherwise.

The apparent connection between goodness and desire satisfaction has led to the economic notion of expected utility: the product of a number assigned to how much the individual wants a given outcome (its utility for that person) and the probability of its occurring, given a certain action. The presumption is that what is most rational, and most in one's interest over the long term, is to act so as to maximize expected utility.

There are, however, major difficulties with this scheme. First and foremost is that people do not always want what is good for them, or want what is better for them more than they want what is worse. In order to get around this obvious problem, numerous philosophers have proposed that what is good for people is not their actual desires, but the desires they would have under certain conditions. These conditions always include *full information* about what the results of all possible alternatives would be like to experience. R. B. Brandt, for example, has suggested, as a way to measure goodness and happiness, that something will be good for us if — given this information — we would prefer our lives with it to our lives without it.[9] Since we cannot be aware of all the consequences in the future of having something, what we would prefer with full information cannot be an actual preferences. Consequently, if our preferences determine what is good for us, they can only be preferences we *would* have *if* we knew what all these consequences would be.[10]

If you knew that continuing to eat rich food would lead to your early death from heart disease, then perhaps you would want that hollandaise sauce just a little bit less. Or perhaps not; if a great quantity of rich, delicious food really means more to you than a long life with less of it, even after you are fully aware of all the consequences to you of all possible sorts of eating habits, then, according to the full information view of the good, it really *is* better for *you* to eat large quantities of gourmet foods. With the same information, other people might choose differently, and what is good for them will, accordingly, be different.

Thus the full information theory of the good (FIT) fits the first two desiderata of variability and commonality: it allows for individual differences in what is good, yet it also gives a unified account of goodness which shows what is common to the good of all individuals. It also appears to fit the criterion of comprehensiveness in that it allows us to say that the list of those things generally thought good are good because people who understand what having them is like will want them. The comparability desideratum is more problematic, for as it is well known, there are major difficulties with comparing utilities, especially between different individuals. On the other hand, we do make such comparisons, and we need an account of what we are doing when we make them.

Yet some argue that the satisfaction of certain desires — even desires obtained with full information — would not be good for the individual who has them. There are some situations in which having what he wants is not good for an individual. Someone who is perfectly satisfied with what he is or has done, is likely to overlook faults that need correcting or not to accomplish as much as he could. We also think it bad when a person is pleased with, and wants, the misfortunes of others.[11]

Many of these perverse desires are bad because they result in harm to people other than the agent. My particular focus here, however, is on whether the satisfaction of such desires are good for the agent herself. They are not. In all these cases the person's desires are indicative of dispositions which at the very least tend to diminish overall goodness for the individual, as well as for others. Even if my private gloating over the failure of a colleague does not result in any harm done to that person, the enviousness which disposes me to this is symptomatic of deeper unhappiness within myself. People who are self-confident and not threatened by others' successes are unlikely to rejoice in the sorrows of their fellows. In addition, such a malicious disposition shows a lack of the sort of fellow feeling and sympathy which allows us to have loving relationships with others. Such relationships are a source of joy, from which a malicious person is at least to some extent barred by this trait — even if she does not recognize what she is missing. Consequently, even though a malicious person may have brief spurts of happiness when others suffer, this happiness comes at a cost in lesser happiness overall for herself — let alone what this trait could do to others. Here I am not talking about the kind of pleasure we often feel on seeing a person receive his just deserts, but rather pleasure felt at the unmerited pain of another. Nor do I wish to claim that in every case the gratification of a malicious desire would be bad for the person who has it. If that person were incapable of better feelings toward others, this might be one of the few sources of happiness for her, and on a desire satisfaction notion of the good, one would have to say that it would be good for her to have that desire satisfied. None of this entails that her having that desire, or its being satisfied, is good overall, as opposed to being good for the agent. Thus the fact that we think happiness at the misfortune of others is bad is not a counterexample to the thesis that satisfaction of desires is what is good for persons. Any good that might come to the malicious person simply as a result of her nasty desires' being satisfied is generally outweighed by the absence of individual good that having such desires indicates.

Similar arguments apply to the case of persons who are self-satisfied, or who feel happy in spite of deserving to feel guilty. These people, by being unaware of or unconcerned about their deficiencies, fail to correct them and thus risk creating unhappiness for themselves later on. On the other hand, being unhappy over one's failures, sins, and deficiencies has limited value. As most popular psychologists tell us, making oneself miserable over one's defects and past offenses is no better than ignoring them. One is both less unhappy and more likely to bring about future happiness if one can be aware of one's faults and mistakes, but make use of this awareness to correct them or make amends. One should concentrate on what can be done, not on what is past and unchangeable. Dwelling on one's failings beyond what is needed to correct them and make amends as far as that is possible, tends to inhibit one's ability both to do good and to have a rewarding life. The religious concept of forgiveness offers relief from continued misery over one's failings beyond reasonable repentance.

In short, many of these 'bad' desires are such that if we could see the consequences of satisfying them, as compared with the satisfaction of more respectable desires, we would have reason to want to change them. Whether we would change them, and what not changing them would do for the FIT's is a matter to be considered more below.

A FIT has further advantages. For example, it allows, as the simple view that good is the satisfaction of actual desires does not, that a person's life could be either better or worse by having desires or purposes he does not have. It will be made better if the desire is satisfiable and its satisfaction is either compatible with his other purposes or, if not, it would outweigh those with which it is incompatible. A new purpose would make his life worse or more unhappy if it could only be satisfied at the cost of losing many other things that contribute to his happiness.

This consideration provides an answer to Jon Elster, who has claimed that the satisfaction of individual desires cannot be the criterion of justice and social choice because many of our desires are artificially induced, and other desires, the satisfaction of which would have enhanced our happiness, may be artificially extinguished.[12] For example, if a person, seeing that she cannot have something she desires, or that its attainment would be too costly, may cease to have that desire. She increases her happiness by decreasing her desires; this is what Elster calls an 'adaptive preference.' This process is usually unconscious, and is to be distinguished from character planning, in which the agent would deliberately attempt to extinguish a desire which can lead only to frustration. Adaptive preference is also to be distinguished from manipulation by others, in which the agent is mendaciously persuaded that the desired object is worthless, and thus ceases to desire it. And it may also be distinguished from the case in which the agent learns new information on her own, and infers from this that the object is of no worth to her and consequently loses her desire for it. Another form of desire change is when a person, by committing herself to a certain plan of life, does not allow herself to desire objects inconsistent with it. As in character planning, she might, whenever she began thinking fondly of the object she desires, but does not want to desire, attempt to direct her attention elsewhere. By not allowing herself to pursue the object, the desire is likely to fade. Elster does not appear to think that commitment, character planning, or acquisition of new knowledge diminish the value of satisfying the desires that result from them — but adaptive preference and manipulation do.

A proponent of a full information theory can, however, argue that the history of one's desires is not particularly important. After all, none of our desires are entirely free of causal processes over which we have no direct control. What counts for an FIT is what one would desire given all the information about what would happen if those desires were satisfied. If an artificially induced desire, or the suppression of a desire, leads one to live in a way that she will ultimately regret, then that artificial process was clearly harmful. On the other hand, one might be glad of the consequences of having, working for, and satisfying a desire that was induced by, say, advertising. And likewise, having a desire extinguished by the utter inability to realize it, might be a good thing, if retaining it would produce wishful thinking or pursuit of a will o' the wisp that would lead a person to waste years of her life in frustration.[13]

A major objection to the full information theory of the good, and one which is, I think, ultimately fatal, is that people are not always apt to choose rationally. Most smokers know that their lives will be shortened and their health impaired if they continue with that habit. Yet even many doctors and nurses, who see on a daily basis the consequences of smoking in others, are unable to stop smoking themselves. For this reason, Brandt has suggested that rational desires are those which survive "cognitive psychotherapy" — a process by which one comes to understand the origins and maladaptive nature of certain of his desires.[14]

Such a program has a number of difficulties. Much of it has to do with what is an irrational preference. If it is simply one whose satisfaction will harm us, then we have to know what constitutes harm in order to know whether a preference is rational or not.[15] Besides, it is not obvious that all preferences which do not lead directly to our own good are irrational. For example, there are people whose lives are dedicated to the happiness of others, or to some discipline or cause, and this devotion may entail significant personal sacrifice. It is certainly not obvious that all such people are irrational, or that they are really doing what they do only for what they themselves get out of it.[16]

Perhaps an irrational preference can be defined as one which cannot be satisfied, or which can only be satisfied at a cost which is too high. But then we must be clear on what sort of cost *is* too high. Merely having a preference that can't be satisfied is not necessarily irrational. I might prefer to have the figure of a certain film star rather than my own, and this is surely not irrational. What *would* be irrational would be for me to starve myself, exercise for hours on end, and spend a fortune on plastic surgery to rearrange my shape. It is not the preference itself which is irrational, but the actions I might take to try to realize them. And these actions are irrational because engaging in them precludes my obtaining things and engaging in activities that contribute to my overall good or the good of others. If I go bankrupt, ruin my health, and neglect the development of my abilities in order to pursue a trivial objective which — even if achieved — would not make me or anyone else happy, this would be stupid. But what makes us able to judge that such an effort would be stupid is our sense of what is and isn't good for a person. Thus in order to know what is irrational, we must know what costs are too high. But in order to know this, we must know what is and is not good. Hence it seems that we cannot define good in terms of rational preferences without being guilty of circularity.

One further point. If any of us were to know everything about the possible consequences of our actions, and to have perfectly rational preferences, we would not be the people we are. As human beings, we are fallible and have little quirks which make us individuals. Besides determining our individuality, these quirks affect our preferences. If we didn't have them we wouldn't be the same people, so to say that what is good for us is the preferences *we* would have if perfectly rational and totally informed may well be meaningless. If we were so perfect we wouldn't be ourselves.[17] Difficulties posed by Sobel include *who* is to decide among alternative lives and *when* (or after what experiences). If the person herself, as she is, is to decide, then her desires are bound to be affected not only by her personality, but by the experiences she has had before. If she experienced different lives, not only would these experiences alter her desires, but the way in which they would be altered would depend upon the order in which those lives would be experienced. If we suppose that rather than the person herself with all her quirks and prejudices making the decision, some neutral judge decides, then we have moved away from what the *person* would want. How do we characterize the judge so as to avoid this? If the judge is different from the person, then he would want something different from what she wants. We must suppose that he chooses from some perspective and has certain attitudes to avoid this, but to suppose that he has the proper evaluative perspective seems to presuppose that we already know where our good lies.

Rosati takes these considerations even further to argue that the notion of a fully informed person is incoherent. To be a certain type of person experiencing a particular kind of life frequently precludes one from having other experiences and hence from knowing what a life containing those experiences is like. As an example, she points out that a person who is committed to truth above all and who is insensitive to the feelings of others would be incapable of having the experiences of a sympathetic and kindly person. Thus he would be unable to know what it would be like to be sympathetic to the feelings of others and therefore could not be fully informed. His desires would therefore be based on incomplete knowledge. Rosati quite rightly points out that it is not enough for facts to be presented; to have knowledge a person also needs to be capable of assimilating and appreciating those facts. And the facts that one is capable of assimilating depend on one's personality and the experiences one has had before. Having a personality and past experiences are part of what it is to be a person, so that if there were any beings that could assimilate everything relevant, they could not be people with whom we could identify or whose desires we could accept as being those it would be good for us to adopt.

I think the arguments of Sobel and Rosati are unanswerable. While it is surely true that we are most likely to be better off the better informed our desires are, the thought that we can conceive of fully informed desires as determining what is best for us is a chimera.

4. PROBLEMS OF MEASUREMENT

One objection to desire satisfaction as a criterion of goodness is that it is not possible to measure satisfaction. Given this criterion, inability to measure it would preclude us from determining whether one thing was better than another.   Any theory which connects the good of individuals with the satisfaction of their desires, or the desires they would have under certain conditions, must deal with the problem of measurement.

The classic procedure for comparing preferences and desires was devised by Frank Ramsey.[18] According to his method, we let which of two or more objects the person acquires depend upon some chance event like the throw of a die. The method is based on the assumption that our choices of action are based both on how much we like what we intend to get by that action, and also by the probability that the action will achieve the desired result. We choose to do what will give us the product of these, i.e., the greatest expected utility. If the expected utilities of two actions would be equal, a person would, presumably, be indifferent between them.

Ramsey's method allows us to determine the relative magnitudes of preferences for more than two items. For example, suppose you prefer a Toyota to a Subaru, and a Subaru to a Nissan. Using Ramsey's method, we could set up an even bet in the following way. Suppose that you will get a Subaru if you get heads on a coin toss, and, if you toss tails, you will have a chance to gamble between getting either a Toyota or a Nissan. To make the first draw an even bet, we have to adjust the odds of the second bet in accordance with how much better you like Toyotas than Nissans. For example, if you would be equally willing to have a 1/3 chance of getting a Toyota and a 2/3 chance of a Nissan as you would to have a Subaru, then you could calculate the relative utilities for you of the three kinds of cars by the equation:

$$U(S) = 1/3 U(T) + 2/3 U(N)$$

By assigning a number, say 3, to the utility of a Nissan, you can calculate that the utility of a Subaru to you is 6 and that of a Toyota is 12 — but you could assign any number you happened to fancy. Ramsey's method can tell us the relative magnitudes of utilities and even the ratios between them, but not their absolute numerical value. We know only that you have a strong preference for Toyotas over the other cars, and that your preference for Toyotas over Subarus is twice as great as your preference of Subarus over Nissans, but we have no absolute measure of how much they are actually worth to you.

Problems with Ramsey's method become apparent when we attempt to compare the preferences of more than one individual. Suppose that you and your husband want to buy a Japanese car. If he also prefers Toyotas to the others, then your mutual choice is clear. But suppose he doesn't. It might seem that the best solution then would be the one which gives the greatest combined utility for you both. The choice of utility values, however, is arbitrary. We can, given one value, calculate the others by Ramsey's method. But there is no way to show which is the true set of numbers for your utilities, and none to show which are your husband's. Yet the best mutual choice will be different, given different absolute values, even though the relative magnitudes of your preferences and his are held constant. Because of this, we cannot, in the case of more than one person, even rank choices in order of social preference: i.e., what would be preferred by the group.[19]

Efforts have been made to circumvent these problems. John C. Harsanyi has argued that we do make valid interpersonal utility comparisons.[20] We can imagine ourselves in something like the Rawlsian original position,[21] not knowing what our own situation will be. The preferences we would have for each individual, whose circumstances (including that individual's preferences) we know, although we do not know which of those individuals we are, would be objective in not being influenced by our knowledge of our own life circumstances. Harsanyi maintains that a person making a valid moral judgment would be in this state of objectivity, and that his preferences would be for fulfilling the preferences of each individual, and for the realization of the greatest average utility.

Harsanyi argues that if the strength of your preferences differs from mine, there is an explanation for it. I may not know all the factors involved, but at least in principle I could find out why, for example, you might enjoy sailing much more than I — e.g., you have taken lessons and practiced for years, and you don't hate being cold and wet as much as I do. While I don't dispute the fact that we make these psychological explanations, what is problematic here is *how* we determine what factors strengthen or weaken our preferences. We can observe that the more time Jim spends sailing the more skill he develops; he reacts less to getting doused with cold water than he did before. We conclude from this that his enjoyment of sailing is higher on his scale of preferences than it was before. For the reasons discussed above, however, we do not know from these observations that the *absolute* strength of his liking has increased, or that it is more now than that of others who like sailing. Perhaps Jane likes sailing just as much as Jim does, except that she has an enormous loathing for being drenched with cold water, and doesn't have the physical strength to manage the sails. In short, we make judgments about how much people like or dislike certain things by observing what they will exchange in order to get or avoid them. We can rank their preferences, but unless we have a way of determining a *cardinal* utility value for at least two states, and assume that they are the same for all people, we cannot make these interpersonal comparisons.

A further difficulty with Harsanyi's method is the following. Suppose that X is in the original position and wishes to rank everyone's preferences on a cardinal scale of utility, and suppose further that the difficulty mentioned in the last paragraph can be overcome. X does this by employing what he prefers for each individual. But whose preferences does he use? If his own, these may differ from those of the people for whom he is choosing. If X is using the preferences of each separate individual (which it is clear that Harsanyi intends him to do), then his choice is no different from each of these individual's choosing separately, and we are still left with the problem of how to measure the utilities of the different alternatives for those individuals. If

X uses some generic preference, or no one's particular preference, then he has no basis for choice on an FIT model. The difficulties raised by Sobel and Rosati are equally problematic for Harsanyi.

It might be thought that we could take advantage of the fact that we can rank alternatives (i.e., assign ordinal utilities) for individuals so as to make interpersonal decisions in order to circumvent the problems raised by our inability to assign meaningful cardinal utilities. We know that your preference for Toyotas over Subarus is twice your preference for Subarus over Nissans. Suppose your husband's preference for Subarus over Toyotas is equal to his preference for Toyotas over Nissans. By giving the value 1 to the least valued alternative and numbers in proportion to their higher value for each person, we obtain the following:

	Husband	Wife
Toyota	2	4
Subaru	3	2
Nissan	1	1

According to this method of proportional weighting, a Toyota has the highest utility. You win. But now a difficult problem appears. Suppose Nissans are not available. Neither of you wants a Nissan, but now your preference for a Toyota over a Subaru appears equal to his preference for a Subaru over a Toyota. The choice matrix then becomes:

	Husband	Wife
Toyota	1	2
Subaru	2	1

The Subaru now has the same utility as the Toyota, and there is a tie. Yet it surely should not be that the elimination of one choice that was the least favored for both of you will make a difference in the choice between the remaining alternatives. But as Arrow has shown,[22] the elimination or addition of irrelevant alternatives may have an effect upon the outcome of a 'social' choice for multiple individuals. The reason is that there is no way to gauge the absolute magnitude of your two preferences; you can only compare each individual's relative preferences between pairs of choices.

David Gauthier[23] suggests that, while we cannot compare the utility of a given outcome for one individual with that of another, we can assign utility numbers by taking as endpoints for *each* person the worst circumstances that he can imagine and the absolute best, giving 0 to the former and 1 to the latter, and then using the Ramsey scheme to calculate utilities of any intermediate states. As Michael Resnik has pointed out,[24] however, it is difficult to say — for anyone — that any state is so good or so bad that nothing better (or worse) could be imagined by her. Furthermore, suppose a person is incapable of imagining anything better than a state of perfect physical comfort, devoid of any mental stimulation or emotional attachment to others. Would we be willing to say that this person, if he attained that state, could not be better off with the addition of love for another or some intellectual pleasures? Even supposing that the number 1 is assigned to the state he *would* prefer above all others if he were acquainted with all, we run into the problems already discussed. Furthermore, Arrow makes it clear that the same problem arises for Gauthier's approach as for any other that builds upon ordinal utilities.

Further reflection makes it clear why this interpersonal problem arises. We know that you like Toyotas better than the other cars, while your husband likes them least. You, however, may be relatively indifferent to cars, while they may be his consuming passion. If so, even a Toyota may have a utility greater for him than the utility of a Toyota for you. Well, you might say, if automobiles are a consuming passion for your husband, this is surely knowable. After all, it would be manifested by his spending a lot of time tinkering with them, reading about them, and driving them. He would engage in these activities, when he had leisure, instead of doing other things like reading poetry, jogging, or gardening. He might have chosen an occupation dealing with automobiles, or might even neglect his job in order to do things with cars. He would certainly want to spend more money on cars than you would. We know, in other words, that cars are important to your husband. We can know that he wants them — and wants to perform activities involving them — very intensely because he will give up many other things in order to satisfy these wants.

This still does not tell us the absolute intensity of his desire, however. He might actually have a very mild interest in cars, but barely any in other things like his job, money, or other recreational activities. You, who are a person of great emotional intensity, may have a great concern about cars, but it is outweighed by your still greater passion for your career, your family, and the arts. If so, a car may have more utility for you than for your husband. In short, we can determine the *relative* ranking of a person's desires. We cannot, however, merely by observing someone's behavior, determine the *absolute* strength of these desires. Nor can we compare their strength with the strength of the desires of another person.

We *assume* that if one person pursues an object singlemindedly, giving up many other things in order to attain it, that he desires it more than another person who makes no effort to pursue it at all. But this is an assumption based on another: namely, that people are, if not exactly alike in their desires, at least roughly similar. We assume that all want at least some things to approximately the same degree of intensity: for example, food, shelter, or the respect of others.[25] But this is an unwarranted assumption. Even these basic goods may have different value for different individuals. For example, a person born without the ability to taste or smell may eat simply to stay alive, for he gets no enjoyment from food at all. Yet even for him, food might be more important than it is to another person who can taste it, if staying alive is more intensely desired by him.

Money, or rather the amount of money an individual would be willing to exchange for some item, might be considered a good measure of its value to that person. Money is not, however, an entirely neutral medium of exchange, and hence it is not a perfect measure of the extent to which an object is valued by someone. Not only are there many things money cannot buy, but people differ considerably in the extent to which money has intrinsic value for them.

Finally, according to the law of diminishing returns, the value of a unit of money to an individual depends upon how much money he already has. Consequently, monetary value is not a measure of how much something is valued by a given individual, let alone its *real* value. And similar remarks could be made about any supposedly neutral medium of exchange, such as the tokens that inmates of an institution are given for good behavior.[26]

Does any desire based moral theory suffer the difficulties of interpersonal utility comparisons? Certainly any theory that considered the good, and what we ought to do, to be determined by what satisfies actual desires would have this difficulty. Furthermore, any theory which is based on hypothetical desires meets the same problem. We would still need a way of specifying how an individual would rank the objects he would desire, and by how much, and Arrow's problems with interpersonal comparisons arise for both.

Alternatively, we can observe what people do, but as noted, it is hard to assess strength of desire because the extent to which a desire will lead to action depends not only upon its strength, but on the agent's other wants and his or her beliefs about whether and how the desire can be satisfied. Thus an artificial situation like Ramsey's in which the satisfaction of any of the desires depends only on a chance event, eliminates one confounding variable. The problem of *inter*personal comparisons is at least as great in comparing strengths of hypothetical desires among two or more people as it is in comparing strengths of actual desires. I think, however, that the problems of measurement can be significantly diminished through a different analysis of individual good. This analysis, I shall argue, eliminates the theoretical problem of interpersonal utility, although significant practical difficulties remain.

5. HAPPINESS

I shall now argue that goodness for an individual — i.e., his well-being — is happiness, which, in turn, is consciously living as he wants to live over the course of his life. This is roughly proportional to the net amount of time he spends wanting his current situation to continue. At any given moment a person is happy if he is content with the way his life is going, but if the direction of his life brings later moments of discontent and wishing his life were different, his long-term happiness will be diminished. This theory is desire-based in that wants definitely enter into what is good for us, but it is more akin to hedonism than most desire-based accounts. At the same time it differs from the passive associations of hedonism, by identifying happiness as a kind of living rather than as a mere feeling. A happiness account of well-being does not fall prey to the difficulties of being analyzed in terms of hypothetical desires, for it is determined by the individual's actual states over a lifetime. This account also gives us a rough, but common measure of how happy or unhappy different people may be made by a given alternative. If this is successful, interpersonal utility problems would not arise. On the other hand, this method provides only an approximate guide to how happy an individual is, primarily because of practical difficulties in knowing how people are reacting to their circumstances. We have behavioral clues, but these are inexact. Consequently, the characterization of happiness I am presenting here cannot serve as a calculus. My position must also account for some of the objections which have been raised over the centuries against hedonism — primarily, that it is a shallow and inadequate notion of goodness. I believe this charge and others can be answered, and will attempt to do so in the following chapter.

A happy life is one in which the individual has purposes that he strives to realize and which he succeeds in realizing relatively often. For a person to be considered in a good and happy state, he or she must be conscious of having a life that includes acting and aiming toward desired goals, as well as conscious of succeeding or of having reasonable hope of success at some of these goals, at least. Although the consciousness of activity and achievement is not identical with feelings of pleasure and happiness, it often includes them. Happiness may be experienced as a sense of well being, but it is, as Ryle forcefully argued,[27] no specific sensation. A person often realizes that he has been happy after the fact, since during the happy period he was so caught up in what he was doing as to have been unaware of what he was feeling.

What we consider valuable is not the feeling, but rather the state underlying the feeling, which is living a life that one finds satisfying and enjoyable. To see that this is so, we can consider whether we would think it better for a person to have his basic needs unmet and be functioning poorly, but often feel elated, than for him to lack this feeling, but be acting successfully to obtain what he needs and wants. I think we would believe the person better off in the second situation, unless, perhaps, he was feeling positively unhappy. Another way to look at it is — as Nozick suggests — to ask ourselves if we would consider a good life to be one in which the person could continuously press a button that would create in him happy feelings, regardless of what was actually happening to his body and mind.[28] It might seem that according to the definition of happiness I have presented the person who could live in a state of passively feeling pleasure would be the happiest. Of course, there might be people who would find such a life satisfying. One would expect, however, that if they had a taste of an active life, they would find it far more enjoyable. If they did not, however, perhaps the passive life would be the best for *them as they are*. We could not expect that a person with severe mental handicaps would get any satisfaction from mathematics or that studying math would add anything to his happiness or to his well-being. Of course, he *would* have had a much better life if he had the ability to understand and enjoy mathematics, as well as the opportunity to learn it.

Yet while happiness is not just a feeling or sensation of pleasure, a life which was devoid of any pleasurable feelings would hardly be called happy. Neither is happiness merely the absence of pain and distress, as Epicurus thought.[29] Distress can even enhance contrasting pleasure when it is relieved,[30] provided it does not permanently damage the organism. Happiness is, furthermore, virtually impossible for human beings without activity, which is generally recognized as a basic need for all higher organisms. Activity is primarily purposive; if someone acts, he is usually trying either to attain something he does not possess or to use or enjoy something he already has.

He might also be trying to gain more of something, or secure his grasp of what he already possesses. And while he may engage in an activity simply for its own sake, much of activity presupposes the absence or insecurity of something the agent desires.

Aristotle maintained[31] that happiness is always sought for its own sake, and not as a means to other ends, and while there might be some exceptions to this (e.g., a person who tries to be happy in order to fight the cancer which she has been told was caused by her depression), I think it is basically true. While other things are also often ends in themselves for particular people, they may also be desired as means to happiness. And happiness is, again, not simply a feeling, but a state in which the person is acting for purposes, as well as enjoying the activity and those things which he or she has already attained.[32]   Happiness is not, therefore, the secure (and hence boring) possession of everything one wants at all times. Consequently, happiness is identical neither with pleasurable feelings nor with the satisfaction of all one's desires, although to be happy a person needs to have a large degree of pleasure and satisfaction.

Most of the above, however, is a description of a happy life, rather than a definition of happiness. Happiness resembles that which a number of philosophers (e.g., Ryle, Baier, Penelhum, Narveson, and Brandt)[33] have used to characterize pleasure or enjoyment. If an individual is enjoying his present situation — i.e., wants it to continue as it is in the immediate future — , he is happy at that time. The longer this state of enjoyment, the more happiness. Conversely, a person is more or less unhappy, and his experience more or less painful, when he does not want his present situation to continue as it is in the immediate future. The length of time one spends wanting his state to continue is a rough measure of how much one is living a life that he wants to live. Brandt has, in fact, gone on to identify this notion of happiness with individual good, and so — with qualifications — has Thomson.[34] As we shall see, this concept of happiness has a number of advantages.

It might seem that, contrary to what I said immediately above, I am considering happiness to be feelings. This, however, is not the case. A state of wanting something does not involve constant awareness of the object of desire or of constant activity to attain it. The same applies to wanting one's present situation to continue. Suppose you are engaged in a task and someone interrupts you to ask "Do you want to keep doing this right now?" You could surely make an accurate response, without having been thinking all along that you did or didn't want to continue what you were doing. You would know whether you had been interested in the task or excited by it, or whether you were bored or tired or worrying about some other concern. (You could also tell something by the degree of irritation you felt on being interrupted.)

If our overall happiness is proportional to the net length of time being contented with the way one's life is going, we cannot calculate happiness simply from the number of desires satisfied, or even from the difference between desires satisfied and those unsatisfied. One can, for example, think of people whose lives are dominated by a single purpose, who often appear happier than others who have a variety of purposes. What determines one's happiness is not the number of desires satisfied and goals reached, but by one's living a life that she wants to go on as it is.

An interesting objection to this view of pleasure was raised by Hardy Jones (personal communication). He pointed out that if a person is undergoing a dental procedure, he may want it to continue because he knows this is necessary to his overall well-being. Nevertheless, the procedure is not pleasurable. There are, of course many things that we do from necessity or duty or because we know that they will eventually add to the goodness of our lives (or prevent harm), but our attitude toward them is quite different from our attitude to what we enjoy doing. We find ourselves counting the minutes before the period of pain or tedium is over, or trying to distract ourselves from what is happening by thinking of something else. The dental patient, if offered a pain-free alternative treatment, would jump at it instantly, and he is delighted when his ordeal is over. We can say, therefore, that he wants his root canal procedure to continue only in the sense that he chose it as the lesser of two evils. The minimal sense in which he wants it is surely outweighed by the ways in which he doesn't want it to continue, and hence he finds the experience unpleasant. Moreover, a life filled with such pain would need an enormous number of compensatory satisfactions to be considered good.

We may want things at different levels, as those like Frankfurt have noted in discussing first- and second-order desires.[35] I may want something to happen, even though it is unpleasant, because I know that in the long run the event will bring more pleasure and less pain overall. But the experience itself is unpleasant, in that while it occurs I am also wishing it were over. If I *weren't* wishing it were over, I wouldn't find it unpleasant.

Any experience has many aspects, some of which a person may want to continue as they are and others not. Joe's undergoing dental work is a good example. It is on the one hand physically uncomfortable, but on the other, a step which he has good reason to believe will relieve present — or prevent future — pain. He would like the former aspect of his experience to end, but the latter to continue to completion.

Much of life is full of such mixed experience. We may enjoy the company of family, coworkers, and friends most of the time, but find certain things about them irritating. The work we do may have interesting, challenging, and satisfying aspects, but most also has tedious and frustrating moments as well. We can tease out the different aspects of some portion of our lives by asking ourselves what about them we would like to change and what to keep as is. Thus Joe might enjoy the company of his Aunt Millie more if she weren't constantly complaining about the evils of modern life, but he wouldn't want her to stop reminiscing about the days of her youth. He might love giving a well-prepared lecture, but find it extremely irritating and frustrating to deal with a student's question that shows complete lack of understanding of what he has just said. If he could remake the world according to his preferences, he would make the student disappear, and let the lecture go on uninterrupted. Aunt Millie's complaints and the thick-headedness of some students are unpleasant to Joe, while the old lady's reminiscences and his giving lectures are pleasant. Thus his visits with his aunt and his teaching have differing effects upon his overall happiness.

Given that our lives are composed of such mixed experiences, how can we measure how happy we are? The answer, I think, is that it depends upon how much time we spend focussing on the different aspects of our experiences. If Joe seldom thinks about Aunt Millie's complaints or dull students' questions, but rather concentrates upon the features of his visits with the old lady and his classes that he likes, he will be a happier person on the whole than if he thinks primarily of what he doesn't enjoy. A person who moves about from one job or house to another may do so because she is unhappy with each situation or because she enjoys variety and seeks new challenges. I have been in the situation of hating my job and wanting to get out of it into almost anything else, as well as in the very different one of loving my job, but seeing possibilities for greater fulfillment in a new one. The process of changing jobs was in the two cases very dissimilar; in the one I was unhappy and thinking primarily about ways of escaping the situation, while in the other I was happy, but thinking of ways to become still happier. Because in the latter case I wanted a change, it might appear that — according to my definition — I was unhappy. Yet it does not. My happiness in the second job consisted in my doing many things I enjoyed and would expect to continue doing in the new one. Although there were a few aspects of the old job which I didn't especially care for, these aspects did not oppress me much — that is, I didn't spend a lot of time thinking about them. My unhappiness in the first job consisted in there being numerous features which I wanted to escape and in spending considerable time in discontent. In the first case, I was living a life I disliked and wanted to be very different; in the second, I was living a life I enjoyed and which I wanted to change only in minor respects.

People are never totally contented; no matter how happy they are, there will always be changes that might make them happier — e.g., to eliminate a bit of irritation, or to add some excitement. Thus a person can be very happy, although not perfectly so, and look for changes to make his life even better. A person can be quite contented, but if she were to have some new or different experiences, she might become yet more so. In fact, being highly contented might actually interfere with her ability to become still happier, if this contentment prevents her from looking for new and different experiences that would add to her enjoyment of life.

In general, it has been well-recognized by wise people throughout the ages that one's happiness (and the goodness of one's life) is not proportional to one's material well-being. A person who has everything in the way of life's necessities, and luxuries besides, may still be unhappy and miserable if he spends much of his time thinking of what he doesn't have. And a person who lacks much of what is considered important for happiness may in fact be happier than many who have no such lacks, if she puts her attention on what she does have and is able to do. While someone who constantly worries over small discordant aspects of his life may be far better off materially than a person whose hard existence that allows no time for thinking of such trivia, he may well be worse off on the whole even though he has the *potential* for a much better and happier life than she has.[36] In short, our happiness has much to do with our attitudes toward what happens to us and what we are called upon to do, and with how we focus our attention. Time spent focusing on what we can do and enjoy, as opposed to what frustrates, frightens, angers, or saddens us, adds to our happiness and to the goodness (for us) of our lives.

We can often increase our pleasure and the overall contentment and goodness in our lives by concentrating on those aspects of our duties and situations which are pleasant, rather than those which are unpleasant. Joe can put up with Aunt Millie's complaints better if he looks at what he is doing by patiently listening as giving her a bit of pleasure and companionship. He can tolerate the student's stupid question more easily if he looks at it as a challenge to clarify certain points in his presentation. He might also turn his attention away from what bothers him by thinking of something else — e.g., planning his next lecture while undergoing a dental procedure or while Aunt Millie goes on and on about the bad manners of the young and the poor quality of everything they make nowadays. Joe might also act to change unpleasant aspects of his experiences — e.g., ask for more novocaine, interrupt his aunt's complaints with a request for her to tell about her work with the Red Cross during World War II, or suggest to the student that perhaps she is not ready for a course at this level. In short, we do have some — if limited — control over how much we enjoy our experiences and hence of our overall happiness.

One's motivation for performing an action may be determined by one of its features, yet the act may have other features which one would prefer to avoid and still others which provide good reasons for doing it, although perhaps not the agent's actual reason for doing it. Joe's primary motive for teaching may be that he enjoys working out philosophical problems, but this does not preclude there being other reasons for him to do it, such as earning a living, introducing young people to the joys of philosophy, or making him happier than a different career might make him. These reasons may or may not contribute to his own motives for teaching. Nor does his primary motive preclude the possibility that there are certain aspects of work that he dislikes, such as contending with dull students or grading papers. As we shall see, some objections to theories like mine turn on the point that we are not motivated solely by seeking happiness and that increasing happiness is not the only reason for doing something. The above example shows that increasing happiness need not be one's motive for an action, even though that action may make him happier and for that reason be good for him. For that matter, that I know an action would be good for me (*however* one defines goodness) is not typically my immediate motive for doing it. More often I am motivated by the desire to solve a problem with work or in the family, to get warm or satisfy hunger, to help someone out, to communicate my thoughts or feelings, or simply to enjoy myself. Usually, doing these things are good for me as well; that they are good for me, however, is not my reason for doing them. On the other hand, if one of these actions should actually be bad for me, this fact would be a good and usually sufficient reason not to do it — even if it did not motivate me to refrain from doing it.

Happiness is an effect of a life deeply involved in activities which matter to one. Yet one chooses one's activities, associates, and commitments in part because they bring satisfaction and are in a sense self-reinforcing. For a person with no athletic ability, engaging in competitive sports brings no pleasure and hence he avoids them, whereas one who succeeds often is encouraged to persist. Hence for a baseball star, playing baseball is part of his happiness, and when he plays and plays well he is happy, and the happiness playing brings reinforces his efforts to play more and play better. Meanwhile his unathletic school mates (one hopes) find their happiness in business or the arts or the practice of a profession or trade which they enjoy and at which they are proficient. Happiness — as living a life one wants to continue as it is — is thus both a cause and an effect of engaging in projects for which one is suited. It is thus natural to think of happiness and a good life as one which is acting in accordance with one's interests and abilities; certainly such action is inextricably connected with the desire to continue one's present course. Of course, the best life a person could have would be one in which he has great abilities and succeeds in developing them, and in which he is loved and appreciated, and in which he is deeply committed to certain other people and to disciplines and causes (and where his commitments bear fruit). Such a person is likely to be consistently enjoying himself and wanting his life to continue as it is; if he is not, we would not consider him to be having the best or happiest life. Other people without such talents can attain less and are thus less likely to find the pinnacle of happiness, but if they are content with their lot and make the best of what they have, they may well have a happier and better life than someone who was given much more by nature and society. Thus I think most of us do not identify the goodness or happiness of a life with what the person actually does or has, but rather in how he responds to what that life hands him.

One way to think of happiness is in terms of one's life as a whole.[37] Each person has different interests, experiences, and abilities — all of which determine not only what things, events, and activities would make his life happy, but when and how much. A happy life is one in which all of the right components come at the right time and in the right amounts to give the person joy and satisfaction in what he is doing and experiencing. The extent to which some particular occurrence contributes to or detracts from his happiness depends upon its effects on the other components of his life and on his ability to make the most of his gifts. Thus a particular type of event may at one time add to one's happiness, but at another diminish it. For a given person, what is integral to his happiness may be considered a constituent of it. Thus for a brilliant and creative person, intellectual challenge is necessary to his highest degree of happiness; for one who is by nature sociable, the love and companionship of others is required for him to be as happy as he could be. Once an individual has developed an attachment to another or committed himself to some enterprise, his happiness is partly constituted by the presence in his life of that person or his ability to pursue the enterprise. If he loses either, his happiness will be greatly decreased for a considerable time and perhaps forever.

6. MEASURING HAPPINESS

I have proposed that the measure of an individual's happiness and the goodness of her life is the extent to which she wants her present situation to continue. To see this, we must consider what 'extent' means, and in doing so, once again, the criterion is that which people use who are arguing about whether a person is happy, or happier than another or happier than she was at a different time — not necessarily every belief about degrees of happiness that have ever been expressed. 'Extent' might mean either the relative length of time a person spends in this state, or the absolute length of time, or the intensity of her desire for the state to continue. We consider a person happier and better off the greater the proportion of her life she spends enjoying what she is doing and experiencing, as opposed to wishing things were different. And given the same proportion, we would think her life better the longer it was. In either case, we are assessing the balance of time spent happy over time spent unhappy, and the greater that balance, the better the person's life.[38]

If Jane lived for ninety years and spent one third of it contented and two thirds discontented, we would consider her less happy than John who lived only forty years, but was contented for thirty years of that time. Although her total time of happiness would have been the same, she had more unhappiness in her life than he and thus a worse life overall. We would think it a bad thing for John that he died young, having his potential for further happiness cut off. But we are assuming that the additional years would have been full of contentment; had he lived longer and been miserable nearly all that time, his life would hardly have been better simply for being longer.

I suggest, then, that length of time spent wanting one's situation to continue as it is, minus the time spent wanting things to be different, is what corresponds to the amount of happiness in an individual's life — and the goodness of that life (goodness for him, as opposed to its value for others). We thus seem to have a way of determining how happy a person is, and how happy he is relative to someone else. Knowing when and what a person desires, of course, is not always easy. Since people are not usually thinking about what they want, especially while deeply involved in some experience or activity, they might not be explicitly aware that they want their present situation to continue. On the other hand, if they act annoyed when interrupted, or note such feelings in themselves, or if they are asked later (by themselves or by others) whether they wanted, while they were engaged in the activity, for it to continue, then we would have some evidence that they did want it to continue and that they were enjoying it at the time.

Another difficulty with knowing whether we want a situation to continue is the fact that all situations have many different features, about each of which we can feel quite differently. Nearly all of us have aspects of our lives we'd like to change, but have relatively little concern about, while other things we want very much — perhaps desperately — to change. Thus it seems that the *intensity* of the desire to change has a lot to do with how unhappy we are: consider the difference between wishing the weather were a little warmer and wishing that the person you love most did not have terminal cancer.

Our degree of unhappiness with any given situation, or aspect of it, depends largely on the degree to which we are willing and able to change it, or have hope that it will get better on its own. A dreadful situation that we are helpless either to alleviate or to escape is far worse than one we are actively trying to improve with good hope of success. If a loved one is seriously ill, you will be far less unhappy if there is hope of recovery and there are things you can do to speed it, than if there is nothing anyone can do to save her or relieve her suffering.

The intensity of one's unhappiness — over a whole situation, or over some unwanted aspect of a generally satisfactory situation — appears to be the degree to which one is preoccupied with worry, envy, grief, boredom, anger, or any of the other unpleasant emotions. One's unhappiness can be alleviated by considering and trying possible solutions, or — when nothing can be done — with thinking about other matters, or by trying to make the best of things through concentrating on whatever features of the situation can be enjoyed. One is preoccupied when one's attention is absorbed, and one tends to pay less attention to other things going on around one. What appears important here is the amount of time one is stewing over something one can't (or isn't willing) to do anything about, as opposed to planning ways of changing it, acting on those plans, focussing on the pleasant aspects (if any) of the situation, or getting involved in some other activity or experience. If the intensity of unhappiness is a function of length of time spent in wanting things to be different, then the problem of interpersonal utility comparisons becomes much less.

A possible objection to this is that it may seem that intensity of happiness or unhappiness seems to depend on more than time. For example, it is generally true that one's pleasure in food depends much on how hungry one was before, and that the relief one feels after some great worry is removed is the more intense the greater one's fear had been. But of what does this intensity consist? If I am very hungry, a greater proportion of my time is spent thinking of food, or of how much my stomach hurts, and when I finally do eat, I'll spend that time fully enjoying the meal, and less time talking with others or thinking about unrelated matters. Furthermore, food I would scorn when not particularly hungry might taste wonderful. I would savor the taste — i.e., pay attention to it — when under normal circumstances I might barely notice what I was eating. A great worry is one that I think about off and on throughout a period of time, the more so the less I can distract myself with other matters. And when I find that the dreaded situation will not occur, my joy is proportional to the length of time I spend thinking about how much better things are than I'd feared.

Thus, while it is quite true that pleasures are usually more intense after an intense period of displeasure or unhappiness, the intensity of both appears to be a direct function of the amount of time that one spends immersed in thoughts and feelings about the situation in question. If so, we can ameliorate the problem of interpersonal comparisons. One person is happier than another over a given lifetime or part of a lifetime if he spends less of that time in ineffectively wanting his situation to be different from what it is. He may want things to be different without reduction in happiness if he is willing and able to make changes he has reasonable hope will succeed and focusses his energies and attention into making those changes, especially when doing so brings enjoyment. He may also avoid unhappiness by diverting his attention from those aspects of his life which he would like to be different, but cannot change, and concentrate on others over which he has more control or which he can enjoy.

Bernard Rollin (personal communication) has suggested that people may be very unhappy about things that they have *not* been thinking about, at least consciously. There are a number of ways one can incorporate this possibility into the account I have provided here. Suppose that Alice has lost her only child. She may respond to this in different ways, or different ways at different times. She may think almost constantly about her loss, actively grieving and intensely unhappy. At times she may be in a state of denial; perhaps immediately after the child's death, she may fancy that he is not really dead and may someday be restored to her. When in denial her grief will be blunted.

With the passage of time, even after she has accepted the fact that her child is dead, Alice's unhappiness will, if she is like most people, be less intense as she becomes involved in other concerns, but it will never go away entirely. The residual grief may be manifested at times by actively thinking about the child and at others in more subtle ways. One such effect might be a blunting of her ability to take pleasure in her activities. She might not be consciously thinking of her child, but still be restless and unable to concentrate. She might thus be unable to enjoy her work, the company of other family members, or activities she used to relish. Her unhappiness over the loss of her child is in this situation causally related to a sort of global unhappiness, which she may attribute to boredom with her job, the irritating qualities of her relatives, or lack of energy for pursuing hobbies she once enjoyed. If she is an analytical type, Alice may come to realize that her grief over her child is behind all these other manifestations of unhappiness. But the point I would make here is that whether or not she does, her unhappiness consists in living a life she does not enjoy because the loss of her child casts a pall over everything she does. Regardless of the cause, be it a situation like Alice's that would be devastating to anyone, or some imbalance of neurotransmitters resulting in clinical depression, unhappiness is being discontented with and not enjoying one's life overall.[39]

Rollin's objection points up another matter of importance. This is that wanting is not so much an episodic as a dispositional state.[40] It does not always consist in explicit thoughts that one wants this or that. More likely, we know that a person wants something by her reactions to seeing it within grasp, being deprived of it, and possessing it. Does she pay attention to the object when she has it, or focus on the activity while doing it? Is she saddened or angry when the object is taken away, or she is interrupted in the activity? When a thing or event is close to realization, does she work harder than ever to obtain or realize it? If the answer to these is 'Yes' it is fair to say that she wants the object, wants the event to occur, or wants to engage in the activity. If asked, she would probably say, 'Why, yes, I do want that.'

Even so, it is not a simple matter to measure happiness. At best we can get a rough indication of how happy or unhappy an individual might be on the basis of his behavior. Even our own happiness or unhappiness is not an open book.[41] As Edward Becker has pointed out, however,[42] there is behavior associated with happiness and unhappiness. This behavior is what enables us to make some estimate of how happy an individual is and to have some basis for comparing the happiness of one individual with that of another. The unhappy individual is often restless, tired, hostile, bored, or anxious. She finds it hard to become involved with what is happening around her, but is distracted by other concerns. Neither she nor others may be aware of *feelings* of unhappiness, or specific recognition of a situation that she wishes were different. Both happiness and unhappiness are often more global than that. Both may well have more to do with one's neurotransmitters than with one's actual situation. The same thoughts going through one's head may be accompanied by different moods, depending on one's physiological state, for there is little doubt that what is happening in one's life has much to do with one's mood and the state of one's brain. Nevertheless, while we can have a rough idea of how happy or unhappy someone seems to be, precision is unobtainable.

In attempting to know what is best for a given individual, we would need to know how the alternatives would affect the amount of time that she would be content with her situation, given the realization of each alternative. This would require a knowledge of the person which was, in some cases, greater than her own. Furthermore, people are different enough that the same event might increase the happiness of one, but decrease that of another. Nevertheless, we can compare the extent to which a situation A affects the happiness of an individual X with that to which a different situation B affects the happiness of another individual Y. We do this by observing how X's and Y's lives are changed by A and B, respectively. If we are trying to decide whether A or B would be better on the whole, we must make that decision on the basis of hypotheses about the people affected. These hypotheses, in turn, are based upon past observations of those people. We could recall how much enjoyment X and Y have had from items like A and B in the past. If in fact A adds n hours to the time X spends enjoying his situation, and n + k hours to the time Y spends contented, we can say that A was better for Y than for X. If we could give A only to one person, we should, *ceteris paribus*, give A to Y rather than X.

Let us consider again the case in which you and your husband are trying to decide what car to buy. Let us also make the following assumptions: that any car would increase your happiness, that you both want a Japanese model, that you can only afford one car, and that your main concern is to get the car that will bring the greatest overall happiness. You will be better able to reach a decision by considering how you both have reacted to cars — or similar possessions — in the past. Which of you has been bothered most by the deficiencies of your previous automobiles — that is, who has complained, spent time tinkering, or otherwise taken the responsibility for dealing with its problems? Which of you has taken the most pleasure in driving, who has noticed the good points of cars and how these compare with those of other automobiles? Who has taken the most time to learn about cars, so as to determine which models will best satisfy criteria such as durability, safety, mileage, and comfort? In my family, it is my husband and not I who has done all these things. For me any car which gets me from one place to another is just fine; he is the one who invests a significant amount of time and effort; he is the one who really *cares*. For this reason, I am quite content to let him choose what kind of car to buy.

What of the objection to interpersonal utility comparisons mentioned earlier:

namely, that we cannot determine the intensity of a person's desire for anything as compared with that of another's? Yet here I have said that we can; my husband cares considerably about cars and I don't. But how do I know that my concern for cars is not just as great as his, just that it is less intense than my concerns about other matters? I still don't know. What I do know is that because cars are relatively unimportant to me, they do not, as a rule, contribute much to my happiness or unhappiness. (It would be different, of course, if I should have an accident or be faced with the inconveniences of not having a car at all.) Since I rarely think about cars, the small pleasures and annoyances they occasion for many people don't much affect me. In short, a good car adds more time in contentment and enjoyment to my husband's life than it does to mine, and a bad car, by contrast, would detract more from his enjoyment. Therefore, since he would be more affected, it is better in most instances for him to make the choice — given that the aim is to enhance our greatest overall satisfaction.

What affects a person's happiness most is what she is most concerned about because this is what she pays most attention to. What we are most concerned about is what we think about most, do the most planning for, and in which we invest most of our time and energy. Whether we succeed in the goals related to our greatest concerns is of vital importance and tends to overshadow the goals related to lesser concerns. The absolute degree of concern for some item does not determine the extent to which it affects our happiness. In fact, the absolute degree of concern may be a meaningless notion. As indicated above, it seems impossible to measure it directly, but only in comparison with an individual's concern for other things.

What matters to happiness, however, is the extent to which our *major* concerns — i.e., those which occupy our attention the most — are furthered. We have only a limited amount of time, and can only keep our attention on a limited number of things at once. How we allocate time and attention tells both what we care about and what contributes to or detracts from our happiness the most. We can observe behavior — including what people say — which indicates content or discontent with a situation. While these are not precise, and may often be unreliable, they do give some indication of how happy or unhappy a person is, as well as a handle on whether that person is happier than another.

7. CONCLUSIONS

We can see now that defining good as happiness, which in turn is living in a way that one wants to continue, meets the desiderata outlined in Section 2 for a concept of individual good. It allows us to see why what specific things are good for one person may differ from those which are good for others. Yet at the same time, it is a unified concept, showing what is common to all goods. It enables us to measure — theoretically, if not practically — how good or bad a thing is for someone, what things are better than others, and when one person is better or worse off than another. This concept of individual good shows why the things people have traditionally thought of as goods are good: because virtually everyone wants to have them and is happier when they do. And it also gives us a way of determining whether a given item is good or bad for a particular individual.

There is a close relationship between what people want and what is good for them. (1) As a rule we are happy when we have things we want to have and our lives are going the way we want them to — or at least we have reasonable hope of success in achieving most of our major goals and enjoyment of the process of working toward them — , but of course sometimes we may get something we have wanted and find that it doesn't bring us the satisfaction we thought it would, and it turns out to be not so good for us after all. The key to knowing whether what X wants is good for X is seeing how X feels about having it if he gets it.

(2) Things are goods or good for people generally when the great majority of people are happier when they have them, regardless of whether the things are always wanted. Some people may not care a lot about education or self-respect, but if they had them they would appreciate them. In some ways this is similar to Wiggins's remarks[43] about the similarity of value terms to color terms. Just as 'red' describes things that people usually call 'red,' so 'good' describes things or states that people usually feel pleased to have or to be in. Just as a person can be wrong about whether a thing is red by looking at it in a bad light, she might also be wrong about whether it is good for her because she encounters it under conditions which obscure from her how she will be affected by it. And just as a thing may not look red to those who see it under certain conditions (e.g., through a blue glass), so a normally good thing might not be good for certain individuals in peculiar circumstances.

(3) Nothing is a good if no one ever has or ever would care about having it. If there were never any individuals who could see, the greatest painting and most magnificent natural scenery would have no value. Yet a blind person can recognize that a painting or scenery is valuable, even though he is unable to see and appreciate it himself, because he knows it is cared about by others.

When we are glad to have had an experience, enjoy it while we are having it, want to continue having it or have it in the future, this is partly based on the character of the experience and partly upon our own characteristics. Depending upon the individual's physical and emotional state at a given time, events with certain features will appeal to him, repel him, or leave him indifferent. He wants the experience for its particular features, not for the fact that it appeals to him. But it is its appeal to him that defines it as being pleasant for him. What causes it to appeal and thus be pleasant is its other features. It is these other features which he values, and when many people value those features and find experiences that have those features appealing, and they do not bring consequences unpleasant enough to outweigh that appeal, this makes experiences of that kind *valuable* or good, and those things or institutions that provide such experiences good and valuable.

Yet, once again, a good experience or a good thing may not always be good, or good for a particular individual, in every possible circumstance. What determines that is whether in those specific circumstances the individuals affected will contribute to his having the life he wants to live. Thus we can have too much of many of the goods of life, and they are good for us at a particular time only up to the point of satiety and good for us overall only in so far as we do not indulge with sufficient frequency to bring us more pain than pleasure in the long run. And of course a person can have large quantities of a good, which quantities are good for her, but if she deprives others by gaining them, she may well be doing wrong morally. At this stage of the investigation, however, we are considering only what is good for individuals, independently of moral good or what one ought to do; however, to the extent that a person would be happier being morally good, being morally good will be good for her as well as for others.

As noted, too, whether an experience is pleasing at a given time for a given individual is dependent upon that person's state and circumstances. People doing creative work get intense joy from it, but eventually they become fatigued and the thought of doing more at that point can be quite unpleasant. And the foods one enjoyed as a child differ greatly from those one enjoys as an adult. In these cases, the objects of one's attitude have not changed. Thus our attitudes are caused through a complex relationship between the characteristics of an object and a perceiving subject.

My analysis of what is good for individuals avoids a major problem associated with theories according to which we are better off the more of a particular commodity we have. According to Stocker and Slote[44] not only are people not motivated by maximizing good, but maximization need not even be better. Not only that, but there is something morally suspect about the concern with maximization itself: it smacks of greed.

These claims would have truth in them if maximizing good were simply accumulating the greatest possible quantity of good things or good experiences. But it isn't. While there are some people who have insatiable desires for more and more of some one type of good thing — such as money or recognition — nobody has desires like this for everything, and most people are content with a certain level of goods and recognize that striving for more beyond that level brings diminishing satisfaction and often more dissatisfaction in the long run. Wise people have recognized for centuries that goods sufficient for a good life are relatively few — enough to eat and protection from the elements, good health, interesting work that one does well and can take pride in, and people one loves and is loved by. Other goods are so much gravy — nice if you have them, but it is irrational to strive too hard for them, because then you may risk losing the basic and most important goods. People who, for example, feel a need to have more or be better than others — to be richer, smarter, more powerful, more talented, thinner — are often unhappy, because for anything you name, it is almost always possible to find somebody who has it to a greater extent than you. And to pursue any of these ends to excess may cause you to lose your health or damage your relationships with others.

All of this has been said so often and for so long that it is platitudinous. But the basic point is that increased quantities of goods is not necessarily better. But there is one thing that it *is* consistently better to have more of, and that is time being happy with what you have and are doing. Chronically envious people are unhappy and badly off because they rarely have this sort of contentment. And those who have overindulged in physical pleasures will regret it if they must later spend much more time in the future sick and in pain.   People who pursue fame or riches while neglecting their relationships with others may doom themselves to a lonely and miserable old age.   Being happy with what you have and are doing is as much a matter of having moderate desires as of satisfying desires, and this is a state you really can't have too much of.

In proposing criteria for what is good for people, I have followed the procedure outlined in Chapter 1 — namely, noting how people argue for and against proposals that certain things are good for individuals. We clearly don't think that everything a person wants is good for him, but those things which never are and never would be wanted by anyone are not good. We seem to think good those items which people want over time and are glad they have or have had and would like to continue to have. While they might have had even longer periods of contentment had they had something different, the contentment they actually have makes their lives good, even though under different conditions their lives might have been even better. We need not suppose that a person would choose that which would make her most content, given the impossibility of knowing all circumstances and all alternatives — just that what is best for her would actually give her the most extended periods of living as she wants to live. The test of this analysis will be whether those beliefs that people over centuries and in all parts of the world consider good for them (i.e., well-established beliefs) can fit into it easily. For this reason, I shall spend the next chapter discussing more actual and possible objections.

CHAPTER 4

OBJECTIONS TO GOOD AS HAPPINESS

1. WHAT MIGHT GOODNESS BE IF NOT HAPPINESS?

Assuming the characterization of happiness suggested here, is such happiness identical with what is good for individuals? While I do not think that there is anyone who would deny that happiness is *a* good, many have proposed that there are goods which are sometimes at least as valuable, and which may even be better for a person than happiness, so that if loss of one of these were to increase happiness, it would be better to lose happiness than to lose that good. In discussing these objections I will argue — not that these other goods could not be considered ultimate — but rather that our common beliefs about them can be accounted for in terms of their effects upon happiness as I have defined it. To this end I will suggest the following. (a) While many of these goods are extremely important to a good life — even necessary to the best sort of life — , there are some situations in which they may not be good for one, whereas happiness, suitably characterized, is always good for one. (b) While many of these goods are pursued for their own sakes, they are also pursued for their contribution to one's happiness, whereas the converse is rarely the case. (C) While it is almost always reasonable to pursue any of these goods independently of their contribution to individual happiness, that they contribute to one's happiness overall is always a sufficient reason to pursue them (with the sole restriction that they not create greater unhappiness for another, or be in some other sense immoral). I will *not* try to show that we are always motivated by happiness, or that our only good reason for pursuing something is that it will make us happy.

Nor will I claim that we could not so define some other goods as to make them the only things good in themselves for an individual. If we did, however, such a definition would, I believe, come close to the way I have defined happiness: namely, living a life that is satisfying overall, without regret and discontent. What I do claim is that the analysis presented here of individual good allows us to account for the beliefs about it which have survived centuries of discussion. I do not wish to contend that there could be no other adequate analysis, or even a better one. My primary purpose throughout this book is to show that an adequate analysis is possible by actually providing one. If a different theory can improve upon mine, all the better. The truth of moral cognitivism does not require that there be only one true moral theory, any more than scientific cognitivism requires that there be only one true account of physics or genetics. If the account of language and truth conditions given in the first chapter is correct, different theoretical constructs, using different truth conditions for their most central propositions, may be equally adequate. All that is required is that the theory as a whole account for the data — in the case of science, observed phenomena; in the case of ethics, well established moral beliefs. Of course, in a science its practitioners attempt to decide between competing theories by experimentation. With a primarily classificatory theory — as moral theories are — it is not necessary to do this. Which theory (of those which adequately account for well established beliefs) is preferable is determined by practical considerations.

I shall reiterate here and throughout this chapter that the topic I am discussing is what is good *for an individual*, not what is good overall or what it would be good (in general) for some person to have or to be. What would make a person admirable and good is not necessarily good for him. Nor is it always unreasonable for a person to sacrifice what is good for him, if by doing so he can bring about a greater good for others. In subsequent chapters I will indicate where individual goodness fits into moral right and wrong.

(1) One good which is a candidate for being ultimate is liberty or autonomy. Liberty has been widely recognized to be one of the greatest goods. It is good not only because it is universally desired, but because it enables people to pursue their own interests more effectively. Most of us know better than other people what will make us happy, and even when we don't, we often profit more through learning from our own mistakes than by being prevented from making them in the first place.

No one believes, of course, that we would all be better off if we were allowed to do exactly as we pleased, but in many situations loss of liberty in one area may increase it in others. Yet while liberty is a great good, and there are many people who have even been willing to die rather than lose it, most people are not willing to regard liberty as the ultimate good. Most people will accept major restrictions on their freedom in order to survive, and to obtain those goods which are essential to any degree of well being.[1] For some individuals death may be a lesser evil than loss of freedom — but not just any freedom. No one in his right mind would knowingly sacrifice his life in order to have the freedom to drive on whichever side of the road he wished. On the other hand, many have died fighting against tyrannical governments, and we believe their sacrifices worthwhile and worthy of honor.

Since not all freedoms are equally valuable, there needs to be some other criterion for determining which are the most important.[2] The most valuable, I suggest, are those which enable the individual to obtain those things which are most essential to human happiness. Indeed freedom may be considered one crucial constituent of happiness just because a significant level of happiness is impossible without it.

One might argue that liberty can easily be considered ultimate since the value of a particular kind of liberty depends upon how many other kinds of liberty it affects. Thus political freedom gives people many opportunities (i.e., freedom to do things), while freedom to pick one's teeth in public does not. Hence political freedom is more valuable. The problem with this approach is that it tends to classify every good thing as some kind of freedom. Food gives one freedom from hunger; a house, freedom from exposure. Education and good health give one freedom to do many things one couldn't do without them. An army or police force can give one freedom from fear. Conservation gives us freedom to continue to live on this planet. These assertions seem to stretch the meaning of 'freedom' to make it coextensive with goodness, for they characterize freedom as basically being relieved or protected from all manner of things that would make us discontented, and enabled to do those things which make us satisfied with our lives. Thus 'liberty' would be used in just the same way in which I have used 'happiness.' This assertion, of course, opens me to the accusation that I have stretched the notion of happiness just as much as one who stretched the notion of liberty to cover all goods. I think, however, that my characterization of happiness is more naturally coextensive with what people think of as good than is liberty. To see this, however, it will be necessary to discuss a variety of objections — as I shall do in this chapter.

There is a particular sort of freedom which is considered not only a basic good, but constitutive of a basic principle of morality, such that it is better for a person to respect his autonomy even if doing so might diminish his happiness. This is *autonomy*.[3] Autonomy is, fundamentally, the ability to make one's own choices based on a consideration of all the available information which might be relevant. A person's autonomy may be violated both by ignoring her known desires or by deceiving her so that she will make choices based upon falsehoods. If a doctor puts a patient on a ventilator in spite of a clear advance directive to the contrary, he has violated that person's autonomy. And if he lies to you about your diagnosis to keep you from worry and despair, or gives you a placebo to make you think you're getting a medication you want but isn't good for you, he has just as surely violated it. Our autonomy may also be violated when others manipulate our desires:[4] e.g., by lying or withholding crucial information, or by presenting a one-sided view of a situation. One can manipulate a person by inducing shame or embarrassment for some of her desires — which in turn may cause her to suppress them unjustifiably.

There is certainly wrong involved in all these paternalistic actions. To force something upon a helpless person against his will can rarely be justified, since, unless there is very strong evidence to the contrary, we must presume that what one wants is in one's best interests. But sometimes a person is not in a state where he can assess his interests; in such cases we believe ourselves justified in preventing him from doing what he wants. Most of those who are suicidally depressed, for example, are later glad that they were committed for treatment, even though they were forced into a path they did not desire at that time.

Paternalism is usually not good for people for many reasons. If you aren't given a realistic picture of your situation, you may be unable to take control of your life and do what is needed to realize your goals. If you are told that you are going to die soon, you will no doubt be fearful and sad.[5] Nevertheless, if you can get your affairs in order and make sure you spend your last days doing what matters most to you, this will probably give you some satisfaction. If you are kept in the dark, however, your real situation will probably become apparent to you eventually, but most likely when you have no time or energy left to take care of unfinished business. This would surely be a source of significant unhappiness. If you are asking for a potentially harmful medication, it would be much better for you if your physician explains to you the potential problems with continuing to take it, and works out with you a way to overcome your dependence.

On the other hand, there may be situations in which such deceptive medical paternalism might be better for the person. Some patients might be so devastated by a prognosis that knowing it could bring them nothing but increased suffering: e.g., a severely depressed quadriplegic who is told there is no chance that he will ever move again. A drug addict might be in a violently irrational state, so that explaining his situation to him would be impossible, yet continuing to give him his drug would only prolong the problem. In these cases, it may be better for the doctor to say to the quadriplegic something like, "It's too soon to say how much function you'll regain," even though he is virtually certain that the answer is "None," and to give the addict a placebo for a time. As a rule, such measures are temporary, and designed to time things so that discussing the truth with the patient will occur at a time when he is in a condition to deal with the truth constructively: i.e., in such a way as to protect or advance his interests.

Often it is very difficult to know in a given case whether it is harmful (as distinct from being morally wrong) to withhold truth, or to take a choice out of someone's hands. The same may be said about manipulating desires. With children, parents and teachers quite openly want to encourage desires that will lead them to be happy and socially responsible adults, and to discourage those which will have the opposite effect. We don't usually consider these efforts in any way bad for the child. Of course, it is best to influence his desires by letting the child have experiences from which he can learn that, say, hard work and deferred gratification can lead to both material and emotional satisfaction. This influences a child's desire in a better way than, for example, by slapping him whenever he objects to a parental demand. The difference is, of course, that the first kind of influence shows respect for the child and a desire for his ultimate good, while the second does not. Yet in both cases, the child's desires are being influenced and altered. (The term 'manipulation' has evaluative meaning; manipulation of a person is always wrong, whereas influencing or shaping is not.)

Thus it appears that there are occasions when autonomy may not be good for one (unless, as is likely, 'autonomy' also has evaluative meaning, so that it excludes liberties that might not be good for one), although normally autonomy is a great good because it is an integral part of a person's overall well-being and leads to a happier life. While we generally think that it is better for a person to be allowed to do what he thinks best for himself, even if he is wrong and makes mistakes that cause him some harm, we also believe it better for someone to intervene when his mistakes are likely to harm him significantly. The obvious cases are people who are clearly not capable of appreciating their own good, such as small children or the mentally incompetent. Others are less clear — e.g., adolescence, depression, or addiction. These people usually *do* have some grasp of their interests, but their outlooks may be distorted so that they are unable to appreciate what is good for them. Most think it right and good for our teenagers to give them a large degree of autonomy, but at the same time set limits to prevent them from seriously harming themselves. Even normally rational adults may act contrary to their own interests, and if one person sees that another is about to do something disastrous, she may do him a favor by forcibly intervening. (The question of whether paternalistic acts are justifiable is, of course, another matter altogether; that X would be better off if Y keeps X from doing what X wants does not necessarily justify Y's doing so.) Thus whether a degree of autonomy is good for a person depends upon how much harm he can do himself by acting as he desires. Autonomy is an important component of well being, but it is defeasible.

No discussion of autonomy would be adequate without attention to Kant's conception of autonomy as the basis of human worth. For him autonomy is the capacity to legislate in the Kingdom of Ends — i.e. for all rational beings, considering what acts and ends one could will for all to adopt. According to such a conception, anything that diminished or interfered with this capacity or its functioning would be bad for the individual, and conversely, what would promote it would be good for him. As Barbara Herman persuasively argues,[6] however, it is by no means obvious that Kant would hold that what is good for a person is solely what promotes rational autonomy. Nevertheless, Kant holds that this capacity is the ground for the priceless worth of human beings; its operation and what promotes it, while not the only things which are good, are the only unconditional goods. Hence contentment and enjoyment would not be good in themselves, but only as promoting rational autonomy. Yet while the ability to act rationally might be the source of human dignity, the bare ability need not be best for particular individuals. Having rational autonomy (which Kant thinks all humans have) is hardly sufficient to prevent a person's having a miserable life. While rational autonomy might be what *makes people valuable* and the grounds for treating them with respect, it is distinct from the essence of what is *good for* a person.

In discussing Kantian autonomy it must be remembered that he was concerned with what is good overall, and what is morally good. He clearly distinguishes between what acts are right and what are in the agent's interest, and it is what is in a person's interest that I am discussing here. We might also interpret Kant as saying that the only things that contribute to a person's worthiness, or goodness as a person, contribute to her ability to act as a member of a kingdom of rational ends. But once again what makes someone a good person is not necessarily the same as what is good for her.

(2) Charles Taylor and David Brink argue[7] that certain goods cannot be reduced to satisfaction of desire, and their arguments are applicable to the view that the goodness of a life is measurable by its happiness. As examples, Taylor discusses ideals which guide the lives of human beings. Those who live by such ideals as personal integrity, doing God's will, and freedom, for example, are widely admired, and often thought to lead better lives than people who don't have them. This is true, even if the people with those ideals have lives that are less happy and satisfying than they might have been without those ideals. Brink points out that there are many values — such as pursuit of and realization of the agent's reasonable projects, as well as certain personal and social relationships, which are components of a good life and which would be good even if they did not bring happiness.

But these apparent counterexamples do not refute my views — or, in fact, any desire-based theory. Not all ideals are good to follow. Many of those which have been espoused in the past have fallen into disrepute, some of them deservedly. The worst example is probably the ideal Nazi. Others like the medieval knight, the samurai warrior, and the Victorian lady are not much followed today, although many of us still admire certain of the qualities — such as gallantry, courage, and modesty — incorporated in these ideals. Other characteristics associated with these ideals, such as cruelty and submissiveness, are no longer thought good in our culture.

Both ideals themselves, and living up to them, are typically evaluated by their contributions to the happiness of the individual who lives by them, or to the happiness of other people. Often people will be brought up to aspire to an ideal, and are unhappy if they fail to attain it. Aspiring to an ideal may or may not be good for the person, and independently of whether one accepts that ideal, we are most likely to judge whether such striving is good for the person on the basis of whether his life of striving is happy, and whether attaining the ideal is possible for that individual. Certainly we may admire for his efforts a person who attempts unsuccessfully to live by an ideal — even when we reject the ideal — and his striving unsuccessfully might even be good for him, if continuing to try brings him satisfaction enough to outweigh his dissatisfaction at failure. Obviously, living by a particular ideal might be good for others besides the agent (although not always), but I am leaving that possibility out of consideration at present in order to concentrate on what constitutes individual good.

Jann Benson and Dan Lyons[8] have discussed the difference between aesthetic and moral norms, pointing out that many ideals are not necessarily morally good, or even good for the individual, but that attaining them is crucial to the self-esteem of the person who has them. To the extent that a person's self-esteem depends upon adhering to these aesthetic, or honor, norms, his happiness is also extent dependent on doing so. Therefore, it would be a bad thing, *ceteris paribus*, to fail. The honor of the knight, the samurai, and the Victorian lady depended on their meeting certain standards. Failure to do so, with resulting loss of honor, was considered a fate worse than death. In any such case I think all can agree that failure to live up to the ideal would be bad for the person who holds it. But if one simply *doesn't care* about that particular ideal it is not necessarily bad for him not to attain it. If the ideal is one to which he has not been exposed or which he has not been brought up to espouse (e.g., a modern young man and the ideal of a medieval knight), then there need be no harm *to him* in not living up to it. If, on the other hand, one rebels against an ideal that he has been expected to follow, whether it is good or bad for him to do so depends upon many factors.

It is common wisdom that part of a good life is having ideals and living up to them. And certainly a person who does so is far more likely to be well off than is someone who lives his life merely reacting to circumstances or pursuing immediate wants. Yet there is no necessary connection between having ideals and personal well-being. As noted above, consciousness of having failed to attain an ideal can be very painful. On the other hand, seeking or attaining certain ideals can be contrary to one's overall good. For example, consider young women who attempt to make their bodies fit some ideal of perfection or young men who live by gang codes. Nor does it suffice that an ideal be a worthy one for following and attaining it to be good for a person. Ideals of achievement, service, and courage often lead a person to catastrophic consequences for himself or others. Thus while those who live by no ideals seem less than human, and their lives are surely diminished and less good and happy than they might be, ideals, to be *good for* one to pursue and attain, must be carefully chosen.[9]

One of the good things about having ideals is that they prevent a person from becoming self-satisfied. Yet it might seem that my view that a good life involves wanting it to continue as it is would entail that self-satisfaction is a good thing, even if it is not deserved. Clearly there are people who are happy, or happy for periods of time, when, if they were less ignorant or insensitive, they would be dissatisfied with themselves or with their situations in life. We tend to think more of those people who recognize their shortcomings and the limitations of their lives and strive to overcome them. But let us be clear as to what we are discussing: not what makes a person good or admirable, but what makes *her life* good for *her*. If she grows up in a rural community where women have never been considered anything but drudges for their menfolk, we might admire her for seeking an education or career. And she might by her efforts bring great benefits to other women in her society. She need not, however, be better off herself. Whether she herself would be better off by struggling depends upon the obstacles she has to face, as well as her particular talents, and perhaps most important of all, the extent to which she succeeds in overcoming the obstacles.

Also, if a person has certain defects of character of which he is either unaware or which he thinks of as virtues, he will certainly be happier before than immediately after someone or some event brings his faults home to him. He will certainly be a better person if he recognizes his shortcomings and tries to correct them. Even if he fails, he will still be a more admirable person than one who dismisses the evidence and continues to think himself perfect. But will he be *better off* by facing up to his true self? The answer depends upon many considerations. If he is able to correct his character flaws, or at least avoid falling into the traps they set, he is very likely to be happier in the long run. If he is not able to do so, he may not be better off — will indeed be worse off through suffering not only the effects of his deficiencies, but also the knowledge that he is to blame for those effects and the fear that he is doomed to continue the same behavior. (The question of how what we don't know can make our lives worse will be discussed later in this chapter.)

As for the intrinsic goods of which Brink speaks — pursuit of reasonable projects and personal and social relationships — once again, we must consider: by what criteria do we judge a project or relationship good for the individual. A project may be reasonable, admirable, and good, as I shall argue more extensively below, even if its pursuit or its realization could harm the individual — e.g., investigations of outbreaks of infectious diseases in which the investigators run the risk of contracting the illness. But what makes a project good for the individual? Surely projects which engage his interest and fall within the scope of his abilities to handle it, which either succeed or provide instructive and nondisastrous failure, and which if they cause any damage to that person's other goals and interests, that damage is offset by allowing the overall prospering of his interests, are those which are good for him. And these are just those projects which augment his happiness as I have characterized it; persons engaged in such projects tend to want their lives to go on as they are. Thus if Dr. Jones dies of Ebola fever while investigating an outbreak, her endeavor was not good for her; if she does not become ill and returns home safely, it probably *was* good for her. Of course, if she dies she might actually be happier than if she turns down the assignment, and ever after castigates herself for avoiding her duty. If so, then we might say that her investigating the disease outbreak is good for her as well as morally good. In such a case, doing her perceived duty and living up to her ideal is a necessary component of her happiness.

The same may be said about relationships; those which are good for the individual are those which ultimately bring more happiness than unhappiness. Both projects and relationships are species of commitment, to which topic I now turn.

(3) Some of the greatest goods in life, as Martha Nussbaum argues extensively,[10] can lead to misery and disaster. A good, meaningful life is one filled with concerns *other* than one's own happiness — e.g., devotion to family, a discipline, or a cause. Moreover, many of the things that make life most worthwhile for an individual often lead to great unhappiness. This is surely true: commitments to people, disciplines, and causes are probably the greatest sources of happiness to us. On the other hand, caring deeply about anything sets us up to suffer great pain if that thing is lost. Because they fear loss, rejection, or failure, many people never do fully commit themselves to anyone or anything, and we consider their lives thereby impoverished — less good than they might have been.

Yet while a life without commitment cannot be truly good, it does not follow that every commitment is good for one, or that some commitments may not be better than others. Like ideals — which are, after all, a type of commitment — caring for another person or activity may or may not be good for one. Whether or not it is depends upon how it fits in with the rest of one's life — the consequences of the commitment, such as the opportunities it opens or closes off, the effect on the attitudes of the individual, and the memories it leaves, may reverberate for a lifetime.

A passionate love affair that ends with the death or desertion of the beloved would no doubt be good overall for a person who would otherwise have had no love in her life. On the other hand, if carrying a torch for the beloved or fear of hurt prevented her from forming any other relationships which she might have had, that affair would probably be bad for her overall. If the memories of her beloved bring happiness, if the loving itself brought new perceptions and wisdom, these might be, to her, worth the pain of losing the beloved. Much, too, depends upon the ability of the person to pick up the pieces of her life. If the thwarted lover remains crippled by grief or resentment, the affair will certainly have been bad for her overall. If, on the other hand, she forces herself to become involved in new pursuits she may find happiness again, even though she will never forget her lover or completely recover from the pain of loss. After all, even a love affair that lasts might not be good for one. Her life would be better without it if, for example, the beloved is abusive or if without *that* love, she would have found someone else who would have brought her much more happiness.

A person who devotes himself to a discipline or cause and fails to achieve anything in it may or may not be happier and may or may not have a better life than he would have had without that commitment. If he is bitter and disappointed by his failure, or if he would have been able to succeed in an area which he would have enjoyed more, but which he avoided or never encountered, then his commitment would probably not have been good for him. On the other hand, if he deeply loved his work, in spite of realizing that he was not particularly good at it, and if he could enjoy and honor without resentment the achievements of others, then it *would* have been good for him.

Whether a commitment that results in loss or failure is good or bad overall for a person depends on many factors, and what determines the answer is the extent to which the person lives as he wants to live.[11] For the most part while the commitment lasts, he does, for he is caught up in working and caring for the beloved person or pursuit. While he may be beset at times by fear or fatigue, so long as he has hope that the loved person will be with him, or that he may succeed at the pursuit, enjoyment is likely to outweigh pain. When the commitment is over — the loved person dead or gone, the cause finally defeated — , what determines whether it was good or bad for the person largely depends on what happens thereafter. Does he find new commitments? Does he focus on memories of joy, or on feelings of grief and bitterness? Has he learned anything that will help him avoid future tragedies? Does he have family or friends who can help him through the bad times? Much of his ability to recover will depend upon the circumstances of his loss — does he feel guilt for the loss, did he lose faith in himself or God or the world? The answers to all these questions determine the extent to which the person will be able to find enjoyment again in spite of his loss, and the extent to which his memories will bring pleasure or pain. And it is this that will determine whether he will have more or less happiness on balance as a result of his commitment and whether it will have been good or bad for him to have had it.

(4) Another good that might appear to replace happiness defined as being content with one's situation as the ultimate good for an individual is that of activity or the capability to act. Not only did Aristotle define happiness (and the ultimate good) as rational activity in accordance with virtue, but Amartya Sen has argued that utility should be defined as capabilities to function,[12] rather than in terms of desires or reactions. He maintains that capability is the criterion by which we measure good, since, for example, we would not consider a handicapped person better off (and less deserving or needy) because he is cheerful and happy than one with a comparable handicap who is miserable, nor do we consider well off those who are relatively content with their lots in spite of restricted and deprived circumstances. That we don't think so suggests that the capacity to do things — rather than happiness — is the criterion of utility. This capability includes not only strength and intelligence, but many other factors, such as freedom and opportunity, material goods sufficient to enable one to develop one's natural potential, and education and other help from society in realizing one's capacities. Sen also points out that many goods don't map tightly with

capabilities to do things because some can do more with a given amount than others.

Yet capacity, realizing potential, and even activity itself, while obviously ranking among the highest of goods, has drawbacks as the ultimate measure of individual good. I think anyone would agree that the person who is content with his lot — whatever that is — is better off than a person who is discontented with exactly the same kind of situation in life, provided that there is nothing either could do to change his situation. If through discontent one *can* change his situation, he has the opportunity of reaching a higher level of contentment than he had before — and most likely a higher level than that reached by the contented person who does not improve his situation. For this reason, a discontented person may be better off in the long run than a contented one, but he is so only if he makes changes (or if changes are made for him) that will bring him to a state of relatively greater contentment.

Moreover, not all action is good for us. Jake may have — and exercise — the ability to drink all his friends under the table or to work at his job sixteen hours a day, but this hardly entails that these activities are good for him. One might, of course, argue that getting drunk and working so hard that one fails to develop other areas of one's life are not good because they can interfere with one's ability to act overall. Diminishing one's capacity for action, however, is not the only reason why getting drunk and overwork might not be good for a person. If Joe wrecks his car while driving home from the bar and is badly hurt, he is not only worse off because of any disability he incurs, but also because of the physical pain he feels. If he works so hard at his job that he neglects his family he is worse off by missing the warmth of intimate relationships with them. He may actually *do* more by being a workaholic, but he misses out on valuable *experiences* which may involve action or capacities to act, but primarily do not. Thus events can make a person better or worse off even when they have no effect on a person's overall capacity for action.

The same considerations apply to a view like Aristotle's which qualifies the kind of action that is good for a person. There are many goods that are good for an individual even though they have no effect on whether he acts or can act rationally. Enjoying a sunset or playing badminton, eating a good dinner, and making love may not rank among the highest goods, but they do add to the happiness of one's life and one is worse off without at least some such pleasures, even though they have little to do with rationality. One might say that these pleasures are good only insofar as they are not pursued *irrationally* -- perhaps meaning by 'irrationally' something which interferes with one's capacity for rational action. This, however, is a different criterion; it would only allow that these pleasures are not bad for one so long as they did not diminish one's capacity for rational action, not that they are good independently of their effects on rational action. Likewise with action 'in accordance with virtue;' there are recognized goods that have little to do with virtue. If 'virtue' were to be interpreted as moral virtue, prudence, excellence, or as acting wisely in general, we still need to interpret morality, prudence, excellence, or practical wisdom, and these — being synonymous with what is good for an individual — would seem to require an independent criterion of goodness to serve as part of a definition of individual good.

In short, action, or the capacity for it, is a major part of individual good, but is not suited to be the ultimate criterion. As discussed above, many have maintained that happiness — or any other experience-based criterion — cannot be the ultimate criterion of individual good. I have already argued against some of these challenges. Yet while many things are *goods* which often enhance the happiness of particular individuals, they are not *good for* an individual for whom they do not. They may make her a better or more admirable person, and to the extent that this matters to her she will be more or less happy and better off by possessing them. We may say further that she *ought* to care about these goods. But she herself is better off only if possessing them does in fact make her happier in the long run. Knowledge, for example, while generally enhancing the happiness of people's lives — as well as their richness and usefulness — , may in some cases be detrimental. If a person has enough education, for example, to know that other people have much better lives than she, but she is absolutely unable to better her own situation, or to accept the better life of others without resentment, or to use her knowledge as a means of enhancing her enjoyment of life — e.g. by writing about the more fortunate — , or to put her education to other uses which outweigh any resentment it might promote, she is likely to be unhappier and worse off as a result of this knowledge. The extent of her resentment and the unhappiness it brings is, of course, a feature of her personality. If her material and social circumstances are miserable, resentment will make her worse off than one who is in precisely the same circumstances but is not resentful. Her education does not in and of itself make her so miserable, but if it leads her *only* to resentment, it has not been good for her.

Two related candidates for the ultimate good are self-realization and doing one's best. These like all the others discussed above are certainly important to having a good life. Self-realization is presumably making the most of one's talents, with the implication that the talents are good things and used for good purposes (i.e., a talent for sarcasm employed to write amusing novels or essays, but not to hurt others' feelings and alienate coworkers). Thus 'self-realization' is a value term, implying that it is a good thing. It may or may not, however, be good for the individual, if what she does is great for the world but brings her pain, sorrow, or an early death. To exercise to the full a great gift or to dedicate oneself completely to a worthy cause are paradigmatic of self-realization. Yet either usually necessitates the sacrifice of other goods. Whether the self-realization in such a case is good for the individual depends upon whether her ultimate aim is — to her — worth the sacrifices. If looking back at her life a great poet is glad she devoted her life to poetry at the cost of poverty and loneliness. If she is consumed with regret for not having a comfortable income and family life, then complete dedication to her craft was not good for her, however great the value of her work was for the rest of the world.

Likewise, doing one's best work may be good or bad for one. If it brings pride and joy it is good; if it causes one to lose other goods important to one (e.g., the surgeon who neglects his family and undermines his colleagues in order to gain a position where he may perfect his skills), it may not be. The surgeon's having developed his skills brings immense good to his patients, and it certainly is good for him to take pride in his work. On the other hand, he may ultimately regret the results of his inattention to the needs and rights of others. Obviously both the poet and the surgeon would be *best* off if they could exercise their talents to the highest degree and *also* have a happy family, friendly relations with colleagues, and a good income. But the need for many trade offs is a fact of life which insures that none of us can have everything that would make our lives happy. What is best for us is what makes us as happy as we can be, i.e., what enables us to live in a way we are glad to have lived with a minimum of regrets for what we could not have or do. Of course, self-realization and doing one's best work usually contribute greatly to this end.

One reason for supposing that certain goods like those discussed above are ultimate is that we cannot imagine a satisfactory life without them. To be a slave or have one's thoughts and actions controlled by others; to live in ignorance or passivity; to have neither ideals nor commitments to anyone or anything outside oneself; to be unable to realize one's abilities — all these would be unbearable to any intelligent, active, sensitive human being. For such a person, to preserve and further one's freedom, education, and ability to act for what one cares for, it would certainly be worthwhile to sacrifice some of those things that are traditionally thought part of happiness — such as sensations of pleasure, bodily delights, and self-satisfaction. Yet one way to look at this is that these higher goods are part and parcel of what makes you happy and are more critical to that happiness than some of the "lower" pleasures. You could not be content without them; your life would always seem lacking, especially if you knew what you were missing. Thus love, knowledge, self-realization, and freedom are integral constituents of your happiness, as well as essential to what you conceive of as a good life. Other people whose intelligence and outlook are very limited, however, may not be capable of appreciating some of the more exalted goods. We think their lives worse, and rightly so, because they miss much of what gives our lives meaning. They may not feel a lack, and thus may be contented, but they will not have the rich satisfactions which would lead to a greater enjoyment of their lives. Those who have a lack and feel it may be capable of greater happiness and a better life, but if they are totally unable to remedy the lack, they can be miserable and have worse and unhappier lives than either the contented ignorant or those who appreciate the higher joys and have attained a fair number of them.[13] We can certainly think of love, knowledge, self-realization, and freedom as final goods in the sense that we need them all to find life complete and satisfying, and that they are usually sought for their own sake and not simply because having them will make one happier. But they are not final goods in the sense of being invariably good for every person; at times they might be bad for particular individuals in particular circumstances.

The retort might be that happiness can be bad for us as well, and that it would be better for us to relinquish it at times in order to attain another good. Yet if we look closely at situations where that might seem to be the case the appearance is often due to a misunderstanding of what happiness is. For one thing, happiness in one situation may preclude greater happiness in the future, so that what leads to this temporary happiness is bad overall for the person who experiences it, or where a person is led by this happiness to do things which will undermine his long term happiness. Yet even an event bringing temporary happiness is better for a person than the same event with the same consequences that is not enjoyed by that individual. In other circumstances, we might think a specific good is more important to us than happiness when it is a good we could not be happy without. We may believe that no other enjoyable state or experience could replace that good, and we would be constantly discontented without it. We might also imagine that even if we did not know of the good in question and had not experienced it, or lives would still be worse without it. This would undoubtedly be the case, for if we were to experience it (even with fewer satisfactions of other sorts) our lives would be far more satisfying — and better — than they would be without that good. For those goods that matter most to us we would be willing to sacrifice many other things that add to our happiness. But this is not the same thing as relinquishing happiness itself — or even finding better a life with less happiness overall.

Then, too, a person's being happy — even if good for her — might not be good overall. Thus it is not a good thing for the wicked to prosper and enjoy their ill-gotten gains, for their happiness comes at the expense of that of others. Even if, however, one's happiness does not cost another anything it might still be a bad thing. Suppose Bill has harmed Bob. Is it better or worse for Bill fails to feel remorse? Bob will be just as badly off in either case (we are supposing). Suppose also that Bill's failure to feel remorse does not lead him to act differently than if he were sorrowful for what he had done. It is better for Bill to feel remorse simply because he deserves to feel it. I agree that this is so; I do not, however, agree that Bill *himself* is better off for feeling totally ineffective remorse. If he suffers from feelings of guilt which feelings do not lead him to make reparations or to reform himself or do anything to repair the ruptured relationships he has caused, he is worse off for feeling such guilt and no one's lot is improved by it. Not that it is bad for him to remember and regret what he has done, but it would be bad for him if his guilt were to cripple his ability to obtain satisfaction and prevent future regrets. In short, Bill would be a better person for feeling remorse, but he is not necessarily better off himself. He might be better off if he would not want to be the kind of person who can hurt another without feeling sorry about it; in other words, it is part of his good to be a person who cares about how he affects others. Living up to such an ideal may be absolutely critical to the happiness of particular people; if it is not, however, they themselves are not necessarily worse off for not living up to that ideal. Of course, if a person receives external rewards or punishments for what his character has become, such as in a life after death, the whole story is different. And it seems likely that in any real situation a person who does not feel remorse for things he has done that hurt others would be the sort of person who would miss the joys of real attachment to other human beings and thus would be less happy and worse off over the course of his life.

It might be asked why it is important to look for one common criterion of (individual) goodness, and whether such a search might not be fruitless. First, it would be useful to have a common measure because there are times when we want to compare how good certain goods will be for us. When we must choose between two incompatible things or courses of action, and only prudential considerations are relevant, we would like to be able to determine which would be better for us. The objects between which we must choose may be very different and seem incomparable, and it would be useful to find a rational ground for making a choice. There is much at stake in showing that there is a common criterion for individual good; if there is none, it suggests that goodness is indefinable or perhaps not an objective quality at all, but merely indicates our own endorsement. In other words, being able to find a common criterion of goodness is necessary to the cognitivist position.

For the most part we *do* think we can make determinations about what is best for us among disparate good things. When a young person must decide whether it is better to stay in school or to leave and get a job, for example, he knows that money now as well as a break from academic pursuits would be good for him, but so would more education and the prospect of more money later. Assuming that he earnestly wants to do what is best for himself overall, and not simply what has immediate appeal, he will consider what it is about the two choices that makes one better for him than the other. He needs to think not only that both would be good for him, but how good and why. He would, for example, take into account how close he is to getting his degree, how burned out he is from his course work, and what jobs might be available to him with his present level of education. If he has only one semester to go before graduating, it would probably be foolish to drop out; if, on the other hand, he is so sick of studying that he is unable to do justice to his courses, it might be a good idea to leave for a while. If he could get a well-paying job now, then leaving school temporarily makes much more sense than if he could only flip burgers or be drafted into the army. But why are these considerations relevant? If he has only a little left to do to finish his degree, he can, with a bit of perseverance, soon be in a position to earn much more in a more enjoyable job than any he might be able to get without his degree. By sticking to his present course he can have the best of both worlds — and more satisfaction overall — than if he drops out. On the other hand, if he could spend a year or two in professional sports and earn a fortune, he could return to finish his education without financial worries. He might even be able eventually to work at something he loves but which pays little or nothing. Once again, given different sets of circumstances the young man's greatest satisfaction would be attained by very different courses of action. In both cases, however, what we look to in deciding what is best for him is the probable effects of the alternative choices, given the particular circumstances, upon his life as a whole. Thus he would need to look not only at what would provide for his physical needs or give him the most pleasure, but what would exercise his talents, what would fit in with his values, and what he could be proud of. And in general the sort of life this describes is a life which brings much satisfaction and few regrets.

We all make such choices and we consider ourselves to have grounds for making them. Some choices are easy and we can readily see what will be best for us. Others are more difficult, and it is sometimes not possible to know what is best because we do not know all the effects our actions may have or how we will feel about them over time. But we are able to distinguish the hard cases from the easy ones. When we cannot tell what will be best for us we may still be forced to decide what to do; but we can distinguish forced choices from those we make after careful investigation and thought. The point is that we believe there are criteria for what is best, and that when these criteria conflict we can decide which have precedence — or that in the specific situation none does.

Of course, although it might be useful to have a common ground, this does not guarantee that there is one. I do, however, think that when we are evaluating how good or bad a particular choice has been for someone we look to its effect on the satisfaction or regret she has with her life as a whole as compared with the satisfaction and regret she might have had if she had done differently. This might lead one to suppose that happiness is nothing but a by-product of a good life, not constitutive of it. But as noted in the previous chapter, the causal process works in the other direction as well. Although we may not seek what brings us happiness for the sake of happiness, what we choose to seek — and what matters to us — is largely what has given us satisfaction before, or what we have reason to expect — on the basis of our past experience — may give us satisfaction in the future. And it is living in such a way as to experience this satisfaction that constitutes happiness and individual good, not just the satisfaction itself.

2. HOW DOES WHAT YOU DON'T KNOW HURT YOU?

An objection to the view of individual good as happiness, raised forcefully by Thomas Nagel, is that things can affect a person's good which do not affect his actual enjoyment of life at any time. We can say that a person is better or worse off if certain things happen of which he is totally unaware, for they may impact upon his interests.[14] The sorts of things that immediately come to mind are events which might occur after a person's death — which events have a bearing on what mattered to him in life. Because John cared about his business and his family, part of his good is their prospering not only while he was alive, but after he dies. We think how upset he would have been had his son neglected the business and gone bankrupt. If we believe in an afterlife, we think perhaps he *is* upset, but even if we don't, we think the failure of his business to be a misfortune for John. John's son may feel a great deal of shame and guilt over his failure; he thinks he has in some sense wronged his father — especially if he had *promised* to take care of the business. Similar remarks might be made about a person who is in a permanent coma. We tend to think that living in an unconscious state is something bad for the person, even though the person is not experiencing anything at all.

Another type of counterexample is happiness based upon false beliefs. Part of what makes me happy in my job is that I believe my work is worthwhile. Being happy in my job, I'm better off than I would be if I didn't think the work was valuable and if it didn't make me happy. If my work is *not* in fact worthwhile, my happiness in it is misplaced, and I am — as a result — not as well off as I think I am. In short, we believe that happiness based on illusion is not good.

And yet, while we do sometimes think of a person's being better or worse off when things happen which affect what he cares about, but which things do not have any impact upon his experiences, we don't usually think of them as affecting his well being or what is good for him. There are countless effects which our actions have upon the lives and thoughts of others and upon the world at large of which we are totally unaware, but which, if we should find out about them, could make a large difference to our happiness. Does each of these affect what is good for us? Were we to become aware of all of these, we would very likely be much happier or unhappier, and better or worse off, than we are. But since we are not aware of them, they do not affect our happiness or our personal good. Indeed, we often say things like, "There are some things we're better off not knowing." Parents of adult children living far away often make such remarks to each other. If we don't know, we won't worry about things we can't do anything about.

We seem, therefore, to have a certain ambiguity in our attitude toward the effect of unexperienced events upon the goodness of our lives. Some of this ambiguity can be resolved by comparing an individual's actual degree of happiness with that he would have had, given different outcomes. If Carol lies in a vegetative state for the last ten years of her life, she is worse off than she would have been living those ten years as a normal person. She could have had those ten years, and perhaps many more, living a healthy and active life, enjoying her family and career. Of course, if her life without the head injury would have turned out very badly — e.g., with some devastating illness or the loss of those people she loved most — she might not have been better off. Usually, however, we think of the good things that such people might have had and of what they have lost by losing conscious life, and thus consider life in a coma to be a misfortune.

We may also consider a person worse off for not knowing some facts which would, if known, make him unhappy for a time, but which when known would enable him to change course so as to improve his life overall. Learning the truth at least allows one to act more appropriately and on the basis of reality. If I were to learn that my work was doing more harm than good, I would undoubtedly change careers. My temporary unhappiness would be overcome by my finding new and more valuable work.

Obviously, not all events we do not experience, but which, if we did experience them would make us happier or unhappier, are thought to affect the goodness of our lives. There are things an individual might well want to happen, say after her death, but if they don't, her life was not thereby worse for her. I would like to have world peace lasting as long as humans do. It would make me happy if I thought this could happen. The fact that it will not, however, could only diminish the goodness of my life if I had invested a great deal of myself in obtaining peace. And even then, the diminishment would not necessarily take place. Suppose, for example, that after Jimmy Carter dies, there is a devastating Arab-Israeli war and Haiti is taken over by another military dictator. Was Carter's life worse for him than it would have been if his efforts to promote peace in those places succeeded? I don't think it would be. It might if there were things *he* could have done differently which would have prevented the later disasters. Or it might if, knowing ahead of time that peace in the Middle East and democracy in Haiti were hopeless, he would have placed his efforts on some more tractable set of adversaries.

But in general, we do not think that eventual success or failure of a person's efforts — or the opinions of others about him — is what determines the degree of goodness of his life. Carter might well believe that his efforts were worthwhile in themselves, even if their results were only temporary; after all, for a time at least, many children probably grew up better off than they would have been without his good offices. If he does not believe his efforts were worthwhile, then perhaps he needs a more realistic vision of what he can accomplish. None of us can guarantee the happiness of other people, fame and recognition, or the achievement of long-term ambitious goals (like Middle East peace) which depend on the attitudes and actions of thousands of people. If we let our happiness depend on these, we are doomed to disappointment. For this reason, much of happiness and a good life often requires that we adjust our goals to what we can reasonably hope to accomplish, and that we find pursuits which give us current satisfaction as well as opportunities for ultimate success.[15] This is true whether or not we ever learn the outcome of our endeavors.

If John slaved to build up his business solely to establish wealth and success for his son, then his life has not been as good as it might have been. He would have had a better — and happier — life, had he found satisfaction in the competent day-to-day management of a useful industry. Then his life would have been good — in that respect at least — no matter what his son did with the business later on. Certainly, we can say that his life would have been happier and better if he were to know in advance that his son would make the business into a corporate giant — or if he had known of certain avoidable pitfalls and dealt with them then. He might, for example, not have spoiled his son, thereby contributing to his profligacy, or he might have recognized and respected his son's differences and the fact that he would have much preferred to become a scholar or a musician — and found a competent business successor elsewhere. On the other hand, if there was nothing John could or would have done differently, even given the foreknowledge that his son would ruin the company, then the son's failure does not detract from the overall goodness of John's life. If John really got no pleasure from the business himself, then he would have had a better life in some other line of work.[16]

In general, people tend to be happier and have better lives if they do not aim solely for results that they are unlikely to know and which are outside their control. A parent will be better off now and in the future by giving his children love, attention, and appropriate discipline now, so that the children will have the skills they need to find their own happiness. The parent will get satisfaction all along, whereas if he has his heart set on specific ultimate goals for his children, he is most apt to be disappointed. If he concentrates on making a good life for his children in the present, he and they will have had much enjoyment, regardless of how the children's lives ultimately turn out. A writer will have a happier and better life by aiming for high quality and personal satisfaction than if she works only for recognition. She will have had many happy moments, and a good life overall, which she may miss if she is motivated primarily by a desire for fame.

In short, events which occur after we die, or present facts of which we are unaware, If we knew that matters would turn out as we desired, we would proceed with confidence and not be distracted by anxiety and doubt, and thus we would be happier and better off. If knowing that things will not be as we wish given our present course, we might change our methods or even our goals. The confidence, or the changes in direction would indeed make present life better and happier, as well as making the future more like what we would want. The man whose wife pretends to love him while secretly despising him would be much happier if he were in a different relationship; he would be temporarily devastated, no doubt, to discover what she really thought, but he would then have an opportunity to look for someone else. (On the other hand, perhaps not; maybe he is one of those unfortunates who could never find a happy marriage, and perhaps the deceptive one is the best he can hope for. Such a man, we would think, would have a hard time finding a good or happy life in any case.)

The old lady who is happily senile would no doubt be better off if she still had her rationality. She might have painful moments over the losses of age, but she could, on the other hand, command respect rather than condescension from others. (But again, perhaps not; maybe she is too debilitated to enjoy any activities and has lost all the family and friends she cherished. In such a case, she may well be better off senile; we pity her and think her life sad because of all that she lacks that would make it a good one, but given that these lacks are irremediable, being senile might be the best state for her.) Even a person who is contented may not be very well off because different circumstances might make her life much *more* satisfying. And we must remember that contentment does *not* mean mere passive enjoyment or possessing everything one could want. Few if any people are as happy as they could be without a large measure of purposeful activity toward goals they have not yet attained.

Whether unexpressed opinions or facts affect the goodness of our lives depends largely on what matters to us. Suppose that Meg has devoted her life to what most people she knows think a trivial objective — e.g., becoming a master cake decorator. She is never told what people think. To assess the goodness of her life we must consider what it is about decorating cakes that she cares for. Does the opinion of others matter to her? If not, then her occupation has brought her happiness and been good for her, for she has been doing something she thoroughly enjoys. If the opinions of others do matter much to her, then she might have been better off doing something more socially useful, for if others scorned her pursuits, they would have withheld the admiration she craved, even if they never told her what they really thought — not to mention that a person who craves attention has a built in source of unhappiness.

One might say that a life devoted to something unimportant cannot be a really good one. Remember, however, that the concept we are analyzing here is that of what is good for an individual — not what is admirable or morally good or what contributes to the overall good of humanity. Unless it is part of his personal ideal to be morally good or to live up to some standard, being admirable and morally virtuous may not be good for a particular person. A tortured soul may write great poetry, and he may reach moments of intense happiness, but his overall life may well not be as good *for him* as that of many ordinary folk — no matter what beauty he has brought into the world. Of course, if it is his all-consuming wish to create this beauty, and the periods of misery are what enable him to create it, and if he is aware — with consequent joy —

of having sometimes succeeded, his life would be good for him, as well as admirable and good for the world. Yet if he could have had the same creative achievement without the misery his life would have been even better. We consider a person admirable who has overcome difficulties in order to bring about something good — usually *not* something good only for himself. An admirable person may well be happier than one who isn't because he is conscious of living up to some ideal which it is important to him to attain. On the other hand, he might have been happier and had a better life for himself without having lived up to that particular ideal.

One objection to views like mine that goodness is based on what people actually experience is that most people do not want their happiness to be based on illusions. Suppose there is some fact p which would make S unhappy if she knew that p, but she does not know that p. The objection is that her life is not only worse as a result of p, but worse because of the deceptive quality of her happiness. In discussing this objection we need to break down the badness for S of being in ignorance of p into how bad it is for S simply that p and how bad it is that S is somehow prevented from knowing that p. We have already shown, I think, that the badness for S simply that p is indirect. There are causal connections between p and other events that can affect S's well-being. Thus if p is 'John's son ruins his business after John dies,' the fact that p will not directly make John worse off. But John might be worse off if he had pressured his son into going into the family business and had thereby failed to have a close and warm relationship with him. John's pressuring his son would have caused diminished happiness in their lives, as well as causing the eventual ruin of the business. If p is 'John's wife despises him,' that-p will surely cause multiple small miseries for John as well as an absence of the happiness that could come from a truly loving wife, even though John has not figured out that p. In these respects that-p can be bad for a person without his knowing that p. On the other hand, if that-p has *no* causal connection with S's happiness, then there appears to be no effect on the goodness of S's life either, even if S would be happier or unhappier if he knew that p.

But what if knowledge that p is kept from S? This surely adds a measure of badness to S's life, even if she is no less happy. Deception of one person by another is usually bad for that person (as distinct from being morally bad in other ways) for two reasons. One is that the person might, if she knew the truth, make changes that would better her life. The other is that deception itself erects a barrier between the deceiver and the deceived, which may manifest itself in other ways than through the fact about which the deceived is deceived. For example, the deceiver often has diminished esteem for the person he is deceiving (perhaps by thinking her incapable of dealing with the truth), or he may be deliberately working against her interests by withholding information she needs. Then, of course, lies often require further lies to maintain their believability, creating a network of deception which goes far beyond the specific fact which the deceiver does not want the deceived to know. On the other hand, the deceiver may have the best interests of the deceived at heart and may esteem her highly. If there is nothing that the deceived could do to better her situation by knowledge of the fact in question, and if she can only be made unhappy as a result of the knowledge, then the deceiver is most likely doing what is best for the person he is deceiving, even if not what is morally best.

Similar remarks can be made about self-deception. If S deceives herself, she manages to keep herself from knowing a fact that would make her more unhappy than she is. Usually, she would be better off if she faced up to reality and dealt with the situation from which she is hiding. Furthermore, even if there were nothing she could do about that situation, a habit of deceiving oneself is a bad one to form, and it can develop with particular insidiousness for the very reason that if one is deceiving oneself, one is not (fully) aware that this is what one is doing. On the other hand, self-deception may in some situations be better for the self-deceiver. In Ibsen's *The Wild Duck* Hialmar Eckdal has built up a network of illusions about himself and his relationships, and, as a result, has a fairly happy life. When Gregers Werle attempts to confront him with reality, Hialmar is unable to deal with it constructively, and his life falls apart. Of course, Hialmar might have had a better and happier life if he had been able to face the truth. But since he wasn't, Gregers did him no favor. Hialmar was better off in his self-imposed ignorance. He would, of course, have been a more admirable person, even if less happy, if he could have faced the truth, but we are, once again, not discussing what makes people admirable, but rather what is good for them.

In addition, people who care for truth want to live in the light of reality. They do not want their lives to be based on illusion, and would be horrified to learn that they were. They would prefer to know the truth, and think their lives better for knowing the truth, even though they would be far unhappier knowing than remaining in ignorance. This type of case illustrates the reason that measuring happiness as the net time spent content is only a rough measure of the goodness and happiness of one's life. The happiness which is individual good is not mere feeling, but living the life one wants to live, and there may be times that someone feels content, even though his life is not what he thinks or as he wants it. Furthermore, one may feel discontented even though his life is in fact proceeding as he would like. For the most part, those things of which one is ignorant eventually come to light or affect one's happiness indirectly in some of the ways discussed above, so that the long-term happiness of one's life is eventually influenced by what one does not know at a given time. This, however, is a contingent truth, and there may certainly be exceptions to it.

Yet there does seem to be more to a good life than happiness as I have defined it. It involves being able to view one's life as being *worthwhile*, according to one's own values. This does not necessarily mean that it is admirable or morally worthy, but rather that it includes the agent's having most of what matters to him or her realized. It would include both those things that virtually every human being wants, such as the respect of others and having achieved something, and things which the agent specifically desires, such as the happiness of his children or being a good physician. Whether some of these central concerns are realized is often not known to the person and some may only be fulfilled after his death. If he knew whether or not they were fulfilled, his happiness could be dramatically affected, but since he doesn't it isn't. And yet it might seem that his life was better or worse depending upon the fate of that for which he cared greatly.

There is, however, a connection with happiness, in that, if the agent were to know of these events that impact upon his concerns, he would want — or not want — his life to continue as it is. John would, if he knew that his son would ruin his business, or that his wife holds him in contempt, make, if he could, major changes in his present life and course of action. Even though he is happier not knowing, he would be happier in the long run if he knew and could correct the problems. If he could not correct them, the knowledge would only cause him pain. While we value living in the light of reality, we also believe that we ought to protect people from needless suffering. Therefore, when there is a question of whether or not to reveal a painful truth to someone, we ask, "What good would it do?" If there is truly nothing the individual could do to help the situation, we do not think he is better off knowing. We think he would be better off if the potentially painful fact were not true primarily because if it were not true, he would actually have a greater degree of satisfaction — satisfaction he may not actually miss, but which would increase his happiness, nevertheless.

Much of our sense that these unknown occurrences affect the goodness of one's life is that we can rarely be certain that the person won't find out. If they should happen while he is alive, he might well learn of them, as a man might find out that his wife or professional colleagues do not respect him. If they are events which will in fact occur after he dies, we can seldom be sure ahead of time that he won't live long enough to know what will happen. Thus John may well live long past the time he retires and know full well what his son has done to the business. We rarely, if ever, look back after someone's death and say of some present event, "Because Laura's work has now been recognized, this makes her life better than it seemed to have been while she was alive." Rather we would say, "How happy she would have been to see the recognition; I wish she could still be around to know of it." In other words, we think her life would have been better if she had *known* of the recognition, not that it actually was better because of the recognition of which she was never aware.

We do sometimes think of certain things being in, or contrary to, the interests of a person who is no longer alive or aware of what is going on around her. In particular, the fate of those projects in which the person invested much of her life we think of as being in her interests or contrary to them. And we feel that we ought to respect the wishes of those who are no longer capable of knowing whether those wishes are fulfilled. Thus we acknowledge a moral, as well as a legal, obligation to honor the provisions of a will. And we believe we ought to treat with respect those who are too demented to comprehend what is being done to them, at least in part because they wished, when rational, to receive respectful treatment. Our desires reach into the future, often beyond the time when we can know whether they have been satisfied, and we all want some security that what we want now to happen in the future will happen and that our present wishes will not be ignored when we are unable to see that they are realized. Without an established practice of respecting the wishes once had by those now dead or those who are alive but unable to protect their interests, such security would not be possible. In a strict sense the dead or demented person's happiness and good are not directly affected by the satisfaction or nonsatisfaction of the desires they once had. But because of our uncertainty in some cases as to whether they are aware, because of love for that person and desire to respect what she valued, or because of obligations — based on a social need for security — which we have incurred through promises and wills, we ought, or at least think we ought, to act so as to further the interests the individual had while alive and aware.

In addition, the happiness and good of a person is indirectly affected by things which happen that he is unaware of. The man whose wife or colleagues secretly hold him in contempt would be better off if they did not so regard him. He would be better off, and happier, not because of the absence of contempt per se, but rather because he would most likely be a different sort of person — one capable of commanding respect from others and who receives occasional demonstrations of their esteem. This in turn, would make him a happier person overall. We can see this better by considering a person who deserves respect, but who does not receive it. In this case it is not his deficiencies, but theirs, which are the cause of the contempt. We would only consider the person worse off if he particularly desired the esteem of others and missed receiving it.

We all want to be the sort of people who are capable of fulfilling our projects and realizing our ideals and to be progressing toward these ends. When we believe we are, to that extent we are happy and well-off. If some important end is threatened, we want to be aware of the dangers and position ourselves to remove them. So long as we are able to do so, we are still likely to be happy — the more so, the more secure we are in our ability to overcome the difficulties. On the whole, a person is more likely to be happy if he is acting in such a way as to ensure the realization of those goals which are most important to him. Obviously, unforeseeable events could frustrate them and threaten his happiness. If he happens to be dead — or for any reason is never aware of these events — , however, his happiness and the overall goodness of his life -- for him — is not thereby diminished.

How, then, should we view events (E's) which, if we knew they would happen or have happened, would make our happiness greater or less, but which, by hypothesis, we do not know of and which seem, nevertheless, to increase or decrease the overall goodness of our lives? They are highly likely to cause or be caused by a variety of other events (E*'s) of which we are aware and which do affect our happiness. The E's may include the opinions others have of us, the quality of work we have done, or the fate of those projects most important to us. They are for the most part things that are happening during our lifetimes, but may include events which occur only after we have died, such as the ultimate success of our enterprises, and the happiness of our children and grandchildren.

Although it is in our interests — in the sense that these events are things we care about — for the E's to occur or not occur, it is rather the E*'s that actually affect the happiness and the goodness of our lives. It is in John's interest that his wife love him and that his son succeed with the family business, because these are things John cares about greatly. But what constitutes his misfortune is not the fact that these interests won't be realized, but rather all that he lacks in ways of small attentions and demonstrations of caring from a life partner, and all the things he might have done to insure the success of the business and the happiness of his son. Or, if he is the sort of person that is unable to command the respect of others and see enterprises through to success, these deficiencies are bound to diminish his happiness and the goodness of his life in countless ways.

That it is the E*'s, rather than the E's which affect both the happiness and the goodness of a life is suggested by the fact that if John's business fails after his death, not because of his son's mismanagement or John's own lack of forethought, but as a result of a world-wide depression, we would not think that John's life was any worse for him. Likewise, Carter's life will not have been worse for him if the Middle East blows up after he dies, and the unrecognized author's life will not have been better as a result of achieving posthumous fame.

3. OTHER OBJECTIONS

The following objections to the views I have proposed are worth discussing in detail. (1) Having incrementally more enjoyment does not necessarily make your life better.[17] (2) We are not motivated only by the expected pleasantness of an experience. We play a game to win because we want to practice a skill or defeat an opponent, not because winning is pleasant. Nor do we consider that expected pleasantness is the only rational reason for doing something.[18] (3) Stocker[19] bases his argument for pluralism of goods partly on the claim that different courses of action may be equally reasonable, whereas, he says, if there were only one thing that was good, the only course of action which was reasonable would be that which maximized good. Furthermore, we can also reasonably feel the lack of one particular kind of good, even though another life without that good might be equally satisfying. (4) Anderson maintains that there is no one value that should be maximized and accuses all forms of hedonism and utilitarianism of claiming this. She espouses a pluralist notion of value, according to which such goods as health, love, and accomplishment are all good and not reducible to pleasure, happiness, or any other single thing.[20] (5) Several have argued that goods are incommensurable.[21]

(1) Stocker argues that adding a very small amount of pleasure or pain does not increase or decrease the goodness of a life. He cites a person who fails to take enough warm clothes on a vacation. The vacationer surely would have enjoyed himself more had he been comfortably clad, but is his life really worse as a result of being chilly? It seems not. My answer to this would be that his life probably *is* very slightly worse than it would have been if he'd had warmer clothes, but over the course of a lifetime a few days of being a bit chilly count for very little. For this reason, it seems silly to *say* that his life was worsened by this minor discomfort when the chances are that he — like most people — has experienced some far worse things. It does not follow, however, that it is *false* that his life was just a tiny bit worse.

Moreover, some experiences which are unpleasant at the time add more to one's life than they take away — e.g., by making an amusing story, or by providing one with knowledge that comes in handy on a later occasion. In such cases minor annoyances can make one's life better and happier overall in a way that true disasters such as losing a child or being permanently crippled could hardly do. The fact that people often make something good out of a small setback or unpleasantness provides another reason why we may hesitate to say that their lives are worse as a result of such experiences, yet, *ceteris paribus*, they are just a little worse.

(2) The objection that our activities are not motivated solely by pleasure is true, but fails to show that the goodness of a life is not measured by the amount of enjoyment it contains. Pleasantness, rather than being the end at which we aim, is largely an accompaniment or consequence of the pursuit and attainment of desired ends. On the other hand, pleasure and pain, happiness and unhappiness, contentment and discontent are all signs that our lives are, or are not, going in the direction we want them to go. They let us know whether we should continue as we are or attempt to change.

Pleasure and pain are not just signals, however; they also give us a reason not only for acting, but for altering our desire structure. That a course of action is likely to make one happier in the long run is always a good reason to choose it, and — where moral considerations are not involved — a decisive reason. Consider an alcoholic whose wife leaves him. Because he loves her, he is miserable, and because he is miserable, he knows that to make his life tolerable, he must change his behavior, and that changing his behavior will require moderating his desire for drink at least to the point where he is able to abstain. His misery consists in wanting many things to be different — e.g., the blow to his pride, the loss of companionship, the recognition that he has lost control of his life to alcohol. He wants to get rid of the misery, and this may lead him to deal with his situation constructively and attempt to conquer his addiction, eventually making his life better — by replacing the misery with a sense of accomplishment and new satisfactions that he will be glad of. His satisfaction or greater happiness will consist of his living a life he wants to go on as it is and gladness that he has made changes. Even though he may not think to describe his state as happier, if someone were to ask him if he is happier he would agree that he was — and likewise he would consider his life better. In short, although we do not do what we do solely in order to seek pleasure and avoid pain, pleasure and pain provide spurs to continue, or to change, what we are doing.

Furthermore, that an activity will be *un*pleasant is certainly a good reason for not doing it. So is the realization that the activity will produce no pleasure, while taking up time that could be spent in something that was enjoyable. And that an action will produce pleasure or enjoyment is considered by all to be a reason for performing it. These reasons are not always decisive, of course. If a pleasant activity will likely lead to a long period of wishing things were otherwise, or if a brief period of tedium or pain can be expected to prevent many troubles in the future or to bring subsequent joy, it is surely rational to forego brief pleasures or endure brief pain. Furthermore, as I shall indicate shortly, it may be rational to give up a substantial amount of one's own happiness for the sake of another's good or the promotion of a cause or discipline to which one is committed. Thus what is rational does not necessarily coincide with what is good or enjoyable for the agent.[22]

Certainly, for the most part people do not aim specifically and directly for happiness. Rather they want and work toward particular ends, such as earning a living, bringing up a child well, or playing a good game of bridge. They do not as a rule spend time asking themselves whether achieving these ends will make them happy. They are happy when they succeed and unhappy when they fail, because the goals are things they wanted. One is most likely to think about happiness when one has a crisis — e.g., comes to realize that one's present course of action may lead to disaster, or discovers a new and exciting opportunity. When the need for choice occurs we look at the possible consequences of different alternatives and *sometimes* ask ourselves which is most likely to make us happier. Even then, however, happiness as such does not always enter into our calculations. Rather, we imagine our lives given Alternatives 1, 2, ..., n, and choose the one that has the greatest appeal. The more intelligent, imaginative, and circumspect we are, the more detail we fill in to the different pictures, the more accurate they are, and the more carefully we weigh the consequences our actions are likely to have. At least where moral considerations are either not relevant or not being considered, we then choose the one that appears to be the most satisfying and the least likely to give us cause for regret. That is, we try to follow a path that will make us glad of our choice and not wish to change what we have done and what happens to us. This is, on my definition, the *happier* choice as well as the best for the agent; yet we do not always look for happiness *under that description*. Rather, we seek the things we value, which in turn — with luck — make us happy when we get them and also while pursuing them. But although we do not commonly aim at happiness as such in our day-to-day lives, or even in moments of crisis, when we evaluate our lives as a whole, or the overall effect of a particular happening upon our lives, it is the amount of happiness we have had that we use as a criterion. For anyone, the fact that an event or course of action would lead to a life that had more enjoyment and less regret would make them prefer that life and give them the best of (self-regarding) reasons for thinking it good for them.[23]

(3) Stocker argues that the fact that different courses of action aiming at different goods can be equally reasonable shows that there is not merely one good (such as pleasure), and that measuring goodness by the amount of happiness does not entail that the only reasonable way to act is to maximize happiness. It does not show this. While it is reasonable to act in any way we want which is not positively *un*reasonable, that an action will detract from the overall happiness of someone without creating greater happiness for someone else is a sufficient reason not to do it and makes it unreasonable.[24] It is reasonable to do anything that one enjoys or wants to do, so long as it does not harm one or make one more unhappy, and is not immoral (which typically involves restricting others' opportunities for happiness), and it is also reasonable to act so as to increase one's happiness or overall good, however that should be defined, provided one's action is morally acceptable, and it is, finally, always reasonable to act for moral good.

Elsewhere[25] and in Chapter 2 I have argued that what a person ought to do is whatever is necessary for attaining one of these types of purposes. We can go further, I think, and say that the class of *acceptable ends* are (1) specific objects of desire whose attainment does not harm the agent and is not morally wrong, (2) the agent's own overall good so long as the means to this are not immoral, and (3) what is morally right. It is always reasonable to pursue an acceptable end, although it is not invariably best for a particular agent to do so. Moral ends and demands, for example, often call for the sacrifice of a person's own interests. On the other hand, it is not reasonable for a person to sacrifice her own good for something less than bringing at least equal good to others (or possibly for adhering to a moral principle).

A hierarchy like the one outlined above enables us to see how Stocker's claims supporting pluralism can be compatible with there being one ultimate criterion for what is good for an individual. Even without a hierarchy, a monist about value can supply an answer. A woman who faces the choice between family life and a career must give up something; either she will choose to give herself wholly to one pursuit or the other or she will make certain compromises with both (e.g., stay home while her children are small, or do only that housework which is necessary to prevent a visit from the Department of Health). Whatever she does, she is likely to have some regrets. If she is childless, she will feel sadness at missing motherhood; if she stays home for several years, she will miss career opportunities that may hold her back permanently.

It may well be that two or more paths she could have taken would have been equally satisfying on some scale of value, and thus be equally reasonable for her to choose. Nevertheless, she can undoubtedly imagine, even though she cannot realize, a scenario in which she can "have it all." Such imaginings could lead to a sense of lack, because she can, while reading "The Cat in the Hat" to her toddler for the hundredth time, miss the stimulation of giving a university lecture. Or, coming home to an empty house can be dreary for a dedicated career woman, no matter how exciting her day at work has been.

But Stocker's point is that there isn't any common scale on which you can measure the value of the different goods, because they differ so in character. And he is right to note these differences. The satisfactions of life, as well as its pains, are vastly different from each other. The stimulation of a philosophical exchange in a seminar or with a good colleague is entirely different from the joy of cuddling your child in your lap, and both are as vastly different from eating a beautifully prepared gourmet dinner, finding out that your biopsy showed no cancer, looking at an awe-inspiring Byzantine icon, or feeling the warm sun on your face, as all these experiences are from each other. There isn't any way of holding these good things up against one another and saying that this one is better than that. But that isn't what we do in deciding what is best for us. All of them would add to the goodness of a life, and all are reasonable to pursue at least in some circumstances. Yet there may be times when the pursuit or experience of one of these goods may preclude the attainment of another; at these times a reasonable choice is one which leads to the best life overall. Too many gourmet dinners may lead to cardiovascular disease or certain types of cancer. Lying in the sun instead of meeting a deadline at work could lead to loss of your job. In thinking ahead, we look to how we are likely to feel about our choices in the future. What will we regret? What will we be glad of? Will we be sorry or pleased that we made the choices we did, and will we or will we not wish we had done differently?

The answers to these questions — whether or not we actually ask them — determine how good our lives will be, and what it is reasonable to choose. To choose rationally we need to look at how these choices fit into our lives as wholes — only then can we hope to know what is better or worse for us. We do not compare these various goods pairwise in isolation on some scale. But we do have a criterion by which we can decide which good might be better for us in a particular context or set of circumstances. And this is how we will assess its contribution to the degree to which we are content with our lives over their whole course. And as indicated earlier, this potential contribution is only one feature of any event, and it is certainly not the only reason we may desire it or value it. Cuddling a beloved child in one's lap is a joy in itself which needs no other feature to make it good and desirable. But it has another feature, in virtue of which it is good for a person to cuddle her child — namely that it is something people want to do and are glad they have done and may miss not having had the opportunity to do. That feature is not the reason why the mother cuddles her child; it is, however, the reason why it is good for her to do so.

It is well known that human beings are hard to satisfy. We can miss a good, even though we believe we have chosen the path to the greatest happiness that was possible for us. That we have done what will make us as happy as possible doesn't mean that we might not have been happier had things been different. Suppose that Jane has stayed home with her small children and done her painting whenever she could steal a little time; suppose further that under the circumstances this compromise produced the greatest happiness she could have had. If, however, she had had more money she might have hired a maid to do the household drudgery and thus have been able to spend more time on her painting as well as enjoying her children, thus having a yet better life than the one she has. Such counterfactual considerations can make people regret what they don't have. While it is perfectly reasonable to regret such lacks from time to time (especially if we can think of ways to change what we don't like about our situations), we can detract much from our happiness by dwelling on what we have missed by making the irrevocable choices we have made.

That a thing or event is good does not entail that it is always good for everyone — only that it is relatively rarely bad for anyone. That it is good does not entail that everyone wants it, but if no one had ever wanted, or would ever want it, it would not be a good. The value of great painting is dependent on there being at some time beings who could see it; the value of good food and wine on there having been individuals with a sense of taste. A blind man may not be able to appreciate visual beauty himself, but he can acknowledge that a beautful work of art has value because it enriches the lives of those who can see it.

This hierarchy of acceptable ends is independent of any substantive theory of what is good for an individual or what is morally right. It can fit with both descriptivist and nondescriptivist analyses. What is common to all and to ordinary usage is the hierarchy itself. Everyone recognizes not only that it is reasonable to pursue whatever ends take one's fancy, so long as the limits of prudence and morality are not transgressed, but also that it is foolish or wrong to pursue ends that harm us or others.[26]

(4) Anderson has argued that goods are not reducible to one value. We need to consider, however, what one good's being reducible to another means. In the sense

that health, love, and accomplishment are desired by nearly everyone independently of whether they bring happiness, and that it is reasonable to pursue these even if they don't actually increase happiness, then we can say that these are valuable goods which are not reducible to happiness.

On the other hand, as Anderson herself admits, any of these goods may sometimes *not* be good for a particular person at a particular time. To be in love is wonderful, so long as life with the object of one's devotion is both possible and will not bring more misery than joy. Many women recognize that they would be better off without an abusive partner, even though the love they still have is part of what prevents them from leaving. (Abusers are often very adept at manipulating the feelings of their partners, so as to keep that love alive.) Accomplishment is good for people nearly all the time, but one may accomplish something at too great a cost. If one's writing a book, for example, causes one to neglect and alienate one's family, one may well be sorry in the long run — even if the book brings fame and riches. If so, this particular accomplishment may not have been good for the author.

As indicated in Section I, we need — and have — a criterion for determining whether *a* good is actually *good for* an individual in his or her actual circumstances. In order to know what that criterion is, we need to examine how people actually make those judgments, and — even more importantly — how they argue for and against such judgments. If we do, I think we will see that conduciveness to personal happiness is that criterion. Any thing or event that is a good has, as we have seen, many features. Some of these features are those for which people desire the good. Some of them are directly or indirectly conducive to happiness. Others may in some circumstances lead to harm for particular individuals. We may think of a thing as a good, even though in some cases it may harm people, if most of the time it leads to people's happiness. If it didn't, we wouldn't consider it a good.

(5) Stocker has argued for pluralism on the grounds that goods are generally incommensurable. How, he asks, would we compare the goodness of an afternoon discussing philosophy with one of lying on a beach? The two pursuits are so totally different, that there is no common measure by which we could say one was better than the other. Even in deciding which wine to serve with a dinner, we have no way of measuring which is better or even more pleasurable; the wine which we might prefer alone might not be the one we would prefer with the meal, for the character of the meal would affect the way the wine would 'go' with it. Yet we do make choices about how to spend an afternoon, and these are reasonable choices; what Stocker objects to is the supposition that there is single criterion by which we must make these choices.[27]

I agree with Stocker that we do not have some simple scale by which we can measure the absolute or even relative goodness of two things, activities, or states of affairs. On the other hand, I do believe that we have a common ground for making our choices, and this is what will bring us the greater happiness (or least unhappiness) over our whole lives, or more commonly, over particular segments of our lives when those choices are not expected to have wider impact. In choosing a wine for dinner, we want one which will complement the food served in such a way as to bring out best the flavors of all components of the meal so as to make the eating of the dinner as enjoyable an experience as possible. Any enjoyable experience enhances happiness, provided it doesn't also bring regrets. We can, of course, imagine reasons why choosing the particular wine might lead to regrets on the part of one or more diners — if one guest is tempted to eat so much that he has a heart attack, or if another is consumed with envy at the hostess's culinary abilities and never speaks to her again. Or, it may be that the guests are so undiscriminating that they do not appreciate the blend of delicate flavors and would just as soon have had hamburgers with fries and cheap beer.[28]   But assuming that there are no such untoward consequences, the hostess, by having chosen a wine which complements the meal, will have contributed to her own and her guests' happiness by creating a dining experience which all not only fully enjoyed at the time, but are glad to have had and would not wish to have had otherwise. And the experience would have made all their lives just a little bit better, the right wine having added to the enjoyment and the goodness of that experience.

Some choices are more complex, such as Stocker's example of whether to spend the afternoon lying on the beach or discussing philosophy. Much will depend here on background conditions, such as *with whom* one might be talking philosophy — the bore in the next cottage who, without the slightest philosophical training, wishes to tell you about his philosophy of life, or the Greatest Name in your field. Other factors which might make a difference would be whether you have spent the last few weeks working hard to get a paper finished or spent them on other pursuits and feel a need to get back into doing some serious work; whether your current project is going well and you need some down time to let it gel, or whether you are stuck and need the input or feedback of others.

With most of these considerations you are looking beyond the experiences of this particular afternoon to the progress of your current work or even your career as a whole. If, for example, it is the Great Name who invites you to discuss your and her work with her, and you were to choose to lie on the beach instead, you would probably regret that lost opportunity the rest of your life. Moreover, you would never know what seminal ideas might have enriched your work or what professional opportunities might have come to pass. The choice to lie on the beach would have been bad for you both because of the regret and because of what you would have missed that you would have been glad to have had.

Yet, of course, the choice to lie on the beach, foolish as it would appear under the circumstances, might actually turn out better for you. Suppose that the Great Name is a bitter, sarcastic person who criticizes your arguments and ideas in such a way that you — unjustifiably — lose your self-confidence and give up philosophy altogether. Or, perhaps she makes a suggestion that leads you to take a wrong turn in your own work and diminishes its overall quality. Alternatively, her suggestions might lead you to fame without much affecting the quality of your work, and in the process you neglect and alienate your family to the point that — overall — you regret the direction your life has taken.

In short, how good or bad the choice you make will be for you depends upon multiple factors. But it is possible to see what factors will make for goodness or badness by considering how these might contribute to the happiness of your life as a whole. Again, you are, in making choices, probably not thinking about your overall happiness, but rather about what will contribute to a pleasant afternoon, or to the quality of your philosophical work. Yet happiness and unhappiness are made up of the consequences to oneself of countless choices. We usually only think about happiness when we are faced with the need to consider not only long-term, but wide-reaching, consequences of our actions. If, for example, how I choose is apt to affect only how I get along with a coworker, I will be thinking primarily of that relationship. But if this choice may determine whether or not I keep my job (e.g., if the coworker in question is my boss), which in turn may determine what career I pursue, where I live, and many effects on my family, I may need to think of the wide consequences and of my overall happiness (and that of others as well). In so considering I will try to imagine how I would feel about the various alternatives. While telling off my boss may make me feel good at the time, doing so is apt to have many results — e.g., a long period of unemployment and poverty — which I will regret. If I think about these consequences, I will realize that I would regret them and thus know that telling off the boss will not be good for me. If I choose to do it anyway, or do not stop to think of the consequences, this would be a prime example of an unreasonable choice — one which, while satisfying a particular desire, which desire in itself might not be unreasonable — is bad for the agent and contrary to her interests.

Many goods appear to be incommensurable. For example, how does spending time with a child compare with buying him toys? While we can't directly measure the effects on the child's happiness, however, we can make some generalizations from observing differences between children whose parents emphasize material possessions and those whose parents give much of their time. What counts is which children appear happier; which show fewer obvious and subtle signs of discontent with their lives. Such generalizations could lead us to conclude, for example, that while toys are nice and can be major contributors to a child's development, they are poor substitutes for a parent's personal attention. In other words, we may not be able to compare directly two different kinds of goods, but we can observe the effects these goods generally have on happiness. And we *can* observe signs of happiness and unhappiness (which admittedly are not totally reliable), such as verbal expressions and enthusiasm in performing one's activities.

To conclude, then, what is good for a person is what will add to her happiness, and her happiness in turn is measured by the preponderance of time she spends wanting her life to be as it is, as opposed to wishing it were different. I have argued that this conception of individual good avoids many of the difficulties of other accounts and that such difficulties as it appears to have can be answered.

CHAPTER 5

BENEFICENCE AND FAIRNESS

In Chapter 1 I argued that to determine what is right and wrong, we need to find some moral principles which are so basic to our understanding of moral beliefs that they can be considered truth conditions of moral judgments. I proposed that these can be discovered by examining the ways in which people argue about morals. If this is true, then our next step is determining what are the considerations to which people ultimately appeal in discussions of right and wrong. In this chapter I shall try to show that there are two such fundamental considerations — beneficence and fairness. In the next I shall argue that beneficence and fairness may be combined into a single principle, which enables us to resolve the great majority of conflicts between them.

Much of what follows in this chapter will sound platitudinous, because I shall state a large number of moral beliefs that are so widely held that no one thinks they need defending. They are, in other words, well established, having stood the test of time and having been adopted by people from all known times and places. My aim is to show that these moral platitudes may be interpreted as applications of the broader principles of beneficence and fairness. If any moral theory cannot explain our adherence to these extremely common beliefs, or is inconsistent with them, it will — if my earlier arguments are sound — fail to articulate the meaning of moral oughts. Success, on the other hand, will not prove that moral theory to be the only correct one. This, however, is not a problem for cognitivism, for according to the view of meaning expounded in Chapter 1, it is perfectly possible to have alternative sets of truth conditions for a statement, and which set to accept is a pragmatic matter rather than one of discovery. If, on the other hand, my theory can explain and be consistent with our common moral beliefs, and provide a coherent account of those moral judgments that have near universal acceptance, it will be correct — even if there are other possible correct theories.

Some may find it a weakness in the theory I present that it does not generate new moral ideas.[1] On the contrary, given the linguistic presuppositions of Chapter 1, the substantive principles by which the theory is tested must be principles which are well known and widely accepted. The theory should *not* entail novel and surprising moral conclusions; if it did, it would be inconsistent with the well-established beliefs among which truth conditions (in any area of discourse, moral or otherwise) are to be found.

The only exception to this general statement would be cases in which the theory is applied to novel situations, such as those relating to such technological advances as human cloning, or the ability to prolong life beyond the time that a person is likely to find life meaningful. Even here, however, solutions generated by a moral theory would need a close connection with the more general principles which are already accepted. Thus to conclude that euthanasia would not be wrong in certain cases where an individual remains alive in a state of misery might be justified on the basis of our duty to relieve suffering and on showing that this duty overrides others like that of not killing. Limits to euthanasia would include requiring free and informed consent from the person whose life would be taken.[2] Relieving suffering, not killing, and requiring consent of individuals before something with profound effects is done to them are well known and accepted moral beliefs, even though the question of euthanasia is highly controversial.

There are, of course, some people who have not accepted some of the platitudes to be discussed. Many unusual beliefs have been held by peoples in isolated circumstances; others have been adopted by those of certain religious or political persuasions. In many cases, however, these beliefs have never been subjected to debate and discussion with those outside the membership of such groups; furthermore, when they have been debated, an interpretation consistent with the moral platitudes is in most cases possible. Still, there is no doubt a remainder of instances in which people have had moral beliefs incompatible with the principles of beneficence and fairness to be articulated here. What I am going to argue is not that there is universal agreement with those principles, but rather that they are the principles to which moral debate has consistently pointed over time.

1. BENEFICENCE

Beneficence is making things better. It includes both doing good and refraining from doing harm, as well as the prevention, removal, and correction of evils. While everyone agrees that it is right to do good and wrong to do harm, there has been wide disagreement about what is good and what is harmful. In the last chapter I argued that what determines whether an experience is good for someone depends upon whether it makes him happier overall than he would have been without it. And how good or bad a person's whole life is for him is determined by the balance of happiness over unhappiness it contains. Being happy, in turn, is having the kind of life that brings contentment with its current direction.[3]

There is no question that a fundamental criterion for right action is that it produces good for individuals and that a criterion for wrong action is that it diminishes the good in people's lives. And of two possible actions, if one produces more good or less harm, that one is the better to do in most cases. The exceptions, I shall argue below, are invariably where considerations of fairness enter the picture. That we should do good and avoid doing harm is so obvious that it appears trivial. It may seem less trivial to discuss beneficence in terms of happiness for individuals. Yet we never question whether it is good for a person to be happy or bad for her to be unhappy — with two exceptions. The first is when temporary unhappiness or lack of happiness will bring about greater happiness for her in the future. The second is when she is considered not to deserve happiness, or when her happiness causes diminished happiness for others. The second consideration is a topic to be discussed under the distribution of good — i.e., fairness.

Thus — with considerations of fairness excepted — everyone holds that it is good to make people happy and bad to deprive them of happiness. And we *ought* to act in ways that do not interfere with another's attaining happiness. As noted in Chapter 2, what we ought morally to do is what is required to attain moral ends, and the happiness of individuals is unquestionably a moral end. It should be pointed out, however, that while in nearly all cases we ought not to deprive an individual of happiness, it is not generally true that we *ought* to do whatever makes people happy. The injunction not to make people unhappy is stronger than the injunction to make people happy. We consider it worse to take something away from a person who has it already than not to give it to him when he does not already have it (or have a claim on it). Hence I ought not to steal your car, but — happy as it might make you, it is not the case that I ought to give you a car (unless you have a claim on it because you have paid me for one or I have promised it to you — in either of which cases I would effectively deprive you of a car by not giving it to you, because you expected and counted on it). It is generally worse to take something away than not to give it, because when a person already has something — or has reason to expect to have it —, then not having it causes pain and unhappiness from frustration of expectations over and above whatever one might suffer from the simple lack of that thing. In addition, as I shall argue below, it is also unfair — apart from what harm it does — to take something away from a person, but it is not generally unfair not to give someone something.

For the most part, an individual's happiness is not dependent on the actions of other people, but rather on her own. That I don't provide you with food, shelter, and boosts to your self-esteem hardly prevents you from having these goods. Only if you are uniquely dependent upon me — as a child is on its parents — would this be the case. On the other hand, if I steal your food, burn down your house, or make some devastatingly hurtful remark to you, I have directly interfered with your capacity for happiness. Such actions ought not to be done, primarily because they interfere with a moral end — namely, your happiness. On the other hand, while it would be nice for me to give you food, a house, or compliments, these aren't things I *ought* to do because they aren't necessary for achieving moral ends; for the most part you can obtain basic requirements for happiness on your own and hence others' doing such things for you is not necessary for your good.

In choosing to act for the greater happiness of a group of people, we need to be able to assess their degree of happiness. Although, as I argued in Chapter 3, we have a rough yardstick for saying how happy or unhappy a person is, which is the amount of time he spends contented minus the time he spends discontented, it is never possible to know with certainty how any particular future action will affect the happiness of an individual. Hence there are major practical difficulties in determining what choice creates the greatest amount of happiness, not to mention what would be fair. There are clearly limits upon the extent to which we can know the effects of our actions on people's happiness, and this has important implications for practical ethics. However, it does not follow that we cannot know anything about what actions create the most good, or which are most fair.

There are certain things which people must have in order to satisfy their desires, regardless of the nature and intensity of those desires. And there are others which may not be necessary, but which contribute greatly to the happiness of anyone. Both classes are part of what Rawls called *primary* goods.[4] They include food, shelter, money, good health, education, political freedom, opportunity to develop and use one's talents, self-respect, and the love of others. These may or may not be enjoyed for their own sake by particular individuals, but there is no question that they contribute to the happiness of any person, regardless of his particular desires. Furthermore, being deprived of any of these goods will have an adverse effect on the happiness he is likely to attain. Anyone — no matter what else he or she may want — will want more of these goods rather than less. And this is true, even though particular individuals will care differently about specific primary goods.

There may be other primary goods we do not recognize. Some, in fact, have been relatively recent discoveries. For example, after World War II the importance for infants of being frequently held and cuddled became widely recognized. Otherwise, they fail to grow properly and may even die. Until the extensive experience with displaced children brought by that war, few people knew how necessary touch and handling were for the future development — and happiness — of infants.

Many of the primary goods are measurable, so that it is possible to know how much of them a person has and to compare what he has of it with what another has. We also know, in many cases, how much and what kind of certain primary goods are needed for certain purposes. For example, we know how many calories an individual needs to consume to stay alive and to maintain an appropriate body weight. Further, we know what types of foods are required to maintain good health. We also know that too much food, and particularly too much of certain types, is detrimental to health.

All this knowledge can be used to determine how much and what kinds of food are best for a given individual. That which is best for him, which will be most apt to promote his happiness, is that which will enable him to live, feel as well as possible, and engage in the activities he needs and wants to engage in, and which does not contribute to debilitating and life shortening diseases. While the type and amount differs for different people, everyone agrees that it is of prime importance for each person to have his or her nutritional needs met. Unless they are, the individual will be to some extent hampered in the ability to become or remain happy. Furthermore, having *more* food than is necessary to meet nutritional needs adds relatively little to happiness and overall good; at best it provides pleasures of taste, and at worst, clogged arteries and premature death.

Of course, our understanding of nutrition, as well as other human needs, has changed greatly over the years. It may well be that what we now think we know may turn out not to be so. But given a certain body of presumed nutritional knowledge, we can make decisions about what a person ought to eat for her health. As we shall see, we can also make decisions about what is a *fair* distribution of food. These decisions may be mistaken, but they are more likely to be mistaken because of misinformation about the effects of certain types of food than they are to be mistakes about values. We *know* that shortened life and the diseases of nutritional deficiency and excess are bad for one and ought to be avoided. And we know that feeling well and being able to perform the activities one needs and wants to do are good, even if we do not know how best to attain those goods and avoid harm.

Similar remarks may be made about other primary goods. For example, everyone needs sufficient shelter and clothing to protect him from the elements. While beauty, comfort, and privacy are also cherished, protection from the elements is more necessary to happiness. Health care, too, varies in its value, or the extent to which it can promote happiness. Prenatal care for a pregnant woman is more likely to promote future happiness and prevent sorrow than is keeping a comatose ninety-year-old stroke victim alive with a ventilator and artificial feedings.

We have less precise knowledge about nonmaterial goods like self respect, the love of others, and freedom. Yet we know the harm that can be done when these are distinctly lacking and we know the sorts of actions that can promote or inhibit these goods. For example, we are all aware of the devastating effects of partiality and discrimination on the basis of race, religion, gender, or sexual orientation. Not only are these unfair, but the lack of opportunity is all the more painful when one can see what others have. While we cannot measure freedom or love or self-respect on any scale, we can determine (theoretically, if not practically) the roughly measurable effect on the happiness of a particular person of having a certain form of one of these goods.

In short, we may not be able to tell precisely how happy any individual is, or whether he is happier than any other person. We do, however, know a lot about the *means* to happiness: i.e., the primary goods. We know how they (and their absence) affect happiness, the relative importance of particular types of these goods in promoting happiness, and how to measure them. We know this because we know roughly how these goods affect the amount of time people in general spend in contentment.

Supplying or removing primary goods results in increasing or decreasing happiness by decreasing or increasing the distractors that prevent a person from contentedly pursuing his or her activities. If Ann is ill and Bill can cure her illness, so that she is able to do the things she needs and wants to do, she will be happier. If Clara can give David a job, so that he no longer has to worry about where his next meal is coming from, he benefits. If Ernie picks on Frances and undermines her self esteem, she is clearly less happy. In ways such as these, a person can be brought to spend more or less time content with his situation, and thus made more or less happy.

We are now in a position to formulate the principle of beneficence more precisely. It is that it is morally good to increase the happiness of persons and avoid causing unhappiness; that when we have alternatives, it is better to choose the one which will bring the greater amount of happiness (or least unhappiness) provided that requirements of fairness are met. We ought, moreover, to do certain things which are required for happiness, and ought not to do what will cause unhappiness. We can, furthermore, increase happiness by giving people the means of happiness: i.e., more of basic goods, as well as helping them to satisfy particular desires — provided, of course, that by giving them things we don't do something else that will detract from their future happiness.

Obviously, the same quantity of any primary good may affect the happiness of two individuals to a very different extent, and thus primary goods cannot be the underlying standard of utility. Although the real underlying standard (if I am right) is happiness, practical considerations make it in fact impossible to calculate in most individual cases. In making ethical choices we *assume* that more of a primary good makes an individual better off than does less, and that equal amounts of primary goods have equal effects on different individuals, *unless* we have reason to think otherwise (e.g., have information to the effect that their wants are different). Furthermore, we normally hold that individual differences in how much particular goods will increase happiness are largely dependent upon the differences among individuals — in their attitudes, for example. In Sen's example,[5] the cripple who is cheerful is better off than one similarly disabled who spends all his time feeling sorry for himself. This doesn't show, however, that outside help won't be just as much needed and deserved if given to the cheerful person than it would be if given to the complainer. Rightly or wrongly, we think that people are responsible for their attitudes and outlooks, and that what society does to help or harm people should not take these attitudes into account — not only because we cannot quantify precisely their effects on happiness, but also because we cannot do much to affect them. Although we may be wrong in our assumptions that the possession or deprivation of a given quantity of some primary good will have equal effects on the happiness of different individuals, we are probably better off using those assumptions as rules of thumb. If we were to try to calculate their effects on individual happiness, we would never be able to come to decisions — and might still make erroneous choices because of our ignorance of specific relevant factors.

In fact, because the nature of happiness is so intricately connected with having a purposeful life: i.e., activity in the pursuit of goals, and learning to live with the inevitable limits imposed by reality, it is clear that we don't generally succeed in *making* people happy. Rather, we help to increase happiness by giving people the means to create their own happiness through their own activity toward their chosen goals. And we reduce unhappiness by removing obstacles to peoples' ability to do this. Since the means to happiness consist of primary goods, which can to a large extent be quantified, we are not entirely devoid of the ability to choose our actions on the basis of the magnitude of their effect on happiness. This ability is, however, limited; these limitations I shall discuss further below.[6]

2. WHY BENEFICENCE IS NOT ENOUGH

While doing good and preventing harm or unhappiness is a basic component of what it is right to do, beneficence does not define the whole of morality. That fairness is another fundamental criterion of right action can be seen from some of the classic criticisms of utilitarianism. Utilitarianism appears to have a serious problem in paying too little attention to how good is distributed. If more total good can be created by giving all of it to some people and none to the rest than by giving everyone an equal share, then — utilitarianism seems to imply — we should give to some rather than all.

Almost everyone, however, is uncomfortable with this feature of utilitarianism, feeling that such a way of distributing goods would be *unfair*. Some utilitarians have tried hard to show that their theory does not have this implication.[7] I will not attempt to discuss these efforts here. What I shall stress is that utilitarianism as it is *traditionally* interpreted: namely, as enjoining us to maximize total good, regardless of how that good is distributed, is seriously deficient as a moral theory. Suppose we could make everyone in the world supremely happy by torturing one innocent child.[8] Surely the total amount of good would be increased by such a measure. Yet almost everyone would consider this wrong, not only because of the child's suffering, but because the measure is so terribly unfair.

Utilitarians have tried to show that such actions would be wrong because they would really bring more unhappiness than their alternatives. It is wrong to distribute goods unequally because when people see that others have more it makes them discontented and envious.[9] I doubt that in the case of the tortured child his unhappiness at seeing the happiness of everyone else would add sufficiently to his misery and to the total unhappiness in the universe as to make the situation wrong on utilitarian grounds alone. Furthermore, we could easily remove the envy component by supposing that the deprived individual was ignorant of the happiness of others, or in some way made to think that he deserved his disadvantaged state, or would be rewarded in a future life by enduring it. Such situations are not only possible, but they have been successfully perpetrated — at least temporarily — among many people. Far from making the inequality less wrong, most would agree that the deception makes it *more* so.[10]

Another area in which utilitarianism appears weak is in accounting for our beliefs that certain types of actions like telling lies and breaking promises are wrong even when no one is harmed by them. Certainly most people think there are occasions on which telling the truth or keeping a promise is not the right thing to do — e.g., if doing so could bring grave and irreversible harm to someone. But most do *not* think that doing small amounts of good or preventing minor annoyances is a sufficient excuse for lying or breaking a promise.

Utilitarians have argued that it can be wrong to lie or break a promise, even when no immediate harm is done, because of the effect on the agent's character.[11] Lying or breaking a promise will make it easier for him to do so on other occasions, when actual harm may occur. On balance, they argue, more harm than good will be done, even if there are actual benefits from the particular offense. As for the tortured child, utilitarians would say that the effect on the dispositions of the torturers and those who permit the torturing to go on will be so bad that it will offset the increase in total happiness.

This argument, however, will not work. It is by no means clear that one lie or act of cruelty occasionally committed will inevitably increase the disposition to continue such acts in every person, or increase it in proportion to its wrongness. While some might be more likely to lie in the future, others might, on thinking over what they had done, become ashamed and by making a firm resolve never to engage in such acts again, become *less* likely to do so in the future. Besides, once a person has become thoroughly hardened to lying, etc., telling more lies is unlikely to increase his disposition to do so further. At any rate, there is no formula by which we can calculate the effects of every lie on the character of the liar. And we certainly don't know that the effect will not only be bad, but worse than all, or nearly all, good brought about by the lie.

Another important point which utilitarians have brought forward is that certain practices like telling the truth, keeping promises, and obeying the law create good beyond any good done by particular instances of these actions.[12] There is great value in being able to assume that what another person tells you is true; it would be a great waste of time to have to check on everything oneself, even if one could. When we can count on others to do what they say they will, we can make long range plans and coordinate our activities, thereby accomplishing much more than we would if we could depend on no one but ourselves. Where there are rules, laws, and customs which are generally obeyed, we can usually assume that people will behave in predictable ways. This also enables us to make plans and pursue our goals more effectively.

Where people cannot count on others, much less good can be done. And the more people lie, break promises, and ignore laws and customs, the less people can count on each other. A violation of these principles, then, can produce more harm than the direct effects of the particular violation by reducing our ability to count on certain behavior from other people. A lie or a broken promise, utilitarians argue, harms the practice of truth telling or promise keeping, even when it does not harm any individual person and does good to some.

This utilitarian response has one serious problem, however. It is surely true that if everyone were to tell the truth, keep promises, and obey the laws of society, the total amount of happiness would be greater than it is. On the other hand, we might increase happiness still further if *most* people most of the time were to follow these principles, but some break them under certain circumstances.[13] These circumstances would be such that a person could gain some extra happiness for himself or others by lying, for example, without inflicting harm on others. If enough people told the truth, the benefits of truth telling would be unlikely to be significantly affected, especially if the lie were not detected. Yet most think there is something wrong with people's making exceptions of themselves in this way.

The utilitarian's response to this is that there are some cases where lying is justified. And she is probably right. Few people have been convinced by Kant's argument that it is wrong to lie even to save a life.[14] But I am not talking about such dramatic examples. Suppose that Tommy is playing alone with his baseball and carelessly throws it against a neighbor's window, breaking it. The neighbor does not see who did it, but asks several children in the area if they know anything about the window. When Tommy is asked he says he doesn't know. Let us suppose for the sake of argument that the neighbor has insurance which will pay for the window and that her premium — and those of others — won't be raised as a result. She isn't hurt, therefore, by Tommy's lie, and Tommy is benefited by escaping punishment. His lying and getting away with it might result in his becoming more likely to lie in the future, but as we saw earlier, this need not be the case. Suppose it doesn't. Then the total amount of happiness is greater than it would have been had Tommy told the truth, but he was, nevertheless, wrong to lie. Later in the chapter I shall discuss in detail what exactly is wrong with Tommy's lie. For the moment, it is sufficient to show that the utilitarian position, as it is commonly interpreted, is not sufficient to account for certain widespread moral beliefs.

For readers interested in examining these arguments further, much has been written about them.[15] For now, however, I shall assume that we do recognize a principle distinct from that of maximizing good, or happiness — namely, fairness. Because it is a fundamental consideration that we use to justify or criticize actions, and a criterion that does not itself require further justification, fairness — like beneficence — can be taken as a truth condition of judgments of moral rightness.

3. FAIRNESS AS EQUALITY

While everyone agrees that we ought to be fair, however, there is less agreement about how to define fairness. In what follows, I shall argue that fairness is giving equal weight to the good or happiness of all persons. In accordance with the guidelines of Chapter 1, I shall proceed by pointing out the considerations which people use in arguing that an action is or is not fair. First of all, I shall state a number of widely held views about fairness, as well as some current disagreements. Then I shall indicate what seem to be the common criteria which different parties to those disagreements agree upon and to which they appeal in debate.

Virtually everyone agrees that in some sense everyone is entitled to equal concern or treatment. But just what sense this is, is a matter of sharp disagreement. Positions range widely from radical egalitarians who believe that all transferrable goods should be allocated either equally or according to need, to those who hold that the demand for equality is simply a matter of consistency. The latter maintain that we should treat like cases alike, not because there is any reason why people ought to be equal to each other in well-being or in social rewards, but because to the extent that oughts are based on reasons, if R is a reason for doing A to or for X, it is also a reason for doing A to or for Y.

Most philosophers fall in between, maintaining that equality in some sense ought to be sought, but that there are definite restrictions on this demand. Some examples include that of Joseph Raz,[16] who argues that there is no special demand for equality which we ought to satisfy, but rather that we do more good by helping those who are worst off, and our concern for each individual dictates that we ought to make everyone as well off as possible. Utilitarians, too, maintain that equality requirements are satisfied by having everyone count for one and only one,[17] and some (such as Narveson in his utilitarian days)[18] argue for the utility of equality and maintain that utility is consistently promoted by helping the worst off. Rawls maintains that we ought to give every person the most extensive liberty that is compatible with a like liberty for all, and that inequalities of treatment may be justified, but only when they make the worst off better off. [19] Nozick holds that it is neither right nor feasible to try to make everyone equally well off. Instead we should strive not for equal outcomes for people, but rather for procedural justice.[20] Alternatively, Kai Nielsen,[21] Amartya Sen,[22] Thomas Nagel[23], and Richard Miller[24] point out that inequalities of wealth and social advantages tend not only to perpetuate themselves, but to increase inequalities of status among people; while trying to achieve exact equality of well-being for everyone is hardly possible and can do great harm, we ought to make all reasonable efforts to help those who are disadvantaged in one respect or another.

Discussions of these differing ideas of equality are seen frequently among non-philosophers as well. In the United States, for example, Democrats appear more concerned with equalizing benefits by providing more services to the poor and taxing the rich more heavily. Republicans are more inclined to insist that those who have more have probably earned it and have a right to keep it. On the other hand, few if any in either party would maintain either that all goods should be equally distributed or that there should be no redistribution of goods at all. Even the most egalitarian recognize that no one individual has the power or motivation to treat everyone equally, so the duty of whatever equalization there is falls primarily upon the state. Consequently, fear or distrust of government and the desire to maintain liberty of action often limit what many believe ought to be done to promote equality.

Despite the wide differences among these approaches to equality, there appears to be a common thread. This is the belief that a correct moral theory requires us to show equal regard or concern for people in some way or other. What I propose to do in this chapter is to examine how we justify treating people in certain ways in certain circumstances. Looking to actual attempts at justification will enable us to flesh out the fundamental principle of equal concern which is basic to our conception of fairness. I shall then argue that from this principle of equal concern we can derive many well established beliefs about equality.

People's beliefs about equality are largely incorporated in what they consider to be fair. A person is treated fairly when his interests are given due concern, where 'due concern' is the concern they ought to be given. 'Fairness' is a value term, however, while 'equality' is not, or not necessarily. If a way of showing equal concern, or treating people equally, is morally right, then it is fair treatment. So what we need to find out is what sense of equal concern is equivalent to fairness, and this may be done by looking closely at common beliefs about what is fair, as well as disagreements.

In general, people hold it right and fair to help those less fortunate than themselves. They think it wrong to have extreme poverty side by side with great wealth. We expect more time, money, and effort from persons who have been given more by nature or by society. And those who have given much we consider to deserve much in return. People who have harmed others for their own gain, we think ought to be punished — i.e., harmed — in turn. In any enterprise undertaken for the good of a group of individuals, we think the effort should be shared equally, or in proportion to expected benefit. And those who have shared the effort, we think should share the goods attained: again, equally, or in proportion to contribution. When a good cannot be shared, we think that people should have an equal opportunity to acquire it, that it should be given in accordance with some criterion of desert, contribution, or ability to profit or create, or that those who do not get it should receive compensation in some other area.

All of these common beliefs have been widely held among persons of every time and place, whether or not they have been put into practice. Furthermore, they have been appealed to in order to support particular judgments about what is the fair or just thing to do. Yet some of these beliefs tend to conflict with one another. For example, some persons believe that the principle that we ought to help the less fortunate outweighs the principle that people ought to be rewarded in proportion to their contributions, while others take the opposite position — marking, as noted above, a major difference between liberals and conservatives in contemporary politics.

James Q. Wilson[25] makes an important distinction between *equality*, the principle that people are entitled to, so as to equal benefits, and *equity*, the principle that rewards should be given proportionately to, so as to contribution. He maintains that both are components of our ideas about fairness, and that these components may be difficult to reconcile. Nevertheless, I hope to show in what follows that our concerns for both equality and for equity are based on the broader principle: that persons are entitled to equal concern for their welfare, and that this broader principle can be used to settle conflicts between equality and equity.

To see this, let us consider some of the questions people ask when debating issues such as the following. To to what extent does charity really contribute to the happiness of a person? Should it not be limited to essential goods which the individual helped is unable to acquire by his or her own efforts? But should we not, on the other hand, make sure that the social structure does not seriously limit a person's ability to seek his own happiness? For example, ought we not to make sure that every pregnant woman, infant, and young child has an adequate diet, and that no one who is willing to work is denied a job or the means to work at it (e.g., child care, transportation, etc.)? Those who answer in the affirmative are more inclined to favor considerations of equality.

While it is undoubtedly a good thing to help the poor, ought people be forced to do so, and, if so forced, to what extent? After all, it is generally worse to have something taken away from you than not to have gotten that same thing in the first place, not to mention the deprivation of personal liberty. Moreover, much of what people have they have attained as a result of hard work, which work may have interfered with their happiness. Are they not then entitled to what they have earned, and why should they sacrifice for people who are too lazy to work? Those who agree are more inclined to appeal to considerations of equity.

On the other hand, those who appeal to equality point out that the rewards society gives for work often depend little on either the value of that work, or the amount of effort and sacrifice it entails, but rather upon the whims of the market determined by what the society values (e.g. film stars and athletes in the U.S.A.).[26] Furthermore, according to the law of diminishing returns, an additional monetary unit has less value for a consumer the more money she already possesses. Consequently, if a rich woman gives — willingly or unwillingly — some of her money to a poor one, the amount she loses will be of less value to her than the value of what she gives is to the poor one.

In discussing issues like these we constantly refer to people's *interests* or *welfare* and how their capacity for happiness will be affected by certain actions or policies.[27] We consider, first of all, what is in people's interests and the extent to which those interests will be furthered by what is done. Other things being equal, most people think it better and more fair to help those who are worse off, who have less of good in their lives, than those who are better off. The reason for this is that, if we have equal concern for the interests, good, or happiness of two people, we would like to see them both as well off as possible. If so, then we will have more reason to relieve the distress of the one who is worse off and furthest from that goal.[28] This creates pressure toward equality.

But in determining whether an action or policy is fair, we also look to what people have done in the past. The connection between that and their interests or happiness is less obvious, but it is still there. When people expend time, energy, and money, the usual result is that they have less of these things to expend for other goods. If they do not get some good (tangible or intangible) in exchange for what they have expended, then, in general, they are to some extent worse off by having less of the means for happiness. If a person gets the goods achieved by someone else's work or payment, without giving anything in return, he receives a net benefit at the other's expense.

In general, we consider an exchange (goods for money, one service for another, etc.) between two or more people to be fair when both get something they want and neither is obviously and predictably worse off as a result of the exchange. Thus, for example, the exchange of Manhattan Island by the Indians for a few strings of beads from the Dutch was unfair. Fair exchanges also do not result in obviously large disparities between the net benefits gained by the parties. A example of an exchange which would be unfair in this way is paying a starving, desperate person a pittance for his labor. He is better off than he was, but his employer gains much more. Most exchanges of this sort involve at the very least misunderstanding, and — too commonly — deception or coercion, for few people would knowingly and willingly give up much for little in return. The Indians, for example, did not realize that the Dutch expected the beads to give them not merely hunting rights, but exclusive use of Manhattan Island.

From the above it seems clear that we think it right to achieve balance among the interests and happiness of all the parties to an interaction. Unfairness occurs when one individual or group gives something, but gets nothing, or much less than others, in return, or when someone receives a disproportionately large benefit for his efforts. For the most part people think that unless there is some reason to do otherwise, if there are goods to share among a group of people, they should get equal shares. Likewise, when there are burdens to be shouldered, it is considered only fair that these also be equally shared, other things being equal. In cooperative enterprises, those who participate should share equally (or in proportion to contribution) in the benefits and costs. This notion of balancing also underlies our beliefs about punishment: if one person harms another, he ought to make restitution, if possible, and, if the harm was deliberate, be harmed himself as well. And if one person does another a favor, the second person is considered to owe something to the first. The purpose of sharing benefits and burdens has its roots in the idea of considering the good or happiness of all the participants equally.[29],[30]

An objection to the notion of fairness as equal concern is that sometimes what is fair seems to be equated with what accords with given social rules of distribution, even though these rules themselves may strike others as grossly unfair. Thus Charles Taylor points out that Achilles complained of unfairness when Agamemnon took away his "prize" Briseis.[31] Poor Briseis's interests were not considered at all. The points he makes are two. First, that what is just or fair cannot be determined outside of a given society, and secondly, that the very concept of fairness itself is different from that of equality. There is indeed a component of fairness that enjoins us to follow the rules of our society, other things being equal. I will shortly discuss this along with the crucial role of reciprocity in determining what is fair. But while what specific rules call for is determined by the nature of the society in which they arise, the rules themselves may be criticized in accordance with a higher standard. Our ability to evaluate the rules of a culture (including our own) suggests that such a standard is available and is not relative to a particular society. In fact, the rules may be criticized on several levels. First, they may not conform to reciprocity: Agamemnon the King takes away what his underling Achilles has attained through his efforts on the king's behalf, fighting his war, but what has Agamemnon done for Achilles in return? A social rule which allowed the king to take everything and give nothing in return would violate reciprocity. A powerful tyrant might get away with it, but none would call him just. Secondly, the rules may not treat everyone on an equal basis; even if Achilles were allowed to keep the reward that custom prescribed and was thus treated fairly according to the lights of the time, the captive Briseis counts for nothing in the ancient scheme and is thus unfairly treated by the rules. Finally, a rule might well give the interests of all parties equal consideration, but be defective in that following it brings less good than might other alternatives — or even be harmful. The Kwakiutl custom of the potlatch might be an example of this. Presumably open to all to participate — and thus fair in both the above senses, the competitive giving of expensive gifts might well bring ruin and disgrace to those who lose, as well as a false pride in material possessions and status to the winners. A fair rule may not be beneficent.

The point in answer to Taylor is that while the rules of a society determine what specific actions are considered fair by that society, the acts and the rules both may be evaluated according to broader standards of fairness and of goodness in general; such evaluations are not only made by persons outside the society who have different rules, but by those within it.

4. LIMITS ON EQUAL DISTRIBUTION

The presumption that we ought to give the good of all persons equal consideration might seem to suggest that we ought to try to make people equally well off. Fairness does not, however, usually require distributing goods equally among all persons. It would clearly be impossible to make everyone equally well off. Even to distribute all distributable goods equally to all would have many drawbacks, as certain societies which have attempted to do so have learned. Nevertheless, giving equal consideration to the well being of all persons can often be done best by improving the lot of the worst off in preference to improving that of the better off. And sometimes fairness requires making the better off slightly *worse* off in order to improve the lot of those who were worse off to start with. I will discuss some such situations below.

Aside from its impossibility, there are other limitations on the idea of making people equally well off. Not only is it not possible in practice (even if possible in theory) to determine whether people are equally well off, but much that contributes to good or relieves and prevents misery cannot be given from one person to another. Even of things which can be redistributed, attempts to distribute them equally, and keep them so distributed, can have devastating effects. Among these are loss of individual liberty, loss of motivation to achieve with a resulting decrease in the total amount of good done, and a worsening of the condition of all. The widespread rejection of communism which we have witnessed in recent years demonstrates this. While many people in communist nations were clearly better off than they are at the present time or would have been under pre-communist regimes, communism leaves much to be desired. Even where there are real efforts to achieve equality (and party leaders do not in fact have greater wealth and privileges), the result is not optimal, for the following reason.

We could achieve equality in either of two ways: by making the worse off better off (commonly by taking something from the better off) or by simply taking away from those who are better off. But virtually everyone thinks it wrong to deprive a person of something merely to make him more nearly equal to others who are worse off. The *only* justification for taking something away from a person is that it will benefit someone — either the person himself in the long run, or another individual. If a person has something which cannot be shared, and which she has not attained through any wrongdoing, we would consider it merely spiteful to take it from her or destroy it. Even where goods can be shared, forced sharing can lead to the evils which have afflicted communist states.[32] Since these evils result in losses to all, they are effectively like taking goods from some merely to attain equality. In short, a principle which sets limits on the extent to which we should aim for equal distribution of goods is that we ought not to deprive anyone of a good unless doing so will benefit someone (either the deprived person or another) to a *greater* extent. And even this is not usually a sufficient reason.

Since it is neither possible nor desirable to insure equal distribution even of measurable means to happiness, fairness is thought by nearly all to provide everyone with equal *opportunities* for achieving his or her own good. To do this we ought not to erect barriers and, where possible, we ought to remove existing barriers to these opportunities. In general we ought to avoid allowing one person to achieve greater well-being, or the means to it, at the cost of reducing the well-being of others — i. e., benefiting at their expense.

Joseph Raz argues[33], not only that equality is not the most important feature of morality (otherwise it would be just as acceptable to achieve it by taking away from one person as by giving to others), but that a separate requirement of equality is not even necessary in an adequate moral system. If we suppose that happiness is the basic good for humans and that suffering is bad, then we ought to give to the neediest. Doing so, he says, will relieve more suffering and create more happiness than will giving to people who are already well off. His argument that inequalities are bad, not by virtue of their being inequalities, but because they are an indication that there are unmet needs, has much to be said for it. I shall discuss this matter further later in the chapter.

5. RECIPROCITY

People express their belief that all persons should receive equal consideration through a number of principles. For example, they believe that, if there are goods to share among a group of people, they should — *ceteris paribus* — get equal shares. Likewise, when there are burdens to be shouldered, it is considered only fair that these also be equally shared. In cooperative enterprises, those who participate should share equally (or in proportion to contribution) in the benefits and costs. People also believe that when one individual expends some of his goods, he should get something of equal value in exchange. Our beliefs about punishment are founded on the same principle; if one person harms another, he ought to make restitution, if possible, and, if the harm was deliberate, be harmed himself as well. And if one person does another a favor, the second person is considered to owe something to the first.

Thus society operates on the basis of many rules of reciprocity, and on cooperative enterprises in which each person is expected to contribute: i.e., has duties and obligations. And when a person fulfills these obligations, she is entitled to share in the benefits resulting from the enterprise. Every society has such institutions and practices. Although specific rules and associations differ widely from one culture to another, most are based on the notion that the good of each member of the cooperating group is deserving of consideration equal to that given any other person. Those which are not, as we shall see, are deserving of criticism.

The assumption generally made in reciprocal practices is that — unless we know of some reason why not — the same goods have the same effects on different persons. Therefore, all believe that when a person gives something to another she should get something equivalent in return (unless she voluntarily forgoes the good). Even though she probably is more or less happy than the other party already and the goods in question will affect her happiness differently than they would the other, we normally suppose that a fair exchange is one in which the goods received by one are at least roughly equal to those received by the other. If, however, we are aware of an additional factor, such as one party's being desperately poor and the other extremely rich, we are likely to modify our judgment in accordance with our equal concern for the good of the parties involved. Normally, for example, people would think that it is fair for anyone to live anywhere he desires and that no help or hindrance should be made for one rather than for another. If, however, the only housing some can afford is a cardboard box on a muddy hillside, while others can purchase mansions, most would agree that help for the former rather than the latter would be fair as well as beneficent. In considering whether we are giving equal consideration to the well being of all parties, then, we assume initial rough equality, but we recognize that this assumption can be wrong, and in cases where it clearly is, we modify our judgments about what is fair.

Given the assumption that the parties to the transaction start out from a position of equality, a transaction is considered fair when one benefit is exchanged for another which is at least roughly equivalent in value.[34] In many ways this presumption of initial equality is like the presumption that each person is the best judge of her own interests — often false, but one which generally works for the benefit of all alike. Just as, however, it is justifiable to set aside the presumption that a person knows her best interests when she is clearly irrational, it is also justifiable to set aside the presumption of initial equality when the parties to the transaction are clearly unequal. Where this is so, all agree that it is morally preferable to give more through a transaction to a person who is (at least through no fault of his own) worse off; in some cases, it may even be justifiable to enforce some exchanges which equalize the playing field (e.g., through progressive taxation), although this is more controversial.

Clearly, no cooperative institutions are perfect. In the first place, people are very unequal in their natural and social endowments. And those who are most influential in governing the way goods are actually distributed in a society are usually better off to start with and thus have a vested interest in preserving the *status quo*. They do, however, increase their chances of remaining in power if they maintain at least an appearance of fairness. And this appearance is more likely to be maintained by following rules which do not make the better off improve their position still further at the expense of those who are worse off.

Among the things which help a group achieve its ends is to have some rules or customs to guide the behavior of its members in such a way as to realize those ends. Assuming that the rules do in fact promote the aims of the group, it is in the interest of all the members that all obey the rules and honor the customs — at least most of the time. Many people benefit from these institutions and practices. And if any individual is to benefit, it is only fair that he do his part. If other people go to the trouble of obeying a law or following a custom, even when they are inconvenienced by doing so, then an individual who shares the advantages of their obedience, but who does not obey himself, is acting unfairly. By getting the advantages without paying the costs, he *benefits at the expense* of those who follow the rules.

Among the institutions which require cooperative effort in order to succeed are the communication of information and the making of prospective agreements. In order to communicate information, it is necessary that most people most of the time tell the truth as they see it. If a person tells a lie, she generally takes an advantage for herself at the expense of others. Others have sacrificed something to create trust, which trust the liar uses to benefit herself; yet she does not assume her share of maintaining that atmosphere of trust. Lying is consequently at least *prima facie* wrong because it is unfair — whether or not it causes harm to anyone, and even if it creates a net amount of good.[35]

Similar remarks can be made about breaking promises. We can only count on others to do what they promise in a situation where most people do in fact honor their agreements. In order to have a community in which people can depend on each others' word, it is necessary for many individuals to inconvenience themselves by doing things they promised, even though doing so is no longer in their interest. The promise breaker refuses to accept this inconvenience, while at the same time he takes advantage of the condition of mutual dependence which results in his promise being accepted and relied upon. He therefore benefits at the expense of others.

The institution of private property has a similar role. It is useful to us to have things we can do with as we please and to have some security in knowing that we can keep these goods. For this reason theft has a wrong-making characteristic over and above its harmfulness and its resulting in the thief's obtaining goods at the expense of the victim; the thief also benefits from, without contributing to, the sense of security people have about their property. The value of security in possessing what we have provides a rationale for the common belief that taking something away from a person is generally worse than not giving her an equivalent good.

Reciprocity as part of fairness is also expressed in the way people think of cooperative associations, including families, groups of friends or professional colleagues, businesses, religious or social organizations, nations or individual states, cities, and provinces, and many others. Wherever people have common goals, they increase the likelihood of achieving them if they work together. Since, however, doing so requires both performing tasks and following rules for coordinating activities, there are burdens as well as benefits to membership in cooperative groups. On the other hand, small nuisances like stopping for red lights, getting to work on time, and writing thank you letters are offset by such benefits as greater safety in traffic, efficiently run businesses, and the exchange of gifts. If any individual is to benefit, it is only fair that he do his part in maintaining such institutions.

Fairness is required over and above the requirement that one do good and refrain from doing harm. Not only does disobeying traffic signals risk harm, but it is also unfair, and is thus wrong (other things being equal), even if no one is hurt, because if other people go to the trouble of obeying a law or following a custom, even when they are inconvenienced by doing so, then an individual who shares the advantages of their obedience, but who does not obey himself, is acting unfairly. By sharing the benefits but not the burdens and getting some advantage without paying the cost, he benefits at the expense of those who follow the rules.

For most cooperative enterprises it is possible for the practice to survive when some people do not shoulder their part of the burden. If, however, more than a certain number do not, the enterprise will fail. What this critical number is will vary with the situation, but it is usually possible for there to be some free riders. Even though some free riders can get the benefits of the institution without decreasing the benefits it may give, they are still acting unfairly because they benefit at the expense of those who do their part. This is true, even when they do no actual harm.[36]

It may be fair to allow people not to share the burdens at times, when the opportunities for exemption are equally distributed. For example, when a person takes a vacation, her coworkers must cover for her; yet if they, too, get vacations, there is no unfairness involved. It *is* unfair, however, for someone not to come to work without notification and a good reason, even if others' workloads are not increased, or the company's output diminished. We may also excuse people from taking on what would normally be their share of work or other obligations, if it would be particularly burdensome for them (e.g., when they are ill) or when their efforts are critically needed elsewhere. Thus a brilliant rocket scientist might be excused from military service, provided that he help the war effort through his professional expertise. Such distinctions are fair when the same criteria will be applied to all members of the group in deciding who may be excused.

Thus society operates on the basis of many rules of reciprocity, and on cooperative enterprises in which each person is expected to contribute — i.e., has duties and obligations. And when a person fulfills these obligations, she is considered to be entitled to share in the benefits resulting from the enterprise. Every society has such institutions and practices. Although specific rules and associations differ widely from one culture to another, all, and reciprocity in general, are based on the notion that the good of each member of the cooperating group is deserving of consideration equal to that given any other person.

That it is unfair to tell lies and break promises, violate laws and customs, and, in general, not to carry one's share of social burdens, does not show that such actions are invariably wrong. If one can prevent significant harm or bring about a great good, then such acts *may* be justifiable. But the fact that breaking laws and promises is unfair makes it necessary to have a strong justification for doing so.

6. SUMMARY

What may we conclude thus far? By considering the sorts of treatment that people consider fair and unfair, it is clear that we think fairness involves according each person and his welfare as much respect as that accorded to any other. This leads to a presumption that people should be treated equally. Equity is concerned with maintaining or restoring equality, often by giving more to one individual than to another. To justify giving one person more than others requires that the person have contributed in some way to the good of others, or have lost good in some respect. Contributions may be of many kinds — not only careers of public service and the production of useful commodities, but also the provision of entertainment and small kindnesses. Losses may be either due to natural disadvantage, such as a physical disability or having been born into poverty, or they may be caused by the acts of the agent himself or those of other persons. If the agent himself is responsible for his own misfortune, we are less inclined to consider him entitled to help.

Many question whether a person's meager natural endowments should *entitle* him to the support of others, but virtually everyone agrees that it is a good thing to help those who are worse off than ourselves. Moreover, there is universal agreement that someone who is defrauded is entitled to recompense. We also commonly agree that unless there is some reason to the contrary, it is a good thing to share goods equally when they are distributed among a group. Whether equal sharing ought to be enforced is another question, of course. In short, our belief that people ought to receive equal consideration is reflected in our beliefs that inequalities of treatment require justification. One might say also that an underpinning for this belief is the Kantian notion that all persons are of infinite worth, by which he undoubtedly meant in part to imply that each person is equal to everyone else.

It should be noted that merited punishment is not a denial of equal concern. What a person contributes to or takes from society is relevant to how he should be treated, for the reasons considered above. While the type and size of his reward or punishment depends upon an individual's contribution, the degree of our concern for him does not. Whenever someone gains through an interaction with others, and if his gain causes others to lose, he has benefited at their expense. The fact that it is better to help those whom he has exploited than to help him, or even that it may be right to punish him, does not mean that his interests ought to be of less concern than those of others. He simply is less in need of our assistance. But he is still a person, and his interests should still count equally. This is reflected in the belief that even criminals ought to retain some rights, such as the right to trial and appeal and the right not to be brutally treated.[37]

Although what an individual needs, and what she has done, are relevant to how she ought to be treated, her needs and actions are not relevant to the degree of concern we should have for her well-being. Her happiness is neither more nor less important than that of any other person. But if she is able to secure her own happiness, we do better to help others who cannot. And if she has secured goods for herself by depriving others, it is only fair to take from her in order to restore goods to those she has harmed. It is equally important for all persons to have such things as food, shelter, health, etc., and those who already have them don't need our help, while those who don't — and can't supply them on their own — do. That we don't give to the rich doesn't mean that we don't care about their well being. People *should* help them when needed, e. g., if they suffer a misfortune that their money cannot remedy.

To give equal consideration to the well being, interests, good, or happiness of two individuals is not to give or do for them exactly the same things. If a person's welfare is threatened, then those who have a consideration for it will attempt to remove the threat, whatever that happens to be. If his welfare is not threatened, then no action is called for. But if something should happen to harm or deprive him, then, if his well being is considered, he will be helped, if help is possible. Joseph Raz points out that if making persons well off is good, then making any person well off is good.[38] Unless there is a relevant difference between two people, having equal concern for their interests is simply a matter of being consistent. What the principle of fairness states is that there are no relevant differences between persons which would justify giving the interests of one greater weight than those of another.

I have argued that beneficence and fairness are the two considerations to which people ultimately appeal in moral disagreements and that for this reason they are fundamental to what we mean by moral terms. A reason why these two principles are fundamental is that people all want to be treated in accordance with them. This fact provides significant stability in moral views. While people have many different desires, and different things contribute to the happiness of different people, everyone wants to satisfy those desires he has and to be happy. In addition, everyone wants to count as much as anyone else, regardless of what are the specific ways in which he wants to be treated. In short, we may look upon beneficence and fairness as meta-principles, which can be used to justify more specific actions and codes of behavior. Since these are the fundamental considerations to which we appeal, then, if the arguments of Chapter 1 are correct, they constitute the truth conditions of moral judgments.

7. INJUSTICE

One might point to the widespread prevalence of injustice as a difficulty for my claim that fairness as equal concern for all is well established and thus part of the meaning of moral rightness. There have, of course, been many societies in the past in which there has not even been a pretense of equal consideration for all. Distinctions between nobles and commons, masters and slaves, men and women, and dominating and subjected races, have pervaded history and are still present today. Social rules — far from preserving equality among all persons — were often developed to keep oppressed people in their places.

Several considerations explain these differences in treating different groups without forcing us to reject the view that the principle of fairness as equal concern is well established — and thus part of the concepts of fairness and moral rightness. In the first place, *within* groups, rules preserving equality often hold, even where they are not observed *between* groups.[39] As an example, peasants were always expected to follow rules of reciprocity, and fulfill duties to each other, as well as to do whatever the ruling class expected of them. A medieval serf was not supposed to sleep with another serf's bride, nor was his lord supposed to sleep with the wives of other lords, even where the lord was accorded the right to sleep with the bride of his serf.

Another consideration is that oppressed groups have been viewed as inferior (or as some apologists have claimed, simply "different") either in their abilities or their contributions to the society as a whole. If this were really so, their rewards, rights and privileges might justifiably be less (or "different"). Where oppressed groups are so viewed, the less favored group is not always entirely without some rights and privileges; however, citing differences is often merely an excuse for maintaining dominance of one group over another.

For example, in traditional Islamic society women are viewed as being wholly different in their abilities and needs from men. To Westerners, as well as to many of the Islamic women themselves,[40] their lives appear horribly constricted and oppressed. Yet men have definite duties to women: to protect and support them, to provide them with pleasures, and even, when they have more wives than one, to love them equally. Numerous Islamic women, as well as men, have shunned Westernization. Many women have even returned voluntarily to the veil. Others, of course, have done so out of fear, or because they have found that partial Westernization has resulted only in the loss of their old privileges without their gaining the opportunities and freedom of action enjoyed by American and European women.[41]

The point is, however, that in Islamic society, and many others in which there are groups of distinctly lower status, the ideal of fairness is not entirely abandoned. The professed intent of a social order is to reward those groups who supposedly contribute more with greater status and privileges — or reward those making different contributions differently. While an outsider may consider the rewards of the lower status group appallingly meager, they may or may not be so viewed by members of that society — even those in the group of low status.

A second way in which a low status group may be viewed is as being undeserving of normal treatment, or even as not being persons at all. This has often happened when a conquering race has clashed with an aboriginal one. White settlers in Australia, Africa, and America, for example, frequently spoke of the native inhabitants as "animals," "subhuman," and so on, and treated them accordingly.[42] Such views were facilitated by the very different physical appearance and cultural practices of the original people. And in turn those views eased the consciences of the individuals who enslaved or massacred them.

The oppressors would often use as an excuse behavior on the part of the natives which they didn't understand and which appalled them, saying that you could not deal with such individuals and that they were, consequently, outside the pale of human society. And always there was the excuse that the way of the white man, which included Christianity and productive use (or exploitation) of nature, was best for all people. Furthermore, whatever responses these oppressed people made to their oppression were used as additional justification for enslaving or destroying them. When they rose in armed rebellion, this showed they were implacably hostile savages. If they attempted to submit, as many black slaves in America did, these efforts were seen as exhibiting servility and childishness, and consequently taken as further evidence of inferiority. If they fell into despair, turning to drink and idleness, as frequently happened among Australian aboriginals, South Sea Islanders, and Native Americans, the view that they were inferior was reinforced. On the other hand, those who, like the Cherokees, built a new civilization, combining their own traditions with what they had learned from the whites, were seen as insolent threats to the dominant society.

Over the sorry history of human persecution, many have convinced themselves that certain groups of individuals did not deserve the treatment normally accorded persons in their society. Some, such as the Nazis, have claimed that certain classes of individuals were not persons at all and that it was unnecessary to give their interests any consideration whatsoever. People have so convinced themselves — either sincerely or with a large measure of self-deception — by thinking that the group against which they discriminate either deserved less or was unable to profit from benefits which others enjoy.

The European settler in colonial America might actually have believed that the Native Americans deserved to be killed because they had killed whites, or that blacks need not be educated because they could not learn. When white settlers in America were told that they should exterminate Indians because they were cruel and unteachable, they were, of course, more likely to accept this excuse because they wanted the Indians' land. Or when told that blacks were stupid and lazy, they were glad enough to latch onto a justification for keeping them as slaves. Yet, regardless of how poorly examined such assumptions were, or how much in his immediate interest accepting them might have been, the settler would probably not have thought that he was being unfair to Indians or blacks. When views like these were challenged, people actually used excuses like the above to defend their way of life.

All these excuses are significant in shedding light on our view of what persons are, what is expected of them, and how they should be treated, which issues I have discussed at length elsewhere.[43]   For present purposes it is important to note that in discussing different views of oppressed groups of people I am considering how people have attempted to *justify* such oppression: that is, to argue that it is not morally wrong or unfair to treat these groups in ways that they would consider wrong to treat other groups of people.[44] Such arguments are usually specious, but they shed interesting light on what factors we consider to be morally relevant. They indicate, for example, that we think people should be rewarded in proportion to their contributions, that persons' having different needs from others should receive different treatment, and so forth.

We should not forget, however, that much oppression occurs which no one attempts to justify, or, when some do try, others are not taken in. Consider for example, a child abuser who tells the court that he had to put his toddler in scalding water because she wet her pants. He tries to say — and may even believe this himself — that the child deserved such treatment because she was "bad" and had to be taught better. It is unlikely, however, that anyone on the jury would accept such a defense. It is not in their interests to promote child abuse, so they would have nothing to gain by believing the abuser's excuses.

In short, the fact that people have been treated very unequally does not show that fairness (in the sense of having the good of all persons equally considered) is not a criterion for moral rightness which is universally accepted. That people fail to treat others fairly does not show that they don't think they ought to. Some people simply don't do what they ought — even what they themselves believe they ought — to do.

Obviously there have been many societies over the centuries which have not even pretended to be fair. When some group has sufficient power and can get what it wants without considering the interests of others, it often does just that. I am not for a minute arguing that injustice doesn't exist; what I am arguing is that when it is challenged, those who attempt to answer the criticisms (as opposed to liquidating the critics) use the sorts of arguments to which I alluded above. Furthermore, when oppressed people see that their hopes and expectations are being denied, while others benefit from the system, they believe themselves unfairly treated. When such people learn of how other societies preserve their balances and learn that groups like theirs have a relatively better position than they, they become discontented.[45] If a group is disadvantaged in its own society, compared to its position in others, it comes to believe its institutions unjust. The *alleged* purpose of those social institutions which make an effort to justify themselves is to benefit all and share burdens and goods equally, or proportionately. When they do not fulfill those purposes, they are open to criticism and may often be changed through internal reform or rejected outright by rebellion. Obviously, I have not explored the history of all societies and how all those living in them have reacted, so it is possible that some of the above generalizations are not true — or even if they are, they might not be true of future societies. After all, the vast majority of oppressed people never had a chance to make their opinions known, and many regimes were powerful enough to suppress criticism altogether. What I am claiming is that from what we do know of the ways in which people defend their acts and institutions, it seems clear that they consistently appeal to considerations of equal concern for individuals.

8. OTHER OBJECTIONS

One might object that none of us have equal consideration for all people, and it would be totally impossible for anyone to have equal regard for the interests of everyone. Furthermore, we are perfectly justified in preferring and promoting ourselves, our loved ones, and our personal projects rather than the good of strangers.[46] Not only do we provide higher education, toys, and summer camp for our own children, even though we know there are many children in the world who are starving, but few think there is anything wrong with this.[47] Since no single individual or group is capable of providing for the needs of everyone, it is much more efficient to have limited areas of responsibility. Moreover, there is immense value to each person in being especially cared about by some other people. Thus special affections and commitments create greater good for most. We are not being unfair in showing such partiality, provided that what we do for ourselves or our families, friends, and professional associates does not prevent or seriously hinder others from obtaining comparable goods. Because many persons are special to no one, however, fairness requires that society protect the interests of the helpless and friendless; otherwise they may suffer by the acts of those who can look out for themselves or who have others who will. I will discuss these matters at greater length in Chapter 8.

A society which operates well allows people to pursue their own interests so long as they do not do so at the expense of others' interests. It also has backup measures to assist its members when they are unable to help themselves. In a just society with sufficient resources, such institutions as schools, hospitals, and courts of law will be accessible to all persons who need them. The degree of consideration of the needs of its members which can reasonably be required will depend, of course, upon the total resources available to the society.

In short, more good can be done for individuals, and people as a whole are better off, when individuals take responsibility for themselves and a limited number of others, provided that either society or individuals see to it that none who are unable to care for themselves are neglected and that no one is allowed to obtain excess goods at the cost of depriving others of comparable goods. Hence our recognition of agent-relative prerogatives does not show that we do not believe everyone ought to be treated with equal concern.[48]

There has been an objection to the view that fairness and justice require that those who benefit from an institution must share in the burdens of keeping it up. Robert Nozick[49] has argued that another ingredient is required: namely, consent. If one is presented with something one doesn't particularly want and didn't ask for, he says, one is *not* obliged to pay for it. This is often true. Being compelled to exert oneself when the reward is minimal is very burdensome, and, as a rule, if a person doesn't want the benefit, he shouldn't be forced either to take it or to bear a portion of the burdens of making it available to others. Compulsion is always burdensome and detracts from one's happiness, and it should, therefore, be used only when something important is at stake. Furthermore, a person's (freely given) consent to a measure is *prima facie* evidence that it is at least not contrary to his interests, and therefore obtaining it where possible is a good and wise measure.

There are some situations, however, in which it is justifiable to make people pay a share in common benefits which they themselves profit from only minimally. Sometimes it is not possible for the institution or practice to exist at all without being available to all. A nation's army, for example, cannot defend only part of the population. Even if some people choose not to send their children to public school, or have no children, they still profit from having a lesser degree of ignorance among those who cannot afford private education than there would be without public schools. Having areas of wilderness and other undeveloped land has conservation benefits even for those who do not enjoy outdoor life.

If the benefits of an institution are both great and unavoidable for anyone living in that society, then, if the burdens of upkeep on those who do not want it are not very heavy, it may be justifiable to require all to share them. We could not operate such major institutions simply by making a survey of who wanted them and who didn't, and requiring support only from the former. People who are absolutely unwilling to share these burdens should have the option of leaving the society for another — if any exist — where they are not imposed.

On the other hand, enforcing the payment of taxes for national defense, public education, and conservation is necessary if these goods are to be achieved. Considering their benefits to all, these endeavors are worthwhile, even though they somewhat constrict the liberty and pocketbooks of everyone. The enterprises are too large and too important to be left to the whims of individuals. While nearly everyone would prefer a new car, a vacation cottage, or elegant clothes to paying taxes, we might change our minds if we were conquered by a vicious enemy or ran out of natural resources. In short, liberty to do as one pleases with his time, energy, and property is a great good. But it may be outweighed by some other goods such as survival. And sometimes it is worth sacrificing a small liberty in order to gain a greater one. In these cases compulsion can be justifiable.

Even if the individual who is forced to pay for a given endeavor does not directly benefit, the coercion may be justifiable. If, for example, children are allowed to grow up in extreme poverty which could easily be relieved by the assistance of the well-to-do, initial inequalities usually lead rapidly to still further crippling of such children's ability to achieve happiness. Defective nutrition, poor schooling, and lack of good parenting will permanently hamper a child's ability to work for his or her own happiness, and may well make that child a burden to society. In any case, society as a whole is worse off.

In nearly all societies there are people with more resources than they need to create a happy life for themselves. Many of these people deserve rich rewards for the hard and useful work they have done. On the other hand, most have had good fortune as well. In addition to good genes, good upbringing, opportunities for advancement, and being spared major disasters, the social system has usually favored them. Sometimes this system has included exploitation of the less fortunate. Regardless of how the rich obtained their wealth, sometimes the giving of some of their excess wealth to those who have little is necessary to create minimal opportunities for the poor to act in their own interests. Where this is true, the rich benefit at the expense of the poor if they fail to help them. The rich may not be *obligated* to help the poor and may or may not be individually blameworthy if they fail to do so, but they *ought* to help.[50]

It is thus not unfair for those with an abundance of goods to give to those who are disadvantaged. It is unfair for them *not* to do so in situations where inequalities will cause the further multiplication of inequality. Nor is it always unjust to compel the well off to give to the less fortunate. If private charity were so abundant and well organized as to give all the poor a chance to make their own happiness, compulsion *would* be unfair. Unfortunately, it is not. It is important to remember, however, that giving others so much that they lose incentives to act for themselves is neither beneficent nor fair, and the resentment of the well off who are compelled to support those who could work but don't is justifiable.

It should be noted that even for highly worthwhile enterprises, fairness does not always require that everyone who benefits from them contribute to them. In complex societies, more good may be done when each person contributes to those enterprises to which he is best suited to contribute, rather than spreading his talents and resources in all directions. This is still fair, so long as everyone contributes in a fashion which is roughly equal or proportional to total reward. Thus a system can be perfectly just in which each person has a job which he or she can do well, and, in addition, engages in volunteer work for or gives money to a few selected projects, yet shares in the benefits created by the endeavors of all, even those to which he or she did not directly contribute. What is unfair is someone's gaining these benefits without making a contribution of some sort consistent with his abilities and resources.

9. WEIGHING AND MEASURING

It is all very well to talk about fairness as giving equal concern to the well being of every person and not letting one individual benefit at the expense of another. But in order to apply such a principle, we need to know how we determine whether one person is being treated equally with another, or whose interests outweigh those of another in cases of inevitable conflict. In general, we base such judgments on the relative value of the goods to be lost or gained in a given situation. Thus we think it unfair for John to get a promotion when Sue deserves it more. We assume that when

Sue has worked harder and longer and contributed more to the company, she has sacrificed more. If she does not get the promotion, she ends up with less of value than John would if he didn't get it. (Here we will assume for the sake of argument that John and Sue are equally talented and would do equally well in the more advanced position.) On the other hand, we don't think it unfair of George to break into Patty's mountain cabin when he is lost in a snowstorm, for he may well die if he doesn't take advantage of the shelter. Undoubtedly, he owes her some compensation if he is ultimately rescued, but we believe that life is more valuable than property and that when one or the other must be lost it is not unfair for property to be sacrificed.

To make such judgments we need to have some way of estimating the value of different goods. In general, I think, we consider their value to be roughly proportional to their likely effects on the happiness of those who have them. Thus George's life is more important than Patty's property, because we suppose that — for any person — living is more crucial to his happiness than is the protection of any of his personal property.[51] There may be exceptions to this — my mother used to say that her mother would have starved before she would have sold any of the family silver (fortunately, my grandmother was never put to the test) — but they are rare. It might also be that Sue does not care about a promotion — that a job well done and a living wage is all the reward she wants for her efforts, but such selflessness is extremely uncommon. We would expect Sue to be better off through the promotion, and worse off if her extra work were not compensated.

While tangible goods may differ in value for different people, we can and do make some generalizations based on their usual contribution to happiness. And we use these generalizations in making decisions about how to distribute goods fairly and how to resolve conflicts of interest. One way to set up a system for making such judgments is to classify goods into levels depending upon their usual contribution to happiness. We know that some primary goods are absolutely essential for happiness; others are not necessary, but contribute very significantly to happiness; still other goods contribute only marginally to happiness. We might call these Level 1, Level 2, and Level 3 goods, respectively.

Our beliefs about which goods belong to which level may vary with time, place, and circumstances, but in general Level 1 goods would include life itself, the necessary means to staying alive (like enough food, shelter, and health care to preserve life), and whatever makes life worth living for the person (i.e., when life without it is no better for him than death). Level 2 goods include most of the other primary goods, the possession of which almost invariably enhances happiness and the absence of which nearly always impairs happiness. These include good health, education, enough material resources to protect one from major discomforts and hazards, self-respect, loving relationships with other human beings, employment consistent with one's interests and abilities, and freedom to do and say what one wants except where this compromises the freedom of others. Level 3 goods are those which contribute to happiness, but are not central to it. Few material possessions are essential to any person's happiness, although for everyone there are many such goods which would add to his or her enjoyment.

Level 3 goods are much more variable in their effects on happiness than are Level 1 or Level 2 goods. Depending upon a person's interest in fishing a new fly rod might delight him, please him slightly, leave him indifferent, or be a mere nuisance. At times what is a Level 3 good for most will be a Level 2 good for some people. The fishing rod for a person living in an isolated forest could be crucial for his survival, and hence a Level 1 good. What are Level 2 goods for most might be Level 1 goods for some. Suppose that Steve and Sean suffer brain damage in an accident. Both recover enough to carry out most ordinary activities, are able to earn a living, and are not too bizarre in their appearance or behavior to repel others. On the other hand, they have lost their intellectual edge — are not able to retain information, come up with creative answers to questions and problems, and argue incisively as they were once able to do. Steve and Sean might react very differently to that loss. If Steve had been a scientist or a philosopher, while Sean had had a less intellectually demanding career, Steve would be much more devastated and life might no longer be worth living for him. Sean, on the other hand, would surely be unhappy but might find life worth living for other reasons. Thus intellectual brilliance would have been a Level 1 good for Steve, but a Level 2 good for Sean.

One factor which might make a particular good rank at different levels for different people would be whether there were available substitutes. to lose one's job might be the loss of only a Level 3 good if there is plenty of other work — equally satisfying and remunerative — available nearby. On the other hand, for those living in economically depressed regions their particular jobs are Level 2 goods, since losing them would create major hardship.

For the most part, people think it wrong to seek a Level 3 good for one individual if doing so will place significant obstacles in the way of another person's obtaining Level 1 or 2 goods. If my having a new television will cause someone else to go hungry and homeless, then I shouldn't get it — if, for example, I spent my welfare check — meant to feed my children — to buy it. But even though the money I spend on such a luxury item could feed a stranger and pay his rent for a week, it does not follow that my buying it *caused* — even in part — the stranger's hunger and homelessness, or that I ought not to get the television. My doing without the television is not normally necessary for others not to be deprived. Only if others are dependent on my support — as one's own small children would be — would my merely not providing for them deprive them. In fact, people's acquiring Level 3 goods can often enhance the well being of persons at the bottom economic level of society, by providing jobs, etc..

An economic system in which some people have many goods at all levels while others cannot -- even with great effort -- obtain Level 1 or 2 goods, is unfair. But it does not follow from this that particular well off individuals living in that system are behaving unjustly. It will suffice to point out that the better off are not, by the mere act of acquiring luxuries, placing obstacles in the way of others' obtaining necessities. On the other hand if they give up luxuries so that others may have necessities, there is little question but that they are acting well.

One could argue that the best state of affairs, morally speaking, is that in which all persons attain as many goods at each level as possible without preventing other persons from attaining goods at the same and more basic levels.[52] Thus it is morally good as well as good for any individual to have the bare necessities of life. It is likewise good if she also has things that will significantly enhance her happiness, *provided* that her having them will not hinder others in getting basic necessities or goods significantly enhancing happiness. And it is good as well if she has luxury items that marginally contribute to her happiness, but only if her having them does not prevent others from obtaining Level 1 or Level 2 goods.

From this we can see why it is that equality of distribution can sometimes be morally desirable and why it plays an important role in our conception of fairness.[53] It is sometimes wrong, unfair, and unjust for people to be much better off than their fellows, not because there is a moral evil in having people be at different levels of happiness, but because of scarcity of resources. My having a great deal of something, when supplies are limited, may keep someone else from having any of it. I may not be personally guilty of defrauding others, but a system in which there are people who have little chance at happiness because most of the means to happiness have already been appropriated by others is not the best or fairest possible system. It can be improved by redistribution, even if such redistribution is not obligatory or the responsibility of any particular individuals. Indeed, if it were not for the *scarcity* of goods, we would not have any problems of distribution. If nothing that anyone did would result in the deprivation of someone else, we would not need a principle of fairness.

10. CONCLUSIONS

I have argued that considering the equal moral status of all persons to be the core component of the most widely established moral beliefs enables us to provide a consistent account of these beliefs. This equal consideration of the interests of all is consistently cited as a justification for actions and other beliefs, even when our actual practice falls far short of this, which gives, if my discussion in Chapter 1 is not off the mark, a set of truth conditions for moral judgments. It might be that some other account of how moral beliefs fit together consistently with one another would be equally or even more satisfactory. To prove that my own is the only one is not necessary to defend moral cognitivism — only to show that at least one can do the job required.

We show consideration for people by promoting — or at least not harming — their well-being. However one defines well-being, considering the person includes not harming him or threatening his existence, assisting him when he is in need, not taking from him the products of his labor or the things he cares about, and allowing him the opportunity to reach his goals and follow his ideals.

The problems come when what contributes to the well-being of some conflicts with what contributes to the well-being of others. If we give two people in such a conflict situation equal consideration, we choose in favor of the person who stands to lose the most, but we also, if possible, give some compensation to the other party. If gains and losses are equivalent, then some procedure which gives the two individuals equal chances at winning out — e.g., drawing lots or competition through established rules

— is thought fair.

Equal concern does not entail making everyone equally well off, primarily because attempting to do so probably makes everyone worse off in the long run. But when inequality as such — as opposed to whatever that person lacks — causes harm to a given individual, we ought to reduce it. Thus when those who are wealthy can purchase better education for their children, and their subsequent lack of investment in public schools prevents poor children from receiving a decent education, the rich benefit at the expense of poor children, for the poor will have fewer opportunities to escape poverty.

Nor does equal consideration forbid us to give special treatment to those persons we care about in preference to strangers. It does, however, forbid us to promote the interests of ourselves and our loved ones in such a way as to prevent other persons from having their equally or more pressing interests promoted.

CHAPTER 6

BENEFICENCE AND FAIRNESS COMBINED — THE PRIMARY OBJECTIVE OF MORALITY

1. CONFLICTS BETWEEN BENEFICENCE AND FAIRNESS

Beneficence and fairness — while they are the primary considerations to which people defending their moral views ultimately appeal — are not always in agreement. In this chapter I shall propose a principle which combines them and which enables us to decide in most cases what we ought to do. As in the discussion of beneficence and fairness, the test of this combined principle will be whether it is consistent with our well established moral beliefs; in this chapter the emphasis will be on widespread convictions regarding the resolution of conflicts between doing good and being fair. Again, these well-established beliefs are likely to sound platitudinous simply because they reflect what almost no one questions.

An example of a conflict between beneficence and fairness is a situation where telling the truth (which I have argued is an application of the principle of fairness) would cause harm. Most people believe that in such cases it is sometimes justifiable to lie. There seems to be a general consensus (*pace* Kant) — that is, a well-established belief — that lying, if required to save a person's life, would be justifiable, but that it is rarely justifiable for personal advantages.[1] In other situations, however, it is not so clear whether or when lying might be justifiable. At the very least we must know a great deal about the particular situations before being able to make a valid judgment. In order to decide, for example, whether it might be acceptable to lie about a grave danger to the public, it makes a large difference to most whether the affected people might be able to do something to protect themselves from that danger. Since there are usually things that can be done to reduce risk (e.g., evacuation, avoidance of contagion), there are probably very few situations in which hiding or denying dangers would be justifiable. On the other hand, if some knew that the sun was within a short time to become a red giant, burning the earth to cinders, concealing that knowledge (e.g., by lying to a newspaper reporter who realizes that something is up) might be justifiable. While some people could perhaps face the prospect with equanimity, the majority would be likely to panic and make our last days on earth a hell. Even here, however, it is difficult to predict how people will act and, consequently, to know that concealing the truth might have better consequences —

consequently, to know that concealing the truth might have better consequences —
not to mention that direct consequences alone may not determine the rightness of an
action. In short, much of our uncertainty lies in our ignorance of non-moral facts.

The case of lying to avoid hurting someone's feelings has similar features. Most
people believe that knowing a painful truth will usually enable a person to deal with
his situation in a constructive way, and that for this reason lying to spare someone's
feelings is not justified. There, however, situations where such knowledge will
produce only suffering. For example, if a frail old lady were to learn that the son on
whom she dotes has done something she would find utterly disgraceful, she would be
devastated, and there would be nothing she could do to change the hurtful reality. In
this situation, as well as that in which the destruction of the world is imminent, I
believe that most people would agree that we ought to avoid letting the truth be
known. If one cannot avoid either lying or revealing a truth that will, if told, produce
major, irreversible harm, lying would be justifiable. On the other hand, if the harm
is minor or likely to bring compensatory benefits (e.g., where the person who learns
the truth is able, even though hurt, to deal with it constructively), people generally
believe that no lie should be told.

To take another example of well-established beliefs regarding conflicts between
beneficence and fairness, most people recognize a duty to obey the laws of their
society, but they also believe that there are times when laws need not be obeyed — and
even situations in which it is morally better to break a law, or even wrong to obey it.
While all believe that we ought to obey the laws which forbid murder, rape, and theft,
relatively few think we have any obligation to obey laws forbidding certain sexual
practices done in private between consenting adults. And those who broke laws
imposed by Nazi governments in order to protect Jewish friends and neighbors are
considered heroic. How can we justifiably make such distinctions, and what benefits
from breaking laws would make it excusable or even praiseworthy to violate them?

The relevant considerations have been discussed in the previous chapter. Laws in
a reasonably well run society bring about a certain amount of good and prevention of
harm, and members of the society benefit from having the laws followed. Because
most people's obeying a law is required for those benefits to be secured, and because
losing some freedom of action is the cost of these benefits, it would be unfair for some
individuals to accept the benefits without obeying the law themselves. In doing so
they would profit at the expense of those who do obey. On the other hand, if a law
prevents no harm and brings insufficient benefits to compensate for the freedom that
having it takes away, society does not profit by having it, so those who do obey
relinquish their freedom for little or nothing. If people violate such a law, they harm
no one and are unfair to no one. If a law harms people without bringing
compensatory benefits, then breaking the law may be morally better than obeying it.
Furthermore, if a law harms some greatly while allowing other persons to profit, the
law itself is unjust, and breaking it may be morally praiseworthy.[2]

What seems — according to common belief — to make the difference in both the
cases of lying and of breaking the law, as well as other situations like breaking
promises or following the customs of one's society, is whether or not the harm acting

from principle can do is sufficient to outweigh the wrong of violating that principle — wrong inherent in all such violations, even when they do no harm. In what follows I shall argue that these common beliefs are expressions of an overarching principle which allows us to resolve most conflicts between beneficence and fairness.

2. THE CENTRAL PURPOSE OF MORALITY

The combined principle which appears to answer these questions in a way most in accord with our fundamental moral beliefs — which achieves the right balance between beneficence and fairness — is this. The morally best thing for anyone to do is (1) to bring about as much happiness for every person as one can without restricting the ability of any other person to achieve a like degree of happiness, and (2) to bring about as much happiness for sentient nonpersons as is compatible with (1). Another way of putting this is that the best that we can do is to bring as much happiness as we can to individuals which is compatible with a like degree of happiness for all. In this book I shall discuss (1) only: i.e., how to treat persons; the question of who counts as a person and how those who are not persons (animals and fetuses, as possible examples) ought to be treated I have discussed at length elsewhere.[3]

As indicated in Chapter 2, we *ought* to perform those acts which are necessary for advancing moral purposes. Each individual, when faced with a choice of alternative actions which advance moral purposes to differing degrees, does better either to choose that alternative which best promotes them, or at least some alternative that does not put obstacles in the way of their being advanced — by someone else or in some other way — to a like extent. Since it is difficult to compare the happiness of different individuals, doing what is best and what we ought to do usually boils down to doing things that we know make people happier and which do not at the same time take away others' potential for happiness.[4]

Suppose that there is a state S of the world, which is the best state that I could bring about by my efforts. No doubt the same state, or one equally good, could in many cases occur through the actions of others or through natural events. But sometimes they couldn't, or would at least be much less likely to do so. In these latter instances, I ought to perform the action. If a feeble old man gets on a crowded bus, someone ought to give him a seat. Otherwise, he won't get one, and the best state of the world you (and the other bus riders) could bring about relative to these circumstances wouldn't occur. It may not be that *you* ought to give up your seat, if there are plenty of other able bodied individuals who could do so. On the other hand, if everyone on the bus except you is disabled in some way, then you are the one who ought to give the man your seat. Of course, if no one offers his seat, then all those who could have done so are at fault.

If what I argued in Chapter 3 is correct, what we ought to do is what is necessary for reaching one of a certain set of goals. Each agent's good or happiness is one of these goals (i.e., prudential) for that agent. According to the principle of beneficence, a goal of morality is the greatest possible happiness for all persons (and other sentient beings), but when the happiness of one individual conflicts with that of another, another goal of morality is to insure that one person's happiness is not obtained at the expense of another's. Combining these two goals, we can specify the *central purpose of morality* as the greatest possible happiness for each individual that is compatible with like happiness for all persons. What we ought to do morally is whatever is necessary or strongly required for realizing that central purpose, and the best that we can do is whatever advances that purpose to the greatest extent.

While people rarely have this central purpose of morality explicitly in mind when they make moral judgments, its essential components: namely, beneficence (i.e., making people happy or avoiding and relieving causes of unhappiness), and fairness (or not letting some gain happiness at the expense of others) *are* in the minds of those consciously trying to determine what is right. Those who are concerned with justifying their beliefs and actions are also aware of the need to find a balance between conflicting demands of beneficence and fairness, and they generally do so by using fairness as a constraint on what beneficent actions are allowable.[5] In other words, what we do to make someone happier is good, just so long as making one person happier does not bring others to a lower level of happiness than the beneficiary enjoys. People deliberating about what it is right to do may be, but are usually not, explicitly aware of what I've called the central purpose of morality, but they are almost certainly thinking of its components of beneficence and fairness, and the need to balance them. The central purpose is central in the sense that (1) it is a result which would be attained by everyone's acting for the best, (2) it would be, I believe, acknowledged by nearly all people to be a morally unimpeachable result and not overridden by other considerations, (3) when it is hindered in some way, people recognize that something is wrong, and (4) it unifies the principles which virtually all known societies have recognized in one form or another. That this central purpose has all these functions does not entail that there is only one moral principle. As Audi points out[6] having several fundamental principles is perfectly consistent with there being one theoretical construct — like the Categorical Imperative — that explains and unifies them — and that is precisely what I am trying to provide here.

At any time that people have a purpose or goal and are considering how best to attain it, they use a kind of inductive reasoning. What they are looking for are actions which will, under the circumstances, bring about the desired result: i.e., the attainment of their goal. That is, they are looking for things they might do which would be *causally sufficient* for (or at least give the highest probability of) reaching the goal.[7] Because the same kind of effect may often be obtained through several different sorts of causal processes, there may well be more than one action which would, given existing conditions, lead to the attainment of the purpose. If the purpose is the central purpose of morality, or one of its components, there might be several courses of action which are equally good. For example, of several equally deserving charities, one will do equally well in giving to any of them. Contributions to any one of them would advance the purpose of morality equally well.

That there is one central purpose of morality does not rule out the possibility that there are other purposes for morality.[8] Obviously there have been many such purposes throughout history. Social cohesion and order, fear of God, and the desire to keep the *status quo* are all reasons people have had for adopting a moral code and for choosing one code over others. No one of these purposes, however, has been had by everyone, or even accepted as morally valid by everyone. When a moral code or the reasons for adopting it come under criticism, what is appealed to consistently is whether the code works for the good of all people alike — i.e., whether they are in accordance with beneficence constrained by fairness.[9]

Obviously, the central purpose of morality can never be fully realized, since there is always more that one could do to increase the happiness of almost any given individual. Those trying to do right are mainly concerned with preventing or relieving causes of *unhappiness*, or with making sure that increases in the happiness of some don't result in decreased happiness for others. They want to avoid or remove conditions which would significantly impede the attainment of moral ends. Morally conscientious people wish to do what is in fact causally *necessary* for attaining the purpose of morality or the best balance of beneficence and fairness: that is, actions the omission of which will cause uncompensated unhappiness, or allow some persons to benefit at the expense of others.

Not only can single actions advance or impede the central purpose of morality, so also can general practices, or the following of certain moral guidelines. For the most part observing moral rules prevents impediments to attaining the central purpose of morality and furthers its realization. Sometimes these are well-established moral beliefs, in the sense used in Chapter 1 — principles which are agreed on by nearly everyone who has had a chance to consider them rationally. These include the views that one ought not to lie, break promises, or cause needless pain. Others may be rules held by particular societies, such as a belief that it is wrong to bewitch your neighbor's cattle. General rules can relieve us of some of the burden of calculating the rightness or wrongness of particular acts.

When there is no conflict within or between rules, we usually know what we should do. People who have good moral upbringing also know that breaking rules for personal convenience is wrong; rules are not always easy or pleasant to follow.[10] Conscientious people quite rightly avoid and disapprove of the breaking of rules, and following the rules is usually morally right. On the other hand, to follow them blindly, failing to recall the point of having the rule in the first place or to acknowledge when it needs to be overridden by other considerations, is often wrong. Some rules, in fact, may lose their whole reason for being when the circumstances that made them once promote the purpose of morality no longer obtain.

In applying the central purpose and the principles and rules derived from it, however, we encounter major practical problems in comparing the happiness of different individuals. For this reason, I proposed in the last chapter that the applications of moral principles be stated in terms of their effects on the *means and conditions* of happiness, rather than quantities of happiness. Many of these means and conditions can be measured and compared fairly readily.

Moreover, while I can seldom directly increase or decrease your level of happiness,

I could affect your *chances* of happiness by, for example, giving you money or taking it away from you. One can never really know whether one's children are equally happy, but one *can* give them comparable attention, resources, and advantages. A parent who spent much more time with one child than another, and gave the one better food, education, and medical care, would clearly be acting unfairly. We can *know* this, even when we cannot determine exactly how happy the children are.

As noted in the last chapter, some goods are necessary for attaining happiness or a good life (Level 1), and others will almost always make life better and enable one to satisfy more of whatever particular desires one may have (Level 2). Everyone is better off if he or she has at least a certain quantity of these goods (although more may or may not be better). Others (Level 3) are not essential to, but may enhance, one's happiness. Where goods in one group conflict with those in another, decisions are not particularly difficult. If we must choose between curing a child of a potentially fatal disease and sending him to school, we will surely choose the former, for the latter will be impossible if he dies.

The hard questions come when we must decide between Level 1 goods for the same person or for different people, or between Level 2 goods, when all the needs cannot be satisfied. For example, life itself is required for any individual to satisfy any desires or to realize any purposes. This would seem to be an argument in favor of maintaining life at whatever cost. If this is correct, then we should prolong medical treatment for a sick person as long as he lives, no matter what he suffers or what price others may pay.

On the other hand, suppose the patient had no reasonable hope of enjoying any further experiences or activities, or that he has no prospects for anything but physical or mental suffering so severe that no human being would find a life containing it worth living. Then his life will no longer bring satisfaction of desires or realization of purposes; in such a case, the person might well find continued life nothing but a burden. And if the cost of prolonging such a person's life will risk depriving others with a greater hope of a life worthwhile to them of the chance to live it, it would seem both cruel and unfair to do so. What we have here is not a conflict between a person's life and lesser goods, but a conflict between one person's life and the lives of others, or between a person's life and that which would make that life valuable to him.[11]

Another place where measurement can be difficult is in determining the value of following certain moral principles when this may create inconvenience and even harm. Thus if by telling the truth concerning your whereabouts to a potential killer, I may cause your death, I know what harm I can do, but how do I weigh this against the moral wrongness of telling a lie? If someone lies, she benefits at the expense of people who have inconvenienced themselves — and perhaps even lost their lives — to tell the truth. Their doing so has created an expectation that people will tell the truth, even when it may hurt their interests. This may make the liar's lie believed and thus give her the benefits of others' trust. But there is no way to measure how much good is done by the general practice of truth telling, or how much harm individual people have suffered from telling the truth. It does seem, however, that while an atmosphere of trust is a great good and maintaining it costs us all something from time to time, it is rather a Level 2 than a Level 1 good. It is, therefore, probably less wrong to lie if doing so can prevent loss of life or grave injury to some individual. On the other hand, if a lie prevents no major harm, it is wrong. It must, of course, be remembered that the classification of goods into levels is only a rough one, and that a good that is at one level for one person at a given time might be at a different level, or not even a good at all, for other people or for the same person at a different time. All this detracts some precision from these efforts to rank the rightness or wrongness of specific actions.

By considering goods at different levels we may express the combined principle in a more practically useful way. The best state of affairs, morally speaking, is that in which all persons attain as many goods at each level as possible without preventing other persons from attaining like goods at the same level or goods at more basic levels.[12] Thus it is good for any individual to have the bare necessities of life. It is good for her also to have things that will significantly enhance her happiness, *provided* that her having them will not hinder others in getting basic necessities or goods significantly enhancing happiness. And it is good for her to have luxury items that marginally contribute to her happiness, but only if her having them does not place obstacles in the way of others' obtaining necessities or goods that significantly enhance their happiness or luxuries they desire. In some cases Level n goods would be — in aggregate — a Level n minus 1 good. Thus such recreational items as sailboats, stereos, and computer games, or time and money for vacations, would surely count as Level 3 goods, but if we considered the consequences of having no recreational opportunities, we would no doubt rank them collectively as Level 2 goods.

Furthermore, if there are not enough goods at any particular level for all, then it is not necessarily unjust for some to have them and others not. It is better for some to have a chance at happiness than for none. That all cannot live or be happy would not excuse an attempt to make none live or be happy in the name of equality. If everyone has sufficient Level 1 goods, but there is a dearth of Level 2 goods, it would be better for some to have these Level 2 goods and others not than for none to have them. Where there is truly no way for the needs of all to be satisfied, and some must go without, there are some restrictions on the means by which it is decided how and for whom those needs are to be met.

A fair decision procedure will give each individual an equal chance at receiving them, or a chance proportional to potential contribution to the general welfare. For example, if there are seven people on a lifeboat who will all die unless one goes overboard, and where six have a good chance of surviving until rescue, they could draw lots to decide which one to sacrifice. It would also be fair, and more likely to produce a better outcome, if those who have special skills which might improve the group's chance of survival would be exempted from the lottery. Where there is only one job, but several applicants, a fair procedure might be to draw lots. It could also be fair to choose the person who has the largest family to support. However, on the grounds that everyone is better off by having jobs filled by the best qualified people, it is not only fair but more generally beneficial to choose the applicant who is most likely to do the best work. In general, a business is not responsible for the welfare of individuals other than its customers and employees, and even in these cases only in a restricted sense, so that hiring those most qualified generally seems the best way overall of selecting employees. There is nothing wrong, either, with business owners doing the best for their enterprises, provided their practices do not hinder others.

Any system in which some have Level 2 goods, and their having them makes others unable to attain Level 1 goods is unfair in that some would be better off at the cost of others being markedly worse off than they. It does not follow from this alone, however, either that any particular person is obligated to correct such inequalities or that correcting them should be enforced.

3. RESOLVING MORAL CONFLICTS

We now have some general guidelines for resolving moral conflicts. We know that it is always morally good to do things which increase the happiness of any individual, unless by doing so we prevent other persons from achieving goods at the same or lower — i.e., more basic — levels. If whatever we do someone will be deprived, we must try to deprive those who will be least harmed and not reduced to a lower level of well being than those who benefit will reach. If this cannot be done, and — whatever we do — one or more persons will be markedly worse off than those who benefit will be, a decision procedure which either gives everyone a chance at the better off positions, reduces the number of those in the worst off positions, or gives the goods to those whose needs are greater or who can make the most use of them for the benefit of others, should be used.[13]

In addition, where there is an institution such as a law, a moral practice like promise keeping, or a cooperative enterprise whose operation benefits a group of individuals and whose maintenance requires the efforts of a large proportion of the members of the group, it is unfair for any person benefitting from the institution to shirk her efforts. There may, however, be situations in which some individual or another institution benefitting individuals will be harmed if she does her share. A person living in a grossly unjust society may be justified in breaking some of its laws. Not every law, however; one would have been no more justified in breaking traffic laws in Nazi Germany than anywhere else.[14] But if the violation of a law could have rescued anyone from death in a concentration camp, then that violation would have been justified. The test is whether anyone will be worse off if the law is obeyed than people generally will be if it is violated. If so, then a law, or a moral practice, or the duties of an enterprise, may rightfully be breached.[15]

There may be difficulties in making decisions about how to measure and distribute even primary goods. Isaac Levi discusses some of these.[16] Many goods are incommensurable. How, for example, does having shelter compare with having food? If you can't have both, which is more important? How much food is equivalent to a certain amount of shelter? Is it better to give Gena a roof over her head for one night than it is to give Harry food for one day? Which is more important: to educate our children well in school, or to ensure for them a stable family life? In particular, where should we be spending public money — on education or family services, or which combination of these, or should it all be left to private charity?

In some of these cases we can find answers by knowing some of the surrounding circumstances in which such questions might be asked. If the weather is clement, Gena might be all right sleeping in the park, whereas, if the temperature is 40 below she might die. Circumstances make a difference in the answers to these questions because they indicate what the effects are likely to be of doing or not doing certain things on the ability of the individuals concerned to achieve happiness. If Gena will die without shelter for this night, and Harry will die if he doesn't get fed today, their needs are equally urgent. If Irene can help only one, and there are no sources of help for the other, then she must make a tragic choice. She might choose by some chance method, like flipping a coin; this would at least make her decision procedure fair.

On the other hand, Irene might choose on the basis of circumstances which might indicate that either Gena or Harry would lose more by dying tonight. For example, suppose Gena has a terminal illness and will die soon anyway, while Harry, who would be healthy if only he had food, might be able to fend for himself and live a long time if he can obtain enough to get him through today. It would then be better for Irene to give Harry food than to give Gena shelter.

Likewise, one can argue about allocating funds for education as opposed to family services. One hopes that both can be provided, but even where they can be amply funded, there are always limits upon what is available. We may not always be able to decide which of a number of ways of allocating the available funds is best, but as Levi points out, there are some options which are *admissible* and others which are not. An option which would not be admissible would be to spend nothing on either education or family services, but give it all to Senators for yachts and private planes. Another inadmissible option would be to spend all the funds available on family services, leaving nothing for education; after all, only a minority of children are in need of family services, but all need education. Since a given amount of most goods usually benefits those who have little of them more than those who already have much of them, it would seem reasonable to suppose that any admissible option of distributing funds for education and family services would provide a certain basic education for all children but some additional services to help children at risk because of their home situation. Any system which gave many extras in one area but few or none in another would not be admissible because it would seriously hamper the ability of a significant number of children to live a good and happy life.

Although such diverse goods as food, shelter, education, and family services may appear to be incommensurable, they are not entirely so. If the arguments in Chapter 3 are sound, the feature of all of these different goods which is relevant to moral argument is their contribution to happiness, which is, in turn, living a life with which one is content. Since by this criterion a person's happiness is proportional to the amount of time she spends wanting things to be as they are, and quantities of time are measurable, we can — theoretically, at least — compare goods in terms of the increase in happiness having them would bring to specific individuals. Thus shelter is better right now for Gina than food, while food is currently better than shelter for Harry, if immediate shelter is required for Gina to live and Harry will die without food now. At other times, however, the contribution to their happiness of food and shelter would for each of them be more or less, depending on circumstances. Relative contributions to happiness also enable us (in principle) to judge the fairness of actions and policies. Education presumably contributes greatly to the overall happiness of all children, while family services are essential to the happiness of a small proportion of them. Hence a fair distribution of funds between these institutions would provide enough for family services to level the playing field for deprived children — i.e., put them in a better position to attain the happiness that other children enjoy — but spend the rest on educational opportunities for all.

Such calculations are possible in theory, but in practice there are too many unknowns for exactitude. This is why I have suggested that we make determinations of what to do in terms of the generally expected contribution of particular goods to happiness. The assumption — which, of course, need not always be correct — is that the more one has of a particular good, the better off one is, subject to diminishing returns. Among different goods at each level, there may be differences in the extent to which one will enable people to attain their goals. Of two different kinds of goods at the same level, which one is most needed or helpful will depend on the individual persons in question, and the circumstances in which choices must be made.[17] Where social policies must be made, however, or quick decisions involving even a very few individuals, these differences must sometimes be papered over by assuming that each good contributes equally to the happiness of all individuals who receive it. Where we know this not to be the case, however, adjustments are called for, but more often than not we do not know. Obviously, these considerations alone do not solve all moral dilemmas. Some may, in fact, be insoluble. I think, however, that the greatest part of the difficulty of resolving moral conflicts lies in determining the facts in particular cases, especially those determining what would make people happy.

4. OUGHT AND CAN

That the best a person can do is what, of all the alternatives open to him, will best promote the central purpose of morality entails by definition that whatever is best for one to do is something it is possible for one to do. The only actions individuals will perform that increase happiness, forestall harm, and prevent injustices are those alternatives which are open to them — alternatives which are internally consistent, compatible with laws of nature, and are within the powers of the agent. On the other hand, what we *ought* to do is what is necessary, or strongly required, for promoting the central purpose, and there are occasions when we may not be able to do what is necessary. At times whatever one does harms an individual or is unfair to someone, so that one is unable to do what he ought to do.

The existence of moral conflict is evidence that we sometimes ought to do what we can't. In such situations a person has two things he ought to do, but he cannot do situations the agent clearly ought to do one of the actions rather than another — e.g., to save a life rather than keep an appointment — sometimes, to use Sinnott-Armstrong's terms,[18] neither duty is overridden by the other. In such cases, the agent *ought* to perform both duties, but which is *better* for him to choose may be determined by what does the most moral good or least harm, and — if there is no difference — by what is in his own best interests or most in accord with his personal tastes. Because in such a conflict he cannot avoid doing moral harm, he ought, if he can, to mitigate that harm by making amends to anyone injured or offended by his failure to perform the duty. Audi makes a useful distinction between a duty's being overridable and its being cancelable. It is cancelable when the ground for the duty is no longer present (e.g., when the person to whom you made a promise releases you from it). A duty for which the ground is still present still exists (is "ineradicable" in Audi's terms), but may be overridable by a more stringent duty which — under the circumstances conflicts with it.[19] The agent still ought to do what he cannot — i.e., both duties — but since one is more important, it is better that he do that one.

That there is such a "moral residue" does not, however, as Bernard Williams suggests,[20] constitute a sound argument against moral realism. As Guttenplan points out,[21] in most moral dilemmas it is particular circumstances that make our performing one duty incompatible with performing the other. The reasons for each duty's being a duty are unchanged; if things were different we could and should perform both of the acts that we ought to do. Because of those reasons we should regret the failure to perform one of those acts and mitigate where possible any harm we have done through that failure.[22] It does *not* follow that there is nothing to choose between the two acts or that one is not less bad than the other. Thus I ought not to burn your antique Chippendale chair, but if I am freezing to death and my using it as fuel is necessary to save my life, I would be justified. It is *true* that it is better for me to burn the chair than to die, even though it is also true that I ought both to feel sorry for causing your loss and to provide whatever recompense I can. There is such a moral remainder just because it *is* wrong to destroy the property of others, since this causes hardship and sorrow, and because it is a failure to uphold one's share of maintaining the institution of keeping property secure. The sorrow and unfairness resulting from my burning your chair is just as real as it would have been had I done so for no good reason, and thus it causes moral harm. The difference is that in the particular circumstances it would have been even worse for me to have frozen to death when means were at hand to save my life. That failing to take measures to prevent my death would have been worse, however, does not take away the wrongness of my action, which wrongness I can minimize by making amends. That one ought not to allow oneself to die unnecessarily and that one ought not to destroy the property of others are both true, even though in these circumstances it is not possible for me to do all that I ought. But it is also true that one course of action is less bad than the other. There is nothing here to support noncognitivism.

5. WHEN SOME WILL BE HARMED WHATEVER ONE DOES

Sometimes enhancing the happiness of one person makes it impossible for others to have the same amount of happiness. In most such situations it would be wrong to help that individual. If a surgeon could only find a suitable liver for a patient who desperately needed a transplant by killing a healthy person and taking *his* liver, this would indeed be wrong. There are, however, cases where helping one person, or group of persons, *is* considered right, even though doing so will prevent others from receiving equivalent help. For example, Matilda comes across two drowning children. She can save only one by herself, and there is no one else around who could help. To save one, she must let the other drown; but she should surely attempt to save one of the children and not allow both to die because she cannot save both. We will assume for the sake of argument that there is no *prima facie* moral reason why it would be worse for Matilda to fail to save one of the children than it would be for her to fail to save the other: for example, if she were babysitting for one and thus had a special duty to protect him, or if she knew that one of the children was painfully and terminally ill, while the other had every prospect for a long and healthy life.

It is crucial to the sort of case I have in mind that every individual in the case will lose the benefit (or rescue from harm) if no help is rendered, so that no one will gain. The consequences of helping will make no one worse off than everyone will be if no one helps. In this kind of case, I think everyone would agree that help should be rendered to some individuals who can be helped, even though in the circumstances the result will be that others will not be helped. But if different individuals were helped — and, in the proposed type of example, they could be helped just as well as those who are helped — they would gain, while the others would lose.

It seems in this kind of case that whoever is helped, their being helped is incompatible with others attaining a like degree of happiness. In this situation, Matilda ought to help both children, but she can't. Yet we consider it morally *better* to help some than to help none. In such situations where there is no difference in what the individuals involved need or deserve with respect to the proposed benefit, fair procedure is, as noted above, to equalize the opportunity for receiving the benefit — e.g., by competition or by chance.

The case of the drowning children is different in several respects. First of all, there will be no future chance for the child who isn't rescued to get the benefit of having his life saved. Secondly, there is no competitive or chance procedure for selecting which child Matilda rescues; if she stops to flip a coin she may lose precious time and, with it, the chance to save even one child. Even if some such selection process were feasible, the children would have no way of being informed of the rules. Thirdly, they did not choose to be in this situation. But these differences do not entail that Matilda cannot choose fairly. First of all, she can scream for help in the hope — however unlikely — that someone else might hear and come to save the other child. Or she might throw a floatable object to one of the children, if something like that is available — even if this does take time. In short, she will, if she can, do something to improve the chances of the child she cannot rescue herself; because she ought to save both, she won't give up trying as long as possible to do so. Secondly, she can avoid choosing which child to save on the basis of some irrelevant characteristic, such as its race, its sex, its looks, or the wealth of its parents. Rather she should make her selection on the basis of which child seems more able to hold out longer, or which is closer to shore. These characteristics are relevant to maximizing the good or minimizing the harm for the two children. In real life it is rare that a rescuer can *know* with *certainty* that no help can possibly come for the second child, or that there is *no* relevant difference between them or in her chances of saving them. But where the rescuer is aware of no such difference and where she is as nearly certain as possible that one and only one child can be saved, the only fair way to make the selection is a negative way; that Matilda *not* make the choice on the basis of some irrelevant characteristic. She should just jump in and start swimming toward one or the other; in this sort of situation what will be fairest is also what will maximize her chances of saving either child: namely, *not* to think or calculate which child to rescue, but start acting immediately. This is as close to impartiality, i.e., considering the interests of each child equally, as she can come in such a situation.

The points to be made in all cases — from races to drowning children — where only some can benefit, is that, first, the benefit *should* be made available and not withheld just because it cannot be shared, and, secondly, the opportunity for receiving it should be made equally open to all, or on the basis of some characteristic which makes one party more likely to benefit from the act. In this way, the interests of all are given equal weight without the benefit being lost entirely. In a case like Matilda's the rescuer *cannot* be right to do what is often acceptable in other cases of moral conflict — namely, to choose on the basis of self-interest or personal preference. This would be to bias the selection in such a way as not to give equal opportunity or equal consideration to all.

It is important to note that, while Matilda's choosing one of the children will in the circumstances result in the other child's drowning, and thus the happiness she preserves for the child she saves is incompatible with the happiness of the other, her putting her efforts into saving the first child is only one of many factors that brought about the death of the second. Left to themselves, both children would drown. She puts no further obstacle in the way of the rescue of the second. She would greet joyfully the appearance on the scene of another person who could help, and if, after she gets the first child to safety, there is the slightest hope of saving the second, she will pursue it. In real life there is rarely certainty that *nothing* can happen to allow the rescue of the other members of a group whom the rescuer cannot help. In short, cases where the provision of happiness to one individual results in its being very difficult or impossible for another to attain like happiness are rare, unless the provider of the happiness for one does something directly to harm the other's chances over and above what is present in the situation.

Given three individuals, A, B, and C, such that without A's assistance, B and C will lose their future chances of happiness, but where A could rescue either B or C, but not both, from disaster, A ought to assist either B or C, so long as he chooses impartially and does nothing to make the chances of the one he does not choose worse than they would have been without his intervention. While A *could* have chosen to help C rather than B, his not choosing C is usually only one of several factors causing the disaster that overtakes C. In the case of the drowning children, it is the dangerousness of the water, their own foolhardiness, or the negligence of their parents that would be the real causes of their deaths. In this situation, it seems clear that Matilda ought to save one child rather than neither, and that there is no reason why she ought to save one rather than the other. Only in a remote sense does Matilda's action allow the child who is saved to benefit at the expense of the one who drowns, for the causes of the child's death include so many factors over and above Matilda's rescuing the other.

Similar remarks apply to certain policies, such as response to terrorism or foreign aggression. Thomas Hill argues that a government can be justified in adhering to a policy of not giving in to terrorists, even though it is virtually certain that some innocent people will be killed as a result of its refusal to give terrorists what they demand.[23] Hill maintains that rational legislators in a kingdom of ends would be able to accept maxims which would allow even the sacrifice of innocents to save the lives of others. They could do so while knowing that they themselves might become victims, if — and only if — the probability of any particular person's benefitting from such a practice is much greater than the probability of his being killed. Thus we should not give in to terrorists, since this will encourage them; that some innocent people will surely die when terrorists are resisted is an unfortunate result of this policy, but on the whole people can expect to be much better off and have fewer chances of being victims of terrorism. In a situation where a terrorist has taken hostages whom he threatens to kill if his demands are not met, particular individuals stand to lose their lives in order that others may live. A case can, however, be made for the view that the hostages have themselves benefited in the past from the policy of not giving in to terrorists — i.e., they might have been killed earlier had other terrorists not been resisted.[24]

Likewise, when a country is invaded or threatened in such a way that citizens' lives are apt to be lost, some of those who fight will inevitably die or be crippled. If, however, no resistance is made to such aggression, many more would die, including perhaps those soldiers who die in the present war. Moreover, if a country has a reputation for fighting back, which reputation can only be sustained by actually doing so when threatened, invasion is much less likely, so that even those who die in a particular war have probably benefited from past wars of defense. (None of this, of course, can be justifiably used as an excuse for starting a war for territorial expansion, ethnic hatred, or furthering business interests. Moreover, the fairness of allowing some soldiers to be killed in the national interest depends also on a fair means of selecting who is to serve — e.g., volunteers, or a truly random draft system.)

There are, however, cases where there is no alternative that the agent ought to choose. In William Styron's novel *Sophie's Choice*, Sophie, — together with her small son and daughter — is a prisoner in a Nazi concentration camp. She is told by the camp commandant that if she chooses one of her children to be killed, the other will be saved. If she does not choose one, both will be put to death. Faced with this agonizing dilemma, she hesitates until it is clear that both children really will be killed unless she chooses one — at which point she tells the commandant to take her daughter away but save her son. As one might expect of such an individual, the commandant fails to keep his promise to save the boy, and she never sees either child again. What ought Sophie to have done? To have chosen neither child would have doomed them both. To choose either would have been unfair to the other, and — as it happened — saved neither. In this case whatever she did would result in evil to her children. Knowing the consequences of her actual choice, we can say that it might have been slightly less wrong to have refused to choose one child over the other, thereby not showing partiality between her children. But that this would have been the least bad alternative does not imply that she ought to have chosen it. She was placed in a horrible situation where anything she could do would be wrong. Although the least bad thing she might do was something she ought not to do, Sophie surely could not be blamed for any choice she might have made — either a desperate attempt to save one child or an inability to doom either.[25]

6. OTHER MORAL VALUES

In the above I have concluded that there is one overriding moral principle which has two major components: beneficence and fairness. This claim entails that this principle and its components provide all the criteria we need to justify our moral beliefs. There is evidence, as the work of James Q. Wilson shows,[26] that human beings in all cultures past and present, to the extent that we have knowledge of their moral thinking, have used these criteria at least in some rudimentary form.

I think it more likely that examples of *additional* criteria, rather than the absence of those of beneficence and fairness, may be put forth as equally fundamental. I shall now argue that some such possible criteria, while certainly of great importance, are entirely justifiable in terms of beneficence and fairness. Not only do beneficence and fairness supply universally recognized reasons why these other criteria are generally accepted, they may also override those subsidiary criteria in cases of conflict. I do not want to claim that it would be impossible to provide another correct account of morality in which one or more of these other criteria was counted as basic. As long as beneficence and fairness were fully included in the system, it could certainly be adequate. What I *am* claiming is that no other principle to which we commonly appeal *needs* to be considered as basic.[27]

Let us consider these possible competitors for a position as an ultimate criterion: respecting liberty or autonomy, love, treating humanity as an end in itself, respect for human life, and authority or tradition.[28] Liberty, as noted in Chapter 4, is good not only because it is universally desired, but because it enables people to pursue their own interests more effectively. Respecting autonomy might also be considered a requirement of fairness, in that it is good to be able to count on having our freedom of action respected, and our ability to count on it requires that people in general not impair this freedom. Consequently, a person who restricts the freedom of another for his own purposes takes advantage of the practice of respecting autonomy at the expense of others.

Not all freedoms are equally valuable, however, and there needs to be some other criterion for determining which are the most important.[29] The criterion people appear to use is the degree to which the freedom in question tends to enhance human happiness. Moreover, restrictions on freedom are considered justified when necessary to implement the principle of fairness — e.g., when people are not allowed to do things they might want if their doing so prevents others from attaining goods or acting as they wish. What determines whether such a restriction is morally acceptable are the relative effects of the restricted activity and the effects of the restrictions themselves on the overall good of the parties involved.

It has often been argued that we ought to respect a person's autonomy even at times when doing so is against his best interests.[30] In Chapter 4 I argued that autonomy is an extremely important primary good, but that there are times when a person may in some situations be better off if freedom of action is at least temporarily withheld. The question at issue here is whether in situations where it is given that acting against the person's desires or withholding information which might influence his desires would be better for the person, violating autonomy is morally justified — i.e., whether autonomy can override beneficence and fairness.

On my view, if there is *no* reason to doubt a person's ability to make an informed and rational choice, we should allow him to do as he wishes so long as his so acting will not harm others. Autonomy does not, however, override fairness. It is also clear that a person who is obviously irrational — insane, severely retarded, or an infant — is incapable of autonomous choice, and hence others who have her good at heart should make decisions for her. The examples discussed in Chapter 4, however, are largely concerned with people whose rationality is basically intact, but who can act quite irrationally. Persons who are depressed, addicted to substances, who have undergone recent traumatic events — such as major physical injury or loss of a loved one — may have impaired rationality in some areas; they are, however, able to make most decisions quite reasonably. People in these situations may do foolish things which they will later regret; for the most part, however, we don't think we ought to forcibly prevent them from doing such things.

It might appear then that we believe autonomy to override considerations of beneficence. On the contrary, however, we sometimes keep a basically rational person from a course of action which is apt to cause irrevocable harm — e.g., committing a suicidally depressed person to a hospital temporarily; insisting that a woman who wants a tubal ligation (which would result in permanent sterility) immediately wait thirty days before having the surgery; refusing to accept a gift that we know would ruin the donor financially; withholding a medication from an elderly person that she wants, but which is likely to increase her risk of falling; or continuing to give medical care to an accident victim who says he only wants to die — when that care can be expected to bring reasonable recovery. Most would, I think, agree we are justified in doing so. We realize that allowing the person to do as he wants at the time will not only result in serious harm, but will take away future options.

These examples might be interpreted as showing that we can only justify restricting autonomy for the sake of preserving autonomy in the future. If so, then respecting and enhancing autonomy could be considered (one of) the fundamental moral principles from which all others could be derived. Again, I do not deny that this is possible, but only that it is not necessary. Nevertheless, there are examples to suggest that we have other justifications for restricting autonomy than fostering greater autonomy in the future. Most of us would think it justifiable to take away a teenager's car, telephone or television privileges until he does his chores; refuse to give an insistent patient a medication which could cause him slight, though not irrevocable, harm; or withhold a gift of money from a relative until she can present guarantees that she will not spend it foolishly. It would be difficult to claim that these reasons for not giving a person what he wants is for the sake of greater autonomy for that person or others.

Respecting autonomy is, fundamentally, allowing an individual to make his or her own choices based on a consideration of all the factors which might impinge on such a decision. A person's autonomy may be violated both by acting in certain ways against her known desires or by deceiving her so that she will make choices based upon falsehoods. Violating autonomy in the second way is *prima facie* wrong if for no other reason than because it involves deception and hence is a breach of the principle of fairness. Not every way in which we act against a person's known desires, however, constitutes a violation of autonomy. Rather, we consider it a breach if there is actual prevention of that person's carrying out an action or policy. This often involves force — physical, emotional, or legal pressure. The person who is committed to a mental hospital because he opposes the government and the patient who is placed on a ventilator in spite of an advance directive to the contrary have clearly had their autonomy violated.

It is less clear, however, that the person who is committed because he is suicidally depressed or the young, previously healthy person with a severe chest injury who is put on a ventilator to save his life, but who says he wants to die because he cannot stand the pain, have had their autonomy violated. We certainly don't think the teenager who is told he can't use the family car until he cleans his room has lost autonomy. All of these people have had something done to them that they do not want, but the cases in which their autonomy is violated are those in which their liberty of action has been *unjustifiably* restricted. This makes 'autonomy' *mean* the freedom a person *ought* to have. To know, then, whether an act violates the autonomy of an individual, we need to know whether that act was morally justifiable in the first place. And this requires prior knowledge of whether it satisfied other moral principles.

In Chapter 4 we noted situations in which even deceptive medical paternalism might be justified: e.g., a severely depressed quadriplegic who is not told the truth that there is no chance that she will ever move again and the drug addict who is given a placebo. As a rule, such measures are temporary, and designed to time things so that discussing the truth with the patient will occur at a time when she is in a condition to deal with it constructively. Here again we are not violating the patient's autonomy, for we consider the temporary deception to be justified by the eventual outcome.

In short, liberty and autonomy are not fundamental principles distinct from beneficence and fairness. Liberty ought to be respected and fostered because it is generally good for people to be allowed to do as they wish. It may, however, be justifiably restricted when one person's freedom of action harms others or when it would seriously harm the person herself. Restricting liberty is justifiable only when the harm is significant and outweighs the benefits of the freedom to act in the manner which will cause that harm. Violating a person's autonomy does not occur in all cases of restricting her liberty of action. Rather it occurs when liberty is restricted in a morally unjustifiable manner — not when it is restricted in order to prevent grave harm to the agent or to others.

Love has sometimes been put forth as a fundamental, distinct, principle.[31] There are, however, different kinds of love, not all of which could serve as a universal law of morality. Those like romantic love, love of one's children, and friendship, all of which require personal knowledge of and affection towards particular individuals, will not do, since no human being can have these relationships toward more than a very limited number of other persons. Morality requires concern for all persons, not just those we know. Acting upon personal affection, while it usually leads to good, can also harm others, or even diminish the long term good of the person one loves — as when a government official gives a job to his incompetent nephew instead of a qualified applicant.

There is a form of love, which Christians call *agape*, that incorporates this universal concern — the kind of love which motivated Mother Teresa to devote her life to the poor of a country far from her own. To love a person in the *agape* sense is to want his or her good, but since it applies to all persons, one's *agape* for X does not allow one to benefit X at another's expense. Love of this sort is exactly fulfilled by following principles of beneficence and fairness, and is not distinct from it.

Another candidate for a fundamental moral principle distinct from that which I have suggested is Kant's second formulation of the Categorical Imperative: namely, that we should treat humanity (or rational nature) as an end in itself, and never as a means only.[32] If we suppose that treating humanity or rational nature as an end in itself to be treating individual persons as ends in themselves, this does not require an additional principle to those I have already suggested. To treat a person as an end is surely to treat *her good*, including her existence and ability to pursue her ends, as having worth simply because she *is* a person. Yet what is this *but* to treat her with fairness and beneficence? When her good conflicts with that of other people, this may demand sacrifices on her part. That this is so does not show that she is being treated merely as a means to the ends of other persons. Where *someone* must sacrifice, then the person who does is being used as a means to the good of others. If, however, every effort is made to minimize the sacrifice, to obtain the sacrificer's consent, to make recompense, and, above all, perhaps, to use a fair means of selecting the person who must sacrifice, that person is not being treated *merely* as a means. To the extent possible, her ends, her existence, and her ability to achieve her ends are being preserved as much as possible in the circumstances, and she is thus being treated as an end in herself. Compare this with the situation in which she is chosen arbitrarily for the sacrifice, perhaps because she is helpless, and that she is starved or beaten or subjected to indignities and pain which are unnecessary for achieving the overall result, and where she is given nothing to compensate her for what she has lost, even when compensation would have been possible. Clearly, in this case she is not being treated as an end in herself, and the laws of beneficence and fairness have also been violated.

It might be argued that what is to be treated as an end in itself is rational nature, not the person's goals and personal well-being. I already argued in Chapter 4 that this position would entail that what was not part of or contributory to a person's rationality would not matter morally. Yet we all think that many things which are not connected with rationality are valuable, and valuable because they enhance human life in all its aspects.

A variation on the view that we should treat humanity as an end in itself is that we should consider human life sacred. This position has been elaborated by Ronald Dworkin.[33] Holding human life sacred, he says, may sometimes conflict with the interests and rights of individual humans. Thus one might maintain that it is wrong to help a very ill person commit suicide, even though he has nothing to look forward to but suffering and wishes above all else to die. It is in the best interests of the patient to die, and yet most people have some qualms about assisted suicide.

There are many reasons why this is so. First of all, the permanence of death makes us rightly reluctant to take a life, no matter how miserable its prospects. A second reason is that many people believe that our lives are not ours to do with as we will — that we were put here by God to fulfill some purpose, and that by ending any life we frustrate that purpose. A third is the wonder that we often feel at the apparently miraculous existence and development of a human being; wasting anything so intricate and marvelous seems a shame. Still another reason is the fear that allowing people to destroy any human life, no matter how limited or full of suffering, can result in a hardening of our attitude toward others and make us less reluctant to kill people when their existence becomes merely inconvenient.

All of these considerations may conflict with our views of what is truly in a person's interest. An embryo which has not yet developed sentience has no interests of its own.[34] Its existence might very well be contrary to those of its mother, society, or even those of the child it would become if allowed to develop. It may be totally contrary to the interests of a hopelessly sick individual to continue to live. What, then, is the status of the sacredness or inviolability of human life which might make it wrong to end these lives? The answers depend on which of the reasons we look at.

The consideration that death is final is not inconsistent with considering the individual's overall interests to be best served by his death. If, to the best of our knowledge, there is no hope whatsoever of an ill person's meaningful recovery, he may well be better off dead, or at least no worse off. For example, if a CT scan shows that there is no cerebral cortex left, or if cancer has left him in unbearable pain, it is futile to hope that the patient can regain any purposeful or enjoyable life. Death would not then be an evil.

The belief that God has a purpose for all of us, which we have no right to frustrate by killing anyone, is dependent upon a particular type of religious belief. But even supposing the correctness of this view, it is justifiable by considerations of beneficence and fairness. If the deity has plans and purposes, they are either good for humans or they are not. If they are not, the only good reason for conducting our lives in accordance with them would be prudential. If God's will and purposes are good, then we have a strong moral motive to participate in that good. Assuming that God cares about our well-being, fulfilling his purposes will bring us good as well, and it is in our best interests to try to do this by doing what we believe to be morally best. In this case determining whether such practices as abortion and euthanasia can be justified must depend on moral considerations other than God's supposed purposes.

The conviction that we should not destroy such a marvelous thing as a human being is more of an aesthetic value than an ethical one, rather on a par with the desire to preserve great works of art. This is not to belittle such values, but when questions of great human suffering are at stake, they should not carry decisive weight. It would be a terrible thing to wantonly destroy a Rembrandt, but if doing so would prevent a maniac from dropping an atomic bomb on Amsterdam, I think almost anyone would agree that the Rembrandt should be sacrificed. We value great masterpieces and the intricacies of nature, including the human body and mind, because they add to what makes life interesting and worthwhile. We also value the fruits of human creativity and effort over and above their artistic worth because of the investment in them their creators have made. As Dworkin suggests, part of our reason for valuing a human life is the investment that the person himself and those who care about him have made in it. Other things being equal, then, it is in the interests of people to preserve human life, as well as human creations and the works of nature. But it is an interest that we may be justified in overriding.

The fourth reason for considering human life sacred is the most important of all. Most people have a horror of taking the life of another human being and a desire to protect such life, even when we may believe that life to be terribly blighted and of no interest to its possessor. When I did hospital and nursing home care, I had many patients who were extremely debilitated, with no hope of recovery. In a number of cases the decision was made by the patient's family (since the patient himself was no longer mentally able to make such decisions) to stop any life prolonging care. Our job nurses was simply to provide comfort measures until death ensued. This was very difficult for us; anything that suggested a remote chance of improvement in the patient's condition made us want to return to a full scale effort to save his life. Even though we knew the patient had nothing to gain from continued existence, the desire to preserve life at all costs could not be extinguished.

And this desire is a very *good* thing. We have seen the horrors of the failure to value human life in ethnic cleansing and in the actions of the so- called "conscienceless kids" who shoot and torture their victims for thrills. But as Dworkin points out, valuing human life involves more than simply preserving it. It also involves wanting particular lives to be good and worthwhile for the persons who lead them; this desire may be in conflict with the desire to preserve life.

Again, it is worth pointing out that many desires and values we have are — like ideals — usually good to satisfy because of all the other goods their satisfaction brings. But they may not invariably be the best thing to pursue. Valuing human life fits into this category; whatever interpretation we put on it, whether it is a desire to preserve human life or a desire to enhance it, it brings many goods with it. It keeps us decent and concerned. That we value human life can make us want to be beneficent and fair to everyone. It can make us choose to be moral, even when doing right is inconvenient or even bad for us personally. Like ideals of chivalry, however, it may sometimes be carried to a point where it fails to do good, and can even bring harm or injustice.

I know of no philosopher who holds that we ought always to obey established authority,[35] but one at least appears to hold that adherence to tradition is fundamental to morality.[36] One reason to obey authority is that an authority has the power to promote or frustrate your happiness, so that obedience is likely to get you more of what is good for you than does disobedience. A less cynical reason is that an authority (God for example) is benevolent (desires good), wise (knows how to achieve what is good), just (will see that everyone gets a fair share), and powerful (able to attain its goals). Put all together, the good of everyone will be best promoted, and justly promoted, by submission to the dictates of such an authority. Unless a particular authority is so completely virtuous, however, no one thinks that submission to it is invariably right.[37] If more good and more justice may be done by challenging authority, we think doing so is at least sometimes justifiable, and we praise and admire those who defy a wicked government.

Adherence to tradition, too, is usually justifiable in terms of beneficence and justice. Traditions give a society cohesion and enable its members to get along with one another. Violating them often results in harm and unfairness. On the other hand, traditions can be stifling, and some promote unjust, discriminatory treatment of certain groups of people. Of course, disrupting traditions — even those which are hardly ideal from the standpoint of beneficence and fairness — may cause serious harm to the people who practice them, often much worse than the harm individuals may suffer within those traditions. It does not follow from this, however, that every tradition ought to be preserved and followed.

Thus such criteria for right action as freedom and autonomy, love, authority (including God's), and tradition are themselves justifiable in terms of beneficence and fairness, reinforcing the claim that the latter two are ultimate. There is yet another view of what is right and wrong which rejects all these specific criteria, but holds that what one ought to do is what a person having certain characteristics, or in a particular situation, would do or prefer or advise. Thus Brandt maintains[38] that the Hopi think what a person ought to do is what someone who is completely objective and knowledgeable would choose, rather than what causes least harm or is in line with tradition. He thus attributes to the Hopi a form of *ideal observer* theory, such as that proposed by Frank Chapman Sharp.[39]

Ideal observer theories, however, have a major problem. Certainly a person who is absolutely unbiased and has complete knowledge of all the relevant facts will make the right choice. But why require that the ideal observer be unbiased? The reason clearly is that he must not give one person greater consideration than others — which is, simply, that he must decide on the basis of fairness. We must also suppose that the ideal observer is benevolent — i.e., desires the good of the people affected; otherwise, he may choose evil for them, albeit impartially. In other words, to define the characteristics of an ideal observer whose moral judgments are correct, we must know what characteristics will enable him always to choose rightly. And in the theories discussed, he always chooses according to benevolence and fairness.

For the purposes of this discussion, I would include among ideal observer theories that of John Rawls. Rawls maintains that we should choose principles which an individual in the *original position* — who did not know what his state in life would be, and who did not even know how likely it was that people would occupy particular places in the social order — would want to have govern the actions of everyone.[40] The person in the original position is, unlike the Ideal Observer, ignorant of many things and may care nothing for anyone but himself. Yet in that position he must choose rules which are fair, and give his interests consideration equal to that of others. Otherwise, he will risk having others benefit at his expense. Furthermore, he will want rules which will insure him at least a minimal level of well being. In short, the person in the original position must choose principles consistent with fairness and beneficence. Indeed, if one asks why we should want rules chosen by a person in the original position as opposed to some other conditions is that other conditions would not necessarily result in a choice of fair and beneficent principles.

7. THE NEED FOR GENERAL PRINCIPLES AND THEORIES

A number of writers — particularly some working in the field of medical ethics — have questioned whether *any* general ethical principles or theories can enable us to generate solutions to specific cases, even where the facts of the case are taken fully into consideration.[41] They claim that the various moral rules and considerations we use in making choices cannot be reduced to a single moral theory or principle. As a result, it is necessary to go through a process of balancing. Since there is nothing to determine the relative weights of these rules and considerations, some have suggested that even these lower level guidelines are useless. We need, instead of following moral rules, simply to gather as many facts as possible and allow persons of good will to draw a conclusion about what to do.[42] One writer has suggested that what we ought to do is derive our rules from observed facts, the facts being what consequences are satisfactory to reflective individuals.[43]

When rules conflict, however, a person may find herself in a situation where nothing she could do seems right. Every alternative violates some rule or other. In these situations, the conscientious person will try to find a course of action which does the least wrong possible. To determine what this is, we need to know which rules apply, and which should take precedence in case of conflict. We need to know whether one is justified in making an exception to a rule in a given situation. We need to try to determine which circumstances of the case are morally relevant and which are not.

Far from indicating that general principles and theories have little to do with moral reasoning, we *require* criteria in order to determine how to adjudicate between different rules and considerations. And it is moral theories which attempt to set forth such criteria. Without general theories, we would be at a loss to know which rules to follow when we cannot follow all. Baruch Brody suggests that of several different moral considerations or rules, we weigh their significance in the case in question and then make our judgment.[44] We know which considerations (including the consequences of actions, rights, respect for persons, cost effectiveness, justice, and the relative virtuousness of the given actions) need to be weighed through moral intuition. Brody provides guidelines for deciding how weighty a given consideration is in a given case; thus the weight assigned to a patient's right to care depends in part on the burden to others of providing it, and the respect we should give his right to make decisions concerning his own health is partly dependent upon his rational competence. Yet we are then left with the questions of why *these* considerations and not others. Are the considerations all of equal importance, or should some take precedence over others? If a moral pluralism like Brody's is really true, these questions can't be answered. Brody states very definite views as to what adds to the weight of the given considerations. Yet an explanation of why these considerations have the weight they do is missing. If there is no basis for why the burdens to others of giving a person something he has a right to might diminish the weight that right carries, if this is just one more intuition to balance against all others, we will have a hard time defending a judgment that such a right is limited.

It might be objected that we only feel the necessity of determining the relative weights of different moral decisions because we must decide how to act; it does not follow from this that we are any more *justified* in deciding one way rather than another. There are two lines of response to this. First of all, in making moral decisions we usually consider some choices better than others — and for reasons. When we are unable to decide which course of action is better we know that the moral considerations are closely balanced or that we don't have enough facts to decide which we ought to follow. We can, in other words, tell the difference between a case in which we choose an action simply because we must make a decision and are not sure we are acting for the best and one in which we believe our choices are clear and justified. Second, if a theory which explains the relative weights we give to particular moral considerations is defensible, this will strengthen the view that one choice can in fact be better justified than another and need not be made simply because we are forced to choose.

According to the theory I have proposed we *can* give some answers to these questions by an appeal to the central purpose of morality. This central purpose explains why we have the principles we do and why virtually everyone ascribes to some principles of beneficence and fairness. And these principles in turn explain why our well-established moral beliefs are what they are. Furthermore, the central purpose helps us to determine whether specific rules are good ones to keep and when exceptions to them are justifiable. As we shall see, it also helps us to decide whether, given that a rule is a good one to follow, it ought to be enforced.

While people do not typically think of this purpose when they make moral judgments, its essential components: namely, beneficence (i.e., making people happy or avoiding and relieving causes of unhappiness), and fairness (or not letting some gain happiness at the expense of others) *are* in the minds of those consciously trying to determine what is right. People are also aware of the need to find a balance between the demands of beneficence and those of fairness when one consideration conflicts with another, and they generally do so by using fairness as a constraint on what beneficent actions are allowable. In other words, whatever we do to make others happy is good, just so long as making one person happier does not bring others to a lower level of happiness.

Nevertheless, these objections suggest a need for a detailed account of how we can make and justify moral decisions in complex cases, using the central purpose of morality as I have stated it. I shall provide an account in the last chapter of this book.

CHAPTER 7

AGENT-RELATIVE RESTRICTIONS

In[1] recent years criticisms of views like my own have focused on the objection that it ignores both the demands of moral principles and certain *agent-relative restrictions* (or *constraints*). The critics contend that because of these demands and restrictions, what an individual ought to do is at times *not* to bring about the best consequences — however 'best consequences' is to be interpreted. Rather the person ought to refrain from violating certain moral principles, even if by violating one he can prevent others from violating the same principle to an even greater degree. Looked at from either a consequentialist or an agent-neutral point of view, it would seem to be worse for ten innocent people to be killed than for one, no matter who did the killing. And it would be worse for ten lies than for one to be told, regardless of who the liar was. But those who favor agent-relative restrictions point to an additional consideration: from the point of view of the agent, it is worse to *be* the liar or the killer than to fail to prevent others from lying and killing.[2]

There are actually two separate issues here. One is whether the consequences of an action always determine its rightness or wrongness, and the other is whether the moral character of an action is independent of which person is the agent. A *consequentialist* theory is one that gives an affirmative answer to the first question, while an *agent-neutral* theory gives an affirmative answer to the second. As we shall see, it is possible for a non-consequentialist moral theory to be agent-neutral. Those which are not agent-neutral are never consequentialist; although such a theory might be imagined, it might not be coherent.[3] In what follows I shall argue for agent-neutrality; my views are consequentialist only in a modified sense, and I shall continue to try to show (as I have in the last two chapters) how both consequences and principles interact to determine whether or not an action is right.

As commonly viewed, both non-consequentialism and agent-relative restrictions would make morality more demanding than most sorts of consequentialism. Here we may be held to standards that require major sacrifices, of not only our own interests, but the interests of others. Proponents of both positions sometimes appear to maintain that there are certain things that no one ought ever to do, no matter what. A person of integrity and good moral character simply does not do certain things, *whatever the consequences.* Even when you could do an enormous amount of good by going against such a tenet — e.g., save many lives by killing one unoffending individual — you ought not to. While neither view entails absolutism — that an act is the breaking of a promise or that *I* would be the one to break it might be considered only one additional reason for me not to do it —, their proponents often talk that way. And it is sometimes hard to see the limits on the force of these restrictions when the role of consequences is disvalued.

There certainly is a strong element in common moral thinking for both non-consequentialism and agent-relativity. Sticking to principle is widely admired; those who suffer for the sake of an ideal are often considered among the greatest heroes. We all honor people who have gone to prison or have been tortured or executed rather than betray their comrades or recant some belief, even when we have not agreed with the causes for which they sacrificed so much.

Even when a person believes that he must — for good moral reasons — lie or break his word, he is apt to feel besmirched and dishonorable. In the C. S. Forester novel, Admiral Hornblower felt utterly disgraced after he swore on his word of honor that Napoleon was dead in order to stop a ship full of French soldiers headed to rescue the emperor from St. Helena.[4] He believed, quite justifiably, that when it was discovered that he had lied, he would be ruined and have no recourse but to resign from the Navy. Even though he believed that his lie was necessary to avert a new war, this did not erase the stain on his honor.

All proponents of both non-consequentialism and agent-relative restrictions hold that what one ought to do is not necessarily to bring about the best consequences. There are several other themes which appear in their discussions, which themes will be addressed in this chapter. First, there are certain considerations which constrain or outweigh the value of the consequences of an act. Second, some at least maintain that what is morally relevant in an action is the expression of, or effect upon, the agent's character, not the value of the states of affairs he brings about. Third, most espouse the view that it is worse to do something wrong than to allow that wrong to happen (or allow other people to do it). Yet while there is truth in all these positions, I shall argue that what is true does not entail either the need for agent-relative restrictions or a fully non-consequentialist position.

1. CONSEQUENCES AS COMMODITY OR AS OVERALL VALUE: THE ROLE OF DISTRIBUTION

Most moral theories — including consequentialist theories — have a place for the common belief that an agent ought sometimes to sacrifice the greatest good in order to avoid being the doer of harm herself. While some classical act-utilitarians appear committed to the view that if you can do more good for a greater number of people by telling a lie, it is better to lie, not all types of consequentialism define the best consequences in terms of maximizing some commodity like pleasure, happiness, or the satisfaction of desires or preferences. Some forms of consequentialism include in moral good the *distribution* of commodities, thus making room for considerations of fairness and justice.[5] If my own view is correctly characterized as consequentialist, it is certainly of this type. Such versions of consequentialism can, I believe, accommodate the possibility that one ought sometimes to follow moral principles rather than maximize a commodity.

Any theory that takes adequate account of distribution can acknowledge the value of institutions like moral practices and interpersonal commitments. It is unfair — and hence wrong — to lie or to shirk the duties imposed by one's roles in society. This feature of social roles takes the sting out of an argument which has been raised by Garcia[6] in favor of agent-restrictions and non-consequentialism. Garcia maintains that a person often assumes a special relationship with another person which then makes it worse for him than for others to take certain actions. Thus a parent is not generally required to go out of her way to help the children of strangers, but she is always morally bound to do what she can to help her own. Even if she could increase the amount of pleasure or desire satisfaction in some neutral sense by doing good for several children not related to her at the cost of neglecting her own child, she would be guilty of an additional sin. Over and above the harm done by neglecting *a* child, she would have violated the relationship of motherhood.[7]

A distribution-sensitive theory — consequentialist or not — can acknowledge that there is something wrong with violating special duties, even when the violation causes less direct harm to individuals than not violating these duties. These violations are worse because of (a) the immense benefits that accrue to having institutions of family, friendship, government, business, and so on, and (b) the fairness requirement that any person who accepts the benefits of those institutions share in their upkeep. But this wrong is not due to an *agent-relative* restriction; rather it is the result of a characteristic of the agent, such that it would be equally wrong for any agent with the same characteristics (i.e., being in the same relationship) to fail in those duties. It is not *who* the agent is that is relevant, but rather her role.

In short, I am distinguishing here between two sorts of value — namely, the happiness or good of individuals, and moral goodness or value. Because of the requirements of distribution, moral value does not consist in maximizing the total quantity of individual good. Distribution requirements in turn are centered in the principle of fairness and based upon the equal moral status of all persons. Nevertheless, other things being equal, the more individual good is attained, the more moral value is realized.

However individual good is defined, any distribution-sensitive consequentialism sets limits on the pursuit of that good — which limits are grounded in the basic equal worth of persons. What is critical to recognizing equal worth is not letting one individual's pursuit of his good infringe upon the chances of another person to attain hers. This is certainly consistent with Kant's second formulation of the categorical imperative that we ought to treat humanity as an end in itself, and it sets definite limits on increasing individual good. Whether this is called a deontological rather than a consequentialist position is not important. Regardless of labels, what matters is that we acknowledge that every person's good is worthy of pursuit for its own sake because every person is valuable, and that because everyone has equal value, no person should attain greater good at the cost of another's not being able to attain a comparable good. While this imposes restrictions on maximizing the good of particular individuals, however, these are not *agent-relative* restrictions.

Distribution sensitive consequentialism appears consistent with well-established moral beliefs. Most people believe that since keeping to moral principles brings major benefits, they ought to be followed in all but exceptional circumstances. When we stand to lose only Level 3 (or even some Level 2) goods (i.e., those which are not critical to any person's well being, the principle should be followed. Breaking moral rules, however, may be excusable when the cost to individuals of following it in the particular case is clearly and substantially greater than the benefits those individuals and others obtain when the rule is generally followed. Thus one may be permitted — even morally required — to lie to save a life since the primary benefit of truth-telling — being able to rely on what others say — is probably a Level 2 rather than a Level 1 good. One ought not, however, to betray one's comrades to the enemy when this would cost them their lives, even though one stands to suffer torture and death by keeping faith.[8] Well established moral opinion allows us to consider saving lives more valuable than truth-telling, but truth-telling more valuable than getting out of minor inconvenience, so that we may be justified in lying to save a life, but not to protect ourselves from slight inconveniences. According to my theory, the final test of whether it is permissible to violate a moral principle is whether doing so satisfies a more fundamental principle — namely, that of beneficence within the bounds of fairness -- which principle can be expressed in the central purpose of morality. This principle should never be violated, since it is the source of justification for all the other principles.

There are a number of considerations which make it usually wrong, even on purely consequentialist grounds, to violate moral principles. One such consideration, which applies especially to telling even 'benevolent' lies, is that of respecting a person's autonomy. As Thomas Hill points out, being in rational control of one's life often requires that we know painful truths. Even if this knowledge does not affect our actions, it may well affect the attitudes we take.[9] Being autonomous is something which nearly everyone considers part of a good life, so that interfering with a person's ability to exert rational control diminishes his good. Yet Hill admits that respect for autonomy may sometimes be overridden. As in earlier examples, if one person has very good reason to think that a particular truth would be utterly devastating to another, and no reason to believe that the other person wishes to know, he might be justified in telling a lie.

Moral rules have been found over the centuries to be useful guides in helping people live together in harmony and in reaping many benefits. We cannot calculate all the possible consequences of our actions; even though it may seem to us that telling a lie may bring more good than harm, we usually can't be sure. So even a strict act-utilitarian can argue, as Mill does,[10] that we ought to tell the truth. A further reason for uncertainty noted by Jonathan Bennett[11] is the ability of a person who is tempted to break a rule to deceive herself about the situation.

In short, when fair distribution of goods among individuals is considered part of moral good, a view which favors maximizing moral good can account for those situations in which specific principles should take precedence over considerations of benefit and harm to individuals and when they should not. In addition, the inclusion of fairness can account for special duties people have resulting from their roles and relationships in a completely agent-neutral way.

2. WHEN SHOULD WE DAMN THE CONSEQUENCES?

There is certainly something magnificent in the picture of a person standing up for principle and damning the consequences. Admirable as it is for a man to sacrifice his life for speaking out against tyranny or endure torture rather than betray his comrades, we should note that in these cases his actions are most likely to save the lives of others. When a person refuses to violate a principle despite the fact that this will cause *other people* — including perhaps some who have no say in the matter — to suffer greatly, our views are likely to change.

There are few deontologists who truly believe that we ought to stick to principle in every situation, no matter what the cost.[12] Certainly few non-philosophers believe this. Hornblower succeeds, through telling a lie and backing it by giving his word of honor as an officer, in averting an action which could well have plunged all Europe into renewed hostilities. He is devastated by what he has done and expects nothing but disgrace for himself. In addition, there might be significant moral costs, as well as those to himself and his innocent family: perhaps Hornblower's lie would make the word of British naval officers less trusted. After all it was the utter reliability of an officer's word of honor that made the French captain accept Hornblower's improbable story. Yet preventing the deaths of thousands was, Hornblower thought, worth these costs. Had another Napoleonic war ensued when he had an opportunity to prevent it, he would surely have felt even worse than he did after telling the lie. And I think most would agree that such feelings would have been appropriate. According to the view proposed in Chapter 6, Hornblower both *ought not* to have lied and *ought* to have done something to prevent renewed war, but in this situation the *better* — or least bad — thing to do was to lie with the intent of preventing war.

Bernard Williams argues, however, that upholding certain principles even at the cost of permitting much greater harm is in accordance with our ordinary moral intuitions. As an example, he poses a situation in which a man named Jim is captured by guerrillas who are about to execute twenty Indian prisoners.[13] The guerrilla leader says he will spare the lives of nineteen Indians if Jim will kill one himself. Williams maintains — and claims that ordinary moral thinking is in accord with this — that Jim ought to refuse.[14]

It will be instructive to discuss in depth Williams' contrived case of Jim and the Indians. I am not at all sure that even a classical utilitarian, let alone anyone whose theory includes a principle of distribution or fairness, would conclude that Jim ought to shoot the one Indian. For one thing, in any realistic situation Jim would have no reason to think that the guerrilla leader would keep his word and spare the other Indians. Nor, on the other hand, could he be certain that the leader really will kill all twenty Indians if he refuses to kill one. The offer might be just a trap to get Jim in trouble with the authorities, or a government army might appear to rescue the expected victims. Since Jim doesn't *know* what the guerrillas will do, and has control only over his own actions, he might well be right — simply on the principle of avoiding least harm — to refuse.[15]

Even if Jim is virtually certain that the guerrillas will kill the Indians if he refuses and will spare the others if he shoots one, there could still be good reasons for refusing. According to my own theory, one factor that would make a crucial difference as to what Jim ought to do is whether the Indian Jim would kill would be among those executed by the guerrillas if he refuses. In Williams' example, he is; if not, however, then Jim ought to refuse, for if he kills the one Indian, he would be taking the life of a person whose life is not already forfeit and who would otherwise live. On the grounds that it is worse to take from a person something he expects to have than to fail to prevent an equivalent loss to others who expect that loss, I would say that in this case Jim ought not to kill the Indian. His doing so would be similar to the surgeon in Harman's example who removes the organs from one healthy person to provide transplants for several people who need those organs to survive.[16]

On the other hand, if that Indian would be among those executed (as he is in Williams's example), I believe that — given very strong probability that the captain will do exactly what he says he will — it would be better for Jim to agree to the deal. I expect that in this scenario all twenty Indians would beg him to accept; who wouldn't prefer to reduce his odds of being killed from 100% to 5%?

Granted, if Jim does kill the Indian, then even if the guerrillas keep their promise to spare the other nineteen, we would hope that he would feel remorse. Any morally sensitive person would have nightmares about having done such a thing. No one who has any concern for doing what is right could help but be shaken by being in a situation where his doing a grave wrong is the only way to prevent worse wrongs. Yet Jim should also feel remorse if he refuses and all twenty Indians are killed. His own sense of moral purity will hardly suffice to wipe out the evil of twenty deaths, of which he might have prevented nineteen. This appears to be much the same sort of situation discussed in the last chapter; whatever Jim does, he harms someone and does something which he ought not to do. The question is, however, whether his least bad course of action is to shoot the one Indian or allow the guerrillas to shoot twenty.

Thomas Hill has forcefully put forth another consideration for cases where one must decide whether to avert evil by committing an evil.[17] One reason for not committing a lesser evil oneself is its effect on one's relationships with others. When we hurt another person, especially a friend, family member, or any individual for whom we have a special responsibility, it damages our relationship. This damage goes beyond the specific injury to the other person and adds to its wrongness. If Jim were, for example, a close friend of the Indian he is invited to kill, the wrong he would do by killing that Indian would be greater than it would otherwise have been. But as Hill also notes, the importance of good relationships to others does not always dictate following principle over consequences; for example, if one tells the truth to a murderer about his proposed victim's whereabouts, this is a betrayal of the victim, which, should the victim survive, would ruin the agent's relationship with him (or with his family if the murderer succeeds).

The case would also be altered if, as in a similar example proposed by Alan Gewirth,[18] Jim would have to torture the Indian to death. In this case, additional wrong would be done to the Indian he would kill, above and beyond the loss of his life. In this variant the Indian would lose more than he would lose if Jim refused the offer, and might lose more than the other Indians would gain. If so, they would then benefit at his expense.[19]

In short, there are situations in which following a principle regardless of the consequences is morally worse than not doing so. Whether it is right or wrong to damn the consequences depends on many factors — the degree of harm to some individual(s) and also the degree of unfairness, as well as the factor of uncertainty about the effects of our actions. Other than the principle of beneficence bounded by fairness, there are conceivable circumstances when any subsidiary principle might justifiably be violated. Nor does the question of whether and when consequences to specific individuals should be overruled depend upon the bare fact that the harm or injustice would be done by the agent rather than by others.

3. CHARACTER AND RULES

Some philosophers, such as Phillipa Foot[20] and Stephen Darwall,[21] maintain that character is central to morality, and that, since this takes precedence over consequences, we ought to take care of our character before looking to the consequences of what we do. Kant, of course, held that not only is a good will good in itself, but it is the *only* thing that is good in itself.[22] On this sort of view, other goods like health, wealth, and political liberty are good only insofar as they contribute to the making of a good character, will, or — if one is religious — soul. Happiness is good only if it is a result of consciousness of good character; it would not be good if undeserved. What happens to individuals' bodies or feelings or possessions is, by comparison, unimportant; what counts is how people respond to the vicissitudes of life and what their response does to and demonstrates about their character. Indeed, according to Garcia[23] the reason that intending a bad effect is worse than allowing an unintended bad effect to occur is that a bad intention is a manifestation of a bad character.

This high-minded view of what is good and the kind of life we ought to lead is vastly appealing, but we need to think a little more about what is involved in the notion of character. What *is* a good character, and why should developing one be of the first importance? Good character has at least two components. One is acting morally as an end in itself; the other is living up to certain ideals or cultivating certain virtues, which virtues include acting morally, but may include additional features, such as courage, gentility, or the improvement of one's mind.[24] It may in fact be difficult to discriminate between what is required by an ideal and what is required by morality.

Let us look at each of these in turn. The requirement of good character that a person act for the sake of doing what is morally right typically involves following moral principles. The morally good person, however, must not only act on the basis of valid principles and not rules that are arbitrary, pointless, or harmful, but he must also be able to weigh conflicting principles in order to follow those which are most important. Any theory which holds that morality consists of following principles or rules needs for its justification to distinguish which principles are *worthy* of being followed from those which are not.[25] Further, the grounds on which principles are chosen also determine which principles should take precedence in those situations where they conflict — e.g., that we may break a promise to attend a social engagement in order to save someone's life. And the grounds — whatever they are — on which principles are chosen in virtually all theories have some reference to the consequences of following the principles. The consequences referred to may be the consequences of everyone's following them, or those of particular individuals' following them. The consequences have reference to what would happen to persons and their ends if those principles were adopted (individually or universally), and the extent to which individuals would care whether they were followed.

If good character is thought to consist of blindly following a set of rules regardless of the consequences, the world might be better without it. Just as a strong-willed or intelligent person is more apt to act rationally than a weak-willed or stupid one, the morally principled are more likely to do good than those who are not. But occasionally they can do much harm, and it is rare that people agree that this harm is justified simply because those doing the harm acted from some principle. While we are more likely to be moral if we stick to rules nearly all the time, being moral also involves taking into consideration the reasons or grounds for those rules, as well as for breaking them on those rare occasions when it is clear that the spirit of morality requires it.

The second aspect of good character involves living up to ideals or in accordance with certain virtues. Foot, for example, says that we ought to act from the virtue of benevolence. But what is benevolence, but desiring, protecting, and working for the *good* of individuals?[26] Surely this means that the benevolent person must act in accordance with the expected consequences of his actions on other human beings. Furthermore, it would seem that we consider benevolence to be a virtue *because* it typically brings good to individual people.

Foot argues, however, that there is no reason to assume that we should judge character traits on the basis of the consequences they are likely to bring. She says that we have no reason to suppose that states of affairs are *morally* good or bad. To characterize them as such is to assume the truth of consequentialism. Yet we must have *some* grounds for judging character traits and some reasons for thinking the traits of generosity and honesty are better than miserliness and deceitfulness. As with principles, traits of character and ideals must be evaluated in accordance with their overall moral worth. In assessing whether a particular virtue or ideal is worthy, we must consider the grounds upon which it is considered good to inculcate that virtue or ideal.

For the most part, virtues are virtues because of the good they bring. As noted in Chapter 4, some character traits once thought virtues have gone out of style because we have come to believe that they are at least sometimes harmful or promote unfairness. Gentility in women, for example, has traditionally been considered a virtue because of the pleasantness it brings to social and family life. Yet gentility is now less prized because some see it as encouraging passivity in women, which passivity contributes to their subordination. Thus we might endorse gentility with limits: i.e., that women — and men, too — ought to be courteous and considerate of people's feelings, but at the same time speak up when their own or others' interests are at stake. In judging whether and to what extent a character trait is a good one to develop or an ideal is a good one to live by, we need to consider whether having or living by it is for the good of everyone alike — or is in accordance with whatever are valid and fundamental grounds for moral judgments.[27]

We need to appeal to these grounds in determining not only what character traits are worth developing and what ideals we should live by, but also the *extent* to which they should be pursued and which to pursue when they conflict. As is well known, Aristotle maintained that we should, as a rule, live by the mean.[28] Courage is the mean between cowardice and foolhardiness; generosity is the mean between stinginess and profligacy. The virtuous mean is not merely a middle ground between the extreme vices (e.g., to flee 50% of the time and fight the other 50%); rather it is doing what is right or appropriate for the situation. In fact, for some character traits, there is no mean, for any manifestation of it is either always bad (e.g., cruelty) or always good (e.g., justice). A courageous person faces those dangers which ought to be faced, and the generous one gives to others when he ought to, and to the extent that a person is virtuous, he is never cruel and always just. In order to know when to face a danger or give something away, we must appeal to standards of right and wrong action. And, as with principles, these standards seem most plausibly to be grounded in what is good for everyone alike, and it is the tendency to promote whatever it is that is morally right that constitutes good character.

The two components of character — i.e., living by the demands of morality and living up to ideals or in accordance with virtues — may sometimes be discordant; sticking to principle sometimes conflicts with benevolence and other virtues. We can admire and respect immensely a person who always acts from principle, even when we disagree with her principles. But we may well think less of her, especially when her principled actions demonstrate a cold or rigid character. For example, suppose she disowns her daughter who has gotten pregnant out of wedlock. We can respect the strength of her convictions — and even share her views on extra-marital sex — but still disapprove of her lack of compassion. How we should balance such conflicts between particular principles and particular virtues has its grounds in the effects of either individual adherence or of everyone's adherence to those principles and virtues.

In any moral system that pays attention to fairness, a person has certain spheres of responsibility so that the work of the world is divided up in a relatively efficient manner. Each person ought to do her share of that work. In accordance with this assignment of work, it seems eminently reasonable to maintain that each person has responsibility for her own character, and thus ought not to allow herself to get out of the habit of obeying important moral rules. It does not follow, however, that this responsibility never allows us to break those rules in extreme circumstances. Moral purity (considered as following the rules) is a great good, but there is no reason to think that it ought always in every circumstance to take precedence over other considerations.

The notion that we ought to care for our character, and live by moral principles and ideals thus has ample grounds in any moral theory, consequentialist and agent-neutral, as well as deontological and agent-relative. If everyone paid attention to his or her character and lived entirely by principle, the world would be a far better place. People do much more good by consistently refusing to engage in morally questionable activities, even if on rare occasions they might do more good by violating a principle.

Williams argues[29] that a person who truly has certain character traits that we all agree are admirable and ought to be cultivated cannot be constantly thinking of the consequences of his actions. Would I be truly honest if every time I opened my mouth I thought first of what the effects of my utterances would be rather than whether what I was about to say was true? Perhaps not, but this is not what even a thoroughgoing consequentialist needs to recommend. Since telling the truth is nearly always best, any moral theorist ought to recommend the development of habits of truth-telling, so that we will be truthful almost automatically. (It might also be noted that saying whatever one thinks is true *without* considering the consequences is not always a good thing — e.g., by revealing information that could gravely harm others.)

Furthermore, as Railton points out,[30] it may be better overall even on a purely consequentialist view for people on rare occasions to bring about worse consequences as a result of sticking to a habit which is generally virtuous. We might even say with Williams[31] that we should regard some possible alternatives as unthinkable, even if on extremely rare occasions we might bring about more moral good than harm by choosing those alternatives. In such exceptional situations, we would have to take into consideration not only the effect on one's character of violating the rule, but also the fact that we would violate the principle of fairness by breaking — even for the benefit of others — a rule which many people have obeyed at significant cost to themselves.

Finally, even if by lying or killing I could prevent more lies or murders, those who would commit the other sins are, after all, responsible for their own actions. My not lying or not killing is not going to *make* them lie or kill. Because human actions are so unpredictable, the possibility that criminals will relent or be prevented from their evil deeds by other events cannot as a rule be dismissed entirely. If I were to kill someone because I believed this to be the only way to prevent five murders, and later discover that those murders would not have taken place anyway, I would have great cause for remorse. And if those murders did take place when I refused to kill, I would surely feel terrible, but probably not to the same extent, because I could never be sure that my killing would have been absolutely required to prevent them.[32]

Some of these issues may be clarified by noting the difference between the moral features of an action and the moral character of the person who performs it. Kant's saying that only those acts done from duty have moral worth should perhaps be interpreted as Barbara Herman does[33] to mean that only those acts which are done with due regard to moral principles indicate good moral character in the agent. It does *not* mean that his action can have no additional motives, such as love for a spouse or devotion to a discipline or any of the innumerable spurs to action that humans have, to have moral worth. In fact, Herman maintains that the Categorical Imperative does not itself motivate any action, but evaluates the reasons for which an act might be done to indicate whether it (or its omission) is morally acceptable. Morally good people want to do what is right and judge their actions and other motives by the moral standards to which they adhere. What they actually do may be judged by others — even objectively — as wrong, but if they have honestly and thoughtfully believed it morally acceptable, such mistakes do not reflect upon their character. Those who do what happens to be right only from selfish motives have no better character than many who do wrong, but their *acts* are still morally good, even if their characters are not.[34]

The moral value of acts depends, then, upon the good or harm they cause, as well as their fairness, and this is distinct from the question of whether the person performing them has a good will — although of course the better his will the more likely he is to do good and not do wrong. Moreover, while the better the person's will the better his moral character, and while nothing can be more central to a person's goodness (as opposed to what may be good for him), no one can have a good will who does not have a conception of what it is to do good acts and what kinds of acts are right and which wrong. Without some such conception of right and wrong, a person's good will acts in a vacuum and has no object — and thus to all intents and purposes does not exist.

In short, the person of good character cannot avoid looking at the consequences of what he does and at what the consequences would be if everyone acted in the same way. These consequences determine both what principles are valid and which should take precedence in cases of conflict. Thus the assessment of character cannot be divorced from the consequences of one's action. Furthermore, each individual has responsibility for his own character, the development of which is dependent upon what he does and not upon the actions of others. Every person *ought* to cultivate a good character since having one will better enable him to do right. This, however, does not make the duty to cultivate a good character agent-relative, for everyone has this duty. The responsibility for one's own character does add an element of badness to doing something wrong, for in addition to the moral wrongness of the act's being performed is the wrongness of having damaged one's character. This may explain the appeal of agent-relative restrictions, but responsibility for character is not agent-relative.

4. INTEGRITY

Closely related to the notion of character is that of *integrity*. Williams maintains that for Jim to kill the one Indian would be a violation of his integrity.[35] The reason is that killing — apart from its agent-neutral wrongness — goes against an important part of Jim's beliefs, which are central to his image of himself and which are part of who he is. An even clearer example Williams proposes is the scientist who has to choose between unemployment and a job doing research in chemical warfare — an enterprise he is against on principle. The scientist has a particularly strong reason — over and above anything objectively wrong with chemical warfare — not to take the job, because doing so would violate his integrity.

I think we can agree with Williams that people have a very important reason not to violate basic principles in which they believe without assuming that this is a special agent-relative restriction. A person with integrity usually has a better character than one who doesn't. A person who has no core beliefs which are part of her identity is not someone you can count on. Nor is she able to take pride in herself as someone who can live by an ideal. Thus any person has both moral and self-regarding reasons to behave in accordance with some basic principles.

Furthermore, the beliefs an individual holds may make what is right for him to do different from what it is right for another to do. If Ron is a firm believer in nonviolence, then perhaps he ought to refuse military service, while Sam, an avid patriot, ought to serve. But I say "perhaps." While one's moral beliefs are an important factor, they may be overridden — especially when those beliefs are in conflict with major moral principles. If their country is in grave danger from a vicious enemy, both Ron and Sam ought to serve — Ron perhaps in the Medical Corps or some other noncombatant role. On the other hand, if their country is the aggressor against a small and innocent neighbor, it would be morally better for them both to refuse to fight in that war.

One's moral beliefs are like many other personal characteristics which may be a factor in determining what one ought to do. If X sees Y being robbed, many facts about X may be relevant to determining what he ought to do. If he is young and strong, or armed, perhaps he ought to intervene directly. If not, perhaps he ought instead to call the police, since direct intervention might only result in two victims rather than one. These characteristics are not agent-relative reasons because *any* agent with the same characteristics would have the same reason to act as X ought to act. Likewise, if Ron's nonviolence is a reason for him not to serve in the military, this reason would count equally for any person with the same beliefs. And reasons based on integrity and personal moral beliefs — while extremely weighty — are not absolute. Should a white supremacist maintain his integrity by following his core beliefs? I think only other white supremacists would approved of such "integrity."[36]

Jonathan Bennett has argued[37] that endorsing personal integrity does not support agent-relativity. Sticking to principle and developing one's character is a special responsibility of agents, and this is true of all agents. If so, any person who violates a rule in which he believes has done more wrong than a person who does not know — or disagrees with — the rule. If I *care* about my character and integrity, then I will also feel shame for my failure; in addition to doing what is morally wrong I will have fallen short of a personal ideal, and my wrongdoing will have greater disvalue for me than it would have had if I didn't care. But the failure to realize an ideal is not necessarily a moral failure, and even when it is, failure does not always add moral disvalue to the moral wrongness of the act.

In other words my regard for my character does not make my breaking a promise any better or any worse than if I had no such regard. Obviously my breaking a promise will say different things about me, depending upon whether or not I care — i.e., moral weakness versus moral insensitivity or ignorance — and it may have different effects on my character. If I don't care, the promise breaking is unlikely to make me any different. If I do, it might make it easier for me to continue breaking promises, or I might be so ashamed that I will make special efforts to see that I don't do so again. These effects are moral consequences, since they will influence my future acts, but they do not seem to be essentially different from other conditions which influence future actions. For example, which specific other people find out about my broken promise — and how much they care — will influence how I may be penalized and thus how I will act in the future.

In short, acting on principle is an important part of moral integrity, but it needs to be balanced with an ability to recognize and follow the more important principles when principles conflict, as well as to take account of circumstances which alter the weight of principles. The value of preserving one's integrity, moreover, does not depend upon agent-relativity. Standing up for what he believes is a trait which tends to make any person act morally. But if his beliefs are false or inapplicable in the circumstances, he may be brought to do worse as a result of them.

5. ACTIVE VERSUS PASSIVE HARM TO OTHERS

One of the persuasive features of the view that there are agent-relative restrictions on our producing the best consequences is that in general, we do seem to think it worse to bring about some evil oneself than to allow the same or greater evil to occur. For example, it is surely worse to drown another person than to fail to save that person from drowning. Thomas Nagel, for example, argues that there is a distinctive moral difference between the evil one does and the evil that happens, and that we are often not justified in doing evil — in aiming at it — even for the sake of preventing worse evils of the same kind from happening.[38] Intending evil adds to the wrongness of my doing the evil; from my perspective, the goodness or badness of what happens and the goodness or badness of what I do count separately.

But this is not necessarily so. Rachels[39] gives an example where it is not. In one scenario the uncle and sole heir of a rich boy holds the child's head under the bath water until he drowns. In another his nephew falls in the tub, hits his head, and is knocked unconscious. The uncle sees it all happen, could easily pull the boy from the water, but instead does nothing and lets him die. I think that most people would hold the uncle equally blameworthy in both scenarios. In both cases the uncle's intentions are thoroughly evil; the only difference is that in the former case he is willing to take a positive action, whereas in the latter he may only be willing to take advantage of a situation which allows the child's death. That the former is premeditated and the latter not may make the degree of punishment greater — not because the uncle's drowning the boy is morally worse than his failing to pull him out of the water but because, in general, someone who actively kills has a greater potential to kill again and is thus more dangerous.

Frances Kamm has proposed an ingenious principle for deciding when it may be acceptable to kill one individual who would not otherwise be killed in order to save the lives of more people.[40]   If the act which will save the many is at least as intimately connected (in a causal sense) to that good as it is to causing the harm, it is justifiable.   On this criterion, it is, for example, morally acceptable to throw a switch that will deflect a trolley from the path by which it will inevitably kill five people onto another track which will cause it to kill only one person; the same act that will kill one will be just as instrumental in saving five. Kamm would by this criterion no doubt agree with me that Jim would be justified in killing one of the Indians who will be killed anyway, since the causal connections between Jim's alternatives and the deaths of the Indians are the same as in the above case.

Both Bennett and Kamm have clearly hit on an important feature of moral relevance: on my theory, if what I am about to do will causally hinder the central purpose of morality, then I ought not to do it. Likewise, if my failure to do some action will causally hinder the realization of that purpose, I ought to perform the action. If the causal connections between my act or my failure to act are relatively direct, so that — given the circumstances — what I do or don't do is bound to make a difference, then the ought is clear. If, on the other hand, the causal connection is indirect, it may be possible, for all we know, that what I do won't be decisive. The guerrilla captain may relent or the Indians may be rescued in time by their friends. Then Jim's killing the one Indian would have no good effect, but it certainly would have had a bad one. In the particular example, however, Williams demands that we *assume* that it is certain that all twenty Indians will be killed if Jim does not kill one. This is hardly an assumption that anyone in a real life situation can make; nonetheless, given this assumption, my theory implies that Jim would do better to kill the one Indian.

I have argued above and elsewhere,[41] that the reason it is usually worse to inflict harm directly than to allow harm to occur or be inflicted by others is that it disrupts normal expectations. In general it is worse to take something away from a person than not to give that same thing to the individual, because the loss of something one possesses is usually harder to bear than not getting a thing one has never had. Furthermore, it is unfair, for the agent benefits at the expense of others by making an exception of himself to the practice of protecting possessions such as life, self-esteem, and material goods. If, however, the person has been led to expect the good in question, then he will be just as disappointed by not getting the good as he would be by having it taken away, so there would be no moral difference.

What we expect is dependent upon many things, including the availability of the good (or capacity to avoid harm), the difficulty of obtaining the good or avoiding the harm, and the traditions in the society in question. In medical care, for example, certain procedures are normally expected; others are considered extraordinary. Which procedures fall into which category depends on the state of medicine in the time and place under consideration. In a poverty-stricken society procedures which are considered routine in North America or Western Europe would be held extraordinary. People consider it worse to withhold routine care than to withhold extraordinary care. People come to expect routine care; indeed, this is what makes it routine. This is why practitioners who violate these standards of care are liable in malpractice suits, whereas they are not held to standards beyond those upheld in their society.

In those cases where the preservation of life may not be a good, it is still a more serious matter to stop routine care — such as feeding and medication to control pain or other distressing symptoms — than it is to stop extraordinary measures such as dialysis. The difference between routine and extraordinary care is largely dependent upon cost. Not only is the monetary cost to society a factor, but even more so is the burden of suffering for the patient relative to expected benefit. Dialysis may be worth the discomfort, time, and expense it entails for a person able to live a full life, but not for one who has no further hope of enjoyment or accomplishment.

In general, then, we tend to think it worse to kill than to fail to prevent a death, to steal than to prevent an equivalent loss of goods, to lie than to prevent deception — *provided* that the things we fail to prevent would normally be expected in the usual course of events and that it would be more burdensome to all concerned for the agent in question to prevent the evil than to avoid inflicting it.

Thus if I could easily throw a life preserver to a drowning child, and do not, I am worthy of blame, for it is only expected of people that they help in such circumstances. Of course, if I had pushed the child into the water, this would be worse. The reason, however, is that, but for my pushing her, the child would not have been in the water in the first place, and would have no expectation of danger. And the notion of expectations explains why it would be worse for Jim to kill the one Indian if that Indian would not otherwise be killed than if he were among those designated for execution.

Similar remarks apply to the trolley cases. If I throw the switch, I know that I will save five people and kill one, whereas if I don't I will allow five to die, but will not kill one. The person who dies if I throw the switch is never in danger unless I intervene; for this reason, I would do relatively more harm to him by throwing the switch than the harm I would do to any of the five I fail to save by not throwing the switch. On the other hand, there is a common notion that numbers *do* count, with an expectation that where several people are in imminent danger of death we might be justified in killing one person (not otherwise in danger) to prevent their deaths. This is consistent with Hill's discussion of how a Kantian might permit harming some to save many — if this is a rule rational people could agree on, as Hill suggests, because it would give them a smaller probability of death over the long run.[42]

Another exception applies to some of Kamm's variations. She imagines a situation where deflecting the trolley sets off a rock slide which in turn kills one person who is not otherwise in danger. Since normally, at least, we don't know that the rock slide will occur or that the one individual couldn't get away, we can't be sure that not throwing the switch is necessary for preventing the death of a person who will not be killed unless the switch is thrown. We could be justified in throwing the switch, given that our doing so is not bound to result in the death of anyone. One problem with such examples, however, is that they are so contrived that it is impossible to know what any given individual would really expect in these situations.

One final point: intending to do evil is usually worse than allowing it to happen, not so much because of the badness of the thing done, but because of the disposition of the agent and the potential his having that disposition has to bring about further evil. If I am the sort of person who would push a child into the water and let her drown, I am much more dangerous than I would be if I would not do that, but would not take minimal trouble to save a child that was already drowning.

6. THE BOTTOM LINE

Kamm argues that a person may have a right which cannot justifiably be violated in order to protect the rights of others, without this protection being based on agent-relative constraints. If, she says, a supposed right can be set aside whenever doing so would provide more good, or even whenever doing so would prevent more violations of the same right, this supposed right is not a real one. Its possessor has no protection, and he is no longer considered a person in the same sense that we usually think of persons, namely as those to whom certain things cannot be done.[43] Kamm points out, however, that respect for rights is centered in the potential *victims* of rights violations, not in the agent. It is not the fact that the agent is doing the wrong that makes it wrong, but what this does to the victim. Thus she argues for restrictions on what we may do in the name of preventing wrongs, but denies that these are agent-relative restrictions.

I agree with Kamm on nearly all of this, most particularly her views on agent relativity. Yet most of the rights we recognize can be overridden in some circumstances, and, if so, consequences matter when one must decide whether to follow a particular principle. My right not to be killed may be set aside if I attack another person with deadly force, or if I am a combatant in a war, or perhaps even if — as in some of Kamm's own trolley examples — my being killed is a necessary result of efforts to save the lives of several others equally in danger. One might say that the exceptions can be written into the description of the right, but this is not feasible. My friend whom I have promised to meet for lunch has a right to my being there, but there are innumerable circumstances which could excuse me from coming. There is no way that these could be spelled out in advance, and a vague statement to the effect that she has this right unless some more important considerations arise is useless as a guarantee.

On the other hand, Kamm is quite correct in supposing that there is a bottom line which people ought to be able to count on and, if this line is crossed, they have a right to be aggrieved. Without this bottom line, a person really is not being treated as a person in the full sense. The bottom line is, I believe, the basic equality of persons, expressed in the general principle that no one ought to benefit at another's expense. What this means is that no one ought to receive goods when his attaining these goods results in others being both worse off than they would otherwise be and worse off than she would be with those goods. In general, particular principles such as truth telling can be viewed as subordinate to the more fundamental principle of beneficence within the bounds of fairness — which principle should never be violated.

In Williams' example, the Indian Jim is invited to kill is no worse off as a result of the other nineteen being saved than he will be if Jim doesn't kill him. On the other hand, if that Indian is not one of the group designated for execution, he *would* be worse off than he would have been had Jim not killed him, as well as worse off than the Indians saved, and this is why in that variation of the case Jim probably ought not to shoot him, even though his doing so would save the lives of many others. On the other hand, if I fail to meet my friend for lunch because I come across an accident where I can offer significant aid, she is worse off as a result, but she is not worse off than those I have helped. Thus I would not have done wrong, although I still ought to try to make amends. Thus the basic right of receiving equal consideration with all other people can explain why we may sometimes set lesser rights aside, while at the same time it places limits on what rights can be set aside and under what circumstances.

The restrictions which are generally recognized are not really agent-relative except in the sense that the agent is typically in a better position than anyone else to do certain things. These things include controlling her own actions and molding her own character. These restrictions apply to *all* agents, however, as does the meta-rule that we ought, *ceteris paribus,* to follow those moral rules which have been shown to bring benefits, reduce harm and insecurity, and coordinate social existence. When Jim is in the dreadful position of having to choose between killing one or allowing twenty to die, what he ought to do is not determined by who *he* is, but rather by his role as *the agent* in the case and by the circumstances — which would apply equally to anyone else in his position. Anyone else in the same situation ought to do the same thing that Jim ought, whatever that might be.

7. CONCLUSION

In short, agent-relative restrictions do not pose a major threat to my theory or any other which gives due attention to fairness. Such a theory allows for individual good to be sacrificed at times for moral principles. But the reason why this may be done, according to such views, is the great moral value (which may include both more individual good or showing equal respect for all) of acting on principle. There may also be occasions when moral value can only be preserved by violating a particular principle, and in such situations, violation is sometimes justifiable. But I also believe that all but the most extreme deontologists would agree that such occasional violations are morally acceptable.

From the above I think we can see that restrictions on maximizing individual good have a place in any distribution-sensitive moral theory, although they do not play the role some recent writers would give them. There are, as we have seen, constraints which nearly everyone recognizes. These restrictions are, however, outweighed when significant harm to a person is likely to result from the agent's adhering to some particular moral principle. Generally, I ought to obey moral principles even though I could bring more happiness to myself or others by violating them, because it would be unfair of me not to. On the other hand, when actual harm to individuals can result, it may very well be worse to follow a moral principle. Again, this does not apply to the principle of beneficence within the bounds of fairness — expressed here as the central purpose of morality — which ought never to be violated.

I have also argued that there are no grounds for believing that there are agent-relative restrictions in the sense that there is wrongness over and above the moral harm produced by the agent, which wrongness results from *his* having perpetrated the act. Certain characteristics of all agents generally, of all agents who occupy similar social roles, and of the expectations people have, make an agent's doing certain things worse than his failing to prevent equivalent harm. These include the fact that people have more control over their own actions and character than over external events and the acts of others, the moral importance based on fairness of people's fulfilling roles which they have undertaken, and the fact that people are more harmed by having something taken from them which they had counted on having than never having it in the first place. These facts, which give rise to the intuitions to which agent relative restrictions appeal, are easily accounted for on nearly all moral theories, and certainly in mine.

CHAPTER 8

OUGHTS, OBLIGATIONS AND THE BEST

The purpose of morality, as I have argued in Chapter 7 is (not including what we should do for sentient nonpersons) the greatest well-being or happiness of each person that is compatible with a like level of well-being or happiness for all. Anything a person can do which helps promote that end is good to do. And whatever is in that person's power which will do the most to promote that end is the morally best thing he or she can do.

What a person ought (morally) to do is for the most part a subclass of what is best for him to do: namely, what is necessary for him to do to promote the purpose of morality. Moral oughts are largely things one ought *not* to do, things that harm others. But they also include doing what is one's fair share in enterprises of the sort discussed in Chapter 6. Furthermore, they include things one could do to benefit others when one is in a particularly good position to help in some specific way. People with special training or who have money or goods which are readily available, ought to put them to use for the benefit of others when they are in a better position to promote the overall purpose of morality than are other individuals.

But what one ought to do may or may not be an *obligation* or a *duty.*[1] There is behavior which we consider so essential for a decent society that we think people ought to be punished if they fail to conform to it. Different societies have different ideas about what particular actions are demanded, but the distinction between what is required and what is good and morally important, but not demanded, is widely recognized across cultures.

For example, if you are hard up and I have money to spare, it would be nice of me to lend you some. If I am in a particularly good position to help you, I probably ought to do so, but if I choose not to, no one will blame me. On the other hand, if I have *promised* to lend you money, the situation is very different. Then I am *required* to do so, even if it becomes inconvenient. If I don't, I have behaved badly and am considered worthy of blame. I may even be punished by law, if the promise was a legal contract. I am *obliged* to lend you the money, and you have a *right* to get it. In this chapter I shall try to spell out the distinctions between what is best to do, what we ought to do, what we are obligated to do, and what we have a right to. I shall argue that these distinctions enable us to resolve the contemporary debate about

193

agent-relative prerogatives.

What I shall try to do in this chapter is to indicate how this three-way distinction between oughts, obligations, and the best one can do accounts for many well-established beliefs. This distinction, moreover, can be used by any moral theory, even though the specific cases of what is and is not obligatory, etc. may vary from one theory to another.

1. OBLIGATIONS AND SANCTIONS

1.1 Obligations Are Required

Obligations and rights involve oughts with something added. The something added has to do with requirements or coercion or being bound. People who violate their obligations and ignore the rights of others are open to criticism and penalties, which are not meted out to those who are simply not as good as they ought to be. Elsewhere,[2] I have argued that what we are obligated to do is what we not only ought to do, but what there both is and ought to be a sanction against our *not* doing.[3]

If I break my promise to lend you money, I will at the very least be subject to your indignation and that of others, and I may even have to suffer a legal penalty for breach of contract. Furthermore, there *ought* to be such penalties because keeping promises is very important to achieving whatever goals people happen to have. Furthermore, since keeping promises is often inconvenient, people are tempted to break them. If they could do so with impunity, we would not be able to count on the performance of others often enough to make the institution of promise keeping useful. If we are going to rely on promises at all, we need to have some way of applying pressure on people to keep them. And since the institution of promising *is* so helpful, we ought to maintain it, and maintaining it requires having penalties for breach of promise.

Because social pressure, coercion, and punishment are unpleasant and detract from the happiness of those subjected to them, they must, if they are to be justifiable, do more moral good than harm. Hence they are only justified if the actions which they enforce bring about a great deal of good or prevent significant harm. The institution of promising is such a good. So are not killing or maiming others, not stealing from or cheating them, and not lying to them. So are fulfilling certain functions in society, whether or not explicit promises have been made, which functions include obeying the law, doing one's job, and fulfilling certain roles in family life.

It is not only important that people behave in accordance with these standards if society is to be tolerable, but there will be many occasions when individuals are tempted to violate them. Without sanctions, the good will not be achieved, and because the good of having people behave in accordance with these rules is very great, the sanctions are justifiable. And in virtually all societies, there *are* sanctions against killing, stealing, promise breaking, lying, and neglecting certain social tasks.

Obligations do not exist if either there is no sanction or there ought to be no sanction, no matter how valuable the action. It would, for example, be a morally good thing if everyone were to tithe: i.e., give one tenth of one's income to charity. But, except for members of a few churches, people are not expected to do so. For the rest of us, there is no sanction, or any form of pressure to tithe. Perhaps there *ought* to be a more well-developed sense of concern for the needy, resulting in an established custom of tithing and at least disapproval and criticism of those who fail to do it. But since there isn't, most people don't have an obligation to tithe. People who *do* tithe are thought to be going above and beyond the call of duty.

What is obligatory is highly dependent upon the social climate. For example, until recently those who have been deeply concerned with environmental issues have been considered by the average American to be rather fanatical. Certainly people who recycled their trash were not considered to be merely doing their duty. The climate of opinion is changing, however, and it may be that in the near future people who *don't* recycle will be the exception and will be criticized. Indeed, it may become *illegal* to throw away such reusable items as paper and aluminum. In any case, even now, most thoughtful people recognize an urgent moral claim to protect our environment, even though there are many specific things we could do in this direction which are not — yet at least — obligatory.[4]

1.2 What Counts as a Sanction?

There is a sanction for doing or failing to do a type of action when some group exacts a penalty against (or withholds a reward from) individuals who fail to perform as required. Actions which are tokens of that type — assuming they are actions which members of that group ought to perform and that the sanction ought to be imposed — are obligatory for those persons. Almost any group of people who are united by common enterprises and concerns can exert a sanction. These include not only the obvious sorts of groups like nations, families, and corporations, but also informal groups loosely organized, if organized at all.

All the people using campgrounds, for example, are expected to conform to certain standards of behavior — e.g., clean up after themselves and not make noise late at night. Those who don't conform will probably not be punished (even if signs are posted) unless their offenses are particularly flagrant. But other campers may ask them to behave properly or take them to task for not doing so. Most campers will not think the critics to be meddlesome busybodies, and that they do not is an indication that there is a sanction for the behavior in question. By contrast, if one camper were to criticize another for using a particular kind of tent or trailer, everyone else would think his remarks totally out of line. There are no sanctions governing what type of camping gear one uses, only for behavior which interferes with the pleasure of others.[5]

Sanctions need to be generally endorsed by the group which imposes them. Criticism by an isolated individual which does not have the endorsement of the group is not a sanction. Such an individual may be justified in trying to stop behavior which is harmful, but he is not imposing a sanction, and he is not enforcing an obligation.

1.3 When are Sanctions and Their Enforcement Justified?

There are limits to what sanctions ought to be imposed. If you show me lavish hospitality, then I have an obligation to do something for you in return. If I never do, then you have a right to be aggrieved and to criticize me. It would, however, be excessive to have me beheaded for such a social lapse. A sanction, in short, ought to be appropriate. And what makes a sanction appropriate is that having a sanction of *that kind* is needed to achieve moral ends. Hence if a sanction is too severe, the harm done to the offender and others offsets any good which might come of his and others having conformed.[6] Or, if a sanction is too lenient, it will be ineffective. If it doesn't deter people from failing in their obligations, it is worse than useless. Not only will it do no good, but it will do harm to those few who on whom it is imposed, cost something to be enforced, and create disrespect for law and custom generally. If some type of action produces so little good that even the small disvalue of an extremely light sanction outweighs it, then there ought not to be any sanction. In that case actions of that type are not obligatory, even if there *is* a sanction.

That there is a sanction against a particular type of action does not mean that it is, or ought to be, enforced every time someone in the group which imposes it performs a token of that action. Others may not, for example, find out that she has done it. Or, someone may not be able on a specific occasion to carry out the sanction. In other cases, there may be extenuating circumstances that make mercy and forgiveness more morally appropriate. If one's child is tired or sick, it might be better to overlook obnoxious behavior that one would and should normally punish. Or a felon who is terminally ill might be released from prison to spend his last days with his family. Likewise, a soldier may not be punished for deserting his post if remaining there would have meant certain death. If, however, a penalty is never exacted, or exacted so rarely that it deters no one from the behavior for which it is supposed to be a penalty, then there is no sanction and no obligation.[7] And if a sanction ought never to be enforced against failure to perform a type of action, then there is no obligation to perform such an act.[8]

Even when it would normally be necessary to have a sanction, or to enforce an existing sanction, circumstances are occasionally such that enforcement — or even the existence — of a sanction may not be justified. It might, for example, be morally important for someone to perform an action, enough so that something should be done to see that the action is carried out, but sanctions might not be the best way of promoting these acts. For example, people ought to support their children, and, where they do not, something should be done to see that those children are supported. Yet if the parents have difficulty earning and keeping money — e.g., if they are struggling with poor health, inability to find work, mental retardation, or drug addiction — and if society is in a position to help, then help is more appropriate than punishment. Because punishment (including even simple criticism) hurts, the only justification for it is that it is necessary for achieving moral ends. If the same ends can be achieved by kindness, then that should be tried before penalties are invoked.

Whether there is an obligation depends upon whether sanctions are justified if helpfulness fails.

If a person ought to do something, but doing it is very difficult (although not impossible), and others in society are in a position to help him, but do not, the person may or may not be obligated. If others did provide the help they could, and if all were held to the same standards, then if the person still failed to do what he ought, a sanction would be justified and he would be obligated.

Sometimes a person remains obligated, even though the usual sanction ought to be withheld. If the person *ought* to perform the action, and even if those who normally would impose the sanction ought to use help and encouragement rather than punishment, the person could still be deserving of criticism if he were to fail — even without help. Furthermore, if the person is truly obligated, some sanction is justified even when the usual sanction is not. Thus the criminal who is terminally ill was still obligated not to have committed his crime. Even though his sentence ought to be mitigated, he still should have been imprisoned and served at least part of his time. Moreover, the fact that he came from a disadvantaged background does not excuse him from his felony. Society ought to have done more to help him in his youth, but the fact that it didn't does not void his obligation.

Furthermore, a person may normally be obligated to do something, but not be obligated when placed in a situation against her will. A person who is hired to do a job is expected to perform up to certain standards and is obligated to do so. But if, let us say, the person who normally does the job is absent or otherwise unable to perform it, and another employee is forced to take over his tasks even though she is not qualified, she cannot rightly be held to the same standards. Let us assume that either she is threatened with loss of her own job if she does not fill in or that the work she is expected to do is such that if it isn't done at all more harm will be done than if it is not done up to the standard (i.e., it isn't a case where a nurses' aide is ordered to fill in for a brain surgeon). In either case, the employee is being pressured into a situation she did not want, and this voids the normal obligation to perform according to the usual standards associated with that job.

Not only are there no obligations where there are no sanctions, but an action which never ought to be enforced is not an obligation, even if people are actually punished for failing to perform it. Where an action ought not to be enforced, this is either because the action itself is wrong or because the harm brought about by enforcement is worse than any good the action might do. For example, today we would consider the sacrifice of one's firstborn child to Moloch wrong.[9] Even though the ancient Carthaginians believed it their duty to do this, and were punished if they didn't, *we* don't consider that they had any such obligation. We might say that they *were required* to sacrifice their children, or that they *thought* they were obliged to do so, but not that they *were* morally obligated to. That this is so is indicated by the fact that if we were to hear of parents who had refused to give up their baby to the flames, we would admire them for their courage, and not hesitate to think they had done right.

Many actions would have their best effects if performed in cooperation with a group, for example, a system of care for the sick and elderly. A person who did so individually, but where there was no system, would be doing what he ought, but would not be obligated. Also, if someone is uniquely able to assist others, i.e., the only person with the skills or resources immediately available, she would be obligated to do so in situations where people with her capabilities are required to assist in that way. But if she would not be punished or criticized for not assisting, then she is not obligated. Yet she ought to because only if *she* does will moral ends be furthered. When a system of allocating tasks exists, however, people are pressured to fulfill their roles and thus have obligations within the system; without a system, there is little or no justification for sanctions.

As another example, actions which are not normally obligations may become so if one stands in a special relationship with another. People have, for example, duties to family members which are prescribed by the customs and laws of their society. We are also obligated to do what we have contracted to do, e.g., in our jobs. For example, a public official has an obligation to hire the best people to fill positions for which he is responsible. In many parts of the world, however, public officials are also expected to give family members whatever available jobs they can. The view of most Americans is that nepotism is not only not obligatory but wrong. In some countries, however, where government is largely ineffective (perhaps in part *because* of nepotism), and people rely more heavily upon their families for life's advantages, it may in fact be the only way for some people to get along. No doubt the system ought to be changed, but it is the duty of no particular individual to change it, and in the given situation, engaging in nepotism may bring about more moral good than not doing so, and may even be obligatory.

Often sanctions are imposed by one group of people upon those who are not members of that group, for example, the nobility and landed gentry's imposing certain behavior on the peasants in a medieval society. Ought there to be such sanctions, and hence obligations (over and above prudential reasons) to conform? The answer depends upon whether good can result from performance of the actions in question for those upon whom the sanctions are forced, and not only for those who enforce them. For example, parents impose sanctions against misdeeds of their children. The children rarely endorse the sanctions, but they are, for the most part, obliged to act in accordance with what their parents tell them to do. Assuming the parents to be kind and reasonable, what they want the children to do is usually good for them, for the family, and for the larger society, not simply to satisfy the parents' whims.

On the other hand, sanctions imposed by a conquering power on another nation are rarely justifiable, and then only if having them creates substantial good for the conquered people. Only then might the vanquished be morally obligated (as opposed to being obliged by force alone) to obey. For this reason, resistance to very oppressive regimes is generally considered morally praiseworthy. As long as the relationship between the conquerors and conquered remains one of exploitation, there is no moral obligation of the latter to the former.

If, however, there is assimilation, intermingling, and the establishment of cooperative relationships between the two groups, there may well begin to be common interests, followed by mutual obligations and sanctions which are justified. Thus all citizens of present day Italy ought to obey their laws and be punished if they violate them. Yet over the past several thousand years, this land has been overrun by a number of conquering peoples. Most of these, however, have been assimilated and are no longer distinguished from the indigenous population. Before assimilation, however, the conquered people would have been justified in resisting.

1.4 Obligations and Ability to Fulfill Them

It also follows from this characterization of obligation, that we are rarely obligated to do what we can't, for we ought not, in general at least, to punish people for doing, or failing to do, what they cannot help doing or failing to do. Since punishment causes unhappiness, it can only be justified if it diminishes the punished individual's own unhappiness or that of others to a greater extent.[10] For example, punishment as a deterrent or rehabilitative measure may bring a greater balance of happiness over unhappiness for the person punished and justify his pain. A child may not have the self-control to avoid committing offenses against others and putting himself in danger; but his mother is justified in punishing him not only to prevent immediate harm, but to teach him better behavior. One may justify making him go to his room when he pulls the cat's tail, even though he doesn't know any better and can't be expected to refrain now, just because a mild penalty will help him to know better, and control himself better, in the future.

In cases, however, where we are preventing an irresponsible individual, whether a small child or one who is criminally insane, from doing harm, this is not generally considered *punishment* or even a sanction. For the child, until he is able to control his behavior, it is called *discipline*, and one hopes that what is done to him causes minimal pain and unhappiness — just enough to give him an incentive to act differently. For the woman who hacks her guests to death and stuffs them in the freezer so that she will have enough to eat when the aliens invade Earth, her being committed to a mental hospital is not so much a punishment as our simply protecting ourselves against such people. She ought to be treated with as much kindness and dignity as is compatible with seeing that she doesn't have a chance to repeat her performance. Still, the methods by which we control the behavior of irresponsibles are both morally necessary and, since usually aversive, are not very different from punishment.

Often morally responsible individuals will be unable to do things which are normally obligatory for them. In most of these cases, we do not think it right to penalize them, and thus do not consider them obligated. One type of case is a genuine conflict of obligations. For example, suppose Martha tells Nellie that Ollie is cheating on Pauline, and then makes her promise never to reveal this to Pauline. Later Pauline asks Nellie directly: "Did Martha tell you that Ollie is cheating on me?"

Nellie has a genuine conflict of obligation. She is normally obligated not to break promises and not to lie. But it is hard to see how she can avoid doing one or the other in this situation. (Let us suppose that a return question like, "Now why on earth would she tell me anything like that?" might simply inflame the suspicions of an already anxious Pauline, and prompt her to say, "Well, *did* she? Just answer my question!") Now granted that no matter what Nellie says to Pauline she does something she ought not to do, no neutral observer will blame her for failing in one or the other of these *prima facie* obligations. If she decides that Martha's gossip is no more than that, she might simply lie, but keep her promise. If she believes on independent grounds that Ollie *is* cheating, and that Pauline would be better off finding this out and acting to protect herself, she might break her promise by telling the truth.

In either case, Nellie is trying to minimize the moral harm done. By looking beyond the standard rules which are important — indeed essential — guides to life in society to the purpose which lies behind them, she may resolve her conflict. And any objective person who can see her predicament will sympathize and not blame or criticize, much less punish, her for her efforts. She will no doubt already be unhappy at being in this dilemma, and it would be wrong to make it worse by subjecting her to some sort of penalty, especially since doing so will in no way amend the situation.

Occasionally, however, a person ought to be punished for doing things that he couldn't help. Examples of such situations might include those where it was not clear that the person could not have avoided the offense — either by finding some way around it, or by avoiding the situation which made him unable to help it. Thus a drunk driver who kills others by causing an accident — as Aristotle would have told us — is still guilty of manslaughter because he could have avoided driving while drunk.[11] Likewise, one might think that Nellie has violated an obligation because she should never have promised Martha not to tell Pauline what Martha had said. Yet the circumstances may well have been such that Nellie would have had no reason to think that it was a promise she might not be able to keep. Where there was nothing the agent could reasonably be expected to have done to avoid the offence, there is normally no justification for punishment.

There may, however, be situations in which a responsible person ought to be punished for some act or omission even where he or she did not do anything objectively wrong, or did something wrong unavoidably. I think such situations are rare and the circumstances in which they arise would be most unusual. If an individual was forced to choose between two incompatible obligations, both of which are extremely important, it might be right to punish any violations, even inadvertent ones, in order to avoid setting a precedent.

Suppose an American bomber pilot is charged with destroying a Taliban target, but soon receives a message informing him that the target is in fact a school; there may or may not be children inside. On the one hand, he knows that harming Afghan children is both wrong and contrary to the American mission, and he has strict orders to avoid doing so; on the other, if he does not bomb the target, the enemy will undoubtedly harm friendly troops. If he hesitates and radios back to his commanding officer for instructions or attempt to learn whether there are children in the building, he will probably fail to destroy the target, for the Taliban forces are likely to see the plane and get away. The pilot has two duties: to carry out his mission and to avoid harming innocent civilians. Fulfilling one may make it impossible for him to fulfill the other.

Whatever the pilot does, he is apt to bring harm upon some individuals he has an obligation to protect or at least not to hurt. If he does kill innocent children, or alternatively, if he does not and the ground forces on his side are attacked and killed, it may be that whatever he does he ought to be punished, so that other officers may not be tempted to take that course in circumstances where it is less clear that the dilemma is not resolvable. It is of prime importance both that pilots follow orders and carry out their missions, *and* that they not harm innocent civilians. These considerations are both so important that pilots who in some circumstances could not help violating one or the other of these normal duties ought to be penalized to avoid setting precedents. Assuming that it is clear that the officer was in a true dilemma, however, the punishment ought to be as light as possible.

As another example, a person may be morally justified in breaking a law — in certain cases of civil disobedience, for example. Yet it might be that punishment of those who do so ought to be inflicted in order to prevent disrespect for law and order. In this case the protester ought not, and would not be obligated, to obey because the higher moral demand would be more consistent with the central purpose of morality. Nevertheless punishment might sometimes be justified so that others might not be tempted to break laws for lesser reasons. As in the case of the army officer, however, punishment should be light.

1.5. Release from Obligation

Sometimes a person who is obligated to perform an action for another may be released from that obligation. It may or may not be that the person still ought to perform the act in question. For example, suppose Paula promises Ramona to meet her for lunch, but later finds that it will be inconvenient for her to do so. She calls Ramona to explain her predicament, and Ramona says, "That's OK, why don't we try for next week." Ramona might have said, "No, you promised, and I was really counting on this particular day." In this case, Paula is still obligated, although such a response is likely to put a strain on their friendship. Even when Ramona releases Paula, it may be that Paula still ought to have kept the lunch date. Suppose, for example, that she knows Ramona is going through some rough times and could use the moral support that getting together with a good friend might provide. Assuming then that her conflicting business is not as important, she ought to keep her promise and not seek to be released from it.

There are occasions, however, when one cannot be released from an obligation. For example, one may have obligations which are not owed to a specific individual, such as, perhaps, obligations to those yet unborn. Since these individuals don't exist yet, we don't owe anything to specific persons, nor, even if we did, could they release us from our obligations.[12] Also, sometimes the beneficiary of an obligation may not be in a position of releasing someone from that obligation. Suppose that Susan and Tom get divorced. Susan is awarded custody of the children, but Tom agrees to take care of them two weekends a month. If the children do not want to be with their father, this by itself does not release Tom from his obligation. He is obligated to Susan (and perhaps to the State as well), not to the children, for what he agreed to do in the divorce settlement.

At other times, a person cannot be released from an obligation because what he is obliged to do is of vital importance. Suppose that Andrew is severely depressed and asks Bruce to shoot him. Bruce is not thereby released from his obligation — to Andrew, his family, and to society — not to kill him or anyone else. Should he accede to Andrew's request, he would be, and ought to be, convicted of murder. What makes the difference between Bruce's case and that of Paula is that if Bruce kills Andrew, Andrew's interests will be permanently and totally harmed, whereas Ramona's will not be drastically affected by Paula's not having lunch with her.

I say "generally" because there may be circumstances in which Bruce might be justified in killing Andrew at the latter's request. Suppose Andrew is not just temporarily depressed, with a good chance of recovery through antidepressant medications and psychotherapy. He is a person once very physically active, who is now a quadriplegic as the result of an accident. He has found nothing worth living for since he became disabled, and all the miseries of his condition make his life a burden which he wholeheartedly wishes to shed. This is not the place to consider whether euthanasia or assisted suicide is ever justified, but if it is, this might be a situation that would qualify. On the grounds that this was truly what Andrew desired and truly in his best interest, it might be that Bruce was, by Andrew's request, released from his normal obligation not to kill.

We are sometimes thought to have obligations to ourselves: e.g., to care for our health, to develop our talents, etc. — apart from obligations we may have to others to do these things because our ability to function well helps them. On my theory, one has a self-regarding obligation to do A, if one ought to do A and if there is and ought to be a sanction against failing to do A. There are some thing which we are and ought to be required, by law or by social pressure, to do, which primarily affect ourselves. Often others are affected as well; for example, laws requiring seat belts and motorcycle helmets protect one's family and society from the burdens of caring for a human vegetable. And while there neither are nor ought to be laws forcing adults to further their education, work hard, and care for their health, there can be a significant amount of social pressure on people to conform to certain standards, even when conforming affects only the agent. At times we may intervene directly to prevent individuals from doing certain things to harm themselves — e.g., jumping off a tall building or giving away life savings to a total stranger. One would be thoroughly justified in preventing such acts in virtually all situations.

Assuming that such coercion is justifiable, it follows from my own analysis at least, that we have some duties to ourselves. It does not follow, however, that these are absolute, any more than our obligations to others are absolute. In the first place, one person can release another from many obligations owed to the first by the second.

Although we do not release ourselves from obligations to ourselves, we can achieve the same effect simply by choosing not to do certain things. As a rule, you have no right to my property, but if I give you something, then you are no longer obliged not to take it. Nor do I normally have an obligation to myself to keep what I own, just because I have a perfect right to give it away. But there may be things which I ought not to give away because doing so will seriously harm my interests, and others ought not to accept such gifts. And where the law or social pressure should and does intervene, we may say that you have an obligation not to accept my gift and I have an obligation to myself not to give it.

In short, one has obligations to oneself when one's wish to do something affecting oneself alone or most particularly does not suffice to release others from preventing one from doing it. Some might claim that there are in fact no such duties, and I do not wish to argue the point here. I only want to say that duties to oneself can fit easily into my analysis. I also maintain that where an individual will not be obviously worse off by doing something normally harmful and which he normally has a duty to himself not to do, there is no duty in that particular case, and others should refrain from coercion. Thus a person who is terminally ill and in great pain may be justified in suicide, even if she normally has a duty to herself to preserve her life. Or, she might be justified in selling herself into white slavery, if she and her family will otherwise starve.[13]

To summarize thus far, actions which are good or which we ought to perform may either be obligatory or non-obligatory. If obligatory, there is some group which enforces sanctions against nonperformance of the action, and there *ought* to be such sanctions.

2. SUPEREROGATION

Good actions which are neither obligatory nor required for achieving the central purpose of morality are known in ethical theory as *supererogatory* — actions above and beyond the call of duty. Those who do more than is expected of them are worthy of praise. People who do what would normally be their duty under conditions which people cannot normally be expected to perform it, or who do more for others than they simply ought to do, are considered to be better, morally speaking, than average. And those who engage in supererogatory behavior on a large scale are the stuff of saints and heroes.[14]

Certainly many persons *feel* themselves obligated to do what most others would think supererogatory. They may feel shame and guilt for omitting some act of personal sacrifice which would have helped others — for example, not entering a burning building to save a child, or not having become a missionary to a primitive tribe. Those who do more than they ought or are obliged to do have done something supererogatory. A person who fails to stop at the scene of an accident has failed in an obligation. A person who provides first aid, enlists other passing motorists to stop traffic and call an ambulance, and comforts the victims does what needs to be done in the situation and thus what he ought to do. He has also gone beyond the bare minimum, and if there were others nearby who could have done what he did just as well, his acts were supererogatory. He might, indeed, do even more — such as to visit the victims in the hospital, make arrangements for their affairs to be attended to, or help them financially. Other people could probably do these additional things as well as this Good Samaritan, so he would have done far more than what he is obligated to do or what he ought to do.

Whether an action is obligatory , what ought to be done, or supererogatory depends in part upon the person's roles in his or her society and in part upon the conditions under which the act would have to be performed. Much would depend upon whether the person belonged to a group which exerts sanctions against failing to perform the act, or whether he was especially well suited to perform it. For example, firemen are *expected* to enter burning buildings; it is one of their duties. Other people without a firefighter's training or equipment who did this would be considered to have gone far beyond the call of duty. And those who do what is normally only what they ought or are obliged to do under particularly difficult or dangerous conditions — such as the emergency workers who entered the World Trade Center on September 11, 2001 — have behaved in a supererogatory manner.

Another advantage of the three-way distinction enables us to deal with the problems raised by *moral luck.*[15] The problem is that the moral worth or lack of the same of an action seems to depend upon external circumstances, not of the value or disvalue of the action itself. For example, if Steve gets drunk and drives home without having an accident he has supposedly not done anything as bad as he would have if he had gotten no more drunk and driven no more carelessly, but killed a pedestrian who happened to be in his way. Many of those who lived in Nazi Germany did things which many people in other countries might have done had they been exposed to the same pressures, such as reporting a Jewish neighbor to the authorities knowing that this would almost certainly ensure his death. Those people from countries that would not countenance such betrayals were never put to the test; yet some of them would, under the same circumstances, almost certainly have cooperated with the Nazis. Since they did not live under a Nazi regime, however, they did not cooperate or do the evil cooperation required.

The society into which one is born and spends one's life creates circumstances which strongly influence what one is able to do, what one knows and believes, and what one is tempted to do. All these factors are matters of moral luck, and since they play a major role in what a person actually does, how we evaluate those actions appears to be very much a matter of fortune. On the other hand, however, it does not seem true that the drunken driver who got home safely or the weaker citizens of the United States or England were any better people than the driver who killed someone or the Germans who cooperated with the Nazis.

The significance of moral luck depends upon which component of evaluation of actions and persons one is considering. If we are considering the worth of an individual's *character* it has a relatively small effect. The drunk who drove home without incident is no better morally than the one who killed a pedestrian. We might, however, not *know* or be able to assess someone's character apart from the consequences that stem from his overt actions. Thus none of us who have lived in democratic societies know how we would behave had we lived under Hitler. We may hope we would have resisted, and the way we have responded to smaller challenges may give some indication as to whether we would, but — for all we know — our courage might have failed. On the other hand, what we have experienced also affects our character and these experiences are also a matter of luck. A child who has been brought up to hate members of another race or ethnic group will certainly have a different character from one who has been taught tolerance. And a child who has been subjected to abuse or neglect is less apt to develop a warm, sympathetic personality. While we normally do not look for all such influences in judging a person's character, if we are aware of some salient background information we are usually willing to make some allowances and admit that they are not fully responsible for what their character has become. (This does not, of course, entail that we should excuse their behavior, not protect ourselves from what they might do, or refrain from punishing their misdeeds.)

In short, then, we tend to take into account the effects of moral luck in evaluating a person, and this is relevant to whether we consider them worthy of praise or blame, and whether — and what degree of — sanctions ought to be imposed. It is, however, otherwise with judging what a person ought to have done. No one ought to turn an innocent neighbor over to people who will persecute him, regardless of the circumstances. This applies just as much to those who live in democracies as to those who live under dictators. We would, of course, blame an American citizen who went out of his way to get a Jewish neighbor into the hands of a hate group somewhat more than we would blame a German under Hitler for doing the same. The latter was very likely influenced by fear or hope of gain, while the former could hardly have been motivated by anything but hatred. For the German, such an act might be the line of least resistance; the American would have to go out of his way. Likewise, we would have much more admiration for a German who risked death by refusing to betray his Jewish neighbors to the Nazis than we do for present-day Americans who don't persecute Jews. On the other hand, for all of these people it remains true that they ought not to do what will result in the persecution of anyone else. No driver ought to kill another person by driving recklessly or while drunk. Driving drunk *and* killing someone compounds the offense. Even though the character of the unlucky driver is no worse than that of the lucky one, what he has done is worse, for he has done two things that he ought not to have done. What one ought to do is at least relatively independent of one's luck, whereas whether and what sanctions are appropriate, and what counts as worthy of praise or blame, is not. Thus a part of determining obligation is dependent upon considering circumstances of moral luck, while oughts are not so dependent.

Some acts felt to be obligations are not actual obligations. For the most part, these are actions which are not required by any group to which the person belongs.

Rather they are actions which would be needed to achieve some particular ideal. Thus a very religious woman whose ideal was to give herself totally to God's service, but who had become sidetracked by marriage, children, and a comfortable job might blame herself for *not* becoming a missionary. In such a case, I would say that perhaps she *ought* to have become a missionary, simply because doing so was needed to fulfill a major personal goal. It might even be that she ought *morally* to have done this, had she been uniquely suited to it and if her doing so would have been needed for advancing the central purpose of morality. But in neither case would there have been an obligation.[16]

On the other hand, a person may do more than she is obliged or ought to do. As an example, we may use a situation in which someone needs help, and there are several persons about who might supply this aid without any great trouble. There is no reason why one specific individual ought to help rather than anyone else. Suppose that a child is lost in a crowded mall. Many adults are available to help. It isn't the case that any particular person ought to assist the child; since moral ends can be equally well served by anyone's doing so, Alan's helping the child is not necessary to serve these ends, nor is Barbara's helping. *Somebody* ought to, but it needn't be any particular person. If Alan volunteers, he is going a little beyond what is expected and is doing something supererogatory. If Alan is the sort of person who generally makes such small sacrifices for others when there is no need for *him specifically* to do so, we tend to think of him as a bit better than the rest of us.

Of course, if no one helps the lost child, we would find the whole group of adults at fault. As Russell Jacobs pointed out to me, we hold all the people who witnessed Kitty Genovese's murder without doing anything — even calling the police — blameworthy. In such situations each individual would share the blame, even though no one of them had the sole responsibility for helping. In group situations there seems to be a gap: those who act are considered to have done something supererogatory; yet if no one acts, all have failed to meet an obligation or do as they ought. Thus Peter Singer can rightly say [17] that the affluent people of the world are, collectively, morally at fault for allowing preventable hunger.

What others do, and what they could do, is highly relevant to what a particular individual ought to do. As I suggested above, whether one ought to perform an action depends in part upon the likelihood that the effects of that action will be brought about by other processes — either natural events or the acts of others. It also depends upon what acts of others or natural occurrences will counteract the good we try to do. We know perfectly well that not enough is being done to relieve the hungry, and that nearly all of us ought to do more than we do.

Nevertheless, we also know that what we give of our surplus will often not reach those who need it and may in addition (although this is controversial) compound the problem by causing overpopulation. If the food sent to famine-stricken lands ends up rotting on the docks or stolen by roving bands of guerillas, our charity goes to waste. We do better to give where we know that our gifts will be effective. We are inundated by requests for donations to countless causes, most of which are no doubt worthy, but we must make difficult allocation decisions; even the richest cannot give everything that is asked of them. And the problem of hunger is immensely complex; in different places causal factors and likely solutions vary widely. Further, if we neglect our families and communities to help those in distant places, we risk not only making life hard for those near to us, but hurting the valuable relationships we have with them. So there are good — although not decisive — reasons for acting locally rather than globally.

In short, people ought to help others when they have sound reason to believe that there is something they can do which will really have a good effect and when that effect is unlikely to occur if they fail to act. Those who step forward without waiting to see if others will do the job, as well as those who make substantial sacrifices for the good of others, have done something supererogatory.

Likewise, actions which ought *not* to be done may be divided into the forbidden and the morally offensive. What we are forbidden to do is what we are obligated not to do; what is morally offensive is what we ought not to do, but for which there is no sanction or for which there ought not to be a sanction. Since we are generally justified in criticizing any behavior that does real harm, even though we may not be justified in punishing it, most offensive, but not forbidden, behavior is such because there is no sanction against it. Slavery or human sacrifice in a society where these practices were not only customary, but where they would not be questioned by the establishment, might be of this sort.

Sometimes a good act which is not a duty or obligation takes precedence over doing a duty.[18] When you have a business appointment, but on the way you come upon the scene of an accident and aid the victims instead, you have failed an obligation, but everyone would agree that you did better by helping. On my view, the central purpose of morality was better served, and, moreover, (if there was no one else who could have helped, or helped as well as you) it couldn't have been so well served had you passed by. Thus you ought to have aided them. Indeed, if there was a clear need for your aid specifically, so that the victims' misery would have worsened, and their chance for survival perhaps decreased had you not helped, you would have been deserving of criticism if you had ignored their plight and met your friend on time; you would then have been obligated to stop. This obligation would have outweighed your obligation to your associate, and your associate and others would be wrong not to excuse you. Even if others could have helped, your doing so was, not only on my view but on that of common sense morality, morally preferable to your keeping your appointment.

Performing or avoiding a whole range of actions would make our world a better place, but constraints on our time and energy make it impossible to do them all. Knowing what our obligations are enables us to organize our time and to insure that we will do what is most important. On the other hand, there are undoubtedly occasions on which we would do more good and prevent more harm or bring about more justice, by neglecting minor obligations for some project which is supererogatory.

3. AGENT-RELATIVE PREROGATIVES

In recent years a number of philosophers have argued that traditional moral theories — and especially consequentialism — ignore the common belief that an agent is allowed to count his own commitments and projects more heavily than those of persons in general.   According to their view, we have *agent-relative prerogatives* (or *options*). They claim, moreover, that what an individual ought to do is at times *not* to bring about what is from an impartial standpoint the morally best consequences — however 'best' is to be interpreted. At times, they say, a person is not required to act for the best, when to do so would mean that he would have to abandon certain deeply held interests or commitments of his own.[19] Thus the fact that I might be doing more good if I were now working to feed the hungry instead of writing a book which only a few people are likely to read is not a sufficient reason for me to turn off the computer and head down to the local soup kitchen. I have a prerogative or option to engage in activities that are important to me, even though alternative actions might bring better results.

In this section I shall argue that agent-relative prerogatives, properly understood, are perfectly compatible with most agent-neutral theories — at least with any moral theory which offers an adequate distinction between obligation and supererogation. I shall try to show that while we are not always obligated to act for the highest moral goals or principles in preference to pursuing our own commitments and projects, there are definite limits on what we have a prerogative to do. The account below will, I hope, allow us to spell out what these limits are.

3.1 Agent-Relative Prerogatives are Compatible with Agent-Neutral Theories

There are certainly reasons for acknowledging agent-relative prerogatives. We don't as a rule believe that people are morally required to devote their entire lives to doing good. Those who do are considered above — and apart — from the rest of humanity. We admire them, but may also be somewhat repelled by them.[20] Anyone who, for example, leaves her family in order to devote her life to the unfortunate may do tremendous amounts of good and we may honor her for it. At the same time, we may wonder if she is quite human with normal affections. Thus we may well believe that not only do people have a *right* to favor those they love and to follow their own interests and concerns, but those who do may in some ways be morally superior to those saintly folk whose whole intent is to do the greatest possible good, but whom we may suspect of not really *caring* for other people. Hence we definitely appear to believe in the validity of agent-centered prerogatives.

We normally do not consider a person morally at fault for doing more for his spouse, children, and parents than for strangers, even when those strangers are much needier. Nor would anyone blame a person for following a harmless career which utilized his abilities, even though he might be able to do much more good in some other occupation. Yet this is the position which several contemporary writers have attributed to consequentialists.[21] This view of consequentialism may have been promoted by such statements as Smart's assertion that the right action for an agent in given circumstances is that action which produces better results than any alternative action,[22] and Shelly Kagan's claim that we are morally required to do the most good[23]. It is not only consequentialists who have suggested that our special commitments and affections are as nothing to an overriding moral ideal; consider the Biblical injunctions to be perfect and to leave family behind to follow the Lord.

To say as Smart and Kagan do that a certain action is *the right action*, and presumably morally required, suggests that to do anything else is *wrong*. Most consequentialists, however, do not maintain that failure to bring about the greatest good is wrong. Mill, for example, calls wrong only those actions which promote *un*happiness.[24] Sidgwick allows that acting on the special affections and commitments between people is the best way to bring about the greatest good.[25] Mill and Sidgwick do not, however, deal directly with the question of where we draw the line between what is wrong to do and what is simply not the best we could do.

Yet although there is a place for agent-relative prerogatives, I do not believe there is anyone who maintains that they are a primary moral consideration. Our obligations to others frequently outweigh them. Suppose that Joe's most central personal goal is becoming as rich as possible. Suppose also that his Uncle Fred has willed him several million dollars. Joe's goal of becoming rich hardly outweighs his duty not to murder Uncle Fred.

I believe that any moral theory which draws an adequate distinction between what we are morally required to do and what it would simply be good to do can make room for agent-relative prerogatives without violating commonly held moral beliefs. There have been a number of accounts of this distinction which allow us to determine the proper scope of agent-relative prerogatives. These include the work of Kurt Baier, Joel Feinberg, and D. A. J. Richards, and — more recently — that of James Forrester, as well as my own.[26] All have proposed that an act A is obligatory for X if some sort of coercion or sanction to see that X does A is justifiable.

The three way distinction I have outlined above among what what is best to do, what one ought to do, and what one is obliged to do easily takes care of a recent complaint against consequentialist types of moral theory.[27] Bernard Williams,[28] Samuel Scheffler,[29] and Jonathan Dancy[30] maintain that any view according to which one is required to bring about the greatest amount of good (however good is defined) also requires a person to violate his integrity. The reason for this somewhat astonishing claim is that if we must spend all our lives constantly pursuing the greater good, we will not have time to spend on the things we value and the projects dear to our hearts.

In what follows I will demonstrate that my three fold distinction is applicable to any moral theory, and that it allows any theory to draw the line which separates behavior that is minimally decent in fulfilling one's obligations from that which is good and from that which is saintly. It allows any type of moral theory — teleological or deontological — to distinguish what is demanded from what is basically morally needed and both of these from what is the best that one can do. No reasonable moral theory will demand that everyone constantly strive to maximize good on pain of punishment, but any adequate one will also indicate what is needed to attain the highest moral good.

Thus if the greatest moral good is to bring about the greatest happiness for the greatest number, then one whose goal in life is to do what is best will constantly work toward that end. What she ought to do is only what is required *from her* for that end to be achieved; if others can do these things just as well as she, then it is not the case that *she* ought to do them. On the other hand, she *ought* to work to further her own interests and those of persons close to her, including people she is in an especially good position to help. Yet she is not *obligated* to do even all this, but only those things which the object of bringing about the greatest good for the greatest number not only requires, but requires that people be pressured to do. If, on the other hand, what we ought to do is what we would not want anyone to fail to do — if the maxim of our actions were a universal law — then what is best is what we will for everyone to do, and what we are obligated to do is what we want everyone to be penalized for not doing.

Thus both of these two kinds of moral theory allow us to make distinctions between those who do no more than they are required to do, those who do what is needed to be a good person, and those who go far beyond and make doing good one of their life's priorities. No one is required to sacrifice his or her integrity, or give up favorite goals on either a utilitarian or a Kantian theory except insofar as pursuing these goals interferes with the good of others.

The distinction between what is obligatory, what one ought to do, and what is, from a moral point of view, best to do can enable us to see just where agent-relative prerogatives lie. I do not think it matters to the main points I am trying to make in this chapter whether or not the above analysis is the best available. *Any* moral theory which distinguishes between what is morally required and what is simply good to do will serve that purpose. Primarily what is needed is a distinction between those acts which are crucial from a moral standpoint and which, moreover, can normally be expected from human beings and those which are good — perhaps *very* good —, but beyond what a person should be required or expected to do.[31] [32]

On any such theory, we don't have prerogatives to harm others, or gain advantages at their expense. If we fail in our obligations, i.e., those things which are especially important, we deserve at the very least censure and perhaps outright punishment. If we do what we simply ought not to do, but are not obligated not to do, the case is less clear. I may not be blamed for failing to help a stranger when I, and I alone, could do so easily, but I am certainly not as good a person as I should be. In this sense, I don't have a prerogative not to help; I have a prerogative to hurry on about my business only in the sense that others do not have a clear right to criticize or put pressure on me to behave differently.[33] Another way to put it is that anyone who fails in his oughts or obligations falls short of what is normally expected in the way of moral behavior from human beings. Those who honor their obligations and do what they ought to do are good, decent human beings. If everyone were so, the world would be a far better place than it is.

Yet many people do extraordinary things for the good of others which go *far* beyond what is expected of them. A soldier who falls on a grenade in order to save his comrades, and either dies or is horribly wounded, or a missionary who spends her life in a poverty-stricken part of the world, giving up all personal comforts and opportunities for family life, do much good at great cost to themselves. They do things we have *no right to expect* from anyone, and they have a perfect right — an option or prerogative — not to act as they do. Each could instead have justifiably lived an ordinary life, decent and good, not meriting any blame and fulfilling all obligations. People like the soldier and the missionary are better, from a moral perspective, than the rest of us.[34] Nevertheless, being the best person one is capable of being is extremely difficult; since few of us hold ourselves to that standard, we hardly have a right to require it of others.[35]

Granted, saints and heroes can be hard to take. One reason may be that we feel ourselves inferior to them, knowing that we would be incapable of such sacrifices. Or we may wonder if they have normal desires and attachments. In some cases we may be correct in thinking that a person who gives his life for another may not value his life highly, or that one who gives herself to the service of God does so because she cares little for other humans. But it would be presumptuous in the extreme to think this is always so.

From the above we can see that agents have a prerogative to pursue their own concerns under certain circumstances. They have a prerogative in the sense that they are not deserving of criticism or of being thought lacking in moral fiber, even in some situations when they might do more good by an alternative course of action. On the other hand, if they do not choose that action which does the most good, they have not done their moral best. And there are times when pursuing our own concerns is not only not the best we can do, but something we have no prerogative to do.

For the most part, so long as we harm no one else or fail to shoulder our share of the enterprises from which we benefit, we are not obliged to act for the general good rather than our own or that of our loved ones. Often we do more good by caring for ourselves and those we know than we would do by helping strangers. But if we can do more good or prevent more harm by setting aside our projects and commitments, we may do better than be just ordinarily morally decent.[36] We can do more than just not do wrong. We can strive to make a greater contribution to the well-being of others than we are expected to do. We can volunteer to fill a need or prevent a disaster, even though there is no reason why we rather than someone else should do so. We can choose careers that emphasize service rather than profit. We can give of our surplus to help the unfortunate. One hopes that we would be motivated by caring and sympathy and not merely by promoting our image as great benefactors, superior to others. Yet regardless of motive, the supererogatory good we do has moral merit. In fact, only those who go above and beyond the call of duty and what they simply ought to do are doing the *best* they can do. Those who perform such supererogatory acts deserve praise, but we cannot expect or require everyone else to behave in a similar fashion. Obviously, what is obligatory under some moral systems might not be under others; the examples of the distinctions between obligations, oughts, and supererogation I have used here are drawn from what most contemporary Westerners appear to think. What I maintain here is not so much that those specific examples show what is actually obligatory, etc., as to illustrate the distinctions which any moral theory can and should employ.

In this way the distinction between what is morally required and what is morally best shows the proper role of agent-relative prerogatives. We have a prerogative not to do our very best, but none to fail to do what is required. All of this is perfectly compatible with agent-neutral moral theories. If more moral value — however this is defined — can be achieved by imposing sanctions on those who fail to perform a certain type of action, then it is obligatory. If not, then that type of act may still be better than what people are required to do. The best situation is one in which everyone does what he or she can to bring about the moral best. But given that many people don't care about morality as such and would have to be forced if they were to act for it, we would surely do more harm by requiring that people act for the best. Thus the best policy, on any moral theory, is to let people alone — i.e., allow them the prerogative — to follow their own inclinations except where their doing so will impair the ability of others to do the same. But even though they have room for agent-relative prerogatives, all credible moral theories set limits on partiality to those people, disciplines, and causes one loves.

3.2 Objections to Objections to Agent-Relative Prerogatives

3.2.1 It's Not So Good to Seek the General Good

Some have suggested that a person who always acts so as to bring about the greatest good, whatever that happens to be, *could* not be the best sort of person.[37] If I did things for my family and friends not because I loved them, but because I thought I could do the most good by these favors, and would never do anything for them if I believed I could do more good by helping someone else, they would have serious reason to feel hurt. It would be clear that I didn't love *them*, and was only interested in some moral abstraction like the greatest good for the greatest number. Perhaps this behavior would indicate an egoistic preoccupation with becoming better than others. Stocker, for example, maintains that if one is motivated only by doing the most good, he cannot be essentially committed to the person for whom he is doing the good.[38] As Stocker admits, this objection could apply not only to utilitarianism and other forms of consequentialism, but just as well to any moral theory. A person who directed her life *only* by the Categorical Imperative or the tenets of some religion would be equally insufferable.

Not only would a person like this be most unattractive, but there are good reasons for thinking that people do more good when they aim not at maximizing good or being perfectly moral, but at taking care of their own needs and those of the people they care about — provided, of course, that they avoid making it difficult for those to whom they are not close to achieve *their* own happiness.[39] 'Do-gooders' are often criticized as meddlers who don't understand the real needs and interests of the people they are trying to help. If, as seems likely, people who aim at maximizing good or being perfectly moral are not in fact taking the best means to doing good, then anyone who is solely motivated by this desire will not do as much good as he might if he had other motives. The fact that aiming to achieve the greatest general good is not the best means to achieving that end, however, does not show that attaining it cannot be the best result, morally speaking.

3.2.2 The Greatest Good Isn't Won by Aiming for It

Several philosophers have maintained that there is something paradoxical about the fact that maximum good is best attained by people aiming at things other than maximum good, and that this is somehow a failing for a teleological theory.[40] But there are many goals which are best achieved by not aiming for them directly. Happiness is one, and another might be winning at tennis. You are more likely to become a winning player by concentrating on developing your skills and coming to love the game for its own sake than by focusing on winning alone. This in no way indicates that there is something wrong with the goal of winning at tennis.[41] That indirect methods are the best way of achieving goals hardly impugns the goals themselves.

Besides, there is much interplay between the achievement of greater overall good and the pursuit of the specific good of individuals. A person who loves his own children deeply is much more likely to become sympathetic to the plight of children suffering in distant lands. He is better able to imagine the pain of those mired in war and famine because he is in tune to the feelings his children would have if they were hurt or hungry. This would in no way make him care less for his own children, but would make him more likely to extend aid to others. He might even help to develop empathy in his children by suggesting that they, too, give up small luxuries to help the unfortunate.

The process may work the other way, as well. Suppose that Dora's chief ambition is to do more good than anyone else. She throws herself into charitable work with great abandon, not from any feelings of concern for the people she helps, but merely because this will enhance her self-image as a superior person. Such people can, admittedly, do a lot of harm. Yet it is also possible that Dora will be moved by the predicaments of some of the recipients of her bounty or touched by the affection she receives in return. This may cause her to develop deep feelings and real concern for specific individuals. Moreover, the fact that a person wants to be a certain kind of individual — in particular, a morally good individual — does not necessarily involve a self-centered concern with one's own image.[42] Dora *might* want to be morally good, not because she is aiming for sainthood, but because she is appalled by the suffering in the world and believes that she can best help to relieve it by doing as much good as possible herself. She wants to help because she also believes that unless people generally pitch in, things won't get much better. It is unlikely that such a person will be totally devoid of self-regarding motives like the wish to feel useful or enjoyment of the gratitude of those she has helped. But her motives need not be entirely selfish.

3.2.3 The General Good Does Not Always Trump the Good of Individuals

A third objection involves situations in which the good of people to whom one has special attachments is incompatible with the achievement of the greatest overall good. According to most moral theories it appears that I ought in such circumstances to sacrifice individuals for the common good, whereas we ordinarily think it right to put individuals first. A possible example is the use of a commons. Here the families in a community own in common property all can use — e.g. land on which they can graze their sheep. It is to the advantage of all that the land not be overgrazed, but each family also wishes to maximize its profits, and so has a powerful motive to put as many sheep on the common pasture as possible. Of course if everyone overgrazes, the land will soon be worn out and all will suffer.

But suppose that one family is able to take its profits and move on to another place, leaving the others to shift as they may. Is it wrong for that family to do so? I believe that it is. This family has benefited at the expense of the others. If there is no central agency to enforce limits on grazing and everyone is acting in the same way, there may be no *obligations* for restraint. Yet those who overgraze and then move on have done harm, and I think most people would agree that they have acted wrongly.

Yet whether a person ought to put an individual before the good of all persons, impartially considered, is not always obvious. When one is faced with a choice of whether to harm an individual to whom one is specially committed or to harm people generally depends upon many factors. These include the nature of the special relationship and what would happen if everyone violated such relationships, the extent of the harm done, and also questions of desert. For example, if I discover that my friend is planning to bomb an airliner, I ought to turn him in. On the other hand, if he is an illegal alien who will be politically persecuted if deported, I should not report him. In general, such decisions should be based upon whether protecting one's friend would result in greater moral harm, according to the theory being used, than failing to do so. In my view, if the moral harm done by breaking the law (which includes the unfairness of making oneself an exception) would be outweighed by the direct harm done to my friend by obeying it, then breaking the law would be justified. In the case of the bomber obviously it would not; in the case of the political refugee it almost certainly would.

In making such choices, some allowances should, of course, be made for human weaknesses; we are not generally considered obligated to do or bear more than humans normally can. Thus we can say that a man in a concentration camp *ought* not to grab extra food for his child to save that child from starvation when other children are equally desperate. But assuming that, since almost anyone would do the same punishment would be inappropriate, he would not have an obligation not to try to save his own child at the expense of others.

3.2.4 Agent-Neutral Theories Ignore the Personal Point of View

Samuel Scheffler argues[43] that consequentialism ignores the personal point of view — that is, the fact that each individual cares specifically about his own interests, projects, and commitments out of proportion to his concern for overall good. These matter more to the individual than they matter in the overall calculation of what is the best state of affairs overall, even when the pain to an individual of having to relinquish something that matters to him is taken into the calculation of overall good. There is a sort of moral independence of the personal point of view; it should count in determining what an individual should do, over and above the extent to which it counts in weighing overall good. Thus each member of each family that is grazing its sheep on the commons has his or her own personal point of view which contains a desire that he or she, and the family as a whole, be as well off as possible, and this desire weighs not only in the impersonal calculation of overall good, but again in each person's calculation of what is best for him or her to do.

Nagel makes a similar point:[44] that the value to an individual of a private ambition like climbing Mount Kilimanjaro which is shared by few others may, for him, far outweigh a goal — like freedom from pain — which people generally have and which has agent-neutral value. Yet while others have a good moral reason not to cause the mountaineer pain, they do not have any moral reason to help him climb Mount Kilimanjaro. They have an objective, agent-neutral reason not to cause him pain, but only the mountaineer has his agent-relative reason to climb this peak. Moreover, the climber has a weightier reason to try to climb Kilimanjaro than he does to avoid pain, just because of the importance of that goal to him.

There is no question but that people do care more for themselves and certain others, as well as for some deeply-held commitments and cherished projects, than they do about the overall good of humanity. The relevant question, however, is to what extent does this caring determine what people ought to do or what is best for them to do.[45] That a person wants or cares for something does not determine conclusively that it is right or best for him to have it, although the wanting or caring is very important in determining what good or harm will depend on his having it or losing it. As long as it does not insist that everyone is *always required* to act for the best, any moral theory can give each person permission to pursue his own concerns, so long as they do not infringe unduly on the concerns of others.

The distinction between levels of good discussed earlier allows an answer to Nagel's objection and clarifies what is legitimate in the personal point of view. For a person who wants to climb Mount Kilimanjaro, doing so would usually count as a Level 3 good. As such, others would have a moral reason to at least not interfere in his effort, and perhaps even to help in some circumstances. But they have a greater reason to help him achieve those goods — such as his health — which are either required for him to attain happiness or are major contributors to his happiness, and no reason to promote this goal on his behalf if doing so would interfere with the abilities of other persons to attain their goals. Now in Nagel's example, the mountaineer's happiness seems to be highly dependent upon his climbing this particular mountain, so this would be a Level 2 good for him. If so, others have more reason not to interfere, or even to help him. Still, it must be remembered that a person's particular aims may not always be good for him to attain. If the mountaineer ruins his health as a result of climbing Kilimanjaro, he may regret this later on. Of course, at the end of his life he may believe it was worth the sacrifice, in which case climbing that peak was probably good for him despite the consequences.

And we must also remember that one's attaining his ambition ought not to take precedence over the crucial needs of others. If the mountaineer can only afford to make the climb by neglecting the safety of his native bearers, for example, he ought not to try it. Thus we can see how the way an action or goal of action is described can clarify its moral importance. Described as 'climbing Kilimanjaro' the goal does not seem to have any moral importance at all. Described, however, as 'attaining a life-long ambition,' it has much significance not only for the agent's personal good, but as a reason for others not to get in his way. Described as 'endangering the lives of native bearers,' it becomes an action to be avoided for strong moral reasons. Actions have multiple features and consequences, of which some may have moral importance. When they are described in terms of morally important features, we can see reasons for or against doing them which may not be immediately apparent.

That an impartial moral theory sets limits on prerogatives does not entail that it cannot take into account the differences between individuals' interests, talents, and commitments. No reasonable moral system would require a talented artist to give up work on his painting in order to perform some community service like picking up trash on a highway. On the other hand, he would not be excused from obeying anti-littering laws, paying taxes for highway upkeep, or doing *something* for his community. He might, for example, donate some of his paintings to be auctioned for charity — a contribution that would not only be consistent with his integrity as an artist, but would do more good than his collecting trash.

3.2.5 If Consequentialism Were True, Competition Would not Be Legitimate

Another argument for the primacy of agent-centered prerogatives is our recognition of the legitimacy of competition.[46] Since not all can win, my gain is your loss and conversely, and we both have, if the common view is correct, the right to pursue our own good, even though it seems that one of us benefits at the expense of the other. Thus one's personal good is in direct conflict with the common good, and in these cases would not any moral theory that is fundamentally impartial demand that one give up one's personal good?

Competition, however, as I showed above, need not involve one person's benefiting at the expense of another, if certain conditions hold. If the competition is voluntary and fair, and if no one is excluded because of characteristics irrelevant to the nature of the competition — e.g., skin color or one's parents' social position

— then no competitor necessarily benefits at the expense of another. Furthermore, if the society at large provides a variety of opportunities for all, winning and other forms of success are more evenly distributed. Moreover, when competition is not forced, people engage in it because they think the chance of winning or the pleasure of the contest outweigh the pain of losing; thus even the losers usually do not sacrifice much happiness. Finally, even those who fare badly in competition still gain benefits from the performance of those who do win out; a great musician provides pleasure for many who have no hope of achieving the recognition she attains.

3.3 Conclusion Regarding Agent-Relative Prerogatives

From the above I think we can see that agent-relative prerogatives have a place in any reasonable moral theory, although they do not play the role some theorists would give them. There are, as we have seen, constraints on agent-relative prerogatives. These constraints apply when significant harm to persons other than the agent is likely to result from the agent's exercise of his prerogative. I have a right to favor my family and friends over strangers just so long as I do not hinder the ability of strangers to further their interests; I am not morally required to work for their happiness, but I have no right to deprive them of the means for achieving their own. I have a right to pursue activities I find valuable and enjoyable, even when I might do more good by serving others, but I have no right to engage in activities that bring harm to others. My life and actions might, however, be more meritorious if I did some things which I have a right not to do, such as contributing large amounts of money and time to the service of the less fortunate.

An agent-neutral moral theory can make room for all these factors.[47] One which assigns value to a person's fulfilling certain responsibilities and commitments, showing love for specific other individuals, and having aspects of his life protected from the violations of others can allow certain agent-relative prerogatives. At the same time, such a reasonable theory also sets proper limits; while one's rights to pursue his own concerns are extremely valuable, they do not override certain other moral considerations.[48]

4. RIGHTS

Rights are intimately related to obligations. For the most part, if Person A has a right to X, then some other person, or group of persons, B, has an obligation at least not to interfere with A's possession of X. If A has a right to life, then all other people have a duty not to kill him. If A has a right to vote, others are forbidden to prevent him from voting. If A has a right to an education, his parents, or the state, or some other group is obliged to see that he at least has the opportunity to get one. Anyone who tries to kill A, or keep A from voting or out of school, is and ought to be punished in some way. In some cases A has a positive right, in that there is some B who is obligated to do something for A; for example, children have a right to certain basic care from their parents, and parents who fail to give this care may be penalized.

4.1 Rights and Obligations

It is not, however, always true that if Person A has an obligation to do something, there is some Person B who has a right to his doing it. There usually is. For example, if Joe is an employee of a firm, the owners, other employees, and customers of the firm have a right to Joe's fulfilling the duties of his job. Below, however, we shall see some examples in which obligations and rights are not correlated.

Like obligations, rights involve an element of coercion. If I have a right to something, it is not merely something that it would be nice if I had. My seeking or having it ought to be protected. As with obligations, since sanctions and a credible threat of them have costs, the good to be achieved by protecting a person's possession of a thing must be relatively large if there ought to be a sanction.

Although everyone agrees that rights are *usually* correlated with obligations, this is not always so. One way to approach the issue of rights is through an example proposed by Joel Feinberg.[49] Feinberg maintains that people often have claims to receive certain sorts of treatment. He considers claims virtually equivalent to rights. He argues that sometimes these claims are not claims *against* anyone, and, for this reason, do not involve obligations on the part of some other person. He considers an example of such a claim to be the case of a starving baby in an impoverished country. This child has, Feinberg says, a right or a claim to food, yet no one identifiable individual or group has an obligation to feed her.

Two points can be made in response to this. First of all, it is not clear that *no one* has an obligation to provide food for this baby. Secondly, even if no one has this obligation, there may still be a stringent moral demand, whether we call it a right or not, that the child be fed. Certainly the child ought to be fed. But in saying that she ought to be fed, we are claiming simply that there is something wrong in a world where she goes hungry. This — as James Forrester has pointed out — does not logically imply that any particular agent ought to do so or should be blamed for not doing so.[50]

But now, suppose that some people having more than they need would like to help hungry children. As it happens, there are millions of hungry children. Presumably, each charitable individual would be doing what he ought by providing food for some of them. But no one person, and very likely not all of them together, could feed all the hungry. Is there any reason why I, as opposed to my next door neighbor, ought to feed the *particular* child in Feinberg's example and not her brother, or another child in a different country?

The answer is clearly no. We surely ought to give of our surplus to those who are needy. In addition, we ought to try to give where we can help the most. If the money we give is pocketed by venal bureaucrats, we have not helped anyone. We may do more good by helping our relatives and neighbors whose needs we know directly, and where we do not have to depend on others to distribute the goods we provide. On the other hand, those people may not be the most needy. Hence, in attempting to do good, we have to make complex decisions, and it is not always clear that one charitable act will be better than alternatives. Hence it is not clear that I, and I rather than someone else, ought to help a particular hungry baby rather than a different one.

Certainly those who have plenty ought to give some of what they do not need to others who are in need. And they ought to target their charity to those who will profit from it. Furthermore, well off people are to some extent obligated to give something of their surplus to the needy, for public opinion does — and ought to — pressure them to share their wealth. But as a rule a given individual has no obligation to assist some specific needy person.[51]

On the other hand, even though there is no one individual who has a duty, or even ought, to feed the starving baby in Feinberg's example, we think there is something wrong with a world in which children are hungry. It *ought to be* that all children are fed. Furthermore, assuming that through adequate birth control, sustainable agricultural techniques, and just distribution of goods we *could* feed everyone adequately, then we, collectively, *ought to do* so. Individuals and groups who feed some of the hungry are, generally speaking, doing something good.[52]

A hugely complex problem like world hunger cannot, however, be resolved by piecemeal efforts. What is needed is a well thought out plan which can fit in with other human enterprises. If a plan conflicts with too many other projects and ways of life, it will not be accepted to the extent necessary to get it to work. Acceptance is crucial, since a plan of that magnitude would require the coordinated efforts of many individuals. Only when some plan is in place, can we start talking about obligations of specific individuals to feed other specific individuals. We may certainly have smaller plans which can effectively alleviate hunger among certain groups. Where people are committed to helping certain specific individuals through such plans, then those people have obligations to those specific individuals. If the baby in Feinberg's example is covered by such a program, then particular persons do have an obligation to *her* to see that she is fed.

Most such programs, however, help as many children as they can, but they have no commitment, and no obligation, to help all, even all those in one specific area, such as the slums of a large third world city. And only if there comes to be a world wide plan with the capacity of reaching *all* children, and a mechanism for doing so, will there be, for every single child, a particular individual or group which has an obligation to feed him or her. There could, of course, be national programs committed to feeding all children of that nation, and some countries have them. Within such a country each child would have someone obligated to see that she is fed.

In short, there ought to be such a system. Furthermore, it would be good to work toward creating such a system, and those who are in a particularly good position to work for such a system *ought* to do so. In the meantime those who can ought to alleviate hunger for individuals, so long as their efforts do not create still greater problems.

We certainly recognize obligations of charity, but these are not obligations to perform specific actions for the benefit of specific individuals, unless and until we commit ourselves to a particular program which covers those particular individuals. Then our duties are defined.

4.2. Background versus Institutional Rights

What, now, are the *rights* of the child in Feinberg's example? If there is no specific individual or agency who has the responsibility — i.e., the duty, to see that she is fed, and if there were no rights without corresponding obligations, then it seems that she would not have a right to be fed. For unless responsibility can be allocated, it is not possible to have and enforce sanctions to guarantee her being fed. If it is not possible to enforce sanctions in a particular case, then there *are* no sanctions in that case. For a completely ineffective sanction, as we saw above, is no sanction at all.

Yet it does seem that people can have rights to things for which there are not, in fact, sanctions to protect those rights. People who are oppressed are said to have a right to freedom and self determination. And this would be true even if there were nobody (including the downtrodden themselves) who recognized such a right or was critical of the oppressors. The moral evil would be the same, and so would be the fact that there ought to be some way of preventing such tyranny.

On the other hand, unless there ought to be sanctions, there is no right. Rights, as we saw earlier, are not just things that it would be good to have or bad not to have, but things that should be protected. If a starving baby has a right to food, then something ought to be done to at least make it possible for her to receive it. It seems reasonable that every nation that can ought to have agencies whose job it is to make sure that all its children have enough to eat. Some, however, may be too poor or disrupted by war or other problems to manage this. If so, the nation — or rather its citizens collectively — are not obligated to feed every hungry child.

There are, moreover, nations which have sufficient wealth, and no major disruptions which would prevent them from having agencies to guarantee food for all their children. If they do not do so, this is a fault of which the citizens, collectively, are guilty. They are worthy of blame, and *are* blamed, by world opinion, their underclasses, and their own citizens who do care, but whose efforts to change things have not prevailed because of the apathy of the majority. In *this* case, there ought to be sanctions, although they may consist solely of criticism. Should such criticism not exist, however, this surely does not take away the right of hungry children to food.

On the other hand, we sometimes say that people *ought to have* a right to something, where their possession of the thing is not protected (e.g., in the nineteenth century, some said that women ought to have the right to vote). This suggests that in certain contexts, the term 'right' is used to refer to some good against which there *are* sanctions for depriving people of it. This further suggests that there may be an ambiguity in the term 'right,' or at least two different types of rights.

Ronald Dworkin[53] proposes a distinction between *background* rights and *institutional* rights. The latter are actually protected in a particular society; in the United States, for example, institutional rights would include the right to vote, the right to collect Social Security, and the right to read pornography. Even the definition or promulgation of such a right may depend on certain social structures and laws. A background right, on the other hand, might or might not be protected in a given society. If it is so protected, it might take very different forms in different political systems. A background right corresponding to the right to vote might be the right to have a say in social policy. In some cultures, voting is not the form which this right takes, even where it is protected. For example, there are some parts of the world in which no action is taken unless a consensus is reached. Everyone has been able to have a say in what is done, but there is no voting. Likewise a background right to care when one is old and helpless may be realized as an institutional right to getting a pension from the government or an institutional right to direct support from one's children. Some societies do not take care of the aged; in these places, the old may have a background right to care, but no institutional right at all.[54]

What of background rights to things which cannot be obtained? Suppose that a full range of the best health care known to medical science is such a great good that everyone ought not only to have it, but should have special efforts made to ensure that they get it whenever they need and want it. Assume also that the world does not have the resources to provide such care (which might include mechanical replacement, at great expense, of any defective body part, so that life of a sort might be indefinitely prolonged). Then does everyone have a background right to optimal health care? I would say that we do not. The reason is that if a good cannot be provided, then punishing, or even criticizing, anyone for not providing it, is wrong and thus there ought not to be a sanction against failure to provide.[55] So if a good can't be provided, there is rarely a right.[56]

The upshot of all this discussion is that rights, like obligations, require the moral justifiability of sanctions. Without them, there is no right. On the other hand, unlike obligations, some rights (namely, background, as opposed to institutional, rights), do not require the existence of sanctions.

4.3 When Can Rights Be Overridden?

That a right is of great moral importance does not, however, entail that it may not be overridden by other considerations. Some rights are more important than others, and when two rights conflict, the more important should be protected. If having my property protected would mean that my life, or that of others, would not be, my right to property is overridden.

Just as it is possible that we may be excused from what would normally be a duty if we would be able to do great good which is not obligatory by violating that duty, some rights may also be overridden by moral (or even prudential) considerations which are not rights. Returning to a previous example, if Steve is lost and seeks shelter from a storm by breaking into in Samantha's mountain cabin when she is not there to give permission, he surely is justified in using the cabin without permission. Samantha's right to have her property let alone unless she gives permission to use it is overridden by Steve's urgent need.

Even if one's possession of some item is protected, this does not guarantee a right. The medieval lord who exercised his *droit de seigneur*, was allowed to sleep with the wife of his serf. Assuming, as I suppose everyone now does, that he was wrong to do this, he did not really have such a right. Those who believed that such activities were morally acceptable and should be allowed, no doubt *believed* that the lord had the right. If they were wrong, and the practice shouldn't have been permitted, the lord had no right to sleep with the serf's wife; rather in that time this practice was tolerated, allowed, or guaranteed.

4.4 When Are Rights Relinquished?

An individual may have rights that he or she does not exercise, and, as with obligations, a person may release others from their obligation to give him that to which he has a right. In every election, millions of Americans waive their right to vote. This does not, as Feinberg recognizes,[57] mean that they have lost their right to vote. If they chooose to vote in the next election, they may. If Samantha is home she may release Steve from his obligation not to trespass on her property by inviting him in. Release by the person affected, however, may not always mean that the right is no longer in force. As in the case of obligations, my asking you to kill me or take my life savings does not by itself waive my right to my life and my property. Only if it is obvious that I will not suffer significantly by giving up what I have a right to, might you be no longer obliged not to take it.[58]

H.L.A. Hart has argued that there are no rights for individuals who cannot by their own choice limit the freedom of action in some area of some other person or persons.[59] He concludes from this that individuals who cannot choose to restrict the actions of others, such as infants and animals, do not really have rights. It is, however, not the actual choice that constitutes the right, for a person may have a right which he himself does nothing to enforce, because enforcement is better left to others. If you are mugged on a city street, the pursuit of the mugger is up to the police, and his prosecution and punishment up to the courts. You might attempt to take the law into your own hands and punish him yourself, but this would be foolish. Not only are you likely to get badly hurt, but private vengeance is explicitly forbidden by the law. The most you can do is call the police and testify in court, but anyone else can do this for you.

In short, even though you have a right to walk the streets in peace and a right to your money, *you yourself* are not the one who limits the freedom of others with respect to your rights. In some cases, of course, you may. You may inflict social sanctions on people who violate your right to proper respect, and you may bring suit against a person who has cheated you. But we have many rights that we ourselves do not or cannot or ought not to enforce by our own action. Since this is so, there is no reason for supposing that being in a position to limit the action of another by our own choices is a necessary condition of having a right. Hence Hart's argument provides no reason to suppose that those who cannot so choose have no rights.

In this chapter I have argued that the distinction between what is best for one to do, what one ought to do, and what one is obligated to do can be used by any type of moral theory and allows the resolution of those objections raised by the proponents of agent-relative prerogatives. Rights can also be accommodated into theories that provide the distinction. When this distinction is applied to my own theory, I believe it is consistent with a wide variety of well-established moral beliefs and not obviously inconsistent with any.

CHAPTER 9

SOLVING MORAL PROBLEMS

I have now completed my defense of the view that moral judgments are capable of truth and falsity, and that we can have moral knowledge. In the first chapter I argued that moral judgments are no different in principle from statements of fact in other areas of discourse. In Chapters 2 through 8 I have expounded a moral theory which I believe would be acceptable to almost everyone, philosophers and non-philosophers alike; in fact, most of what I argued in Chapter 2 and Chapter 8 could apply to any moral theory, even a non-cognitivist one. Throughout I have tried to deal with objections which have been raised against similar specific tenets in the past. While other possible theories might be equally coherent and equally able to accommodate all well established moral beliefs, I do maintain that any such theory would — as I believe mine does — incorporate the fundamental truth conditions of moral judgments.

My views do not support moral absolutism. Because the fundamental purpose of the moral enterprise is to promote equally the happiness of all persons (and to some extent that of other sentient beings), and because happiness can, in turn, be achieved in many different ways, different moral codes and practices can be equally good. On the other hand, my theory is not relativistic, for it affirms the universal validity of two basic principles that are in one form or another held by people in all known times and places. Further, it provides ways of combining these two principles that avoid the appearance of conflict between them. As noted in Chapter 1, these principles might be abandoned; this could, however, happen only under one of two conditions. Either human nature would be so altered as to be unrecognizable, or people would have little interest in promoting what would then be called moral behavior.

There remains a major objection against which I must contend. It is that general moral principles are too vague to carry the burden of showing us the solutions to moral problems. Several philosophers have argued that any proposed moral principles are either so vague that they provide no solutions to concrete moral problems or so specific that they generate counterexamples.[1] In what follows, I shall argue that general moral principles *can*, when knowledge of non-moral facts is sufficient, be used to solve specific moral problems. The argument here will be brief; elsewhere[2] I have applied the basic theory defended in this book to the resolution of a number of practical moral issues.

1. A MORAL PROBLEM

There are many difficulties in applying basic moral principles to specific cases. While most everyday instances of applying moral principles are fairly straightforward, other situations are astonishingly complex. For example, when two persons suffer cardiac arrest simultaneously, the hospital personnel and equipment needed for a "code" may be sufficient for only one.[3] This came close to happening on my first job after finishing nursing school, in a small county hospital in Rawlins, Wyoming. One night two people were brought into the emergency room in full cardiac arrest; luckily, however, the second did not arrive until after the unsuccessful efforts on the first had been stopped, so that it was not necessary to make any decision about how to allocate the code team's resources.

A later situation brought home to me the difficulties that might arise if two patients "coded" simultaneously. Rawlins is the home of the Wyoming State Penitentiary, and the inmates are frequently brought to the hospital. Violent criminals were then (and no doubt still are) kept in rooms apart from other patients, shackled to their beds, and provided with a twenty-four hour guard. For a time two penitentiary prisoners who had both had mild heart attacks — not severe enough, evidently, in their physician's opinion, to warrant their being placed in intensive care — shared a room on the general medical floor.

Apart from being prisoners and having had heart attacks, the two men, whom I will call Jones and Smith, were very different. Jones had been convicted of a particularly brutal rape and murder; Smith had been sentenced for armed robbery but had not, so far as I knew, inflicted bodily harm on anyone. Aside from his heart condition, Jones was in good health; Smith, however, was suffering from terminal lung cancer. Even with pain medication, he was wretchedly uncomfortable. Jones, on the other hand was in high spirits, attempting jokes with everyone who entered the room. He evidently enjoyed life, to a point that most of us on the staff found repugnant. We couldn't help but feel that given his hideous crime he ought to be ashamed and keep quiet. Certainly no one felt like being friendly with Jones or responding to his overtures.

Since both Jones and Smith had suffered mild heart attacks, cardiac arrest was a distinct possibility.[4] Although it never happened, it has been interesting to speculate as to what we should have done if Jones and Smith had suffered cardiac arrest simultaneously. Obviously, the staff on the floor would have begun CPR with both patients, but the full effort could only have been carried out for one of them. For which one — Jones or Smith — should it have been made?

There are a number of morally important considerations here. First of all, Smith was not going to live long in any case and his present life was probably not very pleasant for him. Given his very poor condition, resuscitation efforts would not have had a high probability of success; if he survived at all, he might well have been left with severe brain damage. Jones, however, was in basically good health, and resuscitation would have a good chance of restoring him to full functioning. So far as anyone could tell, he had good prospects for many more years of life. Jones seemed to be enjoying life much more than Smith was. These considerations would favor resuscitating Jones before Smith. It is, however, important to note that Smith had never expressed a desire to die or not to have life-saving efforts made on his behalf. It was only through minimal observation and projection of our own feelings that we could have inferred that Jones's life meant more to him than Smith's did to *him*.

Then there is the question of desert. Both Jones and Smith were convicted criminals. Yet Jones's crime was much worse than Smith's. Jones had inflicted terrible harm, including death, on other human beings. Smith had threatened violence and stolen money, but he had not physically harmed a person. While neither man had earned much from society, Jones clearly deserved less than Smith. Or, at least, this appears so from what we knew of their reasons for being in the Pen. We *didn't* know anything about other aspects of their lives. Given the nature of Jones's crime, it is most unlikely that his character and behavior prior to committing it were exemplary. But he might not have been all bad. He might also have had dreadful experiences in his childhood, which would hardly excuse what he had done, but might provide mitigating circumstances. As for Smith, he might have committed his robbery under desperate circumstances which would have tried the soul of any man. On the other hand, his crime could have been only one of a long series of misdeeds, some of which might have been worse than Jones's but were never found out. In short, it is unlikely but not inconceivable that Smith was a worse person than Jones, had done even more evil, and was therefore less deserving of having his life saved.

Also relevant might be the effects on others of saving Jones versus saving Smith. Since they were both in prison, they could hardly be supporting any dependents, but they might have had family who cared. Furthermore, Smith's term was (so far as I know) limited, although it was most unlikely that he would survive to see the end of it or be able to support anyone if he did. Jones was a lifer, but he was in fact later released on parole. So it is possible that his family might have profited from his being released and enabled to earn money.

There are other powerful considerations which would point toward saving Smith. Both men had shown themselves dangerous. But given Smith's debilitated condition, he was not as dangerous as Jones. Jones might kill a guard while imprisoned or an innocent civilian after escape or release on parole. Moreover, even if he never hurt anyone again, we cannot dismiss the fear induced by his getting free among those whom he had harmed or might harm. As it happens, I later heard that after Jones's parole, his one surviving victim committed suicide from terror and depression. In short, Jones's continuing to live was a not inconsiderable threat to other people, although the degree of the threat was hardly calculable in advance.

Another element to consider is the economic cost to society. Both convicts were being supported at public expense while in the Pen, and their medical care was also being paid for by the State. Smith, because of his other illness, was likely to have the more expensive care in the short term, but Jones would be around for longer and be supported by the public longer. On the other hand, Jones might possibly have been required to do some useful work in prison once he recovered, thereby offsetting some of the public expenditures.

Given the fact that decisions to resuscitate must be made instantaneously, it would have been, of course, impossible to calculate all these factors, some of which depended upon information which no one at the hospital had available. No doubt, given the antipathy which the staff by and large felt for Jones, Smith would have gotten the code team, but, of course, this antipathy wouldn't have made the decision the *right* one. Yet all these factors are morally relevant and need to be taken into account in order to determine what would have been the best decision — in this case and in others — and to enable guidelines to be developed which would make future immediate decisions more likely to be correct.

Another important consideration has nothing to do with the effects on the two criminals or the costs to other individuals, but the responsibilities of medical personnel. Partly because of their inability to know many of the relevant facts, but even more so because of the scope of their duties, they have no right to let their moral judgments about their patients affect the care they give. Or, if they cannot avoid doing so, they should, if possible, step aside and let others take charge of the patient in question. (For example, a black nurse on our unit discovered, when she went to offer a different prisoner an evening back rub, that his back sported a huge tattoo of a Ku Klux Klansman. She refused to have anything more to do with this individual, but there were others who could take over his care. Had there not been, she would still have had an obligation to do what she could for him, despite her entirely understandable revulsion.) In the situation under discussion, of course, a decision would have had to be made — but our moral assessments of the individuals should not have had any affect upon it. After all, there is an expectation on the part of patients that medical staff will care for them regardless of their moral failings — without which expectation they might well be reluctant to give them great control over their lives.[5]

2. WHY SOLVING MORAL PROBLEMS IS DIFFICULT

What has been said of this case is equally applicable to many of the thorny problems in applied ethics. What makes these questions so difficult? Students in applied ethics classes often complain that knowing the theories of Mill, Kant, or Rawls doesn't help them decide whether life-sustaining treatment should be withheld from a patient in a permanent vegetative state. The theories seem to them quite irrelevant. They maintain you can use any given ethical theory to defend different and incompatible answers to the same question. And they have a point.

Suppose, for example, we choose to resolve the dilemma of which convict to resuscitate by the principle of the greatest happiness for the greatest number. We could say that Jones has more to live for than Smith, so that more happiness will be created if he were saved. Yet Jones is more likely to harm others and be a drain on the public treasury; saving him will probably create more unhappiness than saving Smith. A thoroughgoing utilitarian would calculate *expected* utility here. If one makes many choices under uncertainty, acting on the basis of expected utility should let one maximize happiness in the long run, if not always on specific occasions. Thus a utilitarian might choose to "code" Jones or to "code" Smith, depending upon his assessment of how likely each, if resuscitated, was to survive and obtain some happiness, as well as how likely each was to harm others. There would be many unknowns here, and even slight differences in either one's estimate of probability of some outcome or the value or disvalue one would place on it, might tip the balance.

The matter of desert is a difficult one for utilitarians. Punishment, according to classical utilitarianism, should not be based on the nature of the criminal's offense but upon the effects of that punishment upon him and upon the rest of society. Rehabilitation, protection of the innocent, deterrence, and restitution are all recognized by utilitarians as legitimate grounds for punishment. Retribution, however, is not.[6] That Jones deserves less would not be a reason in itself to withhold lifesaving care from him. The only acceptable related reason would be that Jones is less amenable to rehabilitation or is more dangerous to society than Smith, so that less good would be done by saving him. This by itself would allow the utilitarian to argue that saving Jones would produce a lower level of expected utility than would saving Smith. Yet it still might be outweighed by the greater expected utility to Jones himself of being resuscitated. Thus utilitarians might answer the dilemma either way, not merely because they might assess probabilities in several ways, but because they might place different values on the possible outcomes. And these values are difficult to measure, so it is difficult to see how a utilitarian would decide.

A Kantian would approach this dilemma quite differently. A Kantian holds that considering the interests of other persons in deciding which criminal to let die is never justifiable, for we ought never to use any person as a mere means.[7] The life of any person has value because of its rational nature, and its being saved should not depend upon that life's effect upon others. Indeed, differences in the prospects for future happiness of the two criminals themselves should not be considered, for the value of our lives is independent of our happiness. Kant would have us decide on the basis of what the agents could rationally will, and this seems inevitably to depend on considerations of the effects on human beings of universally applying the maxim of action. Hence our Kantian might decree that he could rationally will that in situations where the life of one person only can be saved, we must save the one who has the best prospects for future happiness. In this instance, he would probably choose Jones. But the Kantian might equally well determine that he could rationally will that in all cases where we can save the life of only one dangerous person we must save the person who would be least dangerous. In that case, he would probably choose Smith. No matter which decision he makes, the Kantian considers consequences — not the consequences for the specific individuals affected, but the consequences if the maxim of action were universally applied. For Kant says that in order to decide which of two maxims whose recommended actions conflict we ought to follow, we must decide which one we could most rationally will as a universal law. And to figure out what the consequences of universal application of a rule or policy is, if anything, even more difficult than to determine the probable consequences in the particular case. Now Kant himself was a strong believer in retributive justice.[8] He might very well argue that *neither* man deserves to be saved, but Jones less so than Smith. Yet, as I shall argue below, there are major difficulties with adding to an individual's punishment which has been prescribed by law either ill-treatment or the withholding of benefits.

This brief discussion suggests that definitive solutions to difficult practical problems are not always obviously derivable from an ethical theory. If different answers can be derived from the same theory, and if the same answers can be generated by different theories, the skeptical student will ask why we should care which ethical theory we adopt. And if there is no reason to prefer one theory over another, does it matter whether or how a given moral viewpoint may be justified? No wonder many students view both ethical theory and metaethics as no more than academic speculation!.

These difficulties provide an argument against the possibility of ethical truth; if moral judgments are neither true nor false, this would explain why answers to practical problems are hard to come by.   Nevertheless, we can give other explanations for the failure of theories to give obvious solutions to hard problems. For instance, the facts which we need to know are so numerous and complex that we cannot in our present state of knowledge make the necessary calculations. Moreover, the data are not sufficiently complete, and it is unlikely that they ever will be. Hence, trying to decide whether it is better to "code" Jones than to "code" Smith is rather like predicting the weather in New York City exactly ten years from now: theoretically easy but impossible in practice.

One can justifiably argue that the same problems arise whenever we try to predict the effects of human behavior. Because we do not have sufficiently precise and detailed knowledge of initial conditions, our actions may have effects that we could never have predicted and which are markedly different from what we intended. This can happen even when we think we know all the relevant facts. When we are dealing with a problem in which we *know* that we cannot possibly discover many of the critical facts, it is no wonder that we are often at a loss as to what we ought to do. Agreeing on principles does not suffice for agreement on a solution.

I don't think anyone doubts that lack of factual knowledge is a significant handicap in solving a complex problem in applied ethics. It does not, however, seem to be the whole story. The reason for much of the complexity of moral theory is that what is good for people is so intimately connected with human desires and purposes. Almost all major ethical theories acknowledge this connection. Mill, for example, maintains that the most pleasurable (and hence, in his view, the best) experiences are those preferred by people who have experienced them.[9] Even Kant tells us that we ought to act according to maxims we could *will* to be universal laws.[10]   And a recent ethicist, David Brink, who has argued that human good is independent of what is desired, still maintains that the ability to pursue (and, presumably, sometimes attain) one's goals and purposes is an integral part of that good.[11]

People's desires and purposes, however, are notoriously difficult to assess. For any individual, what he wants and how much and how he ranks the objects of his desires differ from day to day and even minute to minute, so that he may not even know himself what he wants. Often a person can find out what he wants, or wants most, only by a complex process of self-analysis, and of observing not only his own behavior, but his reactions to real and hypothetical situations.

Even when a person knows perfectly well what he wants, he may not candidly express his desires to others. Consequently, it is even harder to know what others want than to know our own desires. When peoples' desires clash, so that satisfying those of one necessarily frustrates those of another, most theories have no decision procedure because we cannot measure how much we would satisfy or frustrate the parties concerned; the difficulties with interpersonal utility comparisons discussed earlier makes this clear.

But the difficulties with recognizing, measuring, and comparing actual desires and purposes are only part of the story. There are no ethical theorists who have maintained that all *actual* desires ought to be satisfied; most ethical theorists tell us that we ought to be somewhat selective in our striving to realize our purposes. Mill thought we should pursue the pleasures we would prefer if we had experienced all. Kant says we should act on maxims that we could *rationally* will to be universal laws: i.e., those that would not be impossible, self-defeating, or against what any person is capable of wanting if everyone tried to follow them. Ideal observer theories maintain that we ought to act as an all knowing, impartial, and benevolent individual would want all human beings to act.[12] Rawls's contract theory says we should choose principles that we would prefer under certain rather specific choice conditions.[13]

In Chapter 3 I argued that what is good for us is happiness, which is proportional to the net amount of time we spend wanting our lives to continue as they are. This may or may not occur when our actual desires are satisfied. Where we have purposes that will inevitably be frustrated, happiness is best realized when one is able to give up or modify these purposes. Furthermore, our lives might be better and happier if we had purposes we do not in fact have, if they would lead to a happier life overall. This view, I think, reduces but does not eliminate the problems of measurement.

In short, according to most ethical theories, what is good for us is not necessarily what we want here and now but what we would want under certain conditions, or what would satisfy certain criteria. As if the task of knowing actual desires is not - hard enough, that of knowing hypothetical wants or the effects of their being satisfied is extremely difficult, if not in many cases impossible.

All this suggests that if valid ethical principles are closely tied to wanting and desiring, we have a good explanation of why it is hard to solve complex moral questions, especially those affecting large numbers of individuals. For some, this may indicate a reason to reject desire-based ethics. The alternatives are not promising, however. They tend to degenerate into absolutist principles, or spur-of-the-moment intuitive decisions, which fail abysmally in complex situations. In the example of the prisoners just discussed we can see that such intuitive decisions could be far from right or reasonable. And when such tenets as "Never take human life" conflict with central human concerns, people who disagree require justification. One who appeals to this tenet as a reason for opposing all abortions, for example, will be challenged by those who point out that an absolute prohibition would result in deformed, retarded, starving, unloved, and abused children, whose lives might be worse than no life at all.

If the anti-abortionist is to justify his position, he must find reasons why all of this suffering is more morally tolerable than is allowing abortions. And it is difficult to see how he can do this except by appeal to other human concerns — i.e., things that people want or could be expected to want under certain conditions. For example, the principle of absolute sanctity of life might be based on the view that life is desired above all by everyone, or that because God has created life, we would risk our relationship with God by destroying it. (A good relationship with God, presumably, is what we would desire above all, if we were sufficiently rational.)[14]

Thus far the issues discussed involve only individuals whom all acknowledge as existing persons. Other issues concern how we should treat those like fetuses, animals, and future generations, which are either clearly not existing persons or not so recognized by everyone. There is less of a consensus on what makes an individual a person than there is on what principles ought to govern our treatment of persons, so debates on abortion and animal rights are even further from resolution than debates on allocation of scarce medical resources.[15]

To summarize, even where we have clear principles which offer guidance in ordinary circumstances, the facts needed to apply them in complex situations can rarely all be known. Even the basic morally relevant features, like happiness, desires, and equality of treatment, are extremely difficult to assess. Add to this that it is of great importance to us to solve these problems correctly, and it is no wonder that we find them so difficult.

In spite of these difficulties, there are many cases of obvious wrongdoing: e.g., inflicting burns on a small child, cheating an old lady out of her pension, and genocide. Even though there are persons who attempt to justify such atrocities, and gullible individuals who fall for their arguments, a rational and impartial observer can easily see the fallacies. Likewise there are clear-cut cases of doing what is right. Even though many of the great heroes and heroines of the past were criticized by their contemporaries, future generations can assess objectively the value of what they did.

The above discussion suggests, moreover, that our uncertainty in so many less clear cut cases is fully explicable without supposing that there is no solution. Certainly for many moral dilemmas there is no *good* solution. Every alternative brings moral harm, and at times no one alternative is less harmful than the others. Still, even to conclude that there is nothing to choose, morally speaking, between two or more alternatives is to find an answer.

Disagreements between people who sincerely want to do the right thing, and who are trying to apply the principles of beneficence and fairness, are most often based upon disagreements over facts and the relative probabilities of the outcomes of different courses of action. Other disagreements may be based on their ways of comparing the value of different outcomes for different people – comparisons which have grave difficulties, but which can be lessened by the suggestions I have made in earlier chapters, such as classifying goods on different levels by their usual effect on happiness. And finally, their disagreements may result from different notions of who is to count as a person.[16]

Another proposed explanation for the difficulty of applying moral principles to specific situations is that there is an irresolvable gap between the value terms in which general principles are stated and the factual terms in which problematic situations are described.[17] Such expressions as 'good,' 'happiness,' 'freedom,' 'interests,' 'fairness,' etc., in which general principles and theories are stated are value terms. When we try to apply such principles to specific cases, we need to interpret facts in such a way as to indicate whether these value terms apply. According to the argument under discussion, there is no way to do this without changing over from factual language to value terms.

The facts of a case, for example, might tell us that a certain medical procedure would cost a given amount of money, have a given probability of curing the patient, and have particular probabilities of causing specific side effects. But, the argument goes, only by changing the meanings of some of the terms used could we restate these facts in such a way as to say anything about what is in the patient's best interests or what is most likely to make him or her happy or whether spending the money on the treatment is fair to others. In making these changes, indeed, the person drawing the inferences would incorporate his or her own values by interpreting the facts in the light of those values. Thus if I were to think that too much money was being spent on a treatment, I might say that it was unfair to other persons, or not in the patient's own best interests. On the other hand, if the costs did not seem excessive to me, I might describe using the treatment as fair and in the patient's best interest.

This objection poses a formidable challenge. To meet it one must show that defensible practical solutions *can* be generated from a theory in combination with the known facts. I have tried to do this earlier in *Persons, Animals, and Fetuses*. For now it should suffice to recapitulate two points for which I argued earlier in this book:

(1) Individual good can be defined in terms of happiness, which is living as one wants to live, and which is proportional to the net length of time one spends wanting one's situation to continue — a theoretically measurable quantity. This notion does not incorporate value concepts such as benefit and fairness; and

(2) Because actual comparisons of happiness are difficult — even when possible — , we can give rough estimates of what is good for people and make judgments of distribution in terms of the more easily measurable means and conditions of happiness.[18]

Because many of these means and conditions *can* be measured and compared, they allow us to make rational decisions about what is best for individuals and what is fair to do when we are unable to give everyone what would benefit him or her. While I can seldom directly increase or decrease your level of happiness, I could affect your *chances* of happiness by, for example, giving you a job or firing you. A boss cannot ensure that his employees are equally happy, but he *can* apply all rules evenhandedly and pay the workers in accordance with their contributions to the firm. We can *know* that an employer who gives raises and promotions differently depending upon his personal friendships or the employees' looks, rather than ability, is acting unfairly – even if we cannot directly measure and compare how happy his workers are.

Classifying goods into levels helps, but it does not solve all problems. It is usually not difficult to make decisions when Level 1 goods conflict with Level 2 goods, or either of these with Level 3 goods. Conflicts between Level 1 goods for the same person or for different people, or between Level 2 goods are more difficult; I have discussed ways of dealing with many of them in Chapters 6 and 7. At times two or more courses of action may be (as far as the facts can be known) equally balanced, morally speaking. If none is better or worse than the alternatives, the agent is free to choose on the basis of his own interests or personal preference.

Furthermore, because facts concerning what will occur in the future given different courses of action are so difficult to determine, we are well-advised to establish policies ahead of time to deal with situations that commonly arise — such as what to do when a very ill person will die if certain medical interventions are not carried out immediately, or how to allocate certain expensive medical procedures (such as organ transplants) when the society cannot give them to all who might need them. Policies may not always work for the best or give the fairest results; however, if they have been decided upon by informed and impartial persons, those who carry out the policies will make relatively few mistakes — certainly fewer than if there were *no* policy and people were forced to make decisions anew whenever an emergency occurred.

3. SOLVING MORAL PROBLEMS

We may use the methods discussed in earlier chapters to shed light on the particular problem of which of the two convicts we ought to resuscitate. Assuming that each has a chance for a life that is even minimally satisfying, they both have a Level 1 interest in living. If not, as might be the case with Smith, since he is terminally and painfully ill , then death would not be a bad thing for him. In this case we do not know what Smith's desires are for continued life in his situation, and we do not know what he would want in the way of life-saving procedures or what his experiences might be after resuscitation or how he would feel about them. Since, however, no one had asked him these questions and he had not expressed a desire not to be resuscitated, it is best — given the irreversibility of death — to assume that he wanted to live and that continued life, even one so curtailed, was valuable to him. Because advance knowledge of a person's wishes in these matters is so important, patients are now asked on admission to the hospital about their wishes for resuscitation. There is no question, however, that Jones had better prospects for future personal happiness than Smith, and if we had to choose which to save, then, if this were the only consideration, we would have done better to save Jones. It is remotely possible that, for all we know, Jones might be so ravaged with guilt that life is a misery for him, while Smith, though ill and in pain, has a few things left that he wants very much to do – e.g., become reconciled with his family. But all this is unlikely, and in the absence of any evidence these remote possibilities can hardly serve as a basis for decision.

The future happiness of the convicts, however, should not be the only consideration. Both men had shown themselves dangerous to other people, but Jones seemed more dangerous than Smith. Both his past crime and his present greater physical strength gave him a larger potential for causing deadly harm to others. Saving Smith would have been unlikely to bring any evil to anyone else; saving Jones might.

Another factor is that Jones, having committed a worse crime than Smith, deserves less from society. But what exactly does this mean? According to the theory of obligation which I spelled out in Chapter 8, it is so important for people to conform to certain oughts that sanctions for failure to conform both exist and ought to exist. Part of the value of having sanctions is that people can know what to expect if they violate their obligations. If these sanctions are vague, then people cannot be expected to adjust their behavior in accordance with what may happen to them when they offend.

When a person has been properly convicted of a crime and given a certain sentence, he or she has been sanctioned in accordance with the laws of that society and not capriciously. Other people do not have the right to impose additional punishments on the lawbreaker. Although they certainly have the right to express disapproval and to avoid the company of criminals, they are not justified in inflicting additional harm upon them. For this reason, that Jones has committed a more hateful crime than Smith has is not a reason for justifying the withholding of lifesaving medical procedures; this would be the infliction of new punishment by unauthorized persons. He is serving his sentence, and while we at the hospital may have thought that sentence was not severe enough, we would have been wrong to take into our own hands the imposition of more penalties. It is certainly possible to imagine that the sentence for a vicious crime might include not getting certain sorts of medical treatment. If so, then withholding CPR from convicted murderers might be justified in a society which had such penalties. Regardless of the nature of his crime and his punishment, a convicted felon is still a person.[19] Because of his crime he has forfeited certain rights and society has the right to inflict certain harms upon him; but apart from these he is entitled to moral consideration from others.

Thus the choice between resuscitating Smith and resuscitating Jones should depend not upon desert,[20] but rather upon questions of harm and benefit. The fact that Jones poses a danger to others, while Smith does not should carry relatively little weight in the situation. Presumably, the judge and jury did not think Jones dangerous enough even to withhold the possibility of parole, much less impose the death penalty. Their estimate of his dangerousness may have been wrong, however. Many prisoners who, like Jones, have been in maximum security escape, or kill guards and other inmates. We must, however, remember that the harm to others a given criminal might inflict is very much an unknown, and thus an unsuitable basis for deciding which convict to save.

The decision then boils down to the relative effects of resuscitation on the prisoners themselves. The balance of reasons seems to favor resuscitating Jones, for it is more likely that Jones would benefit from more time living than Smith would. Indeed, attempted resuscitation upon Smith might easily inflict more harm on him than allowing him to die. Life support measures in very debilitated people most often result in only brief survival of a brain damaged individual.

We cannot be certain, however, that this would be the result. Since we know nothing of the inner lives of either convict, or what matters to them, knowing which would benefit more would be impossible (unless, as it is not, it were certain that Smith could survive CPR only as a vegetable).

In short, we must conclude that there are too many unknowns to decide whether it would be better to save Jones or to save Smith. The uncertainty is, however, about facts, not about moral principles or how to apply them. If the hospital staff were to know in advance that CPR would allow Smith to have a visit with family resulting in reconciliation, and if they were to have known what did in fact happen to Jones's victim after his parole, it would be more likely that resuscitating Smith would have a better outcome.[21] Likewise, we could conclude that it would be better to give Jones rather than Smith CPR if we were to know that Jones would repent and live a law-abiding and useful life but that Smith would die with even more misery.

In short, we can have hypothetical knowledge of what we ought to do or what would be best to do, given certain sets of facts, and we can gain this knowledge with any number of moral theories. When we do not know the facts, we are uncertain, but this does not raise a problem for moral realism or for the usefulness of moral theories. We make decisions under uncertainty on many non-moral matters as well. Thus when we have experience which allows us knowledge of the probable outcomes of certain kinds of actions in certain conditions, we can make policies — based on recognized moral considerations — that will give us better outcomes overall and avoid disasters, even if the actual results are sometimes less than desirable. Such policies are particularly helpful in medical emergencies, when there is no time to ask philosophical questions or look for further information.

For example, what we knew at the hospital was insufficient to tell us whether Smith could benefit from CPR. If, however, someone had discussed with him the probable result of this measure and whether he would desire it, this would have given Smith the opportunity to think about what a resuscitation attempt might mean for him and to choose in advance what he considered in his best interest. If he believed that his present suffering was great enough that further life was not worthwhile, he could then let this be known to his physician, who would then have written a "Do not resuscitate" order. Otherwise, in case of his undergoing cardiac arrest, he would receive the same efforts any other patient would have, and in the case of simultaneous arrests, discovered simultaneously, he and the other patient would have equal rights to the code team's efforts. If there are no moral grounds, because of the uncertainty about future events, to choose or not to choose Smith over Jones or any other patient, the choice could be based upon convenience or personal preference. Hence the code team might resuscitate Jones because they believed that Smith's case was futile, or, because of their revulsion for Jones, they might put their efforts into saving Smith. Neither alternative would be clearly better, morally, than the other.

On the basis of probabilities of various outcomes, we can, as individuals and as societies, plan ahead rationally. Since hospitals are now discussing with patients when they are admitted what they would want done should they suffer cardiac arrest, this can prevent the tragedy of having someone resuscitated against her wishes, or, alternatively, of not being resuscitated when this could be of benefit to her. We need not be completely at the mercy of impulses which may only compound the tragedy. Yet because we are working only with probabilities and not certainties, we may make mistakes. And because these are weighty matters, any mistakes are grave and costly. We may be just as uncertain which horse will win the Kentucky Derby, but unless we have bet far more than we can afford, the uncertainty does not bother us greatly.

Yet the mistakes can be minimized. Suppose I know that the chances of my leading a life that has any worth to me are minimal if my cortical neurons become like a bunch of twisted wires. If I make a living will now telling my family that once I am diagnosed by two physicians as having Alzheimer's disease I want nothing done to keep me alive beyond basic comfort measures, then they will have a good estimate of what will be best for me (at least as I am now and to the extent that I am able to project what I might feel as an Alzheimer's patient; these people typically behave as if extremely sad, angry, or fearful). For I will have made it clear what makes life valuable to me. And suppose that the general consensus of a society which has observed many Alzheimer's patients is that their lives are such that no one would want to live that way. Then surely it makes rational sense to allocate scarce resources for other medical uses than for prolonging the lives of Alzheimer's patients. As in the case of terrorism discussed in Chapter 6, a policy that uses limited funds for medical care to provide a healthy start for children, rather than ventilators and other forms of intensive care for those who have irreversible dementia, is only what rational beings would desire for themselves and those they care about.

4. ANOTHER CASE

A tragic situation which has recently gained the attention of the media illustrates the sort of complex ethical problems we face in today's world. I shall indicate how this problem might have been handled using my theory. The situation is this. A pair of Siamese twin girls was born with one heart shared between them. They could not survive long while joined, as the burden of supplying blood to both their bodies is more than the single heart can carry. On the other hand, separating the twins could save only the twin whose heart is now providing circulation for both; the other would die. Separation would mean certain death for this twin, while not to separate them would mean certain death for both.

The twins' parents brought their daughters to Great Britain from Malta in hopes of saving them through expert surgery and medical care. When told the dilemma, they refused to allow the twins to be separated. As devout Roman Catholics, they believed that the teachings of their religion would forbid it, for the operation would effectively kill one of the girls. Even though separation would save the other, and even though both would die without the surgery, the parents thought it would go against Catholic teaching to permit the separation (and at least one Catholic priest was quoted as agreeing with them). On the other hand a high court in Britain ruled that the separation should go ahead in the interests of the girl who could survive. The surgery was performed and the weaker twin died, while as of this writing the other has so far survived.

There are at least three questions here. (1) Ought the doctors to have performed the surgery? (2) Ought the parents to have refused it? (3) Ought the courts to have enforced it? Let us examine each in turn.

(1) Leaving aside for now the issues of the extent to which what the doctors should do is affected by the parents' refusal of permission or by the state's ordering of the separation, we may make two observations. First, the surgeons ought not to kill a person and they also ought not to allow a person to die when their actions could save her, since both courses of action would make it impossible for at least one girl to have a happy life (or life at all). Given that they ought not to take either course of action, the question is — since a decision must be made — which is the least bad choice? And I think it is clear that performing the surgery would least impede the central purpose of morality and is thus the better or least bad course of action. Assuming that there is no doubt that the twins would both die without it and that there was no chance that the twin without the heart would survive if the surgery is done, more moral harm would be done if the girls were not separated.

There are obvious parallels with Williams's case of Jim and the Indians, discussed in Chapter 7. The major difference is that the known medical facts in this situation make the outcomes of performing the surgery and of not performing it appear to be virtually certain, whereas in Williams's case the outcomes of Jim's killing or of his not killing the one Indian would not be known in any real life situation. In the case of the Siamese twins there were no other people or natural events that could intervene to save either the unseparated twins or the twin left with no heart after separation.

Of course, we need to consider other facts than that with surgery one girl would die and without it both girls would die. Are there questions of fairness, as well? Certainly on the surface it seems unfair for one child to live at the cost of the other's dying. But without the surgery that child would have died anyway, and as already noted in Chapter 5 fairness is not simply equality. To deprive one person simply to bring her down to a level of well being equal to that of someone less well off is not justifiable. Since nothing that could be done would have saved the weaker twin, and since saving her sister would not have caused her to die, the surgeons would not, by operating, appreciably change the outcome for her, it was not unfair in this sense to separate them.

Could it be unfair to separate the twins in the sense that doing so would violate a moral rule such that it is unfair to make oneself an exception? Clearly this applies to active killing. Yet it also applies to failing to save a life when one could do so without grave risk to oneself. Of course, as noted often above, it is worse to take something away from a person that he or she has or expects to have than to fail to give it to that person. Therefore, in most ordinary cases it is worse to kill than to fail to save a life. In this case, however, the one twin lost nothing as a result of surgery that she would not have lost if it were not performed. On the other hand, the other twin would have lost her life if not separated, but now has a chance of living. This argument from fairness, then, does not count against separating the twins.

The distinction between withholding a routine procedure and withholding a heroic one — noted in Chapter 7 — could be applicable here. Evidently in Malta a separation of this complexity is not routine; perhaps it is not routine in Great Britain, either. If not, then it would — if my earlier arguments are correct — be less bad, *ceteris paribus*, not to have performed it, since it would not be normally expected, than it would be not to perform some routine life saving procedure. This point is, however, unlikely to carry much weight in this case. The twins are too young to expect anything. Their parents brought them to England seeking a procedure that might help; they were obviously expecting something that would save their daughters. Unfortunately, the surgery that was possible could save only one. Furthermore, in estimating whether or not a complex, extraordinary procedure ought to be withheld depends in large part upon the burden to the patient of having it done. To the twin who died it cost much, but nothing that she would not have lost anyway; presumably she did not suffer more, as she never woke from anesthesia. For the other, there will no doubt be a long period of recuperation with considerable discomfort, with the possibility that she will not survive anyway. The burden of *not* performing it, however, would have been certain death.

Another factor which might lead one to think it better not to have performed the surgery could be the possibility of the effect upon the character of the surgeons and other operating room staff — or what doing such surgery would say about their characters. Would doing a procedure that would kill one person (who would die soon in any case) in order to save another be likely to harden them and make it easier for them to kill a person who might live in order to save someone else? As noted in Chapters 5 and 7, the effect upon character of performing any action is something that can rarely be predicted without detailed knowledge of the agent and his circumstances. In this case it seems unlikely that doing this surgery would have a bad effect on the characters of those performing it. Their intention was not (as the priest who criticized the court for ordering the operation maintained) to kill the weaker child. If there were anything that could save her (e.g., to give her a heart transplant at the same time as the separation occurred), they would surely have attempted it. At least we do not have any reason to think they would not.

The key to knowing whether a consequence of an action is intentional is what the agent would do to avoid that consequence if the opportunity arose. The agent does not intend an effect which he would prevent if he could avoid it short of jeopardizing the effect which is his primary intention in doing the act. An unwanted side effect is voluntary if the agent proceeds with the action knowing that the effect will, or is likely to, occur, but it is only intentional if he would do nothing to prevent it even if he could. Thus the uncle who allows his nephew to drown intends his death, for he fails to save him when he easily could. Any action (including choosing inaction) has multiple descriptions and consequences, only a limited number of which are desired and probably even fewer are reasons why — or the intention with which — the act is performed. Obviously other effects and consequences are foreseen but unintended and allowed because whatever might be bad about them is outweighed by the overall good the agent expects. So long as the surgeons' intentions are purely to save the one child, other situations where they might be tempted to kill a baby for anything less are highly unlikely. Of course, we know nothing of the characters of the babies' doctors; perhaps they are heartless and cruel. Yet in the absence of evidence to the contrary, we may presume a modicum of decency which would forbid taking a child's life in any circumstances that would allow her to live.

Hence I think that my own theory would favor the doctors' performing the separation, aside from the relevance of the parents' refusal to allow it and the court's ordering it. The relevance of these factors will be discussed below.

(2) Should the parents have refused the surgery for their daughters? The primary reason for their refusal is religious; they believed that their Church would forbid such a thing, and at least one Catholic priest agreed with them. According to the guidelines discussed in Chapter 7, a person should as a rule be guided by his conscience, for this usually results in good actions. Most people know the basics of what is right and wrong, so they are more likely than not to do right if they obey the principles in which they believe. Furthermore acting conscientiously helps to build one's character and develop habits of doing what one ought.

On the other hand, people are sometimes mistaken about what they ought to do, especially in complicated and novel situations. If they follow some authority rather than their personal sense of what is right, whether they actually do right is dependent upon both whether the authority is correct *and* whether they have properly interpreted the authority. Now I do not know what the consensus of Catholic thinkers would believe right to do in the case of the Siamese twins. There is, however, a Catholic tradition which would allow the doctors to go forward with the operation: namely, the principle of double effect.[22] That is, if some evil occurs which is not intended, but is a necessary consequence of an act which brings a greater good, then it may be allowed. And we have seen in this case that there is no reason to think that the doctors' intention is to kill the weaker twin; if they could have saved them both, they would.

Even if, however, Catholic doctrine is clearly against the surgery, the question remains as to whether the parents ought to have done as the Church told them. If the Church is wrong, then if my earlier arguments are sound, they ought not to have obeyed. So whether or not they ought to have refused the surgery depends upon whether the doctors ought not to have performed it. Again if I am right in my conclusions here, the doctors ought to have performed the surgery and the Church (if it would indeed have refused permission) would have been wrong. If this is so, the parents ought not to have refused. In saying this, I do not imply that the parents are hard-hearted and did not care about their children. Obviously they did; otherwise they would not have brought them so far in an effort to save them. They may believe that because the babies' souls are immortal, death is not necessarily an evil for them. They may also think that since the twin who has now so far survived the surgery may die later, even she may be worse off as a result of the separation. With such a complex procedure, that possibility cannot be ignored. If she does die, the pain and discomfort of surgery which would have preceded her death would make this option worse for her than if she and her sister had been allowed to die together. The parents also might have hoped for a miracle that would have permitted the twins to survive joined together.

Given the parents' refusal, should the surgeons have proceeded with the operation? As a rule, no medical procedure should be performed without the patient's consent, or, in the case of a patient who cannot make rational choices, the consent of her guardian. There are several bases for this. First is the great value of being free to do with one's life as one chooses, even when one makes occasional foolish choices. Second, we presume that each person is best suited to know what is good for him, and that guardians are best suited to know and want what is best for their wards. Obviously these presumptions are not always true, but there is great value in having the freedom of choice they espouse protected. And with regard to medical procedures, which frequently involve pain and risk, it is particularly important. Consequently, no medical professional ought to impose any treatment on a patient without that patient's or his guardian's informed consent — with one notable exception, to which I shall now turn.

(3) Should the courts have ordered the twins to be separated, overruling the parents' objections? Parents are normally presumed to have the right to decide what may or may not be done to or for their children. There are two major reasons for this. First of all, parents generally have the best interests of their children at heart and know those interests better than others. Secondly, children are traditionally considered to *belong to* their parents, giving them rights over their children and rights against the interference of others in ways similar to people's rights to manage their property as they see fit.

Such rights are not absolute, however. The idea of children as their parents' property is losing its hold — as indeed it should. There are few parts of the world where parents are now believed justified in selling their children into slavery, in keeping them out of school in order to work in factories, in donating them to religious institutions to be raised as monks or nuns, or in betrothing them to a partner they have never seen. Such practices still exist, but they are increasingly deplored, primarily for the reason that, apart from any direct harm they may do to the child as a child, they grossly restrict the child's future choices as an adult. Often such things are done, not because parents think it good for themselves or their children, but out of desperation when they cannot support their families.

Another point, however, might be made in favor of using children in some respects as property. This is the primacy of the community or family over the individual which is seen in many cultures. I have discussed this to some extent in connection with Wong's criticism of moral cognitivism, where I argued that there are good aspects to both individualism and communitarianism. Putting the family or tribe first makes sense in a situation in which the survival of the group (and its members) depends upon its cohesion. In such circumstances what is best for the group is also what is best for individuals. Most of us also understand the importance of intimate personal relationships, which have for the most part been found within families or small communities. Without these relationships, the lives of individuals are impoverished, but these relationships also demand much from each person involved in order to maintain them and their benefits. A good marriage demands that both husband and wife be faithful to each other and cooperate in the work that needs to be done for the family. Neither is free to follow whatever whims he or she may have. Where married people feel no such obligations to each other, and social and legal pressures are not sufficient to enforce them, marriages are unstable and hence the great benefits of marriage can be lost.

It also needs to be pointed out, however, that subordination of individuals to a group is in practice all too often simply an excuse to allow the dominant individuals to have their way and exploit those with lower status. In many traditional societies women are expected to be faithful to their husbands and do all the hard labor around the home and village, while the same is not required of men, who can go where they want and have whatever women they can get. And it is becoming increasingly clear that women the world over are not happy with such arrangements and are glad to change them when possible. In the days of powerful royal families children were married off to whatever prince or princess would enable their fathers to make the most advantageous alliances. In many cases, no doubt, these kings had the good of their countries in mind — e.g., by keeping a balance of power that would prevent enemies from conquering them. On the other hand, all too many monarchs were interested only in personal power, exploiting their subjects who lived in grinding poverty while themselves enjoying the greatest luxury, and looking for opportunities to conquer and enslave weaker nations. For many rulers in all parts of the world and throughout history, family ties meant nothing; brothers and nephews who posed a threat to the throne were commonly murdered or thrown in dungeons, and wives who failed to bear sons were divorced or even killed.

In short, family and community cohesion, with subordination of some individual wishes to the good of the group, is good so long as all benefit from that society, and where benefits and burdens are shared equitably. On the other hand, when dominant members of a group exploit those who are for some reason weaker, community cohesion and individual subordination are no longer good. In other words, communities and the obligations they entail are good, so long as they work for the good of all alike — i.e., are consistent with the principles of beneficence and fairness.

Given that children-as-property is no justification for not interfering with what parents do with their offspring, the case for non-interference rests primarily on the belief that parents care most about and understand best what is good for their own children. While in most cases this is no doubt true, it is all too clear that in many others it is not. But as we saw in the last two chapters, that parents may sometimes fail in caring or in understanding does not suffice to justify interference, since sanctions carry additional burdens both to those on whom they are imposed and upon the society which imposes them. For sanctions or compulsion to be justifiable, not only must the behavior they enjoin be such that people ought to act that way, but they ought to be pushed toward doing so by some means — e.g., public opinion, legal measures, or brute force. Furthermore, in a given situation some types of sanctions may be justifiable while others are not — depending on which would do more moral good than moral harm.

Most people believe that there are limits upon what parents should be allowed to do with or to their children, but do not believe that simply disagreeing with a family's methods of child-rearing is a legitimate reason for interference. We tend to draw the line at the point where we think it clear that the child is being harmed by the parent's action. When this point is reached, criticism of a neighbor's physical or verbal punishments of his children no longer brands one as a busybody. For the law to intervene, however, more justification is required than for private criticism. To offset the burden of legal penalties on the offender and the costs to society of imposing them, the harm against which the legal measure is a sanction must be obvious and substantial.

It would have been, I think, an obvious and substantial harm to the stronger twin in the case under discussion to have denied her a chance at life, just as nearly all believe that parents belonging to some religious sects have no right to keep their sick children from receiving life-saving therapy. The grounds are similar to those condemning the sale of a child into slavery or marrying her at the age of three to a boy she has never seen: namely, that her normal range of future choices are cut off before she is of sufficient maturity to make them. In the case of the twin, all her choices will be cut off forever if she is allowed to die. There is no question here of supposing that the parents of these twins were abusive and uncaring. They obviously cared, but they do appear to have been misguided and clearly acting against the best interests of one of their daughters. In such a case, the normal right of parents to do as they choose with their children and to act as their consciences dictate is overridden.

Many will ask, "Who has the right to decide what is best?" "Why must we suppose that the British courts are better judges of what morality dictates than the girls' own parents?" If this were a corrupt court, such as those under Hitler or Stalin (or even one run by stupid justices), giving immoral injunctions, it might very well have been better for the parents to choose for the babies and disobey the court. What should be done is not, however, determined by the source of the authority, but by the rightness of the judgments — and this in turn is determined by their conformity with principles of beneficence and fairness. Obviously, anyone's interpretation of what is fair and beneficent may be mistaken, certainly not excluding governmental authorities. There is, however, a presumption that certain authorities, especially judges, have an intelligent and unbiased perspective (which is or should be a reason for selecting them over others) and therefore have been invested with the authority to make such decisions in cases of conflict. There is great advantage in having such authorities who can bring an end to conflict, although obviously their dictates should not be accepted uncritically. For this reason there are systematic values in having and obeying court injunctions, with the proviso that where the courts are seriously mistaken they can sometimes be justifiably disobeyed.

Thus I think that the conclusion best supported by my own theory is that the court did have the right to overrule the parents' objection to separation and order the surgery to proceed. And the doctors had at least a *prima facie* obligation to follow the court's order, on the grounds already discussed — namely, that we ought (other things being equal) to obey the law as a matter of fairness to those who have given up benefits to themselves in order to uphold it as a beneficial institution.

To conclude, then, the fundamental moral principles which are virtually universally accepted allow us to make not only everyday decisions, but even to solve some complex cases. They also give us guidelines for policies which will help us make the best choices in situations where many factors are unknown. Hence the objection that the most general and fundamental principles of morality are not sufficient by themselves to be of use does not harm moral realism. Certainly finding answers requires not only principles but facts — and complex facts at that, but that does not show that the principles are useless.

5. GENERAL SUMMARY

In this book I have developed a case for moral cognitivism. First I have argued that the ways in which truth conditions of moral judgments is determined are not fundamentally different from the ways in which truth conditions in general are determined. The truth conditions of moral judgments are, I maintained, incorporated in the fundamental principles to which people trying to defend their moral beliefs ultimately appeal (when pressed to the limit in debate), under circumstances allowing free and open discussion. An adequate moral theory will use these fundamental principles, showing that they are consistent with all well-established moral beliefs. A well-established moral belief is one which has stood the test of time. It is held in some form by many societies over long periods of time, including societies which have been exposed to others and have been free to accept or reject the standards of those others. Well-established moral beliefs have this importance because they have stood up to criticisms over time and thus either incorporate fundamental principles or can be viewed as applications of them. Hence an adequate moral theory will be consistent with those common sense beliefs that have been widely adopted. It should also be capable of helping individuals to make specific moral choices in complex situations — at least to enable them to know what should be done given particular facts (which may or may not be discoverable).

If no such theory can be developed, then moral cognitivism will be impossible to defend. I think, however, that I have succeeded in presenting such a theory here. I do not claim that it is the only adequate theory or even the best, but only that it does meet the demands outlined above. One point for which I argued is that in general there can be alternative classifications of phenomena, which, so long as they are consistent with the data, are equally acceptable. The same is true of ethics, since an ethical theory is classificatory rather than explanatory, and different theories may be equally valid.

The theory I have presented here is that there are two fundamental principles, namely beneficence (i.e., bringing good and preventing harm to individuals, where individual good is defined as happiness, which is proportional to the net length of time the individual spends wanting his situation to continue); and fairness, which is based on the equal worth of all persons, so that no one ought to receive good at the cost of decreasing equivalent good available to others. I also argued that the two principles can be combined into the overall purpose of morality, which is to provide the greatest good to all persons which is consistent with a like degree of good for all (and as much good for sentient non-persons as is compatible with this end). Doing what he can to best promote this purpose is the best that any person can do; he ought to do what his failure to do would impede realization of this purpose, and he is obligated to do what he ought when there is and ought to be a sanction against his failing to do. Throughout this book, I have tried to show that well-established moral beliefs fit comfortably with this theory and that none are obviously inconsistent with it. In this last chapter I have argued that this theory can be used to provide actual or hypothetical solutions to specific moral problems.

NOTES

Notes to Chapter 1

1 What I present here is a modified version of the more detailed argument I put forth in *Moral Language* (Madison: University of Wisconsin Press, 1982). Since that book came out in 1982, there have been other works which support moral realism from some different perspectives. I will not discuss these here, but will give a few references for the interested reader. The anthology edited by Geoffrey Sayre-McCord, *Essays in Moral Realism* (Ithaca: Cornell University Press, 1988) includes a good selection of these efforts. See, for example, Richard Boyd, 'How to be a Moral Realist' (187-228), Nicholas Sturgeon, 'Moral Explanations' (229-255), and Sayre-McCord's 'Moral Theory and Explanatory Impotence' (256-281). Three other interesting works defending the possibility of moral knowledge are those by Bernard Gert, *Morality: A New Justification of the Moral Rules* (New York: Oxford University Press, 1988) David O. Brink, *Moral Realism and the Foundations of Ethics* (Cambridge: Cambridge University Press, 1989) and James Forrester, *Why You Should: The Pragmatics of Deontic Speech* (Hanover and London: Brown University Press, 1989).

2 See A.J. Ayer, *Language, Truth, and Logic*, 2nd ed.(New York: Dover Publications, 1950), Chapter 4.

3 Hare's main exposition of this theory appears in *The Language of Morals* (New York: Oxford University Press, Inc., 1964), see especially Chapter 11. Other well known nondescriptivist theories include the following. C. L. Stevenson held that value judgments had both descriptive and emotive components. Words like 'good,' 'wrong,' etc. primarily express some favorable or unfavorable attitude toward a person, action, or thing; they also suggest certain descriptive characteristics of the item in question (e.g., that Susan is thoughtful of others). Yet different people might ascribe different characteristics to people they call good; what they have in common is the attitude and the attitude is central to the meaning. [*Ethics and Language* (New Haven: Yale University Press, 1944), esp. Chapters 4, 5, 7, 9 and 10]. Roger Scruton maintains that value judgments are basically expressions of an attitude of commendation or condemnation. In evaluations the attitude is held on the basis of certain characteristics of the evaluated item. One can like a person, but one considers him good only if he has certain characteristics of which one approves ['Attitudes, Beliefs, and Reasons,' *Morality and Moral Reasoning*, John Casey, ed.(London: Methuen & Co., 1972), 25- 110]. Patrick Nowell-Smith held that evaluations are indications of choice, or having a pro (or con) attitude toward something [*Ethics* (Baltimore: Penguin Books, 1954), Chapters 7 and 8]. But we have these attitudes on the basis of characteristics of the item in question.

In all of these theories, moral judgments, as well as judgments of the goodness or badness of things, have two components. First and foremost there is the expression of an attitude (e.g.,approval) or an injunction to do something, but secondly there is an implicit or explicit indication of certain characteristics had by the thing, person, or action evaluated. Anything having those same characteristics will, if the evaluator is reasonable and consistent, be evaluated in the same way. The reason behind these judgments is that the evaluator has the requisite attitude toward things with those characteristics.

4 See Paul Ziff, *Semantic Analysis* (Ithaca, NY: Cornell University Press, 1960), 228; John Searle, 'Meaning and Speech Acts,' *Philosophical Review*, 71 (1962): 423-432; Hector-Neri Castañeda, 'Imperatives, Decisions, and Oughts,' in *Morality and the Language of Conduct*, Hector-Neri Castañeda & George Nakhnikian, eds. (Detroit: Wayne State University Press, 1963), 230-239; and P. T. Geach, 'Assertion,' *Philosophical Review*, 74 (1965): 449-465.

5 A number of people have attempted to get around the presumption that the use of evaluations in arguments indicates their descriptive nature by proposing a logic of imperatives. See, for example, Alf Ross, 'Imperatives and Logic,' *Philosophy of Science*, 11 (1944): 30- 46; R. M. Hare, 'Some Alleged Differences Between Imperatives and Indicatives,' *Mind*, 76 (1967): 309- 326; Nicholas Rescher, *The Logic of Commands* (London: Routledge and Kegan Paul, 1966); Robert P. McArthur and David Welker, 'Non-assertoric Logic,' *Notre Dame Journal of Formal Logic*, 15 (1974): 225- 244; André Gombay, 'Imperative Inferences and Disjunction,' *Analysis*, 25 (1965): 58-62; and Hector-Neri Castañeda, *Thinking and Doing* (Dordrecht: Reidel, 1975), Chapters 4 and 5. In *Moral Language* (Madison: University of Wisconsin Press, 1982), Chapters 3 and 4, I argued that such efforts to construct logics were dependent for their validity on the validity of assertoric arguments; i.e., those using statements that have truth value, whereas logics using evaluations are not so dependent.

6 To avoid this conclusion, Blackburn has suggested that conditional evaluations are themselves expressions of an attitude about the connection between evaluations. Thus 'If it is wrong to lie, it is wrong to get your little brother to lie,' should be read as Hooray! (or some other appropriate attitudinal operator)[Boo!(Lying), Boo!(Getting your little brother to lie)]. In other words, what one approves (or disapproves) of is the

247

conjunction of certain attitudes with one another. [*Spreading the Word* (Oxford: Clarendon Press, 1984), 193-196] Blackburn applies this to conditionals where both antecedent and consequent are evaluations. But what does he do when the consequent is not an evaluation, but a declarative sentence, or perhaps an imperative? Are 'If she ought to keep that promise, she will keep it,' and 'If you ought to be in Denver by noon, leave now' also expressions of attitude about the relations of the components? And if so, what attitude? What about purely declarative conditionals, such as 'If she makes promises, she keeps them?'

The main problem with this approach, however, is that the attitude one has to a conditional is not the attitude one has to each of its parts, but the attitude toward the relationship between them. This relationship is a *logical* feature of the sentence, not a moral one. If I approve someone's holding that if it is wrong to lie then it is wrong to get one's brother to lie, I'm not approving his moral stance, but the fact that his attitude is consistent. I could approve this, even if I didn't like his moral beliefs at all. We sometimes say of a person with whom we mightily disagree: "At least he's consistent!" And there is some approval in that, but it isn't moral approval. Thus if a conditional evaluation is an expression of attitude, it isn't an expression of a moral attitude.

Conditionals in general, however, are *not* expressions of attitudes. Rather they assert that if some state of affairs obtains — i.e., some statement is *true* —, then some other state obtains or some imperative is operative.
[7] *Spreading the Word*, 168.
[8] See Richard Price, *A Review of the Principal Questions in Morals*, in *British Moralists*, 2nd ed., Lewis A. Selby-Bigge (New York: Dover Publications, Inc., 1965),105-184, especially Sections 587, 605, and 609; G. E. Moore, *Principia Ethica* (Cambridge: Cambridge University Press, 1962), Chapter 1; and R. M. Hare, *The Language of Morals*, 83-86.
[9] *Spreading the Word*, 183-189.
[10] See *Moral Language*, 18-19, Chapter 7, and pp. 151- 165.
[11] Chapter 7, especially.
[12] See Wittgenstein, *Philosophical Investigations*, trans. G. E. M. Anscombe, (New York: Macmillan, 1953), 241-242; *Remarks on the Foundations of Mathematics*, ed. G. H. Von Wright, R. Rhees, and G. E. M. Anscombe, trans. G. E. M. Anscombe, (New York: Macmillan 1956), II, 70; *Zettel*, ed. G. E. M. Anscombe and G. H. Von Wright, trans. G. E. M. Anscombe, Berkeley: University of California Press, 1967), 348 & 351, and Davidson, 'Belief and the Basis of Meaning,' *Synthese*, 27 (1974): 309-323, and 'Thought and Talk,' in *Mind and Language*, Samuel Guttenplan, ed. (Oxford: Clarendon Press, 1975), 7-23.
[13] My thanks to Ms. Nicola Berridge of Kluwer Academic Publishers for checking this information on tulips for me.
[14] See 'Two Dogmas of Empiricism,' in *From a Logical Point of View* (Cambridge, MA: Harvard University Press, 1953), 20-46.
[15] One may well wonder what distinguishes claiming that a sentence is analytic from pigheadedness. If we refuse to accept evidence against the truth of a particular sentence, how does this differentiate us from people who simply will not recognize that some pet belief — e.g., in the faithfulness of one's lover or in the truth of a theory one has spent one's life developing — can no longer stand up? The two most important features of analytic beliefs are (1) that agreement upon them is general: i.e., they are widely accepted among speakers of the language, especially among those who are expert in the area of discourse in question; and (2) that anyone who disagrees finds it difficult to make others understand what he or she is talking about.
[16] See *Moral Language*, primarily Chapter 7 for more extended argument.
[17] The need for seeing how moral arguments play out in free and open discussion, rather than under some restrictive circumstances, is due simply to the fact that — in general — truth is more likely to be reached when those investigating and arguing have broad access to facts and opinions, and when no one is intimidated, so that all are free to say what they think.
[18] John H. Barnsley points out that clashes between cultures forces a reconsideration of previously unquestioned values and rules with a search for sounder foundations for moral judgments. (*The Social Reality of Ethics: The Comparative Analysis of Moral Codes* (London: Routledge & Kegan Paul, 1972), 323-324.
[19] See *Moral Language*, 151-173. Others who have argued that morality receives its justification from its fundamental purpose include Kurt Baier, *The Moral Point of View* (Ithaca, NY: Cornell University Press, 1958), 200-204, 309-310; Stephen Toulmin, *The Place of Reason in Ethics* (Cambridge: Cambridge University Press, 1964), 137; and G.J. Warnock, *The Object of Morality* (London: Methuen & Company, 1971), Chapter 2.
[20] In *The Moral Sense* (New York: The Free Press, 1993), 29-117.
[21] See Edward O. Wilson, *On Human Nature*, (Cambridge, MA: Harvard University Press, 1978), Chapter 4; Fred R. Myers, 'Always Ask: Resource Use and Land Ownership among Pintupi Aborigines of the Australian Western Desert,' in *Traditional Aboriginal Society*, 2nd Edition, W. H. Edwards, ed. (Macmillan Educational Australia PTY Ltd, 1998), 30- 46; and James Smith (an account of his experiences between 1755-1759), 'Prisoner of the Caughnawagas,' in *Captured by Indians*, Frederick Drimmer, ed., (New York: Dover Publications, 1985), 25-60: "It is seldom that Indians steal anything from one another. They say they never did until the white people came among them and taught some of them to lie, cheat, steal, and swear" (p. 51).
[22] Wilson, *The Moral Sense*, 191-221. Cross-cultural contact is, of course, not a strictly modern phenomenon. George F. Hourani [*Reason and Tradition in Islamic Ethics* (Cambridge: Cambridge University Press, 1985), 95-97] points out that early Christians in trying to convert pagans, as well as early Muslims trying to convert Christians and Zoroastrians, would appeal to the moral views held by all in common. Amartya Sen, in 'Will There Be Any Hope for the Poor?' *Time* 155 (May 22, 2000): 94-95, discusses the growing craving

for democracy throughout the world.

[23] In 'Off on the Wrong Foot,' in *On The Relevance of Metaethics*, J. Couture & K. Nielsen, eds., *Canadian Journal of Philosophy*, suppl. vol. 21 (1995): 67-77.

[24] See 'The Meaning of "Meaning",' as well as 'Meaning and Reference,' *The Journal of Philosophy*, 70 (1973): 699-711, and 'Language and Reality,' *Mind, Language, and Reality: Philosophical Papers*, Vol. 2 (Cambridge: Cambridge University Press, 1975), 271-290.

[25] In 'The Causal Theory of Perception' *Proceedings of the Aristotelian Society*, Supplementary vol. 35 (1961): 121-152.

[26] *Moral Language*, Chapter 2

[27]. 'Meaning and Speech Acts' *Philosophical Review*, 79 (1970): 3-24.

[28] Others who have made a distinction between these two components of meaning are Erik Stenius, 'Mood and Language Games,' *Synthese*, 17 (1967): 254-274; S. Schiffer, *Meaning* (Oxford: Clarendon Press, 1972), especially Chapter 4; John Searle, *Speech Acts*, (Cambridge: Cambridge University Press, 1970), *passim*; and Michael Dummett, 'What is a Theory of Meaning?' Part II, in *Truth and Meaning*, Gareth Evans and John McDowell, eds., (Oxford: Clarendon Press, 1976) 75-76.

[29] William P. Alston (*Philosophy of Language*, [Englewood Cliffs, NJ: Prentice-Hall, 1964) Chapter 2] argues that meaning is determined by illocutionary act potential. My primary objection to this is the immense complexity of such an analysis, since any given sentence can be used for such a large number of illocutionary acts. Deirdre Wilson and Dan Sperber ['Mood and the Analysis of Non-declarative Sentences,' in *Human Agency: Language, Duty, and Value*, ed. Jonathan Dancy, J. M. E. Moravcsik, and C.C. W. Taylor (Stanford, CA: Stanford University Press, 1988), pp. 77-101] make a sharp distinction between mood and illocutionary force, noting that the former is preserved in non-typical uses such as irony and fiction, whereas the latter is not. They argue that mood and meaning generally are not determined even indirectly by illocutionary act potential. Their case is complex and not one I shall attempt to discuss here.

[30] Charles Taylor has argued, ['Theories of Meaning,' *Human Agency and Language: Philosophical Papers*, I (Cambridge: Cambridge University Press, 1985), 248-292] that propositional content is not the fundamental basis of meaning, as there are many functions of language which are not depictive and many utterances which have no propositional content. For example, a person may, while wiping his brow, say "Whew" to a fellow traveler on a hot day; he is not describing anything or informing the other person of anything she does not already know. Rather he is indicating a desire to start up a conversation. In addition to expressive uses of language there are invocative uses, where a person in a primitive society utters the name of another and thereby all suppose that he has gained power over that person. In addition, one can call upon a god or speak of animals not as they are in nature but as totems or representative of certain qualities or forces. These, Taylor maintains, cannot be viewed as extensions of a depictive use of language and therefore propositional content is not primary. He goes on to say that finding words for abstract notions like 'equality' does not so much describe anything as shape the standards of those who use them.

Obviously there are many uses of language which are not intended to be descriptive of anything. Understanding verbal expressions presupposes, however, the explicit or implicit demarcation of a state of affairs. Certainly, Pete may say 'Whew" while wiping his brow primarily as an entry to conversation with his pretty seat mate. And it is equally certain that he is not telling her anything she doesn't already know. However his words and gestures convey a belief that it is not only hot, but unpleasantly so, even though stating this belief is by no means his purpose in making the utterance. He is pointing to a state of affairs which both he and his listener are experiencing and finding unpleasant in hopes of generating fellow feeling which might lead to further intimacy. If he had said something like "George Washington was the first president of the United States" — thereby also pointing out a state of affairs that is true and undoubtedly already known to the young lady — this remark would do nothing but make his seat mate think him quite bizarre. In short, it makes a difference *what* is the state of affairs to which the speaker calls attention. In addition a shaman may pray to a god to bring rain or victory over an enemy, but this presupposes some beliefs about what this deity can do and what effects prayer can have. Invocations are done for a purpose — i.e. in order to accomplish something (bring about a state of affairs) through the exercise of certain powers (something supposedly had by and hence a descriptive property) of the supernatural entity. Of course, it is possible that some words — or perhaps noises would be a better term — like 'abracadabra' might be uttered for magical effect. Here we have something which supposedly causes a magical result, but such a causal property is not connected with the *meaning* of the word. The word itself is meaningless, and its meaninglessness lies in its referring to nothing and indicating no state of affairs about which one can take an attitude. Certainly also what words we use for such abstractions as 'equality,' whether in the mathematical or the moral sense, do influence the further development of the standards and disciplines which use them. They nonetheless refer to states, relations, or conditions which may or may not be actually realized; in other words, they have descriptive content. There is no doubt that language has many uses other than describing or representing states of affairs. But without some descriptive content — actual or implied — there seems to be no meaning at all.

That the core meaning of sentences includes propositional content is not refuted by any of Taylor's examples. All sentences are not, of course, descriptions, for they may have other moods than assertoric (e.g., a prayer which has an imperative mood). And even descriptive sentences may be used to perform illocutionary acts that are not assertions (e.g., a statement asserting what one will do in the future under circumstances where it will be taken as a promise), as well as to perform such perlocutionary acts as to get the attention of a young lady.

[31] See my *Moral Language*, Chapter 3.

[32] Similar views were expressed earlier by Dummett ('What Is a Theory of Meaning,' Part II) and Putnam [('Reference and Truth,' in *Realism and Reason* (Cambridge: Cambridge University Press, 1983), 69-87].

[33] Crispin Wright *Realism, Meaning, and Truth* (Oxford: Blackwell, 1986), 55.

[34] *Ibid.*, 260-263.

[35] In *Truth and Objectivity* (Cambridge MA: Harvard University Press, 1992), 159

[36] Putnam, Hilary, 'Reference and Truth,' in *Realism and Reason* (Cambridge: Cambridge University Press, 1983), 69-87.

[37] In *Truth and Objectivity*, 47-48. It is hard, however, to see how, even if a statement were superassertible, we could ever know this. Not knowing what evidence might be out there, how could we be justified in supposing that nothing could be learned which would decrease the warrant we would have for believing it? As Wright quite correctly criticizes Putnam for not recognizing (p. 44), one would have to know everything before knowing that any statement p was superassertible. One way of reading Wright, however, is that when p is superassertible at time t, no further evidence would show that a person S believing p at t would not have been justified in believing p at t. Then even if evidence at t+1 were to disconfirm p and make it unworthy of belief then, S would still have been justified at t in believing that p. If this is what Wright means, then I have no difficulty with his notion of "superassertibility;" however, this notion is as far from the ordinary notion of truth as are any of the other verificationist theories he criticizes.

[38] *Realism, Meaning, and Truth*, 57-58.

[39] In 'Values and Secondary Qualities,' in Ted Honderich, ed. *Morality and Objectivity: A Tribute to J. L. Mackie* (London: Routledge & Kegan Paul, 1985), pp. 110-129.

[40] This point was suggested to me by James Forrester.

[41] See *Moral Differences: Truth, Justice and Conscience in a World of Conflict* (Princeton: Princeton University Press, 1992), esp. Chapter 5.

[42] Miller also espouses here a variant of the Open Question Argument, by saying that any characterization of a moral principle which is specific enough to generate answers to moral questions and resolve moral disagreements will not find universal acceptance. Principles vague and general enough to be accepted by all will be too vague to help anyone settle a moral dispute. These arguments are also made by Bernard Williams, *Ethics and the Limits of Philosophy* (Cambridge: Harvard University Press, 1985), Chapter 8, and James Wallace, *Moral Relevance and Moral Conflict* (Ithaca: Cornell University Press, 1988), Chapter 2. The answer to this objection, like that to the one just discussed, depends on the development of a moral theory which can both resolve disagreements *and* find wide acceptance.

[43] See *The Object of Morality*, 159-162.

[44] Here I am not discussing theories which are merely unconventional, such as those of Nietzsche or Ayn Rand. In these cases, as I shall indicate below, there is still agreement with more standard theories on some basic issues. James Forrester has suggested that a person with a radically different moral view could demonstrate his theory not by argument but by vividly illustrating it with examples or by oracular speech. No doubt this is true, but for a person even to understand what such an individual might be trying to convey, there would need to be some agreement in attitudes (which I shall argue below includes value beliefs). Thus Ayn Rand's characters who insist on fairness and charity are depicted in a most unpleasant light See for example the repulsive characters Wesley Mouch and Bertram Scudder in *Atlas Shrugged* (New York: Dutton Books, 1957). But for a reader to see that they are villains he must have some points of agreement with Rand on what constitutes a bad person, e.g., laziness and deceitfulness.. Her heroes and heroines — who share her views — have characteristics which most of us admire, such as strength, courage and commitment; otherwise we would have no sympathy for them.

[45] Such as those described by Miller in *Moral Differences*, 82-87

[46] This issue was raised by an anonymous reviewer of this manuscript.

[47] In Gilbert Harman & Judith Jarvis Thomson, *Moral Relativism and Moral Objectivity* (Oxford: Blackwell, 1996), esp. Chapter 2.

[48] Of course, many engage in bargaining with the hope that they will get everything they want or to gain time or reduce ill-will in such a way as to improve their chances of prevailing. My point here is that any agreement reached is not one which all parties are likely to accept as morally best, only that it is the best that they can get. My remarks do not apply at all to those in which talks break off because of an inability to reach agreement at all.

[49] See especially *Truth and Objectivity* (Cambridge, MA: Harvard University Press, 1992), 92-93, 144-146, 168-201, 196-197, and 'Truth in Ethics,' in Brad Hooker, ed., *Truth in Ethics*, (Oxford: Blackwell, 1996), 1-8.

[50] See similar objections by Wiggins, 'Objective and Subjective in Ethics, with Two Postscripts about Truth' in Brad Hooker, ed., *Truth in Ethics* (Oxford: Blackwell, 1996), 35-68.

[51] *Truth and* Objectivity, 146.

[52] 'Relativism,' in P. Singer, *A Companion to Ethics* (Oxford: Blackwell, 1991), 442-450.

[53] We shall see a number of examples of this in what follows. Edward O. Wilson points out that in different circumstances people may change their emphasis on group values as opposed to individual values. He presents several examples of members of minority ethnic groups who behaved differently with regard to the group, depending upon their opportunities for acceptance by the majority or the elite. When it was to their advantage to enhance the interests of the group over their own aspirations, they did so, but when they had more scope for entering the mainstream, their individual goals and interests took precedence. (*On Human Nature,* Chapter 7) This suggests that people in general want to promote their own goals, and how they behave with regard to a community depends in part upon whether their primary goals are best realized through subordinating lesser interests to those of a group or by acting on their own.

[54] See for example, George Nakhnikian, 'On the Naturalistic Fallacy,' in *Morality and the Language of Conduct*, eds. H.-N. Castañeda and G. Nakhnikian (Detroit: Wayne State University Press, 1963), 145 - 158, and Hare, *Moral Thinking* (Oxford: Clarendon Press, 1981), 13 and 71-75.

[55] For a fuller discussion of this issue see my *Moral Language*, 151-165.

[56] See especially Hare, *The Language of Morals*, 83-86 & *passim*.

[57] J. L. Mackie, *Ethics: Inventing Right and Wrong* (New York: Penguin Books, 1977), 97-102.

[58] In Stephen Darwall, Allan Gibbard, and Peter Railton, 'Toward *Fin de siècle* Ethics: Some Trends,' *Philosophical Review*, 101 (1992): 115-189.

[59] Although Railton is not in full agreement with that view; see 'Noncognitivism about Rationality: Benefits, Costs, and an Alternative,' *Philosophical Issues*, 4 (1993): 36-51. Issue on 'Naturalism and Normativity,' E. Villanueva, ed., and 'What the Non-Cognitivist Helps Us to See the Naturalist Must Help Us to Explain' in *Reality, Representation, and Projection*, John Haldane and Crispin Wright eds., (Oxford: Oxford University Press, 1993), 279-300, and also his reply to Wiggins, 315-328 in the same volume.

[60] See also David Wiggins ('Cognitivism, Naturalism, and Normativity: a Reply to Peter Railton,' in *Reality, Representation, and Projection*, John Haldane and Crispin Wright, eds., Oxford University Press, 1993, 301-313, and also his second reply to Railton, 329- 336 in the same volume) and W. Fenske ('Non-Cognitivism: a New Defense,' *Journal of Value Inquiry* 31 (1997): 301- 309), who make this point.

[61] Wiggins ('Cognitivism, Naturalism, and Normativity') maintains that the fact that a moral demand constitutes a reason to act (apart from the agent's inclination) cannot be explained by any naturalistic theory. Railton ('What the Non-Cognitivist Helps Us to See the Naturalist Must Help Us to Explain' in *Reality, Representation, and Projection*, John Haldane and Crispin Wright eds., Oxford University Press, 1993, 279-300, and also his reply to Wiggins, 315-328 in the same volume) replies that we have many good reasons to promote aggregate well-being; we all have a stake in it. I think, moreover, that we consider moral reasons to override personal goals and interests because if we do not, social cohesion will be impossible, and without this cohesion the benefits of belonging to a society will be lost. Cohesion often requires that we set aside our own concerns at times in order to maintain institutions that benefit all. I will consider these matters further in the following chapters.

[62] In *Impartial Reason* (Ithaca, NY: Cornell University Press, 1983), esp. Ch. 5, 11, and 14.

[63] See *The Moral Problem* (Oxford: Blackwell, 1995), Ch.. 5 & 6.

[64] Smith himself acknowledges all of this in 'Internalism's Wheel,' in Brad Hooker, ed., *Truth in Ethics* (Oxford: Blackwell, 1996), 69-94, proposing that what is a coherent and rational attitude and what is morally obligatory are mutually interdefinable and what we come up with about what we ought to do is done through a process of reflective equilibrium. To me, however, this seems to abandon the search for what moral judgments mean. All Smith has done is to tie their meaning to that of another expression which is equally ill-defined. This move does nothing to answer the question of whether there are moral facts or just what the connection of moral beliefs and attitudes may be.

[65] An anonymous reader of this manuscript made this observation.

[66] See *Morality, Normativity, and Society* (New York: Oxford University Press, 1995), esp. Chapter 2.

[67] In *Ethics*, 60-63.

[68] Bernard Williams, *Ethics and the Limits of Philosophy* (Cambridge, MA: Harvard University Press, 1985), 141-142.

[69] See 'Attitudes and Contents,' *Ethics*, 98 (1988): 501-517.

[70] 'A Note on Commendation and Approval,' *Ethics*, 85 (1975): 148-150.

[71] Judith Jarvis Thomson [Harman & Thomson, *Moral Relativism and Moral Objectivity* (Oxford: Blackwell, 1996), Chapter 6] has also made a similar point.

[72] There are, of course, performatives of approving and condemning (e.g., approving the minutes of a meeting or condemning a criminal to death), which are official acts and do not necessarily express evaluative (or for that matter any other) beliefs about the item approved or the person condemned. But *expressing* approval or condemnation is a different matter, as I argue below. To suppose that all evaluations where approval or condemnation are indicated are performatives, even in those informal situations where a person expresses how

he values a thing, event, or person, is to beg the question of whether or not evaluations are descriptions.
[73] Blackburn ('Attitudes and Contents') rather cavalierly dismisses as quibbles these difficulties with negation. He seems to allow that commitment' has a very broad scope, which includes belief in the truth of an assertion as well as a pro attitude toward the realization of the indicated state of affairs. Certainly, we can provide an abstract notion of some commitment which is the absence of commitment to p (as opposed to commitment to not-p), but unless this notion can be interpreted, it is of no use in a practical discipline like ethics. If what 'A is not wrong' means is nothing that an ordinary person can grasp — as opposed to something only a logician can comprehend — then few people know what they are talking about. The only interpretation that fits, as I have argued, is that a negation of an imperative, commitment, or attitude is the (assertoric) denial that there is such an imperative, commitment, or attitude. And thus the denial is a description.
[74] 'Attitudes and Contents.'
[75] B. Hale, 'Can There Be a Logic of Attitudes?' in Reality, Representation, and Projection, J. Haldane and C. Wright, eds. (Oxford: Oxford University Press, 1993), 337-363.
[76] See Wright, Realism, Meaning, and Truth, 2nd ed. (Oxford: Blackwell, 1993), 241-246 and Susan Hurley, Natural Reasons, (New York: Oxford University Press, 1989), Chapter 9.
[77] In 'Attitudes and Contents.'
[78] 'Securing the Nots: Moral Epistemology for the Quasi-Realist,' in Moral Knowledge ?, Walter Sinnott-Armstrong & Mark Timmons, eds. (New York: Oxford University Press, 1996)
[79] See, for example, Hare, Freedom and Reason (New York: Oxford University Press, 1965), and Darwall, Impartial Reason (Ithaca: Cornell University Press. 1983), esp. Chapter 7.
[80] See detailed discussions of this in Moral Language, Chapter 6 & Persons, Animals and Fetuses (Dordrecht: Kluwer Academic Publishers, 1996), Chapter 2, and Railton, 'What the Non-Cognitivist Helps Us to See the Naturalist Must Help Us to Explain.'
[81] See 'Errors and the Phenomenology of Value,' in Ted Honderich, ed. Morality and Objectivity: A Tribute to J. L. Mackie,, pp. 1-22, and 'How to be an Ethical Antirealist,' Midwest Studies in Philosophy, 12 (1988):361-375.
[82] e.g., John McDowell, 'Values and Secondary Qualities'.
[83] I do not plan here to deal with the issue of how secondary qualities may differ from primary qualities.
[84] That these properties belong to the first class doesn't mean that how we perceive them is unaffected by our bodies and brains. No perceived property could be so independent. Rather, we consider such properties to be what they are (e.g. dispositions) independently of human institutions and conventions.
[85] Frank Jackson [From Metaphysics to Ethics: a Defense of Conceptual Analysis (Oxford: Clarendon Press, 1998), Chapters 1 & 5] notes that many properties are complex, especially those that supervene on basic physical properties, so that such complexity and difficulty in being analyzed is not solely a characteristic of moral properties. Since we have no reason to suppose that these non-moral properties cannot be known to apply to things or that sentences containing them do not have truth value, this type of complexity should not be taken to show that moral judgments are not descriptions or cannot be known to be true.
[86] An interesting suggestion has been made by Panayot Butchvarov ['Realism in Ethics,' Midwest Studies in Philosophy, 12 (1988): 395- 412]: namely, that moral properties are a kind of generic property. As such, we do not perceive goodness or rightness and their contraries directly, but rather infer them from other characteristics. Just as we cannot directly see the coloredness of a flower, but infer that it is colored from the fact that it is pink, we can infer the goodness of an act by noting its good-making characteristics (e.g., that it helped someone out of a serious difficulty), even though we do not see its goodness directly.
[87] See McDowell, 'Values and Secondary Qualities'
[88] See the debate between Harman ('Ethics and Observation') and Sturgeon ('Moral Explanations'), both in Essays on Moral Realism, Geoffrey Sayre-McCord, ed. Ithaca, NY: Cornell University Press, 1988), pp. 119-124 and 229-155, respectively.
[89] In 'Moral Theory and Explanatory Impotence,' Midwest Studies in Philosophy, 12 (1988): 433 - 457.
[90] See Truth and Objectivity (Cambridge, MA: Harvard University Press, 1992), 196-197; and 'Truth in Ethics,' in Brad Hooker, ed., Truth in Ethics (Oxford: Blackwell, 1996), pp. 1- 18.
[91] I am, of course, indebted to Bernard Williams (Ethics and the Limits of Philosophy, and his contribution to Moral Knowledge?, 1996) for the distinction between thick and thin moral concepts. Williams argues that thin concepts, although apt to be widely accepted, are so empty that they cannot be used to solve moral problems. While thick concepts can be used to generate answers to moral questions, they are heavily dependent on culture and unlikely to be agreed upon by everyone. I certainly agree that many thick concepts are culturally determined and not universally accepted. For example, the notion of what acts are honorable is very much a function of the ideals of a particular society. Consider the differences between what has been thought honorable for a Victorian gentleman and for an Afghan tribesman. This, however, does not show that agreement cannot be reached concerning the moral value of such differing conceptions of honor. In the following chapters I shall discuss the notion of ideals and where they fit into a moral theory, as well as attempting to show that the so-called thin concepts are by no means empty and unsuited to resolving moral dilemmas.
[92] And as Thomson points out (Harman & Thomson, Chapter 6), not all explanation is causal; we can also

explain why an X is F by pointing out the characteristics of X that make it an F. This type of explanation is more what I would call classification.

[93] James Forrester points out that a person could know what wrongness is and what lying is, but still not know that lying is wrong. Certainly. A person can also know the circumference of an object and its diameter, but still not know that c = πd. It is less likely that anyone would not know that causing pain or obtaining a good at the cost of someone else's losing a greater good is wrong, just as it is unlikely that anyone would not know that 2 + 2 = 4. As noted above, even analytic statements may not be known by those whose education or intelligence is insufficient, and that a statement's truth may be obvious to most does not entail that it is obvious to all. A well-established moral principle is not necessarily known to all people, for some have failed to be educated in the accepted moral principles of their societies (e.g., small children, mental defectives, and those who have never been able to form attachments and hence understanding of the needs of others).

Notes to Chapter 2:

[1] A person who simply accepts oughts that are handed down to him without reflecting on the reasons for them may not think of them as having or contributing to something of value. Yet even such people acknowledge oughts as determining what they are required to do, as standards of behavior. Such people value the behavior required by these oughts, even though they might not actually relate their beliefs to values in any way. It is perhaps better to say that oughts *presuppose* standards.

It is also true that there are many people who may have other reasons than good evidence and arguments for holding a belief; such people, however, probably would not use epistemic oughts. Rather they might say to someone, "You ought to believe that p because God said so." I owe these suggestions to James Forrester. But it must be remembered that I am talking about beliefs that are appealed to in argument where people are trying to defend their beliefs in a rational manner -- not like the bumper sticker one sees occasionally: "God said it. I believe it. That settles it."

[2] James Forrester has suggested that a person might say something like "According to the law (customs, standards) of that time (place, certain premises), X ought to do A (or it ought to be that p)" when the person does not himself accept those laws, standards, or premises. Here the ought judgment is being relativized to a set of standards other than those held by the speaker; by specifying those standards the speaker makes it clear that he himself disagrees with them. He might even be trying to show someone else a consequence of her beliefs that she would be loath to accept in order to question her standards. Ought sentences based on standards with which the speaker does not agree are included in what Copp calls type-one normative propositions; they say only that the item meets a standard that has (or had) currency in some society or other. These Copp distinguishes from type two normative propositions which entail that the item meets a *justified* standard [See *Morality, Normativity, and Society* (New York: Oxford University Press, 1995), 22-24]. Unless otherwise specified, my discussion is only of type-two oughts.

[3] It does not follow, of course, that the fact that a person values truth or an ideal world or some particular goal entails that he will value the required means to that goal or that he will not value means which will promote that goal, but are not necessary to it.

[4] See James Forrester's discussion in *Being Good and Being Logical* (Armonk, NY: M. E. Sharpe, 1996), esp. Chapter 4.

[5] See, for example, my 'Practical Reasoning and Historical Explanation,' *History and Theory*, 15 (1976): 133-140.

[6] It is not necessary that the end be valuable in any sense other than its being desired by the agent, so long as it meets the restrictions to be discussed (i.e., is neither imprudent nor immoral).

[7] Frank Jackson has argued this in 'Decision-Theoretic Consequentialism and the Nearest and Dearest Objection' *Ethics*, 101 (1991): 461-482.

[8] I am indebted to James Forrester for pointing out the necessity for clarification here.

[9] I have discussed this hierarchy in *Persons, Animals, and Fetuses*, Kluwer, Dordrecht, 1996, Chapter 2. Thomson also considers that moral oughts override other types (see Gilbert Harman & Judith Jarvis Thomson, *Moral Relativism and Moral Objectivity*, Blackwell, Oxford, 1996, Chapter 8).

[10] Of course, people might (and some do) claim that it is better to follow one's emotions, disregarding one's best interests, or to look out for Number One and let others go hang. I shall subsequently discuss these views, which I think can be shown to be based on misunderstandings of what their proponents are actually claiming. It is much more common to find people who act imprudently or immorally, either despite believing they ought not to do so (akrasia or perversity), or having told themselves they were actually doing the right thing (self-deception), or, most commonly, because they haven't thought at all. None of these scenarios counts against the thesis I am maintaining here.

[11] I am indebted to an anonymous reader of this manuscript for suggesting an example of this type.

[12] James Forrester has pointed out the need to clarify this issue more fully.

[13] In fact, quite a lot has been written against 'consequentialist' moral theories in recent years. As examples, see Bernard Williams, in J.J.C. Smart and Bernard Williams, *Utilitarianism: For and Against* (Cambridge: Cambridge University Press, 1973), 108-118; Samuel Scheffler, *The Rejection of Consequentialism* (Oxford: Clarendon Press, 1982), esp. Chapter 2, and Jonathan Dancy, *Moral Reasons* (Oxford: Blackwell, 1993), esp.

Chapters 10- 13. I will discuss these arguments in various places as the book progresses.

[14] See *Beyond Good and Evil*, ed. and trans. Marianna Cowan (Chicago: Henry Regnery Company, 1955), fifth and ninth articles.

[15] Elsewhere I have argued that such views do not represent the position that it is morally acceptable for some persons to benefit at the expense of others, but rather that not all humans count as persons; rather, some are held to be lesser beings, rather like animals, to whom the superior humans may have some obligations but whose duties do not include treating their interests on an equal basis. See *Moral Language*, Chapter 8. This difference in status has actually been an extremely common phenomenon throughout human history. The names of many primitive tribes actually mean 'the People,' and there have been numerous demonstrations of such tribes treating members of their 'in' group with justice and kindness, while exhibiting dreadful cruelty to those outside that group, sometimes even to the point of considering them game for hunting. (See, for example, the discussion of the Mundurucú headhunters of Brazil by Edward O. Wilson, *On Human Nature* (Cambridge, MA: Harvard University Press, 1978), 111-114). The contrast between exquisite torture for enemies in war and loving relationships with family — including adopted outsiders — among many Native American tribes is frequently illustrated by the accounts in Frederick Drimmer, ed., *Captured by Indians: 15 Firsthand Accounts, 1750-1870* (New York: Dover Publications, 1961). Of course, as will be discussed below, indigenous people themselves have often been considered merely animals by invading "civilized" groups.

[16] See *The Ethics*, Book III, Propositions 3-5 and the Definitions of the Emotions, 1, and Book IV, Propositions 18-37 and Definitions. See the edition edited and translated by Robert H. M. Elwes, *The Chief Works of Benedict de Spinoza*, Vol 2 (New York: Dover Publications, 1951).

[17] 'Ethical Egoism is Inconsistent,' *Australasian Journal of Philosophy*, 35 (1957): 111-118.

[18] See, for example, Ayn Rand's *Atlas Shrugged, passim.*

[19] Personal communication.

[20] That people act without considering the interests of others or may attempt to justify their selfish actions by insincerely citing moral reasons does not go against what I have argued here. I am not discussing what people's real motives are, but rather what sorts of considerations people appeal to in moral argument. That the self-centered use moral considerations to justify their beliefs and actions shows all the more that they recognize the necessity of doing so if they are to convince others that they are justified. That they recognize this necessity shows how widespread is the belief in the crucial importance of moral standards.

[21] In 'Be Ye Therefore Perfect, *or* the Inevitability of Sin,' *Religious Studies*, 21 (1985):1- 19.

[22] Indeed, if Dostoevsky is right, mankind is in love with suffering and depravity, and is *right* to be so, as this shows that he is free and not tied to canons of rationality like some automaton. [See *Notes from Underground*, ed. & trans. by Ralph E. Matlaw (New York: E. P. Dutton, 1960), Part I, Sects VII- X]. But here too, we have a conception of human good which contrasts with what is rational and prudent: the good being exercise of free will.

[23] See, for example, Hector- Neri Castañeda, *The Structure of Morality*, (Springfield, IL: Charles Thomas, Pub., 1974).

[24] See *Fear and Trembling*, ed. and trans. Howard V. And Edna H. Hong (Princeton: Princeton University Press), esp. 52-82.

[25] Kierkegaard does speak of a person's performing an act of faith which goes against the ethical as putting the individual above the universal. This might be read in (at least) two ways. If he is suggesting that an individual should put himself or his particular concerns — including his personal relationship with God — ahead of what is morally right, then Kierkegaard is surely wrong. History has been littered with catastrophes resulting from the acts of those who believed that they had a special relationship with God which permitted them to destroy others. On the other hand, I think it more likely that the primacy of the individual could be taken as an expression of the importance of individual persons — a central notion of Christianity (and other modern religions). It is, I shall argue subsequently, a centerpiece of any defensible moral theory that individuals take precedence over rules because individuals are those for the sake of whom rules exist. This does *not* mean that individuals have the right to break rules whenever they wish, but only when doing so will be more consistent with what morality requires. And this, I think, is consonant with the spirit of what Kierkegaard is saying: that since God is good and cares for all individuals, He may ask of a person that she do something which violates an ethical rule that should normally be followed, but His purpose in making such a demand is righteous. If the command really comes from God (as opposed to being dreamed up by the person herself) it will not be ultimately wrong.

[26] There might be individuals who think that one ought to follow the demands of etiquette or the law regardless of whether they conflict with any other considerations. But if such people are forced to try to justify these views, they would be unlikely to convince others.

[27] See *The Structure of Morality* (Springfield, IL: Charles Thomas, Publisher, 1974), Chapter 8.

[28] Similarly Darwall argues (*Impartial Reason*, Cornell University Press, Ithaca & London, 1983, Chapter 14) that what one ought to do is what is unconditionally rational — i.e., what the person would want everyone to do in the same circumstances — is the overall standard by which moral standards, as well as others, are judged.

[29] Not all of these objections apply to Darwall's version of the ought-all-things-considered, for he brings in

the requirement of universality. No one could rationally want states of the world similar to what Hitler wanted because, in Darwall's view, rationality entails looking at actions impartially, so that we would want that action done to us just as we would want to do it to someone else. On the other hand, what X might want impartially could be in conflict with what Y wants impartially. If X judges that Y ought to do A, is he using his own standards or Y's? The same objection applies here as applies to Castañeda's view.

[30] See R.M. Hare, *Freedom and Reason* (New York: Oxford University Press, 1965), Chapter 5.

[31] For a fuller discussion of moral weakness and perversity, and why it shows that moral judgments are not essentially action guiding in the sense that the belief that one ought to do A will result in one's doing A (unless one somehow cannot do A), see my *Moral Language*, 109-122.

[32] There is moral value in pursuing personal goals and one's own interest. We have seen that it is morally, as well as prudentially, right for agents to act in their own best interests, so long as there is no conflict with the interests of others and sometimes even when there is such a conflict. And it is usually right, morally and prudentially, to pursue one's own individual goals, for, as I shall argue later, what is best for us is closely related to what will enable us to achieve our goals.

There is nothing morally good in itself in finding a special stamp for one's collection, or in winning a marathon. But if you are an avid stamp collector or runner, these things are very important to *you*. To the extent that you attain these goals, you are more likely to be happy, and your happiness has moral value equal to the happiness of all persons. While your finding the stamp is something you value and which you care about, those of us who do not share this interest will, of course, not care about either our finding stamps or your finding them, except to the extent we care about you. But this does not imply that the *moral* value of your finding the stamp is greater for you than your finding it would be for others, as Jonathan Dancy maintains [see *Moral Reasons* (Oxford: Blackwell, 1993), 12-209]. That Joe values something and cares about it lends objective value to his having it, just because that would contribute to his happiness. And for Sue who doesn't care about it, her having it would not have the same objective value. This is not, however, a limitation on moral realism or objectivity; it is simply a recognition of the facts that people have different interests and that their happiness depends on different things. And what is objectively valuable is happiness, and the happiness of one individual is just as important from the moral point of view as that of any other.

[33] This is often what people mean by this question, equating morality with existing social mores. See also Copp's discussion, *Morality, Normativity, and Society*, 242-245.

[34] See the classic paper by H. A. Prichard, 'Does Moral Philosophy Rest on a Mistake?' *Mind* 21 (1912): 12-37.

[35] See *The Sources of Normativity* (Cambridge: Cambridge University Press, 1996), especially Lecture 3.

[36] G. A. Cohen, 'Reason, Humanity, and the Moral Law,' in *The Sources of Normativity*, 167-188.

[37] *The Sources of Normativity*, 227-232.

[38] In *Why you Should*, (Providence, R.I.: University Press of New England, 1989).

Notes to Chapter 3

[1] Strongly required conditions include, as noted in Chapter 2, some set of sufficient conditions or other for reaching the goal in question.

[2] This is the scheme which I proposed in *Persons, Animals, and Fetuses* (Dordrecht, Kluwer, 1996), Chapter 3; since that book was published I have come to realize that certain features of my position need further argument and clarification.

[3] See R. M. Hare *The Language of Morals* (New York: Oxford University Press, 1964), especially Chapter 7, and Anderson, *Value in Ethics and Economics* (Cambridge, MA: Harvard University Press, 1993), 3-4.

[4] See, for example, Michael Stocker, *Plural and Conflicting Values* (Oxford: Clarendon Press, 1990), Chapters 6 & 8.

[5] These standards need not be fixed, but may vary with time and individual needs and purposes. As noted in the previous chapter's discussion of 'ought,' what makes a standard correct or appropriate depends upon which value theory is true.

[6] As Panayot Butchvarov ['Realism in Ethics,' *Midwest Studies in Philosophy*, 12 (1988): 395-412] points out, however, the fact that a thing may be good in some respects but not others enables us to answer a pluralist objection I will consider further below. The objection is that if when we decide on item A over item B we may still regret B, we cannot conclude that A is better overall than B on the grounds of some one standard. If there is even the slightest difficulty, however, in deciding between A and B, it is surely because both have some good-making features, which in other circumstances might make either worthy of choice. That there is some one particular criterion by which we decide that A is better than B in these circumstances is not, however, ruled out by the fact that we may regret losing whatever was good in B. That there is one criterion suggests that it would be better to have both A and B than A alone, so that we can be sorry about what we cannot have while still recognizing that our choice was for the best in the specific circumstances, and this is, I think, what we actually believe.

[7] This, of course, does not necessarily make the item bad for you.

[8] See also Christine Korsgaard, 'Two Distinctions in Goodness,' *Philosophical Review*, 92 (1983): 169-195, where she points out that things derive their goodness from their being chosen or desired by us.

[9] R. B. Brandt, *A Theory of the Good and the Right* (Oxford: Clarendon Press, 1979), Chapter 6. This view resembles both Mill's point that the greater of two pleasures, and greater good, can be determined by the preference of the person who has experienced both [*Utilitarianism* in *The Utilitarians* (Garden City, NY: Doubleday, 1961), 409] and Henry Sidgwick, who maintains that what is best for us can be determined by what we would prefer if we had full knowledge of the consequences of all alternatives [*Methods of Ethics*, 7th ed. (Indianapolis: Hackett, 1981), p. 111]. Two more recent proponents of the full information theory are David Lewis, 'Dispositional Theories of Value,' *Proceedings of the Aristotelian Society*, suppl. vol. 63 (1980): 113-137 and Peter Railton, 'Moral Realism,' *Philosophical Review*, 95 (1986): 163-207.

[10] This was the view espoused by Mill, *Utilitarianism*, Chapter II.

[11] See Plato, *Philebus*, 48 b-c [see *The Dialogues of Plato*, vol. II, B. Jowett, trans. (New York: Random House, 1937), 383], and C. D. Broad, *Five Types of Ethical Theory* (New York: Humanities Press, 1956), 234.

[12] See Jon Elster, 'Sour Grapes — Utilitarianism and the Genesis of Wants,' in *Utilitarianism and Beyond*, Amartya Sen and Bernard Williams, eds. (Cambridge: at the University Press, 1982), 219-238.

[13] Elster also argues that autonomy is an important value which is ignored by utilitarianism, giving yet another reason why artificially induced desires, even when satisfied, are not as a rule good. I shall discuss this point later on, as objections from autonomy are relevant to my own theory of individual good, as well as to FIT's.

[14] In *A Theory of the Good and the Right*, Chapter VI. Brandt does not, however, espouse an FIT.

[15] H. Tristram Engelhardt, in *The Foundations of Bioethics* (New York: Oxford University Press, 1986), 31-37, gives a similar argument against Ideal Observer theories of ethics. If what is right is defined as what a perfectly benevolent, all knowing individual wants, we are unable to translate this into practical conclusions without being able to know what it is that this being would want. And to do this we must know what is right on independent grounds.

[16] See Derek Parfit's excellent discussion of this issue in *Reasons and Persons* (Oxford: Clarendon Press, 1984), Part II.

[17] This point was suggested to me by James Forrester, in conversation. There has also been some excellent recent work criticizing the desires-under-full-information account of the good. See, for example, David Sobel, 'Full Information Accounts of Well-Being,' *Ethics*, 104 (1994): 784-810, and Connie Rosati, 'Persons, Perspectives, and Full Information Accounts of the Good,' *Ethics*, 105 (1995): 296-325. Both discuss the intricacies of how one's personality, one's past experiences, and one's earlier decisions determine what it is possible for one to desire, and both make the point that one might be better off having something that one is not able to desire because of something about one or one's past.

[18] Frank Ramsey, 'Truth and Probability,' in *The Foundations of Mathematics and Other Logical Essays*, R. B. Braithwaite, ed. (London: Routledge and Kegan Paul, 1950), 156- 198.

[19] These matters are discussed by Kenneth Arrow, *Social Choice and Individual Values* (New Haven, CT: Yale University Press, 1951), Chapter 3, and have come to be known as the problem of interpersonal utility. An excellent recent discussion is that of Michael Resnik, *Choices: an Introduction to Decision Theory* (Minneapolis: University of Minnesota Press, 1987), 205-212, which makes very clear the reasons why assigning absolute utility values can only be arbitrary.

[20] 'Cardinal Welfare, Individualistic Ethics, and Interpersonal Comparisons of Utility,' *Journal of Political Economy*, 63 (1955): 309- 321, and in *Rational Behavior and Bargaining Equilibrium in Games and Social Situations* (Cambridge: Cambridge University Press, 1977), 51- 60.

[21] John Rawls, *A Theory of Justice* (Cambridge MA: Harvard University Press, 1971), 17-22. Actually, Harsanyi's discussion of this predates Rawls's.

[22] *Social Choice and Individual Values*, Chapter 3.

[23] In *Morals by Agreement* (Oxford: Clarendon Press, 1986), 240- 243.

[24] In an informal presentation to the University of Wyoming in 1992.

[25] This is Harsanyi's view: that the basic similarity of people is what enables us to make interpersonal utility comparisons. See, for example, 'Morality and the Theory of Rational Behavior,' *Social Research*, 44 (1977): [Also reprinted in Sen and Williams, *Utilitarianism and Beyond*, 38-62].

[26] Alfred McKay, 'Interpersonal Comparisons,' *Journal of Philosophy*, 72 (1975): 535-549.

[27] Gilbert Ryle, 'Pleasure,' *Proceedings of the Aristotelian Society*, Supp. Vol. 28 (1954): 195- 205.

[28] Nozick discusses this in *Anarchy, State, and Utopia* (New York: Basic Books, 1974), 42- 45.

[29] See Epicurus, *Principle Doctrines* and *Letter to Menoeceus*, trans. Cyril Bailey (Oxford: Clarendon Press, 1926), 89 & 95

[30] See Plato's discussion of this in the *Philebus*, 31a - 47e.

[31] Aristotle, *Nicomachean Ethics*, Martin Ostwald, trans. (Indianapolis: Bobbs-Merrill, 1962), 1097- 1098.

[32] While I have some problems with Aristotle's characterization of happiness as "rational activity in accordance with virtue," these are primarily due to ambiguities in these expressions. If 'rational' is interpreted as meaning that one is acting in such a way as best to achieve one's purposes, and 'virtue' as meaning that one's goals are appropriate, i.e., such as to be mutually attainable and provide a large amount of overall satisfaction (an interpretation of Aristotle suggested by James Forrester) then I would be very much in agreement with

Aristotle. Another aspect of virtue, which Aristotle, as well as most moderns, would include would be that one's goals included the good of others. Yet while the happiest people are concerned with the good of others, this is a contingent fact and should not be included in the *definition* of happiness for a single individual.

[33] See Gilbert Ryle, *The Concept of Mind* (New York: Barnes & Noble, Inc., 1949), 108, Kurt Baier, *The Moral Point of View* (Ithaca, NY: Cornell University Press, 1958), 272, Terence Penelhum, 'The Logic of Pleasure,' in *Philosophy and Phenomenological Research*, 17 (1956- 57):488-503, Jan Narveson, *Morality and Utility* (Baltimore: The Johns Hopkins University Press, 1967), 57- 67, and Richard B. Brandt, 'Two Concepts of Utility,' in *The Limits of Utilitarianism*, Harlan B. Miller and William H. Williams, eds. (Minneapolis: University of Minnesota Press, 1982). Brandt (*A Theory of the Good and the Right*, pp. 38-42) defines pleasure as wanting experiences to continue, and on pp. 247-253 suggests that what we want to do for others is not to maximize desire satisfaction, which he considers unintelligible, but to maximize happiness or pleasure. See also his discussion of how to measure happiness (253-265). Similarly, R. B. Perry defined the good life as "harmonious happiness" in which all interests endorse each other, whereas unhappiness occurs when interests conflict [*Realms of Value: a Critique of Human Civilization* (Cambridge, MA: Harvard University Press, 1954), 104 ff].

[34] See Gilbert Harman and Judith Jarvis Thomson, *Moral Relativism and Moral Objectivity*, Blackwell, Oxford, 1996, Chapter 8. The restrictions Thomson poses are that what is good for a person is what contributes to a state that person would want to continue, provided that he is aware of the costs and has chosen autonomously. The first qualification turns her definition into something very like a full information theory, and it would be subject to the same difficulties. The second is similar; among other things, autonomy presupposes being informed, although how fully informed it is necessary to be is unclear. It does seem that awareness of costs and autonomy contribute to one's happiness and the goodness of one's life not so much at the moment being considered, but for future moments. Being aware of the costs of my enjoyment of my Key lime pie while I am eating it would really only detract from my enjoyment and whatever good that brings. The costs of this and similar pleasures will contribute to my unhappiness and worsen my life if I indulge enough to impair my health, and in *deciding* whether or not to eat the pie it would be well for me to be aware of these costs. If I am I will be less likely to choose eating pie too often for my own good. The same considerations apply to the autonomy of a choice. Choosing under coercion certainly detracts from pleasure and happiness, and hence from one's good. One may, however, have had one's choice subtly influenced without one's realizing it. If -- as is likely -- such influences keep one from making choices that will lead to greater overall happiness, they are bad for one. They need not, however, detract from the goodness of a particular state. Under pressure from her boyfriend Tracy gives in and has intercourse with him. She sees the pressure as an expression of love and the act brings her enjoyment. The goodness of that *immediate* period of her life is unaffected by the way it was brought about. If indeed he does love her and she is physically, emotionally, and economically ready for a sexual relationship, then that period of her life may be good for her overall, in spite of the subtle pressure. On the other hand, if the boyfriend only wants sex, and deserts her when she becomes pregnant or contracts a disease, then obviously her choice was a bad one for her in the long run. In addition, if she is the sort of person who easily succumbs to pressure from others, she will tend to have a worse and more unhappy life overall than if she chooses autonomously. Thus even if the particular choice in question brings her more happiness than unhappiness and is good for her, the fact that it was not made with full autonomy is an indication of factors that will detract from the overall happiness and goodness of her life.

[35] See Harry Frankfurt, 'Freedom of the Will and the Concept of a Person,' *Journal of Philosophy*, 68 (1971): 5-20.

[36] An anonymous reader of this manuscript pointed out the necessity for clarifying some of the points made in the last three paragraphs.

[37] Julia Annas argues in *The Morality of Happiness* (Oxford: Oxford University Press, 1993), esp. Chapter 1, that this is how the ancient philosophers thought of happiness.

[38] James Forrester has suggested that some might consider the happiest life to be one which ends at the peak moment of happiness [e.g., Herodotus's example of the two young men who after their mother — whose cart they had pulled a long distance to get her to the festival of the Goddess -- prayed that they receive the greatest of all blessings, fell asleep and never woke up; Solon thought they were the happiest of all, since their lives effectively ended while still happy. See *The Histories*, Aubrey de Sélincourt, trans.)Baltimore: Penguin Books, 1954, Book I, 23-26.] Certainly a person would be better off if his happiest time was never followed by a decline in happiness, which decline might appear the worse by comparing it with what went before — and this was Solon's point. He thinks an even happier person was Tellus, who had lived a long — at least long enough to have grandchildren — and prosperous life, but who died a glorious death in battle. Most people today think it a misfortune to die in the prime of life; at that time at least, we expect the person to have more of the same satisfactions he has at the time of death; if so, he would be better off not to have died. If in fact he were to have had only great suffering instead, then we would certainly think him better off to have died when he did. If a person were to have more than one peak moment, with only minimal valleys between, he would be better off to live through them all than only through the first — unless of course he were to spend the rest of his life bemoaning the fact that things were no longer quite so wonderful.

[39] It does not matter here how many desires the individual has; rather it is the amount of time he spends being

bothered by not having the desires he has satisfied.

[40] An anonymous referee argued that if wanting one's situation to continue is a dispositional state, then it is hard to see how it can be measured in time. Yet an object may have a dispositional property continuously over an extended period of time, even though there are no constant manifestations of that property. Sodium chloride is soluble in water even when it is not actually being dissolved; the properties it has which make it soluble are always present, however. A comparable situation is that of belief. I am not constantly aware of my belief that the ground beneath my feet is solid, but not only is that belief constantly acted upon by my walking on it, but if anyone were to ask at any time if I believed the ground was solid I would affirm this to be so; no doubt the features of my brain underlying that belief remain the same. I can also usually date times at which I change my mind — "I believed that p most of my life until June 10, 1983 when I realized that not-p." Hence it may be true that one is wanting one's life to continue as it is, even though manifestations and explicit awareness of this wanting are intermittent.

[41] Indeed, the whole notion of happiness, and with it the idea of wanting things to be as they are, or different, may not be a concept which applies to something actually happening within a human being, but rather a way of interpreting or rationalizing our behavior. If Daniel Dennett is correct, this is the most accurate way of explaining any mental phenomenon. See his intriguing proposals in *Consciousness Explained* (Boston: Little, Brown, 1991), esp. 101- 138, but *passim*.

[42] See Edward F. Becker, 'Justice, Utility, and Interpersonal Comparisons,' *Theory and Decision*, 6 (1975): 471- 484.

[43] In 'Truth, Invention, and the Meaning of Life' in *Needs, Values, Truth: Essays in the Philosophy of Value* (Oxford: Blackwell, 1987), 87-137.

[44] See Stocker, *Plural and Conflicting Values*, Chapter 9 and Michael Slote, *Beyond Optimizing* (Cambridge, MA: Harvard University Press, 1989), especially Chapter 2.

Notes to Chapter 4

[1] James Q. Wilson in *The Moral Sense* (New York: The Free Press, 1993), 194- 196, points out that freedom has not been particularly valued in most societies throughout history. For many there has not even been a word which could be translated as 'freedom.'

[2] See, for example, Joseph Raz, *The Morality of Freedom* (Oxford: Clarendon Press, 1986), 13.

[3] See for example, Tom L. Beauchamp and James F. Childress, *Principles of Biomedical Ethics*, 4th ed. (New York: Oxford University Press, 1994), esp. Chapter 3.

[4] See Jon Elster's 'Sour Grapes — Utilitarianism and the Genesis of Wants,' in *Utilitarianism and Beyond*, Amartya Sen and Bernard Williams, eds. (Cambridge: Cambridge University Press, 1982), 219-238. Elster, incidentally, recognizes that 'autonomy' is a difficult word to define; it is much easier to say where it has been violated (p. 228).

[5] In some non-Western cultures it is definitely considered better *not* to tell a patient that he has terminal cancer. See, for example Akira Kurosawa's film *Ikiru*, in which the hero is told by another patient in the waiting room what the doctor will tell him if he has cancer, which amount to meaningless reassurances. And of course, these things are just what is said to him, for he does indeed have stomach cancer.

[6] See *The Practice of Moral Judgment* (Cambridge, MA: Harvard University Press, 1993), esp. Chapters 9 and 10.

[7] Charles Taylor, in 'The Diversity of Goods,' in *Utilitarianism and Beyond*, Amartya Sen and Bernard Williams, eds. (Cambridge: Cambridge University Press, 1982), 129- 144, and David Brink, *Moral Realism and the Foundations of Ethics* (Cambridge University Press, Cambridge, 1989), 231-235.

[8] *Strutting and Fretting: Standards for Self Esteem* (Niwot, CO: University Press of Colorado, 1991), 45- 52 & *passim*.

[9] That having ideals (like autonomy, commitments, and activity, for example) is necessary for a truly good life does not entail that having ideals is itself a final (individual) good. Given what people are like, they are far more likely to have satisfaction and fewer regrets if they do have ideals than if they do not. A life without any ideals would hardly be satisfying for any but the most unintelligent, bovine individuals. On the other hand, whether having a particular ideal is good for one — either good to have, good to pursue, or good to attain — depends upon other factors.

[10] In *The Fragility of Goodness* (Cambridge: Cambridge University Press, 1986), esp. Chapters 2 and 3. See also Wiggins, 'Truth, Invention, and the Meaning of Life,' in *Needs, Values, Truth: Essays in the Philosophy of Value* (Oxford: Blackwell, 1987), 87-137.

[11] The degree of contentment may not be directly related to what the person thinks about the commitment itself, but upon the multiple, far-reaching effects of having had that commitment. If his life proceeds in a constructive, satisfying way partly as a result of the failed commitment, it may have been good for him, regardless of whether he was aware of the causal relation.

[12] [23] Amartya Sen, 'Rights and Capabilities,' in *Morality and Objectivity: A Tribute to J. L. Mackie*, Ted Honderich, ed. (London: Routledge & Kegan Paul, 1985), 130-148.

[13] It is perhaps worth mentioning that in my nursing career I have been acquainted with a fair number of

people with such mental handicaps as retardation, brain damage, autism, psychosis, and senility. For the most part these people have not shown signs of being happy; in fact, they are often upset by trivial matters that most normal people would ignore. On the other hand, they do not appear to be enjoying much, even when they are doing what they presumably prefer to do. For example, they are undoubtedly not as bored as the rest of us might be watching television all day, but neither do they seem caught up in what they are watching the way a normal person might be — e.g., by laughing, crying, or showing interest or excitement. In short, people who for one reason or another are mentally incapable of appreciating some of the goods discussed above, do not as a whole appear to be happy either, or seem to care greatly about their surroundings unless something occurs to anger or frighten them.

[14] See, 'Death,' in *Mortal Questions* (Cambridge: Cambridge University Press, 1979), 1- 10. Harman has also made this objection [in Gilbert Harman & Judith Jarvis Thomson, *Moral Relativism and Moral Objectivity* (Oxford: Blackwell, 1996), Chapter 9].

[15] See also James Griffin, *Well-Being: Its Meaning, Measurement, and Moral Importance* (Oxford: Clarendon Press, 1986), 16-17, on the fact that all that we might desire has little import for our well-being. Those endeavors in which we have invested much of ourselves are those whose outcome determines our happiness and the goodness of our lives. Not that we should avoid striving for ends that we cannot accomplish. The effort itself may be both good and enjoyable, and some may prefer a life of hopeless striving to one with smaller, more accessible goals. But if a person is constantly frustrated and made miserable by the frustration, we would scarcely consider his life as good as it would have been had he had less ambitious projects. In the case of a Christian striving to be perfect, he might — if certain of his beliefs are true — be better off making the effort than to give up the attempt, thereby dooming his soul to eternal misery.

[16] James Forrester has suggested that it might be part of a person's individual good to perform the duties of his place in life. There is no question that it is a good thing for people to do their duties, but in what sense is it good for the particular individual to do his duty? It might well be good for him, as well as making him happier overall. Certainly it is good for him when he gets satisfaction from doing well something which he cares about. The enterprise — family, business, community — matters to him, and he wants to do his part well; in such a case he is happier overall if he does what is required of him, even though there may be onerous components of his duty. Suppose on the other hand he doesn't care and gets no satisfaction from doing his duty. It might still be good for him to do it if he will be rewarded in some way or punished if he neglects it — either in this life or the next. Otherwise, I can't see that to forge ahead, grudgingly doing what is unpleasant now and promises nothing he wants in the future, could be good for him at all, however much it benefits others. We might consider also what a person's 'place in life' might be. If it is whatever he has chosen or fallen into, when a different life would have brought him greater satisfaction, then it would have been better for him to have had that different life. If his 'place in life' is what is best suited to him, then of course fulfilling it would be best for him.

[17] See Michael Stocker, *Plural and Conflicting Values* (Oxford: Clarendon Press, 1990), 323.

[18] See Brandt's criticism of hedonism *A Theory of the Right and the Good* (Oxford: Clarendon Press, 1979), 132-138.

[19] In *Plural and Conflicting Values*, Chapter 6. See also pp. 248-272.

[20] See *Value in Ethics and Economics* (Cambridge, MA: Harvard University Press, 1993), especially Chapters 3 and 6.

[21] See Stocker, *Plural and Conflicting Values*, Chapter 8, sect. 4.

[22] See also Peter Railton's 'Alienation, Consequentialism, and the Demands of Morality,' *Philosophy and Public Affairs*, 13 (1984): 134-171 which makes this point well.

[23] It need not be a sufficient reason, however. We desire things other than happiness, and frequently do not deliberate as to what will bring us happiness, but go for what seems most immediately attractive. And even when we have decided what is best for us — will bring us most happiness — we may not have an effective desire for it sufficient to overcome particular passions. (See also Wiggins in 'Weakness of Will, Commensurability, and the Objects of Deliberation and Desire,' in *Needs, Values, Truth*, 239-267, as well as my 'Valuing and Akrasia,' *American Philosophical Quarterly*, 37 (2000):209-225).

[24] What is reasonable/unreasonable is not identical with what is rational/irrational, although these terms are often used interchangeably. I prefer to go with Sibley's distinction [see 'The Rational vs. the Reasonable,' *Philosophical Review*, 62 (1953): 554-560] which uses 'rational' and 'irrational' to refer to actions which promote, or frustrate, the objectives of the agent, without regard to the value of those objectives, and uses 'reasonable' and 'unreasonable' to refer to actions which promote, or frustrate, objectives that have value — i.e., bring individual or moral good.

[25] *Persons, Animals, and Fetuses* (Dordrecht: Kluwer Academic Publishers, 1996), 36-40.

[26] It should also be noted that what we ought to do is a subclass of what it is reasonable to do. We ought to do what is required for fulfilling an acceptable end, but it is not the case that we ought to do all that we might do to promote such an end. This fact, for example, allows us to distinguish between what we morally ought to do and what it would be morally good to do. It is, for example, not true that you ought or are obligated to sell all that you have and give to the poor, even though that might be your morally best course of action. This distinction allows us to account for agent-relative prerogatives and to show that using these prerogatives is,

while morally acceptable, not necessarily the best thing one could do. See also *Persons, Animals, and Fetuses*, 51-57 and Chapter 8 below.
[27] *Plural and Conflicting Values*, Chapter 6.
[28] James Forrester has suggested that the feelings accompanying different kinds of meals, or other pleasures, are as different that they may not all be equivalent to happiness — or that we may have different kinds of happiness, such as the difference between Plato and pushpin. Granted. Yet that there are different kinds of happiness does not show that there is no common feature of happiness in virtue of which we call it happiness, rather than some other state. Plato and pushpin can contribute differently to the happiness of different individuals and to the same person at different times. A person of little intellectual capacity or interest in philosophy will not get pleasure from Plato, so reading him would not add to the happiness of his life, whereas pushpin might. For such a person, pushpin would be better for him than attempting to read a work of philosophy which he would be entirely unable to understand. Even for a philosopher a steady diet of Plato (or anyone else) would eventually lose charm, and a game of pushpin might be one way of taking a welcome break. Yet the philosopher would have a source of happiness that would add much to his lifetime satisfaction, and which is not open to a person who had no interest or ability in philosophy. Not only would there be the immediate pleasure of reading and thinking about Plato, but this activity can enrich his life in many other ways besides — by, for example, giving him new directions in his own work, enlivening his lectures, and bringing him into contact with colleagues in the same field. In short, reading Plato is a potential source of many more satisfactions, and time spent contented, than is a game of pushpin.

Notes to Chapter 5
[1] This was suggested by an anonymous reviewer of this manuscript.
[2] See for example, my discussion in *Persons, Animals, and Fetuses* (Dordrecht: Kluwer Academic Publishers, 1996), Chapter 12.
[3] Again, a little misery can have good effects. It can bring greater overall happiness to a the individual that has it, perhaps by preventing much future misery. It can strengthen the character of that individual; this may make him happier in the long run, but it may not. On the other hand, his having a strong character is for the most part a good thing for other people whose lives he affects. Certainly, a small amount of suffering can lead to someone's being a more admirable — and better — person, and it can lead to his bringing about something good. This, however, will not necessarily increase his own happiness or be good *for* him.
    A person may also derive happiness from contemplation of a future state or memories of past states, and her happiness is thus not entirely bound by her present situation. Whether memories or future prospects bring happiness or unhappiness, however, depends upon the way in which we contemplate them in particular present moments.
    It is also possible that a person's being happy may preclude his doing his best work. Whether this is a bad thing for the individual, as opposed to the discipline in question and other people who benefit from it, depends upon several factors. The most important of these is how much the person's happiness is bound up in the quality of his work. If indeed he has not done his best, he will probably not be as happy as he would have been if he had. We may also say that it is a good thing for a person to do his best work, even if it is not good *for* him. James Forrester has indicated that I need to make all these points clearer.
[4] John Rawls, *A Theory of Justice* (Cambridge, MA: Harvard University Press, 1971), 92-95.
[5] In 'Rights and Capabilities,' *Morality and Objectivity: A Tribute to J. L. Mackie*, Ted Honderich, ed. (London: Routledge & Kegan Paul, 1985), 130-148.
[6] James Forrester has argued that there are some moralists who do not think that enhancing people's happiness is a fundamental moral goal. I would say that these views, if they can really be interpreted in this way, have been widely rejected. One important variant might be that what we ought to do is to do the will of God or do what is right regardless of the effects on human beings. Yet we would hardly suppose that doing the will of God or what is right is totally divorced from considerations of human happiness. Those who do the will of God do, according to virtually all religions, receive rewards in the hereafter if not in the present (and those who do not will be punished). And what determines what is right is, as I shall argue more fully below, determined by what in general promotes human happiness.
[7] See for example Jan Narveson, *Morality and Utility* (Baltimore: The Johns Hopkins Press, 1967), especially Chapter 7. Narveson has since rejected his utilitarian views. See especially *Moral Matters* (Peterborough, Ont.: Broadview Press, 1993).
[8] This objection to utilitarianism was made famous by Fyodor Dostoevsky in *The Brothers Karamazov*, Andrew H. McAndrew, trans. (Toronto: Bantam Books, 1970), 293-296 (Book V, Chapter 4).
[9] See, for example, Narveson, *Morality and Utility*, 216. D. W. Haslett has also presented some persuasive arguments to the effect that treating the interests of all equally is far more likely to increase the happiness of all than is partial treatment [*Equal Consideration* (Newark, NJ: University of Delaware Press, 1987), esp. Chapter 10]. He points out, for example, that discrimination can not only cause pain directly to the oppressing class as well as the oppressed, but by denying opportunity to some many benefits for all may be foregone, as when a black man denied an education might have found a cure for cancer if he had not been so deprived. There are, however, surely instances in which overall benefits might be less as a result of equal treatment, and

these are the cases that are difficult for classical utilitarianism.

[10] A similar point is made by David Lyons in *The Forms and Limits of Utilitarianism* (Oxford: Clarendon Press, 1965), p. 172. I shall also argue shortly that deception can be interpreted as a form of unfairness. Hence the torturing of the child would be both unfair to her and also unfair to all honest persons.

[11] John Stuart Mill, *Utilitarianism* in *The Utilitarians* (Garden City, NY: Doubleday, 1961), 424.

[12] John Rawls held this view, and used it to develop his theory of Rule Utilitarianism, which he has since rejected. See 'Two Concepts of Rules,' *Philosophical Review*, 64 (1955): 3- 32.

[13] For this point and what follows, I am heavily indebted to David Lyons, *The Forms and Limits of Utilitarianism*, 161- 177.

[14] See 'On a Supposed Right to Tell Lies from Benevolent Motives,' in *Kant's Critique of Practical Reason and Other Works on the Theory of Ethics*, 6th ed., T.K. Abbott, trans. (London: Longmans, 1959), 361- 365.

[15] Perhaps the most extensive examinations of utilitarianism, both pro and con, are in Jan Narveson, *Morality and Utility* and David Lyons, *The Forms and Limits of Utilitarianism*. Both have comprehensive references to earlier works. More recently, J.J.C. Smart defended utilitarianism and Bernard Williams criticized it in their joint book, *Utilitarianism: For and Against* (Cambridge: Cambridge University Press, 1973).

[16] *The Morality of Freedom* (Oxford: Clarendon Press, 1986), Chapter 6.

[17] See, for example, Sidgwick, *The Methods of Ethics* (Indianapolis: Hackett, 1987), 416-417.

[18] Jan Narveson, *Morality and Utility* (Baltimore: the Johns Hopkins University Press, 1967), especially Chapter 7.

[19] *A Theory of Justice* (Cambridge, MA: Harvard University Press, 1971), section 46.

[20] Robert Nozick, *Anarchy, State, and Utopia* (New York: Basic Books, 1974), esp.149-182.

[21] 'Capitalism, Socialism, and Justice: Reflections on Rawls' Theory of Justice,' *Social Praxis*, 7 (1980):253- 271.

[22] Sen, Amartya, 'Rights and Capabilities.'

[23] *Equality and Partiality* (New York: Oxford University Press, 1991), Chapter 7.

[24] See *Moral Differences: Truth, Justice, and Conscience in a World of Conflict* (Princeton: Princeton University Press, 1992), Chapter 6.

[25] In *The Moral Sense* (New York: The Free Press, 1993), 55- 78.

[26] See also Charles Taylor, 'The Nature and Scope of Distributive Justice,' in *Justice and Equality Here and Now*, Frank S. Lukash, ed.(Ithaca, NY: Cornell University Press, 1986), 34-67.

[27] There are some — and I will discuss their views in Chapter 7 — who believe that we should follow certain rules because they are right, independently of the consequences or the good or harm done to individuals. In general, I would say to any such objector that we need a criterion for determining which are the right rules and that any plausible criterion has at least indirect reference to the welfare of individuals.

[28] Thomas Nagel's characterization of liberal egalitarianism is similar to this (See 'Equality,' in *Mortal Questions* (Cambridge: Cambridge University Press, 1979), 106- 127).

[29] This is similar to Gregory Vlastos' characterization of justice in 'Justice and Equality,' in Jeremy Waldron, ed., *Theories of Rights* (Oxford: Oxford University Press, 1984), 41- 76.

[30] The enterprise may, if successful, put the participants at an advantage over nonparticipants by giving them something the others don't have. This, however, is not considered a violation of fairness, provided the participants do nothing to exclude nonparticipants arbitrarily, harm them, or hamper their ability to engage in comparable enterprises for their own good. We could hardly expect all persons to agree on what to do, much less organize the activities of people from all parts of the globe. Much more good can be accomplished if individuals alone, or in groups of manageable size, act in their own interest -- again so long as they do not interfere with other individuals' and groups' pursuing theirs. These separate efforts may result in people's not being equally well off, but as we shall see, fairness does not require that equality be achieved. Certainly equality should not be sought through practices that would make everyone worse off, which would certainly happen if all enterprises were required to include everyone.

[31] In 'The Nature and Scope of Distributive Justice.'

[32] Robert Nozick makes a persuasive case for this point, in *Anarchy, State, and Utopia* (New York: Basic Books 1974), 163 ff. Suppose, he says, that we were to achieve an equal distribution of goods. It wouldn't last, because some people might work harder than others. People would prefer (and pay more for) the goods, services, etc. of some to those of others. If this natural process were allowed to continue, some people would soon be better off than others. Equality might be restored, but only at the cost of extensive interference with people's liberty to do what they please. The administrative apparatus required, moreover, to accomplish these returns to equality would be extremely costly. All in all, an insistence on equality would bring about many evils and loss of goods.

[33] See *The Morality of Freedom* (Oxford: Clarendon Press, 1986), Chapter 9.

[34] Ideas of what is roughly equivalent in an exchange differ between times and places, and what is fair is often supposed to be what is customary. Yet in any society people consider exchanges unfair when one party receives significantly more or less than others in the same circumstances. Some (e.g., Nozick) might argue that any exchange is fair if neither party is coerced (or deceived) into participating. I agree that we generally do think this, unless we have strong reason to think otherwise — as, for example, when Ron, knowing that Rick is

addicted to heroin, offers him a hit if he will rob a bank for him. Apart from all the other moral evils in this example, the exchange is surely unfair, even though Rick agrees to it, and is neither forced into it nor kept in ignorance of what he needs to know, for Rick gains only a brief pleasure while risking prison, while providing Ron with a major benefit.

Furthermore, we sometimes speak of an action as being fair or unfair *to* an individual or group. As a rule, an act is unfair to a specific individual when the act is done at the expense of that individual. A shiftless employee is unfair to his colleagues who must do additional work and to his employer who is paying him, but not getting a reasonable return. We also speak of unfairness when goods and services are not involved, e.g. in saying that an accusation is unfair. In this case, we mean that the accused did not deserve it. The accusation was a type of punishment -- causing the accused unpleasant feelings, or worse, when he had done nothing to merit them. I am indebted to James Forrester for pointing out the necessity of mentioning these matters.

[35] David Resnik (personal communication) has suggested that it might be fair to allow everyone to tell a certain small number of 'white' lies, so long as they hurt no one and are not frequent enough to harm the advantages we get from general truth telling. Such a practice would indeed be *fair*. It would not, however, be as advantageous as one in which people were always expected to tell the truth. For we could not be sure whether a given individual was using one of his quota of lies on any given occasion. Many institutions and practices can be perfectly fair, but fail to be as beneficial as they might be, and hence are not as good as some possible alternatives.

[36] For an excellent discussion of this matter, see David Lyons, *The Forms and Limits of Utilitarianism* (Oxford: Clarendon Press, 1965), pp. 161-177.

[37] Vlastos makes this point in 'Justice and Equality.'

[38] See *The Morality of Freedom* (Oxford: Clarendon Press, 1986), Chapter 9. Jan Narveson argues similarly in *Morality and Utility* (Baltimore: The Johns Hopkins University Press, 1967), Chapter 7.

[39] Charles Taylor, in 'The Diversity of Goods,' in Sen & Williams, *Utilitarianism and Beyond*, 129-144, has pointed this out.

[40] As an example of this, see *Princess: a True Story of Life Behind the Veil in Saudi Arabia* (New York: William Morrow & Co, 1992). It was written by Jean Sasson, but recounted to her by a wealthy woman, a member of the Saudi royal family, who is well aware of the ways in which women are oppressed in that country and is full of indignation and desire to bring changes.

[41] See, for example, the fascinating discussion of the lives and status of Islamic women in Naila Minai's *Women in Islam: Tradition and Transition in the Middle East* (New York: Seaview Books, 1981).

[42] Among the many books which have dealt with the inhumanity of so-called civilized people to aboriginals, see Alan Moorehead, *The Fatal Impact* (New York: Dell, 1966), especially Part I Chapters 5 & 6 and Part II, Chapter 6; Kenneth Stampp, *The Peculiar Institution: Slavery in the Ante-Bellum South* (New York: Vintage Books, 1956), especially Chapters VIII & IX; and Dale Van Every, *Disinherited: The Lost Birthright of the American Indian* (New York: William Morrow & Co., 1966), especially Chapter 1.

[43] See *Persons, Animals, and Fetuses*, especially Chapters 6, 7, and 8.

[44] Wilson also points this out in *The Moral Sense*, 241- 242.

[45] See again, Sasson, *Princess*. "Sultana," the author's informant, even as a small child, recognized the injustice of the favoritism shown her brother, and was outraged by the cruelty he and other men perpetrated against women.

[46] See for example Bernard Williams, 'A Critique of Consequentialism,' in *Utilitarianism: For and Against*, J. J. C. Smart and Bernard Williams (Cambridge, Cambridge University Press, 1973), 85-89; 108-118; Samuel Scheffler, *The Rejection of Consequentialism* (Clarendon Press, Oxford, 1982), Chapters 1-3; Michael Slote, *Beyond Optimizing* Routledge & Kegan Paul, London, 1985), esp. Chapters 3, 5, and 7; Thomas Nagel, *The View from Nowhere* (Oxford University Press, New York, 1986), esp. Chapter 9; and Jonathan Dancy, *Moral Reasons* (Blackwell, Oxford, 1993), esp. Chapter 10 and 213-217.

[47] An exception would be Peter Singer. See 'Famine, Affluence, and Morality,' in *Moral Problems: a Collection of Philosophical Essays*, 3rd. ed., James Rachels, ed. (New York: Harper and Row, 1979), 263-278.

[48] There is a difference between what we are obligated to do, what we ought to do, and what is morally best for us to do. In many cases what is best for us to do is to forego our agent-relative prerogatives and help strangers in preference to pursuing our own interests. Yet we might not be obligated to do this, because obligations entail that we are and ought to be in some way pressured by society to act; that we have a prerogative indicates that such pressure is not justified. It might not even be that you or I specifically ought to help others instead of getting some lesser good for ourselves, if there are plenty of other people about who could help just as well. I will discuss these distinctions fully in Chapter 8.

[49] Nozick, *Anarchy, State and Utopia* (New York: Basic Books, 1974), 93- 95

[50] . See Chapter 8 for a discussion of the distinction between oughts and obligations.

[51] None of the appeals to the interests or happiness of individuals made here are intended to rule out the possibility of natural rights as justifications for doing or refraining from certain acts. I will discuss rights in Chapter 8. For now, it is worth pointing out that those things to which we have been supposed to have natural

rights are those which most people would consider essential to or part of their good or happiness. Natural rights have been traditionally supposed to come from one of two sources: divine (e.g., Aquinas) or human nature (e.g., Hobbes). (See Lloyd L. Weinreb, *Natural Law and Justice* (Cambridge, MA: Harvard University Press, 1987), especially Part I for a survey of the history of natural law theory.) If the latter, my own views could be considered a natural rights view, as that to which people have thought they had a natural right are just those things people believe critical to their well being -- and which things these are depends upon what people need, which in turn is determined by their nature. Those who suppose that natural rights come from God usually suppose also that God cares for the well being of humans and grants them rights to what is essential to it.

[52] Goods here include anything which people might desire, either for their own sake or as means to something else. That something is a good in this sense does not mean that it is unqualifiedly good, or could not be bad in some circumstances. See also Chapter 3.

[53] Nozick has argued in *Anarchy, State and Utopia* (New York: Basic Books, 1974), Chapter 7 that justice and fairness have nothing to do with equality of distribution, but rather with procedures. That is, if something belongs to one as a result of some recognized procedure which is not itself unjust, then that person is *entitled* to it. Furthermore, it will be, at least on the face of it, *unjust* to take that thing away from him. It is true that we think this way. The reason is, however, that when a person has acquired ownership of anything, we presume that he has, in Locke's terms, "mixed his labor with it," or paid money, or in some other way relinquished goods in order to obtain it. To take it away without adequate recompense wrongs him because then he loses, not only the item taken from him, but the goods he exchanged for it, leaving him relatively less well off than his fellows, so that they benefit at his expense. That this is normally true, however, and that equality is usually best preserved by procedural justice, does not show that all fairness boils down to procedures alone.

Notes to Chapter 6

[1] There are some situations in which lying is tolerated, and less morally offensive, than in the usual case. These include contexts in which lying is expected — in which case the person to whom the lie is made does not count on the truth of what he hears. It is, for example, conventional to say "I'm fine" when asked how you are — even though you are *not* fine. It is generally accepted that unless you believe the person who asks really wants to know, you will spare him the unhappy details. Likewise people are not expected to tell the truth about certain aspects of their lives when asked about them; those aspects are considered private and none of others' business. To avoid the rude-sounding "That's not your concern" (which may also give the impression that one is trying to hide something) the person may simply deny what he knows perfectly well is true. Such lies are typically excused. Furthermore, we often embroider events in our lives when recounting them to others in order to make a good story, or we hedge the truth in order to make an account easier to follow. These situations, as well, are instances of "excusable" lies, since people do not expect or count on strict adherence to the truth. In some cultures, in fact, lying is tolerated in many instances where it would not be in, say, the United States. For example, my son and his wife were flying standby on their way home from a trip to Kenya. They had called the airport in Nairobi to ask if there was room on a flight that day and were told there were plenty of seats. When they arrived, however, they found out that the flight was full, thereby having to waste some of their vacation waiting around until one was available. In Kenya, as in many other countries, it is expected that people will lie in order to save face or maintain a pleasant atmosphere by telling others what they want to hear. Hence a native Kenyan would not have relied upon the word of the airport personnel about his flight. Thus lying may not be wrong when it neither harms anyone nor takes advantage of a practice to which most people in the society adhere. In such a case it is not *unfair* to lie. I am grateful to James Forrester for pointing out the need to discuss such instances, as well as those in the following note.

[2] Some laws which, when obeyed, do bring benefits are regularly broken (e.g., speed limits on Wyoming highways). What would justify this? I should think that only some harm produced by obedience that was greater than any benefit the law was likely to bring would make it morally right to drive over the speed limit — e.g. when rushing a critically ill person to a hospital. Or, it might be foolish to have speed limits, or relatively low limits, where — as in Wyoming — people must travel long distances and the risk of collision (because of low population density) is small. That people do regularly break such laws for much lesser benefits, however, does not mean that it isn't at all wrong to do so.

[3] In *Persons, Animals, and Fetuses* (Dordrecht: Kluwer Academic Publishers, 1996), Parts III and IV.

[4] One feature of the central purpose of morality is that an individual's own happiness is given equal weight with that of other persons. Whatever one does for oneself, so long as it does not hinder a like degree of happiness for others, is morally, as well as prudentially, good. Thus we may allow that it is sometimes better to do things in one's own interest than to do things for others, without giving up the contention that moral oughts take precedence over prudential oughts. At times what is morally right and what is in one's best interest coincide. See also my discussion in Chapter 2.

[5] Copp suggests an interesting comparison of our knowledge of moral rules with our knowledge of grammar [*Morality, Normativity, and Society* (New York: Oxford University Press, 1995), 240]. In both cases, people may not always be able to articulate the rules, but they know how to use them correctly. People do commonly balance beneficence with fairness and solve other moral dilemmas in accordance with something like the central purpose, even though they may not be aware of using this criterion.

[6] See Robert Audi, 'Intuitionism, Pluralism, and the Foundations of Ethics,' in *Moral Knowledge?*, Walter Sinnott-Armstrong & Mark Timmons, eds. (New York: Oxford University Press, 1996), 101-136.

[7] See my 'Practical Reasoning and Historical Explanation,' *History and Theory, 15* (1976): 133-140. This position is also taken by Stephen E. Norris, 'The Intelligibility of Practical Reasoning,' *American Philosophical Quarterly, 12* (1975): 77-84. A precursor of this view is to be found in Anthony Kenny, 'Practical Inference,' *Analysis, 26* (1966): 65-75, where practical reasoning is looked upon as the search for a plan which will suffice for the achievement of our ends. That actions cannot be universally deduced from ends and circumstances has also been pointed out by Judith Jarvis Thomson, 'Practical Reasoning,' *Philosophical Quarterly, 12* (1962): 316-328, David Gauthier in *Practical Reasoning* (Oxford: Clarendon Press, 1963), 95-99, and R. M. Hare, *Practical Inferences* (Berkeley: University of California Press, 1971), 61-62.

[8] David Resnik pointed out the necessity for me to clarify this.

[9] As James Forrester points out, the response of some people to criticism may be to cite principles or rules that the critics accept, but which they themselves do not. In such a case, however, they can hardly be said to be attempting a sincere justification of their views or actions; rather they are trying to deflect blame or criticism. Citing such principles would in fact be an acknowledgment that they are widely accepted.

[10] When I read a paper taken from this chapter and the last to a practical ethics class of Professor Jann Benson at Colorado State University, several students objected to the term 'good moral upbringing.' They thought it suggested that there was only one right moral system, which all children should be taught. While I do maintain that there are certain general principles common to all acceptable moral systems, I am more than willing to admit that different specific rules in different societies may be equally sound. What constitutes 'good moral upbringing,' as I mean the term here is that the child is taught the moral rules which *that* society accepts, as well as the reasons for them, and that he or she is taught that sometimes personal interest and pleasure must be set aside in order to follow these rules — whatever they happen to be.

[11] James Forrester has proposed a variant on this case in which the patient's life can be not only extended for a few months by some heroic measure, but also be made of reasonably high quality — at the cost of lowering the living standard of a substantial number of people. What would be right to do in such a situation would, I think, depend upon how far the standard would be lowered. Adding a short period of good-quality life to that of a person who will soon die in any case would probably be a Level 2 rather than a Level 1 good. If the lower standard of living for the others affected would mean their loss of substantial Level 2 goods, prolonging the life of the patient probably would not be justified. On the other hand, if the others stood to lose only Level 3 goods, the procedure would probably be justified.

[12] Goods here include anything which a person might desire, either for its own sake or as means to something else. That something is a good in this sense does not mean that it is unqualifiedly good, or could not be bad in some circumstances. See also the discussion in Chapter 3.

[13] See also the discussion in Chapter 5. The similarities of these provisos to John Rawls' second lexical principle will be apparent. See *A Theory of Justice* (Cambridge, MA: Harvard University Press, 1971), 60- 75. I do not, however, agree with him that inequalities are necessarily unfair unless they make those in the worst off positions better off than they would be without the inequality. Clearly, an inequality which made the worst off people still more wretched would be unjust. But if it left them no worse off and did not make the improvement of their lot more difficult, it would not be wrong. This is certainly true if their situation could not be improved with or without the inequality. The simple presence of inequality is not unfair; it is inequalities that hinder the worse off from bettering their position that are unjust.

[14] Bernard Rollin has suggested to me that violating any law of such a regime might be justified on the grounds that it would create chaos that might subvert the government. I agree that this *could* be justified, but only if it were part of a well planned strategy. A campaign by many people to tie up traffic in the capital for days on end might work this way, but my running a stop light on my own would do nothing to bring down a dictator and might injure innocent people.

[15] James Forrester has suggested that my remarks about law do not fit well with common views of punishment. It might seem that it would be unfair to punish a con man with a stiff jail sentence when he has not succeeded in defrauding any particular person of more than an insignificant portion of her resources. If balancing harm and benefit were the only consideration involved with punishment, a jail term of several years would be unfair. Legal punishment, however, can and should (although unfortunately it usually does not) serve a number of other legitimate purposes — including deterrence, protection of the public, and even reform of the criminal. Any of these would justify a sentence that would harm the con man more than he had harmed any of his victims; the burden of crime to society goes beyond simple restitution, and it is only fair that the criminal assume whatever part of the burden is possible.

[16] See *Hard Choices* (Cambridge: Cambridge University Press, 1986) Chapters 1, 5, and *passim*.

[17] Cf. Samuel Guttenplan's excellent discussion in 'Moral Realism and Moral Dilemmas,' *Proceedings of the Aristotelian Society*, 80 (1979-80), 61-80. He points out that while it is no easier to say that food is better than shelter or education better than family services — in general — than it is to say whether Englishmen are taller than Frenchmen — in general — , this does not show that such goods are incommensurable. We can tell whether an individual Englishman is taller than a particular Frenchman, and we can also, by the means

indicated in the text, tell whether giving someone food on a particular occasion is preferable to giving another shelter on that occasion, or how much a society should spend on education relative to family services given its specific circumstances.

[18] In *Moral Dilemmas* (Oxford: Basil Blackwell, 1988), esp. p. 29.

[19] In 'Intuitionism, Pluralism, and the Foundations of Ethics.'

[20] In 'Ethical Consistency,' *Proceedings of the Aristotelian Society*, Supp.. Vol. 39 (1965): 103-124.

[21] In 'Moral Realism and Moral Dilemmas.' See also Simon Blackburn in 'Securing the Nots: Moral Epistemology for the Quasi-Realist,' in Walter Sinnott-Armstrong & Mark Timmons, eds., *Moral Knowledge?* (New York: Oxford University Press, 1996), pp. 82-100, who points out that moral considerations separately contribute to the overall moral quality of a given action. He, of course, does not use this issue to defend descriptivism, but to argue against a sort of situation ethic.

[22] Susan Hurley makes a similar point in *Natural Reasons* (New York: Oxford University Press, 1989), Chapter 9. Each of two or more different sets of reasons would, separately, lead to conflicting conclusions as to what one ought, pro tanto, to do. That one judges that one ought, all things considered, to perform one of these actions rather than the other, does not invalidate the reasons supporting the losing contender. I do not think, as Hurley does, that each of these sets of reasons is a sub-system of the self, and that moral reasoning consists largely of deciding which subsystem we ought to take as primary (see also her Chapter 8). On the other hand, her conclusion that the existence of such conflict between pro tanto reasons does not constitute a sound objection to ethical cognitivism is certainly defensible.

[23] See Thomas Hill 'Making Exceptions without Abandoning the Principle: or How a Kantian Might Think about Terrorism,' in *Dignity and Practical Reason in Kant's Moral Theory* (Ithaca: Cornell University Press, 1992), 196-225.

[24] The prevalence of terrorist acts in the society might be relevant here. In one like Israel, where they occur with great frequency, giving in to terrorists would probably have worse consequences and resisting them be more fair to all citizens than in a society where terrorism is rare and limited to specific situations that people can generally avoid — like flying to nations at war. (This note was originally written prior to September 11, 2001, when the risks of dying from terrorist acts suddenly appeared much more likely for Americans.)

[25] As Judith DeCew has pointed out, however, that there are some insoluble moral dilemmas does not show that there are no objective criteria for determining whether actions are right or wrong. (See 'Moral Conflicts and Ethical Relativism,' *Ethics*, 101 (1990): 127-141).

[26] See *The Moral Sense* (New York: The Free Press, 1993), *passim*. For specific examples from one culture, see those discussed by R.B. Brandt in *Hopi Ethics* (Chicago, University of Chicago Press, 1954), see especially pp. 145-146, who illustrates by many conversations with the Hopi that they think it wrong to do things to hurt others, and that they should return favors, keep promises, and avoid dishonesty, even when it won't be found out. Another interesting example, is the anthology edited by Robert M. Veatch, *Cross Cultural Perspectives in Medical Ethics: Readings* (Boston: Jones & Bartlett, 1989). The standards of behavior, including various oaths, to which physicians in numerous societies, ancient and modern, are supposed to follow are given here. Of course there are differences among them; however, all, (including ancient Greece Ludwig Edelstein, 'The Hippocratic Oath: Text, Translation, and Interpretation,' 6-24, the former Soviet Union (Robert Crawshaw, 'Medical Deontology in the Soviet Union,' pp. 106-112), ancient China (Tao Lee, 'Medical Ethics in Ancient China,' 132-139), modern China (H. Tristram Engelhardt, 'Bioethics in the People's Republic of China,' 112-119), sixteenth century Japan ('The 17 Rules of Enjuin,' trans. by William O. Reinhardt, 140-141), Islamic societies in the days of the Prophet Mohammed, (Abdul Rahman, C. Amine, and Ahmed Elkadi, 'Islamic Code of Medical Professional Ethics,' 120-126), ancient India (K.R. Srikanta Murthy, 'Professional Ethics in Ancient Indian Medicine,' 126-132)) all contain principles of treating patients with kindness and consideration, respecting their confidentiality, and treating other physicians with fairness and respect.

[27] David Resnik pointed to me the need to clarify this.

[28] Natural law might also be considered relevant. However, those items which have been promoted as natural laws or rights seem to be the same as those provided for under other moral systems. The question would be, "What makes a law natural?" Is it simply given with no prior justification, or is it justified on the basis of something about its characteristics and effects? If the former only, there seems no reason for accepting it. If the latter, the tenets of a specific natural law account would appear to receive ample justification from another account. Certainly beneficence and fairness seem to be part and parcel of such natural law theories as have been proposed.

[29] See, for example, Joseph Raz, *The Morality of Freedom* (Oxford: Clarendon Press, 1986), 13.

[30] See for example, Tom L. Beauchamp and James F. Childress, *Principles of Biomedical Ethics*, 4th ed. (New York: Oxford University Press, 1994), esp. Chapter 3.

[31] See, for example, Joseph Fletcher, *Situation Ethics: the New Morality*, 26-31 and *passim*.

[32] See *Grounding for the Metaphysics of Morals* in Immanuel Kant, *Ethical Philosophy*, James W. Ellington, trans. (Indianapolis: Hackett, 1983), 35-37.

[33] See *Life's Dominion* (New York: Alfred A. Knopf, 1993), esp. Chapter 3.

[34] Don Marquis has argued that even a nonsentient fetus has interests, since if allowed to have a full life it will be better off than it will be if it is aborted. [See 'Why Abortion is Wrong,' *Journal of Philosophy, 86* (1989):

183-202.] In that sense I agree that it does have interests, although it does not in the more standard sense of being actually aware of what is happening to it. It is the latter sense I am using and the one which I believe is relevant to the question of whether abortion is justifiable. In Marquis's sense of having interests sperm and eggs prior to fertilization would also have interests, as would any somatic cell of a living creature that might be used to create a clone. Each of these has the potential to become under appropriate conditions a sentient being with a potential for happiness and would thus have interests under Marquis's characterization. If this were to be grounds for preserving such things, then not only abortion, but contraception, sexual abstinence, and failure to go forward full speed with cloning research would be wrong. (See also my discussion in *Persons, Animals, and Fetuses*, Chapter 14.)

[35] Even Hobbes thought a man had the right to resist if his Sovereign attempted to take his life (*Leviathan*, Chapter 14).

[36] Alistair MacIntyre seems to think that tradition forms as good a foundation for morality as modern conceptions of individual rights — or at least that there are no grounds for saying that it is not equally valid. See *Whose Justice? Which Rationality?* (Notre Dame, IN: Notre Dame University Press, 1988), esp. Chapter 18.

[37] A possible exception to this would be a prominent school of Islamic thought, in which the word of Allah (as found in the Qur'an and analogies to it) *is* considered to be the standard of right and wrong. This view has been carried to the extreme that if God were to say that it was right to steal, then it would be right. See the discussion by George F. Hourani, *Reason and Tradition in Islamic Ethics* (Cambridge: Cambridge University Press, 1985). Hourani has an interesting take on how this tradition gained ascendancy (Chapter 5): it was thought that if people were allowed freedom to judge for themselves on ethical matters, they might be wrong, whereas Allah would always be right. Furthermore, if God were to be restricted to following human ethical standards, this could be seen as a limitation on God's power. Of course, as Hourani points out (p. 37), the difficulty then shifts to why humans should owe God any loyalty — as opposed to obeying from fear alone — if God did not adhere to those standards.

[38] In *Hopi Ethics*, 104- 105.

[39] See for example Frank Chapman Sharp, *Ethics* (New York: Century, 1928), 109- 110, and Roderick Firth, 'Ethical Absolutism and the Ideal Observer,' *Philosophy and Phenomenological Research*, 12 (1952): 317-345.

[40] See *A Theory of Justice* (Cambridge MA: Harvard University Press, 1971), 17- 21. Another such view is that of Stephen Darwall, *Impartial Reason*, Cornell University Press, Ithaca & London, 1983, *passim*.

[41] See Glenn C. Graber & David C. Thomasma, *Theory and Practice in Medical Ethics* (New York: Continuum, 1989), especially Chapter 2, and Albert R. Jonsen and Stephen Toulmin, *The Abuse of Casuistry: A History of Moral Reasoning* (Berkeley: University of California Press, 1988), esp. Chapters 1 & 15.

[42] Baruch Brody says that clinicians of his acquaintance have expressed this view, although this radical a position has not been seen in the literature [*Life and Death Decision Making* (New York: Oxford University Press, 1988), 7].

[43] Terrence F. Ackerman, 'What Bioethics Should Be,' *Journal of Medicine and Philosophy*, 5(1980): 260-275. This claim, of course, assumes that what counts as a criterion for ethical rightness is what certain individuals under certain conditions *want*. Although this author claims to be getting away from the dominance of rules and theories he is clearly using a sketch of a theory, which bears some resemblance to an Ideal Observer account.

[44] Brody, *Life and Death Decision Making*, especially Chapter 4.

Notes to Chapter 7

[1] I would like to extend particular thanks to Ed Sherline of the University of Wyoming. His trenchant criticisms of an early draft of this chapter are responsible for much of whatever merit it may have.

[2] Philosophers who have held this position include not only Kant [see especially 'On a Supposed Right to Lie from Benevolent Motives,' in *Kant's Critique of Practical Reason and Other Works on the Theory Of Ethics*, 3rd ed., T. K. Abbott, trans. (London: Longmans, 1959), 361-365], but also Bernard Williams, 'A Critique of Utilitarianism,' in *Utilitarianism: For and Against*, J. J. C. Smart and Bernard Williams (Cambridge: Cambridge University Press, 1973), 93-107; Phillipa Foot, 'Utilitarianism and the Virtues,' *Mind 94* (1985): 196-209, Stephen Darwall, 'Agent-Centered Restrictions from the Inside Out,' *Philosophical Studies 50* (1986): 291-319; Thomas Nagel, *The View from Nowhere* (New York: Oxford University Press, 1986), 175-185, and Jonathan Dancy, *Moral Reasons* (Oxford: Blackwell, 1993) esp. Chapter 10 and 217- 220.

[3] For example, suppose it is a worse consequence for Bill to be a liar than for him to fail to prevent a lie; perhaps lying oneself is -5 utils, while failing to prevent someone else from lying is only -1 util. This, however, might not be coherent, since if Bill doesn't lie to prevent Bob from lying and Bob lies, then the overall consequences are worse since we still have one person lying himself *and* a person not preventing that individual from lying. On such a view we could always increase the number of lies prevented sufficiently to make Bill's lying have better consequences than his not lying; if Bill lies and by doing so prevents ten other people from lying, the consequences are better than if he doesn't lie and all ten of the others lie. Most agent-relative theories would not accept the conclusion that in these circumstances Bill ought to lie.

[4] C. S. Forester, *Admiral Hornblower in the West Indies* (New York: Bantam Books, 1958), 49-59.

[5] Jan Narveson's earlier utilitarian views could be described as a type of consequentialism which takes into account distributional considerations [See *Morality and Utility* (Baltimore: The Johns Hopkins University Press, 1967), especially 158-163 and Chapter VII]. The theory he expounds there illustrates the important point that being sensitive to distributional factors does *not* commit a theory to holding that all goods must be distributed equally. Amartya Sen also proposes a view consistent with consequentialism that includes personal rights as goals which are valuable ['Rights and Agency,' *Philosophy and Public Affairs*, 11 (1982): 3-39. John Broome [*Weighing Goods* (Oxford: Basil Blackwell, 1991), Chapter 1] defines consequentialism in such a way that the value of acts, including their fairness or unfairness, may be included in the value of their consequences. What distinguishes consequentialism from nonconsequentialism (or, as Broome prefers to say, teleological from nonteleological theories) is that the former entails the view that the value of states of affairs should be ranked and weighed against one another to determine what one ought to do, whereas the latter denies this. A nonteleological theory might hold, for example, that certain side constraints make an act wrong regardless of how much moral good its being performed might do.

[6] Jorge Garcia, 'The New Critique of Anti-Consequentialist Moral Theory,' *Philosophical Studies, 71* (1993): 1-32.

[7] It does not follow from this that there would be no circumstances under which a mother might do best from a moral standpoint by sacrificing her own child to save many others (although if she did not, it would be hard to hold her blameworthy or consider her obligated). Such circumstances might include her having some special obligation toward the other children (e.g., as their teacher) or her own child's being unlikely to survive in any case.

[8] It does not follow that a person in these circumstances is blameworthy for breaking down. See further discussion of this issue in the following chapter.

[9] 'Autonomy and Benevolent Lies,' *The Journal of Value Inquiry*, 18 (1984):251-267.

[10] See *Utilitarianism* in *The Utilitarians* (Garden City, NY: Doubleday, 1961), 465-467.

[11] In *The Act Itself* (Oxford: Clarendon Press, 1995), 23. Bennett thinks the possibility of miscalculation — whether or not a result of self-deception — is a reason for adopting a two-level moral system. The theoretical level would determine which rules to adopt based on their probable consequences, but at the practical level people should choose their actions based on whether they conformed to principle.

[12] G. E. M. Anscombe is one exception. In 'Modern Moral Philosophy,' *Philosophy* 33 (1958): 1-19 she maintains that anyone who even considers that there might be circumstances when an innocent person could justifiably be killed to save the lives of many has a "corrupt mind." As an example of a philosopher in the Kantian tradition who does not hold that there are no circumstances when exceptions to moral principles may be made — and who thinks that Kant himself would agree — see Thomas Hill, 'Making Exceptions without Abandoning the Principle: or How a Kantian Might Think about Terrorism' *Dignity and Practical Reason in Kant's Moral Theory* (Ithaca: Cornell University Press, 1992), 196-225.' Another philosopher who thinks Kant would allow exceptions is David Cummiskey [in 'Kantian Consequentialism,' *Ethics, 100*(1990): 586-615]. Cummiskey argues that treating persons as ends in themselves will sometimes dictate that, when some will be sacrificed whatever we do or don't do, we will at least do no worse to cause the sacrifice of the smaller number. I do not know if Kant would accept these interpretations, but I do agree with the positions on this matter which Hill and Cummiskey attribute to Kant.

[13] 'A Critique of Utilitarianism,' 98-109.

[14] John Finnis adds a theological slant to such a position, based on the notion that "Man proposes and God disposes." What we should do, he argues, is make sure that we stick to moral principles and let God take care of the consequences, over which we have little control. Thus we ought to avoid wrongdoing ourselves, even when by doing one wrong we can prevent many others from doing wrong. If we do the right thing, presumably, God will see to it that the consequences are taken care of in accordance with His will ['The Rights and Wrongs of Abortion,' *Philosophy and Public Affairs*, 1 (1971): 117-145]. But as Bennett asks, why should we expect God to be in favor of absolutism about rules, as opposed to wanting people to think though the implications of their behavior? (*The Act Itself*, 163)

[15] Thomas Hill makes this point in 'Moral Purity and the Lesser Evil,' *The Monist*, 66 (1983): 213-232.

[16] See *The Nature of Morality* (New York: Oxford University Press, 1977), Chapter 1. A strict consequentialist might argue that the more Indians who could be saved by Jim's killing one that would otherwise not be killed, the less wrong it would be for him to kill that Indian. On the analogy of the organ donor, I don't think so. Suppose Joe were killed & his body parts distributed to 1000 people instead of half a dozen. Would this make his being killed less wrong? I think not. Of course, if Joe or the Indian were to offer his life for the others voluntarily, the wrongness of killing him would be less. And the more others who might be saved, the more likely it is that a caring person might make such a sacrifice. That still would not make it right to take that person's life without that person's consent.

[17] In 'Moral Purity and the Lesser Evil.'

[18] In 'Are There Any Absolute Rights?' *Philosophical Quarterly*, 31 (1981): 1- 16.

[19] Although of course the effects upon the Indians' survivors — especially dependent children — would also need to be taken into account. Perhaps some of them would starve to death, in which case, they could be as

badly off as the Indian Jim would torture. The more Indians who would be saved by Jim's killing one, the more likely such consequences, and the more wrong Jim's refusing might be.

[20] See 'Utilitarianism and the Virtues,' *Mind,* 94 (1985): 196-209.

[21] See 'Agent-Centered Restrictions from the Inside Out,' *Philosophical Studies,* 50 (1986): 291-319.

[22] *Metaphysical Foundations of Morals,* First Section [in *The Philosophy of Kant,* Carl J. Friedrich, ed. (New York: Modern Library, 1949), 140-208].

[23] In 'The New Critique of Anti-Consequentialist Moral Theory.'

[24] Ed Sherline pointed out to me that Foot and Darwall have very different ideas of what good character consists in. Foot's emphasis, like Aristotle's, is on the cultivation of virtues, while Darwall's is more Kantian in its emphasis on good will. I have distinguished here between two aspects of character which incorporate these different components, but both Foot and Darwall have in common the view that how an action expresses character is of greater importance than its consequences. It is this common feature of their positions that I am examining here.

[25] This, of course, does not entail that every person of good character in either sense will actually be able to articulate a justification of all he does or believes.

[26] Bennett makes a similar point in *The Act Itself,* 182-183.

[27] One can, of course, admire a character trait and consider that it has brought about good without adopting it oneself or even thinking of it as a virtue.

[28] *Nicomachean Ethics,* Terence Irwin, trans. (Indianapolis: Hackett, 1985), 1106b 37-1109b 27.

[29] In 'Utilitarianism and Moral Self-Indulgence,' in *Moral Luck: Philosophical Papers 1973-1980* (Cambridge: Cambridge University Press, 1981), 40-53.

[30] 'Alienation, Consequentialism, and the Demands of Morality' *Philosophy and Public Affairs,* 13 (1984): 134-171.

[31] In 'A Critique of Utilitarianism,' 91-93.

[32] See also the discussion by William H. Shaw, 'The Paradox of Deontology,' in *Rationality, Morality, and Self-Interest,* John Heil, ed. (Lanham, MD: Rowman and Littlefield, 1993), 99-113.

[33] In *The Practice of Moral Judgment,* Harvard University Press, Cambridge, MA, 1993, Chapter 1.

[34] In fact, Kant could thus be right in saying that the person who does good from duty exhibits greater moral virtue than one who does the same good from inclination, in that the grim performer from duty must have a greater motivation to act morally in order to do what comes easily to one with a warm and generous temperament. Of course, generous people are in the long run much more apt to do good than are misanthropes, but this generalization need not hold true of particular individuals. And it is certainly true that even in the best of us such happy motives as love are often sorely tried, so that if the person is to do right consistently, he must often rely solely on the motive of duty.

[35] 'A Critique of Utilitarianism.'

[36] It seems appropriate to put "integrity" in quotes in such a context, because this term is definitely value-laden. We never say that someone whose principles we think are evil has integrity. We may not agree with a person's principles, but so long as we can suppose them capable of being held by a person of good character, we can ascribe integrity to him.

[37] In 'Departures from Consequentialism,' *Ethics,* 100 (1989): 54-66.

[38] In *The View from Nowhere* (New York: Oxford University Press, 1986), 175-185.

[39] James Rachels, 'Active and Passive Euthanasia,' *New England Journal of Medicine,* 295 (1975):78-80.

[40] In 'Harming Some to Save Others,' *Philosophical Studies* 57 (1989): 227-260.

[41] *Persons, Animals, and Fetuses,* Chapter 17, where I discuss the distinction between active and passive euthanasia.

[42] As noted in the last chapter, Hill makes the point that rational people *can* agree to a policy which will almost certainly result in the deaths of some if it will save the lives of many more, thereby reducing the likelihood of any one person's dying. See 'Making Exceptions without Abandoning the Principle: or How a Kantian Might Think about Terrorism.' The same point might be made concerning so-called "collateral damage" — i.e., civilian deaths — in wartime. For the most part people do accept that this is an unfortunate but unavoidable effect of war and thus not necessarily morally wrong (assuming the war in question is justifiable). This, of course, does not apply to the deliberate and unnecessary killing or maiming of innocent people, which all too often occurs even in justifiable wars.

[43] In 'Harming Some to Save Others,' 251-256.

Notes to Chapter 8

[1] For the most part I will use the term 'duty' as synonymous with 'obligation.' There may be subtle differences between the usage of these terms in some contexts. However, duties are similar to obligations in the basic sense discussed here. That is, if an action A is a duty of X's, then X ought to do A and there is and ought to be a sanction against X's failure to do A. Moreover, I recognize that 'obligation' and 'duty' are often used interchangeably with 'ought' in everyday discourse, and 'ought to do' interchangeably with 'best to do.' It does not follow, however, that no distinctions among these concepts are commonly observed; what I am trying to do here is clarify some distinctions that I believe *are* observed.

² 'Some Remarks on Obligation, Permission, and Supererogation,' *Ethics*, 85 (1975): 219- 226. An earlier version of this position — namely, that what one is obligated to do is what one ought in some sense to be compelled to do — was stated by several philosophers. These include Kurt Baier, 'Moral Obligation,' *American Philosophical Quarterly*, 3 (1966): 210- 226; Joel Feinberg, 'Supererogation and Rules,' *Ethics*, 71 (1960- 61):276- 288; and David A. J. Richards, *A Theory of Reasons for Action* (Oxford: Clarendon Press, 1971), 96- 101 & Chapter 11. More recently, Jonathan Dancy distinguishes between obligations and oughts on similar grounds ('Supererogation and Moral Realism,' in *Human Action: Language, Duty, and Value*, ed. Jonathan Dancy, J. M. E. Moravcsik, and C. W. Taylor (Stanford, CA: Stanford University Press, 1988), 170-188. My own view adds the condition that there *is* a sanction against X's failing to do A. This proviso makes what is obligatory partly dependent upon social norms: if some behavior is tolerated in a society, then members of that society are not obliged not to engage in it. That this is so is suggested by cases of the following kind. Although ancient Greeks and white southern Americans of the early nineteenth century undoubtedly *ought* not to have had slaves, it seems incorrect to say that they were *obligated* not to have them. The reason is, I believe, that we think of obligations as something that the people who have them recognize, or at least are expected to recognize. Since slavery was culturally accepted in the above-mentioned societies, it would be unreasonable to expect everyone to recognize its wrongness.
A more recent modification I have made is based on my belief that 'ought,' as well as 'obligation,' is too strong to characterize what it would simply be nice to do, even if 'nice' included whatever was the greatest good we could accomplish.
³ Railton has also maintained that obligations require a network of social practices and sanctions. See his 'What the Non-Cognitivist Helps Us to See the Naturalist Must Help Us to Explain,' in *Reality, Representation, and Projection*, John Haldane & Crispin Wright, eds. (New York: Oxford University Press, 1993), 279-300.
⁴ James Forrester has suggested that we could distinguish between obligations which are enforced and those which are not enforced, but still exist (those for which there is no sanction, but ought to be) by considering what legislators would have required had they known the consequences of what they were proposing. The latter, he maintains are still obligations, just unrecognized ones. It does not seem, however, that we use the expression 'X is/was obligated to do A,' no matter how morally worthwhile and important doing A would be/have been, if doing not-A were deeply ingrained in his society. Thus we would not say that ancient Romans had even an unrecognized obligation not to punish offenders by feeding them to lions; we could, however, say that there was a strong moral need for them not to do so. But whether we call such moral needs unrecognized obligations or not, there is a definite distinction between them and obligations which are actually enforced in a given society. This will be even more apparent when we turn to the discussion of rights.
⁵ Sanctions of this sort, as well as more formal penalties have been grouped together by Haslett (*Equal Consideration*, University of Delaware Press, Newark, 1987, esp. Chapter 4) under the term "social pressure system." He also recognizes the importance of the question of what systems there ought to be.
⁶ Hence our ideas about the propriety of punishments change with considerations of what seems fair. Pickpockets used to be hanged — but this inflicted far more harm on the offender than he inflicted on others and now seems to us brutal. (I am indebted to James Forrester for this example.) Also, our views of what punishments are appropriate changes with social conditions. A country which can afford secure prisons may be less apt to impose — and less justified in imposing — the death penalty than one which cannot and in which dangerous felons are more likely to escape.
⁷ Some laws — like speed limits — are not generally obeyed precisely — or punished. If the limit is 65 mph many will push the limit and drive about 72 mph without being picked up. This does not, however, mean that the law is a dead letter, for it does exert some control on what speeds are tolerated. Someone caught driving 80 mph will certainly get a ticket. In other words, a speed limit is enforced to the extent that anyone going more than about 8-15 mph above it can expect a sanction if he is caught.
⁸ Sanctions may be imposed not only for doing certain things, but also for attempts which fail. These are generally imposed for actions which, if they succeeded, would be very harmful — e.g., murder and treason, so that even allowing people to try them is dangerous, for they might succeed on another occasion.
⁹ I've borrowed this example from Professor James Forrester, although we have some disagreements on the distinction between oughts and obligations. [See his *Being Good and Being Logical* (M. E. Sharpe, 1996), Chapter 14.]
¹⁰ It does not, of course, follow that decreasing unhappiness is *sufficient* to justify punishment; if so, punishing the innocent might be justified. And whether and how much a person should be punished is also partly dependent upon considerations of fairness. A criminal has — in addition to whatever harm he has done to individuals — taken advantage (or attempted to do so) of others' abiding by some important social practice.
¹¹ See *The Nicomachean Ethics*, 1113b 30- 1114a 31.
¹² I have discussed the question of obligations to future generations (which not everyone agrees that we have) in *Persons, Animals, and Fetuses*, Chapter 11.
¹³ James Forrester has questioned whether most of our obligations are obligations to individuals, rather than

general obligations. For the most part, I think most obligations are mixed. We have obligations to those who will be harmed if we fail to perform them and general obligations as well in cases where we will be unfair if we fail. Thus Bruce has an obligation to Andrew not to kill him, as well as a general obligation not to kill. Tom has an obligation to his ex-wife to take the children some weekends, because he has an agreement with her and because she will be inconvenienced if he does not, but he also has a general obligation because the practice of keeping agreements makes it unfair for people to take advantage of this practice without doing their share to support it. I have a general obligation to feed your dog while you are gone because I have a general duty to keep promises; I also have a duty to you because you have an interest in your dog's not starving and in promises to you being kept. Whether I also have a duty to the dog is controversial and depends upon the moral status of animals; I would say (see *Persons, Animals, and Fetuses*, Chapter 10) that I do owe the dog his food. In the case of duties to oneself, we might have one in cases where there is a general duty to act in the way specified, and we would also have duties to ourselves, on my theory, when the harm to ourselves from failure to perform is great and irrevocable, regardless of whether there is also a general duty to perform.

[14] See the classic paper by J. O. Urmson, 'Saints and Heroes,' in *Essays in Moral Philosophy*, ed. A. I. Melden (Seattle: University of Washington Press, 1958), 198- 216.

[15] See the discussions by Bernard Williams, 'Moral Luck,' *Proceedings of the Aristotelian Society*, suppl. vol. 90 (1976): 115-135, and Thomas Nagel, 'Moral Luck,' pp. 136- 150, and the response by Anthony Kenny in 'Aristotle on Moral Luck,' in *Human Agency: Language, Duty and Value*, 105-119.

[16] Unless, perhaps, God exists, demands that she be a missionary, and would punish her if she fails to become one. James Forrester made this suggestion.

[17] In 'Famine, Affluence, and Morality,' in *Moral Problems: a Collection of Philosophical Essays*, 3rd ed., James Rachels, ed. (New York: Harper and Row, 1979), 263-278.

[18] Frances Kamm makes this point well ['Supererogation and Obligation,' *Journal of Philosophy, 82*(1985): 118-138]. She also argues that there is an intransitivity in moral judgments in that personal goals may dominate supererogatory actions, and supererogatory actions may dominate duties, but that duties dominate personal goals, and that this intransitivity shows that there is no single standard along which moral value can be measured. I disagree here, because there are two senses of 'dominate' which may be used. Act A may dominate A' either in the sense of being better, or in the sense of being a morally acceptable choice over A'. Personal goals may dominate supererogatory acts in the second sense; however, given that a supererogatory act does more good than promoting a personal goal (which not all do), then the supererogatory act would dominate the personal goal in the first sense. It is therefore not always true that an agent is obligated to give up his goals for the sake of the greatest good. Nor is it necessarily the case that he ought to, for if there are other ways that good could be brought about, the burden does not fall on the agent. The fact that the agent is excusable does not, however, mean that he wouldn't have done better by performing the supererogatory action. But more of this later.

[19] Bernard Williams is one of the first to argue for this position [see 'A Critique of Utilitarianism,' in *Utilitarianism: For and Against*, J. J. C. Smart and Bernard Williams (Cambridge: Cambridge University Press, 1973), 108-118]. Others who have held it include Samuel Scheffler [*The Rejection of Consequentialism* (Oxford: Clarendon Press, 1982), esp. 56-68]; Michael Slote [*Beyond Optimizing* (London: Routledge and Kegan Paul, 1985), esp. Chapters 3, 5, and 7]; Thomas Nagel [*The View from Nowhere* (New York: Oxford University Press, 1986), especially Chapter 9]; and Jonathan Dancy [*Moral Reasons* (Oxford: Blackwell, 1993), esp. Chapter 10 and 213- 217].

[20] Susan Wolf has pointed this out forcefully in 'Moral Saints,' *Journal of Philosophy*, 79 (1982): 419-439.

[21] See, for example, Williams, 'A Critique of Consequentialism,' 85-89, Scheffler, *The Rejection of Consequentialism*, Chapter 1, especially, and Dancy, *Moral Reasons*, 204-206.

[22] J. J. C. Smart, 'An Outline of a System of Utilitarian Ethics,' in *Utilitarianism: For and Against* (Cambridge: Cambridge University Press, 1973), 45.

[23] *The Limits of Morality* (Oxford: Clarendon Press, 1989), *passim*, but see especially Chapters 2 and 10. Interestingly, he describes this view as 'extremist,' and that of ordinary morality — which he criticizes — as 'moderate.'

[24] In Utilitarianism, in *The Utilitarians* (Garden City, NY: Doubleday, 1961), 407.

[25] See for example Sidgwick, *The Methods of Ethics* (Indianapolis: Hackett, 1981), 432-436.

[26] See Notes 1 & 2 above. Roderick Chisholm also makes a distinction between what we ought to do and what we are obligated to do. The latter he indicates is simply what we have a duty, or are required, to do, while the former is supererogatory. Chisholm also points out that what is supererogatory need not be more praiseworthy than doing one's duty, although it is always something good to do. Sometimes fulfilling an obligation may be truly heroic, depending upon the circumstances. ['Supererogation and Offense,' *Ratio*, 5 (1963): 1-14]

[27] Stephen Darwall hints at such a three way distinction in *Impartial Reason*, Cornell University Press, Ithaca & London, 1983, Chapter 14. He distinguishes first between what reason requires and what it simply recommends, as well as between what is required and what there are sanctions against failing to do.

28 In 'A Critique of Utilitarianism,' in *Utilitarianism: For and Against*, J.J.C.Smart & Bernard Williams, (Cambridge: Cambridge University Press, 1973), 108- 118.
29 In *The Rejection of Consequentialism* (Oxford: Clarendon Press, 1982), Chapters 1- 3.
30 In *Moral Reasons* (Oxford: Blackwell, 1993), Chapters 10- 13.
31 Examples of this include not only the proposals of Baier, Feinberg, and Richards mentioned in Note 8, but that of James Forrester in *Being Good and Being Logical* (Armonk, NY: M. E. Sharpe, 1996), 205-209, who proposes that what we are obligated to do is what there ought to be a sanction against our not doing, but that there are many things which ought to be done that are not the obligation of anyone. Paul Hurley's suggestion that agent-relative prerogatives fall into a "protected zone," where the agent should be free of interference indicates a direction for this kind of distinction ['Getting Our Options Clear: a Closer Look at Agent-Centered Options,' *Philosophical Studies*, *78*(1995): 163-188].
32 Some accounts of supererogation are less satisfying. Joseph Raz ['Permissions and Supererogation,' *American Philosophical Quarterly*, 12 (1975): 161-168] and Jonathan Dancy [*Moral Reasons*, 213-217] have suggested that supererogatory acts are those which the agent has the prerogative not to perform because the cost to him is too great. According to Raz, there is value in an agent's pursuing his own projects, which value may counterbalance the amount of good lost by his doing this rather than the act which will do the greatest good. Dancy maintains that the view that some acts are supererogatory just is the acknowledgment of agent-relative prerogatives. He says that an agent is entitled to count twice the cost of his acting for the greatest good: both its disvalue for him as one person among all and again its disvalue to him personally. Neither Raz nor Dancy goes very far, however, in spelling out how we can tell when we are justified in favoring our own concerns over the good of all.
33 Kagan points out that an action's being morally decisive does not necessarily mean that others require it of one (*The Limits of Morality*, 206-209). Thus he recognizes what can form a basis for a distinction between what we ought to do and what we are obligated to do. On the other hand, he does not appear to distinguish between oughts and supererogation (see note 5 above).
34 As Frances Howard-Snyder says, the behavior of a Mother Teresa or Martin Luther King is preferable to that of a typical law-abiding citizen. ['The Heart of Consequentialism,' *Philosophical Studies*, *76*(1994): 107-129].
35 Despite the exacting standards he sets for moral behavior, Shelly Kagan acknowledges this in *The Limits of Morality*, 402-403.
36 Barbara Herman ('Agency, Attachment, and Difference,' *Ethics*, 101 (1991): 775-797) and Frank Jackson ('Decision Theoretic Consequentialism and the Nearest and Dearest Objection,' same volume, 461-482) also point out the fact that we are usually in a better position to help those close to us rather than strangers; we know the needs of our families, friends and neighbors, and our concern for them will make us more likely to follow through with what we start out to do for them. Thus we are likely to do more good by helping our nearest and dearest. However, both point out that there are times when what we ought to do for ourselves and our loved ones is overridden by the needs of those we do not know, and that there are limits to our agent-relative prerogatives.
37 See, for example, Williams' discussion of integrity, where he maintains that a person who is thinking only about doing the greatest good cannot really have integrity, for he would be unable to consider his commitments as anything but one desire among all the desires of all the people in the world, and give them no more weight ('A Critique of Utilitarianism,' 113-118). Wolf ('Moral Saints,' 431) says we have reason to hope that a person does not wholly direct his life by the consideration that such a life would be morally good, for such a person would probably be cold and indifferent to other people and have no real concerns or commitments.
38 In 'The Schizophrenia of Modern Ethical Theories,' *Journal of Philosophy*, *73*(1976):453-466.
39 Thomas Nagel points out that altruism is "too general a motive to run a society with" [*Equality and Partiality* (New York: Oxford University Press, 1991), 60]. Most of the endeavors that advance our interests require considerable concentration of effort. Surgeons, physicists, and musicians must exert intense effort to perfect their skills. Those who work primarily with human beings, either in the family or professionally, must spend much time thinking about and helping specific individuals. Most of us cannot work effectively if we spend too much time thinking about or pursuing the greatest overall good as such.
40 See, for example, Adrian M. S. Piper, 'Utility, Publicity, and Manipulation, *Ethics*, 88 (1978): 189-206, Michael Stocker, 'The Schizophrenia of Modern Ethical Theories,' D. H. Hodgson, *Consequences of Utilitarianism* (Oxford: Oxford University Press, 1967), 60, and Bernard Williams, 'A Critique of Utilitarianism,' 124-135.
41 Peter Railton has persuasively argued this point in 'Alienation, Consequentialism, and the Demands of Morality,' *Philosophy and Public Affairs*, 13 (1984): 134-171. The tennis example is also his.
42 Bernard Williams made this point in 'Utilitarianism and Moral Self-Indulgence,' in *Contemporary British Philosophy, Personal Statements*, 4th Series, H. D. Lewis, ed. (London: Allen and Unwin, 1976), 306-321.
43 In *The Rejection of Consequentialism*, 56-68.
44 In *The View from Nowhere*, 166-175.

[45] Kagan makes this point in *The Limits of Morality*, Chapter 7.

[46] Dancy argues this in *Moral Reasons*, 207.

[47] Sen has argued for this in 'Rights and Agency' *Philosophy and Public Affairs*, 11 (1982): 3-37.

[48] Not all agent-relative values are moral values. For example, suppose that Bert has a family he loves very much and wants to give them not only all they need, but many things to bring them pleasure as well. Anyone's loving other specific individuals is valuable since it brings good to both those individuals and the person who loves them. It is also fair for people to do things for their own families (within certain limits imposed by the needs of other families) because that is how, in most societies, much responsibility is divided. Both loving and taking responsibility are morally valuable; furthermore, any individual in Bert's situation would be equally right to do the things Bert does. But suppose that Bert becomes incapacitated, and Ernie — a relative, or perhaps a social worker with the authority to allocate government funds — takes over the care of Bert and his family. Suppose Ernie is able to give Bert's family all that Bert has been able to do in the past. Bert's family is just as well off, Bert loves them just as much, and the allocation of responsibility is fair. Yet Bert feels miserable because he has taken pride in being able to do these things for his family *himself*. This is a personal goal of his: to be a benefactor and caretaker for his family. It is part of his self-image, his ideal of himself as a person. But this agent-relative value is a personal value, not a moral value. Someone else in a similar situation might not be so devastated by not being able to care for his family, so long as they were cared for by somebody. Of course, Bert's unhappiness would result in diminished good for him, and hence diminished overall moral good; however, the same would be true for anyone else with the same personal values in the same situation.

[49] Joel Feinberg, 'Duties, Rights and Claims,' *American Philosophical Quarterly* 3 (1966): 137- 144.

[50] James Forrester argues in *Being Good and Being Logical* (Armonk, NY: M. E. Sharpe, 1996), 68-73 that there is a distinction between the ought- to- do and the ought- to- be, as well as a number of implications of this distinction for deontic logic. See also my discussion in Chapter 3 of this volume.

[51] The situation is different if one has a special obligation to a particular individual, such as a needy relative or one's foster child in a program like the Christian Children's Fund, or the client of a social worker. Then one ought, and is duty bound, to do certain things for that individual. The reason for the difference is that one has a contractual relationship, or a general duty resulting from kinship to specific individuals.

[52] I say "generally speaking," because not all such efforts have the desired effect, and others may produce more harm than good. For example, if people are simply given food, they may not develop their own ways of producing it, and when help is withdrawn, they will be hungry again. Even worse, there may be many more people to feed, if more children survive to reproductive age. Thus partial assistance, which leaves other problems unresolved, may be worse than none at all. For a discussion of the harm that can be done by simply giving food to other countries, see Garrett Hardin, *The Limits of Altruism: an Ecologist's View of Survival* (Bloomington: Indiana University Press, 1977), esp. Chapter 3.

[53] In *Taking Rights Seriously* (Cambridge: Harvard University Press, 1977), 91

[54]. Both background and institutional rights can include either positive or negative rights. People in all societies have a background right to life (a negative right not to be killed). In particular societies, however, that right may be protected in different ways and under different circumstances. For example, it might be the duty of the police and judicial system to punish murder, but in others this duty could fall on the clan of the murdered person. Also the circumstances which make a person forfeit his right to life will differ: e.g., in some cultures adultery is such a circumstance. I am indebted to David Resnik for insisting that I make clear that my remarks apply to both positive *and* negative rights, as most of the examples in the text are of positive rights.

[55] Although, as Bernard Rollin points out (personal communication), we may well have a background right to whatever is the best health care *we can* provide, or at least to some decent minimum.

[56] This is not a logical requirement. As with obligations, there may be rare circumstances under which someone should be punished for withholding a good from another, even when this is unavoidable.

[57] See Joel Feinberg, 'Voluntary Euthanasia and the Inalienable Right to Life,' in *Medicine and Moral Philosophy*, Marshall Cohen, Thomas Nagel, and Thomas Scanlon, eds. (Princeton: Princeton University Press, 1981), 245- 276.

[58] Even what are generally considered inalienable rights may be overridden. Thus my right to pursue happiness does not allow me to seek it at the expense of the happiness of others, and my right to liberty can be overridden if I become a dangerous criminal. It is possible that even my right to life can be overridden, if, for example, I attack another with deadly force. There are also situations in which I may release another from allowing me what I have an inalienable right to; if my doing so is not permissible even if I want to waive that right, then I have also a duty to myself to retain what I have a right to. If my own views are correct, however, there is one inalienable right: namely, the right to receive consideration equal to that given all others.

[59] See "Are There Any Natural Rights?" *Philosophical Review*, 64 (1955): 175- 191.

Notes to Chapter 9

[1] See Bernard Williams, *Ethics and the Limits of Philosophy* (Cambridge, MA: Harvard University Press,

1985), 116-117, James Wallace, *Moral Relevance and Moral Conflict* (Ithaca: Cornell University Press, 1988), Chapter 2, and Richard Miller, *Moral Differences: Truth, Justice and Conscience in a World of Conflict* (Princeton: Princeton University Press, 1992), Chapter 5.

2 *Persons, Animals, and Fetuses* (Dordrecht: Kluwer Academic Publishers, 1996), Part IV.

3 A situation in which this actually happened: where one person arrested while the code team was engaged in resuscitating another is discussed by Kevin M. McIntyre, Robert C. Benfari, and M. Pabst Battin, 'Two Cardiac Arrests, One Medical Team,' *Hastings Center Report*, 12 (1982): 24- 25.

4 As it happened, neither suffered cardiac arrest, and both were eventually discharged back to the penitentiary. I never heard what became of Smith, but it is probable that he died within a few months. Jones is, so far as I know, still alive and well.

5 An anonymous referee of this manuscript pointed out the need to emphasize this factor.

6 See, for example, Jeremy Bentham, in *An Introduction to the Principles of Morals and Legislation* (New York: Hafner, 1948), Chapter 13, sec. 1. He maintains that punishment, since it is itself an evil, only justifiable when it will prevent a greater evil. Adding punishment of an offender to his offense will only create a greater sum of evil, unless the punishment can do some good as well, such as deterring others from committing similar crimes. Therefore, punishing someone solely for retribution is inconsistent with the principle of utility.

7 See *Grounding for the Metaphysics of Morals*, in *Immanuel Kant: Ethical Philosophy*, James W. Ellington, trans. (Indianapolis: Hackett, 1983), 35- 36.

8 See *The Philosophy of Law*, Part II, W. Hastie, trans. (Edinburgh: T.T. Clark, 1887), 194- 198. According to Kant, punishment is solely for the restoration of equality; it ought never to be imposed on a person — or mitigated — for other ends, such as commuting a death sentence for a criminal if he will submit to medical experiments.

9 See *Utilitarianism* in the *Utilitarians* (Garden City, NY: Doubleday, 1961), 409.

10 *Grounding for the Metaphysics of Morals*, 30-32. Kant attempts to show that all wrong actions have in common that they are based on maxims that no one could will to be universally applied because it would be inconsistent to do so. Making a promise you do not intend to keep in order to gain something could not be consistently given universal application, but the reason for this is not that people could not do so, but that the practice would be self-defeating, and thus something one could not rationally will. And this is a consequence, although not of a specific action, but of a maxim's being universally adopted. Kant may well not have agreed with this interpretation.

But again, why are the moral law, rational nature which recognizes it, and the good will which wants to follow it good? This is a question which I don't think Kant ever satisfactorily answers. But I think an answer is possible, although it isn't one which Kant would like. This is that what makes it wrong to do what, if everyone tried to do would be impossible or self-defeating, is the value of human purposes. Unless purposes had value, it wouldn't matter whether they could be defeated by one's actions or pursued by actions which would be impossible if everyone did them. In addition, as we saw in Chapter 5, it is wrong for anyone to fail to do her share in the upkeep of valuable institutions and practices, such as promising and developing one's capacities to make the world a better place. This is wrong partly from unfairness, but also because of the value of the institutions and practices themselves. If they didn't have any value, there wouldn't be anything wrong with failing to do one's share to promote them.

11 See David O. Brink, *Moral Realism and the Foundations of Ethics* (Cambridge: Cambridge University Press, 1989), 217- 236.

12 See Roderick Firth, 'Ethical Absolutism and the Ideal Observer,' *Philosophy and Phenomenological Research*, 12 (1952): 317- 345.

13 That is, under the veil of ignorance, where we do not know what our life circumstances are. See *A Theory of Justice* (Cambridge, MA: Harvard University Press, 1971), 136- 142

14 See also my arguments in Chapter 6. Others might simply assert that God had said that abortions are wrong and therefore that they are wrong, and would make no attempt to justify their judgments further. Of course, if they did attempt to do so, such pronouncements would need major argument — e.g., how does one know what God said (as opposed to fallible human interpreters), why should we accept God's word as ultimate (e.g., He is the ultimate moral expert, or we will go to Hell if we don't).

15 A discussion of the issue of who or what counts as a person is beyond the scope of this book. I have dealt with this issue in *Persons, Animals, and Fetuses*, Parts III and IV.

16 David Resnik has pointed out that many moral disagreements are based on differences of metaphysical and religious views. This is true, but it does not count against anything I have said here. Either such views are held because they are thought to be facts, or they are held for other reasons. If thought to be facts, they can be used to support a moral view in the same way that facts in general are. One can argue against a moral position based on such a metaphysical or religious view by citing facts to dispute that view. More commonly, religious and metaphysical positions are not treated as facts. Rather, they are positions one holds *in spite of* evidence and observations. Some religious persons say that they must believe, because this is all that makes life tolerable for them, or because it is the foundation of their society, or because it provides a framework for their lives. One

might then dispute the religious or metaphysical position by arguing that these are not adequate reasons for belief in the truth of the view in question, and are thus unable to support the truth of a moral view.

[17] Graber and Thomasma, *Theory and Practice in Medical Ethics*, Chapter 2.

[18] See Chapter 5.

[19] See my discussion of this point in *Persons, Animals, and Fetuses*.

[20] And for this reason the staff's feelings about the two felons — i.e., that Jones deserves nothing but what it is required to do — would be a poor guide to action.

[21] One might argue that Jones did not actually kill the poor woman; he ought not for that reason to be chosen not to get resuscitation. He was, however, responsible for the horrible experience that made her depressed enough to end her life on hearing of his release.

[22] I am indebted to James Forrester for pointing this out.

REFERENCES

Ackerman, Terrence F., 'What Bioethics Should Be,' *Journal of Medicine and Philosophy*, 5(1980): 260-275.

Alston, William P., *Philosophy of Language* (Englewood Cliffs, NJ: Prentice-Hall, 1964).

Anderson, Elizabeth, *Value in Ethics and Economics* (Cambridge, MA: Harvard University Press, 1993).

Annas, Julia, *The Morality of Happiness* (Oxford: Oxford University Press, 1993).

Anscombe, G.E.M., 'Modern Moral Philosophy,' *Philosophy* 33 (1958): 1-19.

Aristotle, *Nicomachean Ethics*, Martin Ostwald, trans. (Indianapolis: Bobbs-Merrill, 1962).

Arrow, Kenneth, *Social Choice and Individual Values* (New Haven, CT: Yale University Press, 1951).

Audi, Robert, 'Intuitionism, Pluralism, and the Foundations of Ethics,' in *Moral Knowledge?*, WalterSinnott-Armstrong & Mark Timmons, eds. (New York: Oxford University Press, 1996)101-136.

Ayer, A. J., *Language, Truth, and Logic*, 2nd ed.(New York: Dover, 1950).

Baier, Kurt, *The Moral Point of View* (Ithaca, NY: Cornell University Press, 1958).

Baier, Kurt, 'Moral Obligation,' *American Philosophical Quarterly*, 3 (1966): 210- 226.

Barnsley, John H., *The Social Reality of Ethics: The Comparative Analysis of Moral Codes* (London: Routledge & Kegan Paul, 1972).

Beauchamp, Tom L. and James F. Childress, *Principles of Biomedical Ethics*, 4th ed. (New York: OxfordUniversity Press, 1994)

Becker, Edward F., 'Justice, Utility, and Interpersonal Comparisons,' *Theory and Decision*, 6 (1975): 471- 484.

Bennett, Jonathan, 'Departures from Consequentialism,' *Ethics,* 100 (1989): 54-66.

Bennett, Jonathan, *The Act Itself* (Oxford: Clarendon Press, 1995).

Benson, Jann and Dan Lyons, *Strutting and Fretting: Standards for Self Esteem* (Niwot, CO: University Press of Colorado, 1991).

Bentham, Jeremy, *An Introduction to the Principles of Morals and Legislation* (New York: Hafner, 1948).

Blackburn, Simon, *Spreading the Word* (Oxford: Clarendon Press, 1984).

Blackburn, Simon, 'Attitudes and Contents,' *Ethics*, 98 (1988): 501-517.

Blackburn, Simon, 'How to be an Ethical Antirealist,' *Midwest Studies in Philosophy*, 12 (1988):361-375.

Blackburn, Simon, 'Errors and the Phenomenology of Value,' in Ted Honderich, ed. *Morality andObjectivity: A Tribute to J. L. Mackie* (London: Routledge & Kegan Paul, 1985), 1-22.

Blackburn, Simon, 'Securing the Nots: Moral Epistemology for the Quasi-Realist,' in *Moral Knowledge?*, Walter Sinnott-Armstrong & Mar Timmons, eds. (New York: Oxford University Press, 1996), 82-100.

Boyd, Richard, 'How to be a Moral Realist' in Geoffrey Sayre-McCord, ed., *Essays in Moral Realism* (Ithaca: Cornell University Press, 1988), 187-228.

Brandt, R. B., *Hopi Ethics: a Theoretical Analysis* (Chicago: University of Chicago Press, 1954).

Brandt, R. B., *A Theory of the Good and the Right* (Oxford: Clarendon Press, 1979).

Brandt, R.B., 'Two Concepts of Utility,' in *The Limits of Utilitarianism*, Harlan B. Miller and William H.Williams, eds. (Minneapolis: University of Minnesota Press, 1982)

Brink, David O., *Moral Realism and the Foundations of Ethics* (Cambridge: Cambridge University Press,1989).

Broad, C.D., *Five Types of Ethical Theory* (New York: Humanities Press, 1956).

Brody, Baruch, *Life and Death Decision Making* (New York: Oxford University Press, 1988).

Broome, John, *Weighing Goods* (Oxford: Basil Blackwell, 1991).

Butchvarov, Panayot, 'Realism in Ethics,' *Midwest Studies in Philosophy*, 12 (1988): 395- 412.

Castañeda, Hector-Neri, 'Imperatives, Decisions, and Oughts,' in *Morality and the Language of Conduct,*Hector-Neri Castañeda & George Nakhnikian, eds. (Detroit: Wayne State University Press, 1963),230- 239.

Castañeda, Hector-Neri, *The Structure of Morality*, (Springfield, IL: Charles Thomas, Publ., 1974).

Castañeda, Hector-Neri, *Thinking and Doing* (Dordrecht: Reidel, 1975).

Childress, James F. And Tom L. Beauchamp, *Principles of Biomedical Ethics*, 4th ed. (New York: OxfordUniversity Press, 1994).

Chisholm, Roderick, 'Supererogation and Offense,' *Ratio*, 5 (1963): 1-14.

Cohen,G.A., 'Reason, Humanity, and the Moral Law,' in Christine Korsgaard, *The Sources of Normativity*,167-188.

275

Copp, David, *Morality, Normativity, and Society* (New York: Oxford University Press, 1995.

Crawshaw, Robert, 'Medical Deontology in the Soviet Union,' in Robert M. Veatch, *Cross Cultural Perspectives in Medical Ethics: Readings* (Boston: Jones & Bartlett, 1989), 106-112.

Cummiskey, David, 'Kantian Consequentialism,' *Ethics*, 100 (1990): 586-615. 226.

Dancy, Jonathan, 'Supererogation and Moral Realism,' in *Human Action: Language, Duty, and Value,* Jonathan Dancy, J. M. E. Moravcsik, and C. C. W. Taylor, eds. (Stanford, CA: Stanford University Press, 1988), 170-188.

Dancy, Jonathan, *Moral Reasons* (Oxford: Blackwell, Oxford, 1993).

Darwall, Stephen, *Impartial Reason* (Ithaca, NY: Cornell University Press, 1983).

Darwall, Stephen, 'Agent-Centered Restrictions from the Inside Out,' *Philosophical Studies 50* (1986):291-319.

Darwall, Stephen, Allan Gibbard, and Peter Railton, 'Toward *Fin de siècle* Ethics: Some Trends,' *Philosophical Review*, 101 (1992): 115-189.

Davidson, Donald, 'Belief and the Basis of Meaning,' *Synthese*, 27 (1974): 309-323.

Davidson, Donald, 'Thought and Talk,' in *Mind and Language*, Samuel Guttenplan, ed. (Oxford: Clarendon Press, 1975), 7-23.

DeCew, Judith, 'Moral Conflicts and Ethical Relativism,' *Ethics*, 101 (1990): 127-141.

Dennett, Daniel, *Consciousness Explained* (Boston: Little, Brown, 1991).

Dostoevsky, Feodor, *Notes from Underground*, ed. & trans. by Ralph E. Matlaw (New York: E. P. Dutton,1960).

Drimmer, Frederick, *Captured by Indians: 15 Firsthand Accounts, 1750-1870* (New York: Dover Publications, 1961)

Dummett, Michael, 'What is a Theory of Meaning?' Part II, in *Truth and Meaning*, Gareth Evans and John McDowell, eds., (Oxford: Clarendon Press, 1976) 75-76.

Dworkin, Ronald, *Taking Rights Seriously* (Cambridge: Harvard University Press, 1977).

Dworkin, Ronald, *Life's Dominion* (New York: Alfred A. Knopf, 1993).

Edelstein, Ludwig, 'The Hippocratic Oath: Text, Translation, and Interpretation,' in Robert M. Veatch, *Cross Cultural Perspectives in Medical Ethics: Readings* (Boston: Jones & Bartlett, 1989), 6-24.

Elster, Jon, 'Sour Grapes — Utilitarianism and the Genesis of Wants,' in *Utilitarianism and Beyond,* Amartya Sen and Bernard Williams, eds. (Cambridge: at the University Press, 1982), 219-238.

Engelhardt, H. Tristram, *The Foundations of Bioethics* (New York: Oxford University Press, 1986.

Engelhardt, H. Tristram, 'Bioethics in the People's Republic of China,' Robert M. Veatch, *Cross Cultural Perspectives in Medical Ethics: Readings* (Boston: Jones & Bartlett, 1989) 112-119.

Epicurus, *Principle Doctrines* and *Letter to Menoeceus*, trans. Cyril Bailey (Oxford: Clarendon Press, 1926).

Feinberg, Joel, 'Supererogation and Rules,' *Ethics*, 71 (1960- 61):276- 288.

Feinberg, Joel, 'Duties, Rights and Claims,' *American Philosophical Quarterly* 3 (1966): 137- 144.

Feinberg, Joel, 'Voluntary Euthanasia and the Inalienable Right to Life,' in *Medicine and MoralPhilosophy,* Marshall Cohen, Thomas Nagel, and Thomas Scanlon, eds. (Princeton: Princeton University Press, 1981), 245- 276.

Fenske, W., 'Non-Cognitivism: a New Defense,' *Journal of Value Inquiry* 31 (1997): 301- 309.

Finnis, John, 'The Rights and Wrongs of Abortion,' *Philosophy and Public Affairs*, 1 (1971): 117-145.

Firth, Roderick, 'Ethical Absolutism and the Ideal Observer,' *Philosophy and Phenomenological Research*, 12 (1952): 317- 345.

Fletcher, Joseph, *Situation Ethics: the New Morality* (Philadelphia:Westminster Press, 1966).

Foot, Phillipa, 'Utilitarianism and the Virtues,' *Mind 94* (1985): 196-209.

Forester, C. S., *Admiral Hornblower in the West Indies* (New York: Bantam Books, 1958).

Forrester, James, *Why You Should: The Pragmatics of Deontic Speech* (Hanover and London: Brown University Press, 1989).

Forrester, James, *Being Good and Being Logical* (Armonk, NY: M. E. Sharpe, 1996).

Forrester, Mary, 'A Note on Commendation and Approval,' *Ethics*, 85 (1975): 148-150.

Forrester, Mary, 'Some Remarks on Obligation, Permission, and Supererogation,' *Ethics*, 85 (1975): 219-226.

Forrester, Mary, 'Practical Reasoning and Historical Explanation,' *History and Theory*, 15 (1976): 133-140.

Forrester, Mary, *Moral Language* (Madison: University of Wisconsin Press, 1982).

Forrester, Mary, *Persons, Animals and Fetuses* (Dordrecht: Kluwer Academic Publishers, 1996).

Forrester, Mary, 'Valuing and Akrasia,' *American Philosophical Quarterly*, 37 (2000):209-205.

Frankfort, Harry, 'Freedom of the Will and the Concept of a Person,' *Journal of Philosophy*, 68 (1971):

Garcia, Jorge, 'The New Critique of Anti-Consequentialist Moral Theory,' *Philosophical Studies, 71* (1993): 1-32.

Gauthier, David, *Practical Reasoning* (Oxford: Clarendon Press, 1963).

Gauthier, David, *Morals by Agreement* (Oxford: Clarendon Press, 1986).

Geatch, P. T., 'Assertion,' *Philosophical Review*, 74 (1965): 449-465.

Gert, Bernard, *Morality: A New Justification of the Moral Rules* (New York: Oxford University Press, 1988).

Gewirth, Alan, 'Are There Any Absolute Rights?' *Philosophical Quarterly*, 31 (1981): 1- 16.

Gombay, André, 'Imperative Inferences and Disjunction,' *Analysis*, 25 (1965): 58-62.

Graber, Glenn C. & David C. Thomasma, *Theory and Practice in Medical Ethics* (New York: Continuum,1989).

Grice, H.P., 'The Causal Theory of Perception' *Proceedings of the Aristotelian Society*, Supplementary vol. 35 (1961):121-152.

Griffin, James, *Well-Being: Its Meaning, Meaasurement, and Moral Importance* (Oxford: Clarendon Press, 1986)

Guttenplan, Samuel, 'Moral Realism and Moral Dilemmas,' *Proceedings of the Aristotelian Society*, 80(1979-80), 61-80.

Hale, B., 'Can There Be a Logic of Attitudes?' in *Reality, Representation, and Projection*, J. Haldane and C. Wright, eds. (Oxford: Oxford University Press, 1993), 337-363.

Hardin, Garrett, *The Limits of Altruism: an Ecologist's View of Survival* (Bloomington: Indiana UniversityPress, 1977).

Hare, R. M. *The Language of Morals* (New York: Oxford University Press, 1964).

Hare, R.M., *Freedom and Reason* (New York: Oxford University Press, 1965).

Hare, R. M. 'Some Alleged Differences Between Imperatives and Indicatives,' *Mind*, 76 (1967): 309- 326.

Hare, R.M., *Practical Inferences* (Berkeley: University of California Press, 1971).

Hare, R.M., *Moral Thinking* (Oxford: Clarendon Press, 1981).

Hare, R.M., 'Off on the Wrong Foot,' in *On The Relevance of Metaethics*, J. Couture & K. Nielsen, eds.,*Canadian Journal of Philosophy*, suppl. vol. 21 (1995): 67-77.

Harman, Gilbert, *The Nature of Morality* (New York: Oxford University Press, 1977).

Harman, Gilbert, 'Ethics and Observation' in *Essays on Moral Realism*, Geoffrey Sayre-McCord, ed.(Ithaca, NY: Cornell University Press, 1988), 119-124.

Harman, Gilbert & Judith Jarvis Thomson, *Moral Relativism and Moral Objectivity* (Oxford: Blackwell,1996).

Harrison, Jonathan, 'Be Ye Therefore Perfect, *or* the Inevitability of Sin,' *Religious Studies*, 21 (1985):1-19.

Harsanyi, John, 'Cardinal Welfare, Individualistic Ethics, and Interpersonal Comparisons of Utility,' *Journal of Political Economy*, 63 (1955): 309- 321.

Harsanyi, John, *Rational Behavior and Bargaining Equilibrium in Games and Social Situations* (Cambridge: Cambridge University Press, 1977), 51- 60.

Harsanyi, John, 'Morality and the Theory of Rational Behavior,' *Social Research*, 44 (1977): [Also reprinted in Sen and Williams, *Utilitarianism and Beyond*, 38-62].

Hart, H.L.A., 'Are There Any Natural Rights?' *Philosophical Review*, 64 (1955): 175- 191.

Haslett, D.W., *Equal Consideration* (Newark, NJ: University of Delaware Press, 1987).

Herman, Barbara, 'Agency, Attachment, and Difference,' *Ethics*, 101 (1991): 775-797.

Herman, Barbara, *The Practice of Moral Judgment* (Cambridge, MA: Harvard University Press, 1993).

Hill, Thomas, 'Moral Purity and the Lesser Evil,' *The Monist*, 66 (1983): 213-232.

Hill, Thomas, 'Autonomy and Benevolent Lies,' *The Journal of Value Inquiry*, 18 (1984):251-267.

Hill, Thomas, 'Making Exceptions without Abandoning the Principle: or How a Kantian Might Think about Terrorism,' in *Dignity and Practical Reason in Kant's Moral Theory* (Ithaca: Cornell University Press, 1992), 196-225.

Hobbes, Thomas, *Leviathan*, Herbert W. Schneider, ed. (Indianapolis, IN: Bobbs-Merrill, Library of LiberalArts), 1958.

Hodgson, D. H., *Consequences of Utilitarianism* (Oxford: Oxford University Press, 1967).

Hourani, George F., *Reason and Tradition in Islamic Ethics* (Cambridge: Cambridge University Press, 1985).

Howard-Snyder, Frances,'The Heart of Consequentialism,' *Philosophical Studies*, 76 (1994): 107-129.

Hurley, Paul, 'Getting Our Options Clear: a Closer Look at Agent-Centered Options,' *Philosophical Studies*, 78 (1995): 163-188.

Hurley, Susan, *Natural Reasons* (New York: Oxford University Press, 1989).

Jackson, Frank, 'Decision-Theoretic Consequentialism and the Nearest and Dearest Objection' *Ethics*, 101(1991): 461-482.

Jackson, Frank, *From Metaphysics to Ethics: a Defense of Conceptual Analysis* (Oxford: Clarendon Press, 1998).

Jonsen, Albert R. and Stephen Toulmin, *The Abuse of Casuistry: A History of Moral Reasoning* (Berkeley: University of California Press, 1988).

Kagan, Shelly, *The Limits of Morality* (Oxford: Clarendon Press, 1989).

Kamm, Frances, 'Supererogation and Obligation,' *Journal of Philosophy*, 82 (1985): 118-138.

Kamm, Frances, 'Harming Some to Save Others,' *Philosophical Studies* 57 (1989): 227-260.

Kant, Immanuel, *Grounding for the Metaphysics of Morals* in Immanuel Kant, *Ethical Philosophy*, James W. Ellington, trans. (Indianapolis: Hackett, 1983).

Kant, Immanuel, 'On a Supposed Right to Tell Lies from Benevolent Motives,' in *Kant's Critique of Practical Reason and Other Works on the Theory of Ethics*, 6th ed., T.K. Abbott, trans. (London: Longmans, 1959), 361- 365.

Kant, Immanuel, *The Philosophy of Law*, Part II, W. Hastie, trans. (Edinburgh: T.T. Clark, 1887), 194-198.

Kenny, Anthony, 'Practical Inference,' *Analysis, 26* (1966): 65-75.

Kenny, Anthony, 'Aristotle on Moral Luck,' in *Human Agency: Language, Duty and Value*, Jonathan Dancy, J. M. E. Moravcsik, and C. C. W. Taylor, eds. (Stanford, CA: Stanford University Press, 1988),105-119.

Kierkegaard, Søren, *Fear and Trembling*, ed. and trans. Howard V. And Edna H. Hong (Priceton: Princeton University Press, 1983).

Korsgaard, Christine, 'Two Distinctions in Goodness,' *Philosophical Review*, 92 (1983): 169-195.

Korsgaard, Christine, *The Sources of Normativity* (Cambridge: Cambridge University Press, 1996).

Lee, Tao, 'Medical Ethics in Ancient China,' in Robert M. Veatch, *Cross Cultural Perspectives in Medical Ethics: Readings* (Boston: Jones & Bartlett, 1989) 132-139.

Lewis, David, 'Dispositional Theories of Value,' *Proceedings of the Aristotelian Society*, suppl. vol. 63(1980): 113-137.

Lyons, Dan and Jann Benson, *Strutting and Fretting: Standards for Self Esteem* (Niwot, CO: University Press of Colorado, 1991).

Lyons, David, *The Forms and Limits of Utilitarianism* (Oxford: Clarendon Press, 1965).

MacIntyre, Alasdair, *Whose Justice? Which Rationality?* (Notre Dame, IN: Notre Dame University Press,1988).

Mackie, J.L., *Ethics: Inventing Right and Wrong* (New York: Penguin Books, 1977).

Marquis, Don, 'Why Abortion is Wrong,' *Journal of Philosophy,* 86 (1989): 183-202.

McArthur, Robert P. and David Welker, 'Non-assertoric Logic,' *Notre Dame Journal of Formal Logic,* 15 (1974): 225-244.

McDowell, John, 'Values and Secondary Qualities,' in Ted Honderich, ed. *Morality and Objectivity: A Tribute to J. L. Mackie* (London: Routledge & Kegan Paul, 1985), pp. 110-129.

McIntyre, Kevin M., Robert C. Benfari, and M. Pabst Battin, 'Two Cardiac Arrests, One Medical Team,' *Hastings Center Report*, 12 (1982): 24- 25.

McKay, Alfred, 'Interpersonal Comparisons,' *Journal of Philosophy*, 72 (1975): 535-549.

Medlin, Brian, 'Ethical Egoism is Inconsistent,' *Australasian Journal of Philosophy*, 35 (1957): 111-118.

Mill, John Stuart, *Utilitarianism* in *The Utilitarians* (Garden City, NY: Doubleday, 1961).

Miller, Richard, *Moral Differences: Truth, Justice and Conscience in a World of Conflict* (Princeton: Princeton University Press, 1992)

Minai, Naila, *Women in Islam: Tradition and Transition in the Middle East* (New York: Seaview Books,1981.

Moore, G. E., *Principia Ethica* (Cambridge: Cambridge University Press, 1962).

Moorehead, Alan, *The Fatal Impact* (New York: Dell, 1966).

Murthy, K.R. Srikanta, 'Professional Ethics in Ancient Indian Medicine,' Robert M. Veatch, *Cross Cultural Perspectives in Medical Ethics: Readings* (Boston: Jones & Bartlett, 1989) 126-132.

Myers, Fred R., 'Always Ask: Resource Use and Land Ownership among Pintupi Aborigines of the Australian Western Desert,' in *Traditional Aboriginal Society*, 2nd Edition, W. H. Edwards, ed. (Macmillan Educational Australia PTY Ltd, 1998), 30- 46.

Nagel,Thomas, 'Moral Luck,' in *Human Agency: Language, Duty and Value*, Jonathan Dancy, J. M. E. Moravcsik, and C. C. W. Taylor, eds. (Stanford, CA: Stanford University Press, 1988), 136- 150.

Nagel, Thomas, 'Death,' in *Mortal Questions* (Cambridge: Cambridge University Press, 1979), 1-10.

Nagel, Thomas, 'Equality,' in *Mortal Questions* (Cambridge: Cambridge University Press, 1979), 106-127).

Nagel, Thomas, *The View from Nowhere* (Oxford University Press, New York, 1986).

Nagel, Thomas, *Equality and Partiality* (New York: Oxford University Press, 1991), Chapter 7.

Nakhnikian,George, 'On the Naturalistic Fallacy,' in *Morality and the Language of Conduct*, H.-N. Castañeda and G. Nakhnikian, eds. (Detroit: Wayne State University Press, 1963), 145 - 158.

Narveson, Jan, *Morality and Utility* (Baltimore: The Johns Hopkins University Press, 1967).

Narveson, Jan, *Moral Matters* (Peterborough, Ont.: Broadview Press, 1993).

Nielsen, Kai, 'Capitalism, Socialism, and Justice: Reflections on Rawls' Theory of Justice,' *Social Praxis,* 7 (1980):253-271.

Nietzsche, Friedrich, *Beyond Good and Evil*, ed. and trans. Marianna Cowan (Chicago: Henry Regnery Company, 1955).

Norris, Stephen E., 'The Intelligibility of Practical Reasoning,' *American Philosophical Quarterly*, 12 (1975): 77-84.

Nowell-Smith, Patrick, *Ethics* (Baltimore: Penguin Books, 1954).

Nussbaum, Martha, *The Fragility of Goodness* (Cambridge: Cambridge University Press, 1986).

Parfit, Derek, *Reasons and Persons* (Oxford: Clarendon Press, 1984).

Penelhum, Terence, 'The Logic of Pleasure,' in *Philosophy and Phenomenological Research*, 17 (1956-57):488-503.

Perry, R.B., *Realms of Value: a Critique of Human Civilization* (Cambridge, MA: Harvard UniversityPress, 1954).

Piper, Adrian M. S., 'Utility, Publicity, and Manipulation,' *Ethics*, 88 (1978):189-206.

Plato, *Philebus, The Dialogues of Plato*, vol. II, B. Jowett, trans. (New York: Random House, 1937).

Price, Richard, *A Review of the Principal Questions in Morals*, in *British Moralists*, 2nd ed., Lewis A.Selby-Bigge (New York: Dover Publications, Inc., 1965),105-184.

Prichard, H.A., 'Does Moral Philosophy Rest on a Mistake?' *Mind* 21 (1912): 12-37.

Putnam, Hilary, 'The Meaning of "Meaning",' as well as 'Meaning and Reference,' *The Journal of Philosophy*, 70 (1973): 699-711.

Putnam, Hilary, 'Language and Reality,' *Mind, Language, and Reality: Philosophical Papers*, Vol. 2 (Cambridge: Cambridge University Press, 1975), 271-290.

Putnam, Hilary, 'Reference and Truth,' in *Realism and Reason* (Cambridge: Cambridge University Press, 1983), 69-87.

Quine, W.V., 'Two Dogmas of Empiricism,' in *From a Logical Point of View* (Cambridge, MA: Harvard University Press, 1953), 20-46.

Rachels, James, 'Active and Passive Euthanasia,' *New England Journal of Medicine*, 295 (1975):78-80.

Rahman, Abdul, C. Amine, and Ahmed Elkadi, 'Islamic Code of Medical Professional Ethics,' Robert M. Veatch, *Cross Cultural Perspectives in Medical Ethics: Readings* (Boston: Jones & Bartlett, 1989)120-126

Railton, Peter, 'Alienation, Consequentialism, and the Demands of Morality,' *Philosophy and PublicAffairs*, 13 (1984): 134-171.

Railton, Peter, 'Moral Realism,' *Philosophical Review*, 95 (1986): 163-207.

Railton, Peter, 'Noncognitivism about Rationality: Benefits, Costs, and an Alternative,' *Philosophical Issues*, 4 (1993): 36-51. Issue on 'Naturalism and Normativity,' E. Villanueva, ed.

Railton, Peter, "What the Non-Cognitivist Helps Us to See the Naturalist Must Help Us to Explain,'*Reality, Representation, and Projection*, John Haldane and Crispin Wright eds., (Oxford: Oxford University Press, 1993), 279-300.

Railton, Peter, 'Reply to David Wiggins,' *Reality, Representation, and Projection*, John Haldane and Crispin Wright eds., (Oxford: Oxford University Press, 1993), 315-328.

Ramsey, Frank, 'Truth and Probability,' in *The Foundations of Mathematics and Other Logical Essays*, R. B. Braithwaite, ed. (London: Routledge and Kegan Paul, 1950).

Rand, Ayn, *Atlas Shrugged* (New York: Dutton Books, 1957).

Rawls, John, 'Two Concepts of Rules,' *Philosophical Review*, 64 (1955): 3- 32.

Rawls, John, *A Theory of Justice* (Cambridge MA: Harvard University Press, 1971).

Raz, Joseph, 'Permissions and Supererogation,' *American Philosophical Quarterly*, 12 (1975): 161-168.

Raz, Joseph, *The Morality of Freedom* (Oxford: Clarendon Press, 1986).

Reinhardt, William O., trans., 'The 17 Rules of Enjuin' in Robert M. Veatch, *Cross Cultural Perspectives in Medical Ethics: Readings* (Boston: Jones & Bartlett, 1989) 140-141.

Rescher, Nicholas, *The Logic of Commands* (London: Routledge and Kegan Paul, 1966).

Resnik, Michael, *Choices: an Introduction to Decision Theory* (Minneapolis: University of MinnesotaPress, 1987).

Richards, David A. J., *A Theory of Reasons for Action* (Oxford: Clarendon Press, 1971).

Rosati, Connie, 'Persons, Perspectives, and Full Information Accounts of the Good,' *Ethics*, 105 (1995): 296-325.

Ross, Alf, 'Imperatives and Logic,' *Philosophy of Science*, 11 (1944): 30- 46.

Ryle, Gilbert, *The Concept of Mind* (New York: Barnes & Noble, Inc., 1949).

Ryle, Gilbert, 'Pleasure,' *Proceedings of the Aristotelian Society*, Suppl. Vol. 28 (1954): 195- 205.

Sasson, Jean, *Princess: a True Story of Life Behind the Veil in Saudi Arabia* (New York: William Morrow & Co, 1992).

Sayre-McCord, Geoffrey, 'Moral Theory and Explanatory Impotence' in Geoffrey Sayre-McCord, ed., *Essays in Moral Realism* (Ithaca: Cornell University Press, 1988, 256-281.

Scheffler, Israel, *Hard Choices* (Cambridge: Cambridge University Press, 1986.

Scheffler, Samuel, *The Rejection of Consequentialism* (Oxford: Clarendon Press, 1982).

Schiffer, S., *Meaning* (Oxford: Clarendon Press, 1972).

Scruton, Roger, 'Attitudes, Beliefs, and Reasons,' *Morality and Moral Reasoning*, John Casey, ed. (London: Methuen & Co., 1972), 25- 110.

Searle, John, 'Meaning and Speech Acts,' *Philosophical Review*, 71 (1962): 423-432.

Searle, John, *Speech Acts*, (Cambridge: Cambridge University Press, 1970).

Sen, Amartya, 'Rights and Agency,' *Philosophy and Public Affairs*, 11 (1982): 3-39.

Sen, Amartya, 'Rights and Capabilities,' in *Morality and Objectivity: A Tribute to J. L. Mackie*, Ted Honderich, ed. (London: Routledge & Kegan Paul, 1985), 130-148.

Sen, Amartya, 'Will There Be Any Hope for the Poor?' *Time* 155 (May 22, 2000): 94-95.

Sharp, Frank Chapman, *Ethics* (New York: Century, 1928).

Shaw, William H., 'The Paradox of Deontology,' in *Rationality, Morality, and Self-Interest*, John Heil, ed. (Lanham, MD: Rowman and Littlefield, 1993), 99-113.

Sibley, W. M., 'The Rational vs. the Reasonable,' *Philosophical Review*, 62 (1953): 554-560.

Sidgwick, Henry, *Methods of Ethics*, 7th ed. (Indianapolis: Hackett, 1981).

Singer, Peter, 'Famine, Affluence, and Morality,' in *Moral Problems: a Collection of Philosophical Essays*, 3rd. ed., James Rachels, ed. (New York: Harper and Row, 1979), 263-278.

Sinnott-Armstrong, Walter, *Moral Dilemmas* (Oxford: Basil Blackwell, 1988).

Slote, Michael, *Beyond Optimizing* (Cambridge, MA: Harvard University Press, 1989).

Smart, J.J.C. and Bernard Williams, *Utilitarianism: For and Against* (Cambridge: Cambridge UniversityPress, 1973).

Smith, James, 'Prisoner of the Caughnawagas,' in *Captured by Indians*, Frederick Drimmer, ed., (New York: Dover Publications, 1985).

Smith, Michael, 'Objectivity and Moral Realism,' in *Reality, Representation, and Projection*, John Haldane and Crispin Wright eds., Oxford University Press, 1993), 235-255.

Smith, Michael, *The Moral Problem* (Oxford: Blackwell, 1995).

Smith, Michael, 'Internalism's Wheel,'in Brad Hooker, ed., *Truth in Ethics* (Oxford: Blackwell,1996), 69-94.

Sobel, David, 'Full Information Accounts of Well-Being,' *Ethics*, 104 (1994): 784-810.

Spinoza, Benedict de, *The Ethics*, edited and translated by Robert H. M. Elwes, *The Chief Works of Benedict de Spinoza*, Vol 2 (New York: Dover Publications, 1951).

Stampp, Kenneth, *The Peculiar Institution: Slavery in the Ante-Bellum South* (New York: Vintage Books,1956).

Stenius, Erik, 'Mood and Language Games,' *Synthese*, 17 (1967): 254-274.

Stevenson, C. L., *Ethics and Language* (New Haven: Yale University Press, 1944).

Stocker, Michael, 'The Schizophrenia of Modern Ethical Theories,' *Journal of Philosophy*, 73(1976):453-466.

Stocker, Michael, *Plural and Conflicting Values* (Oxford: Clarendon Press, 1990).

Sturgeon, Nicholas, 'Moral Explanations' in Geoffrey Sayre-McCord, ed., *Essays in Moral Realism* (Ithaca: Cornell University Press, 1988), 229-255.

Taylor, Charles, 'The Diversity of Goods,' in *Utilitarianism and Beyond*, Amartya Sen and BernardWilliams, eds. (Cambridge: Cambridge University Press, 1982), 129- 144.

Taylor, Charles,'Theories of Meaning,' *Human Agency and Language: Philosophical Papers*, I (Cambridge: Cambridge University Press, 1985), 248-292.

Taylor, Charles, 'The Nature and Scope of Distributive Justice,' in *Justice and Equality Here and Now*,Frank S. Lukash, ed.(Ithaca, NY: Cornell University Press,1986), 34-67.

Thomasma, David C. And Glenn C. Graber, *Theory and Practice in Medical Ethics* (New York: Continuum, 1989).

Thomson, Judith Jarvis, 'Practical Reasoning,' *Philosophical Quarterly*, *12* (1962): 316-328.

Thomson, Judith Jarvis, and Gilbert Harman, *Moral Relativism and Moral Objectivity* (Oxford: Blackwell,1996)

Toulmin, Stephen, *The Place of Reason in Ethics* (Cambridge: Cambridge University Press, 1964).

Toulmin, Stephen and Albert R. Jonsen, *The Abuse of Casuistry: A History of Moral Reasoning* (Berkeley: University of California Press, 1988).

Urmson, J. O., 'Saints and Heroes,' in *Essays in Moral Philosophy*, ed. A. I. Melden (Seattle: Universityof Washington Press, 1958), 198- 216.

Van Every, Dale, *Disinherited: The Lost Birthright of the American Indian* (New York: William Morrow& Co., 1966).

Vlastos, Gregory, 'Justice and Equality,' in Jeremy Waldron, ed., *Theories of Rights* (Oxford: Oxford University Press, 1984), 41- 76.

Wallace, James, *Moral Relevance and Moral Conflict* (Ithaca: Cornell University Press, 1988).

Warnock, G.J., *The Object of Morality* (London: Methuen & Company, 1971).

Weinreb, Lloyd L., *Natural Law and Justice* (Cambridge, MA: Harvard University Press, 1987).

Welker, David and Robert P. McArthur, 'Non-assertoric Logic,' *Notre Dame Journal of Formal Logic*,15 (1974): 225-244.

Wiggins, David, 'Truth, Invention, and the Meaning of Life' in *Needs, Values, Truth: Essays in the Philosophy of Value* (Oxford: Blackwell, 1987), 87-137.

Wiggins, David, 'Weakness of Will, Commensurability, and the Objects of Deliberation and Desire,' in *Needs, Values, Truth* (Oxford: Blackwell, 1987), 239-267.

Wiggins, David, 'Cognitivism, Naturalism, and Normativity: a Reply to Peter Railton,' in *Reality, Representation, and Projection*, John Haldane and Crispin Wright, eds. (Oxford: Oxford UniversityPress, 1993), 301-313.

Wiggins, David, 'A Neglected Position?' in *Reality, Representation, and Projection*, John Haldane and Crispin Wright, eds. (Oxford: Oxford University Press, 1993), 329- 336.

Wiggins, David, 'Objective and Subjective in Ethics,' in Brad Hooker, ed., *Truth in Ethics* (Oxford:

Blackwell,1996), 35-68.

Williams, Bernard, 'Ethical Consistency,' *Proceedings of the Aristotelian Society*, Suppl. Vol. 39 (1965):103-124.

Williams, Bernard and J.J.C. Smart, *Utilitarianism: For and Against* (Cambridge: Cambridge UniversityPress, 1973).

Williams, Bernard, 'Moral Luck,' *Proceedings of the Aristotelian Society*, suppl. vol. 90 (1976): 115-135.

Williams, Bernard, 'Utilitarianism and Moral Self-Indulgence,' in *Contemporary British Philosophy, Personal Statements*, 4th Series, H. D. Lewis, ed. (London: Allen and Unwin, 1976), 306-321.

Williams, Bernard, *Ethics and the Limits of Philosophy* (Cambridge: Harvard University Press, 1985).

Wilson, Deirdre and Dan Sperber, 'Mood and the Analysis of Non-declarative Sentences,' in *Human Agency: Language, Duty, and Value*, ed. Jonathan Dancy, J. M. E. Moravcsik, and C.C. W. Taylor(Stanford, CA: Stanford University Press, 1988), pp. 77-101

Wilson, Edward O., *On Human Nature*, (Cambridge, MA: Harvard University Press, 1978).

Wilson, James O., *The Moral Sense* (New York: The Free Press, 1993).

Wittgenstein, Ludwig, *Philosophical Investigations*, trans. G.E.M. Anscombe, (New York: Macmillan, 1953).

Wittgenstein, Ludwig, *Remarks on the Foundations of Mathematics*, ed. G. H. Von Wright, R. Rhees, and G. E. M. Anscombe, trans. G. E. M. Anscombe, (New York: Macmillan 1956).

Wittgenstein, Ludwig, *Zettel*, ed. G. E. M. Anscombe and G. H. Von Wright, trans. G. E. M. Anscombe,Berkeley: University of California Press, 1967)..

Wolf, Susan, 'Moral Saints,' *Journal of Philosophy*, 79 (1982): 419-439.

Wong, David, 'Relativism,' in P. Singer, *A Companion to Ethics* (Oxford: Blackwell, 1991), 442-450.

Wright, Crispin, *Realism, Meaning, and Truth* (Oxford: Blackwell, 1986).

Wright, Crispin, *Truth and Objectivity* (Cambridge, MA: Harvard University Press, 1992).

Wright, Crispin, *Realism, Meaning, and Truth*, 2nd ed. (Oxford: Blackwell, 1993).

Wright, Crispin, 'Truth in Ethics,' in Brad Hooker, ed., *Truth in Ethics*, (Oxford: Blackwell, 1996), 1-18.

Ziff, Paul, *Semantic Analysis* (Ithaca, NY: Cornell University Press, 1960).

INDEX

LIBRARY OF ETHICS AND APPLIED PHILOSOPHY

KLUWER ACADEMIC PUBLISHERS – DORDRECHT / BOSTON / LONDON